THIRD EDITION

Ansible: Up and Running

Automating Configuration Management and Deployment the Easy Way

Bas Meijer, Lorin Hochstein, and René Moser

Beijing · Boston · Farnham · Sebastopol · Tokyo

Ansible: Up and Running

by Bas Meijer, Lorin Hochstein, and René Moser

Copyright © 2022 Bas Meijer. All rights reserved.

Published by O'Reilly Media, Inc., 1005 Gravenstein Highway North, Sebastopol, CA 95472.

O'Reilly books may be purchased for educational, business, or sales promotional use. Online editions are also available for most titles (*http://oreilly.com*). For more information, contact our corporate/institutional sales department: 800-998-9938 or *corporate@oreilly.co*m.

Acquisitions Editor: John Devins	**Indexer:** Ellen Troutman-Zaig
Development Editor: Sarah Grey	**Interior Designer:** David Futato
Production Editor: Kate Galloway	**Cover Designer:** Karen Montgomery
Copyeditor: Charles Roumeliotis	**Illustrator:** Kate Dullea
Proofreader: Piper Editorial Consulting, LLC	

December 2014:	First Edition
August 2017:	Second Edition
July 2022:	Third Edition

Revision History for the Third Edition

2022-07-12:   First Release

See *http://oreilly.com/catalog/errata.csp?isbn=9781098109158* for release details.

The O'Reilly logo is a registered trademark of O'Reilly Media, Inc. *Ansible: Up and Running*, the cover image, and related trade dress are trademarks of O'Reilly Media, Inc.

The views expressed in this work are those of the authors, and do not represent the publisher's views. While the publisher and the authors have used good faith efforts to ensure that the information and instructions contained in this work are accurate, the publisher and the authors disclaim all responsibility for errors or omissions, including without limitation responsibility for damages resulting from the use of or reliance on this work. Use of the information and instructions contained in this work is at your own risk. If any code samples or other technology this work contains or describes is subject to open source licenses or the intellectual property rights of others, it is your responsibility to ensure that your use thereof complies with such licenses and/or rights.

978-1-098-10915-8

[LSI]

Table of Contents

Preface to the Third Edition

Since the second edition of this book was published in 2017, there have been tremendous changes in the world of Ansible and Python, including several major releases. Substantial changes happened outside the project as well: for example, Red Hat, the company that backs the Ansible project, was bought by IBM. That hasn't slowed the Ansible project at all, of course: it's still in active development and gaining users. The development of cloud infrastructure and containers has also changed the landscape immensely.

We've made multiple changes in this edition, most significantly adding six new chapters that cover containers, Molecule, Ansible collections, creating images, cloud infrastructure, and CI/CD. We've also added much more detail to other chapters, with a focus on using software engineering best practices and test frameworks to validate code and eradicate guesswork. We've updated all the example code for compatibility with the latest Ansible, as well as everything that addresses Python dependencies. Our material was written to reflect the significant changes between 2017 and 2022. We could go on, but we hope you'll dive into the text, try the code, and discover for yourself just how much Ansible continues to advance.

Conventions Used in This Book

The following typographical conventions are used in this book:

Italic
> Indicates new terms, URLs, email addresses, filenames, and file extensions.

`Constant width`
> Used for program listings, as well as within paragraphs to refer to program elements such as variable or function names, databases, data types, environment variables, statements, and keywords.

Constant width bold

Shows commands or other text that should be typed literally by the user.

Constant width italic

Shows text that should be replaced with user-supplied values or by values determined by context.

This element signifies a general note.

This element indicates a warning or caution.

Using Code Examples

Supplemental material (code examples, exercises, etc.) is available for download at *https://github.com/ansiblebook*.

If you have a technical question or a problem using the code examples, please send email to *bookquestions@oreilly.com*.

This book is here to help you get your job done. In general, if example code is offered with this book, you may use it in your programs and documentation. You do not need to contact us for permission unless you're reproducing a significant portion of the code. For example, writing a program that uses several chunks of code from this book does not require permission. Selling or distributing examples from O'Reilly books does require permission. Answering a question by citing this book and quoting example code does not require permission. Incorporating a significant amount of example code from this book into your product's documentation does require permission.

We appreciate, but generally do not require, attribution. An attribution usually includes the title, author, publisher, and ISBN. For example: "*Ansible: Up and Running* by Bas Meijer, Lorin Hochstein, and René Moser (O'Reilly). Copyright 2022 Bas Meijer, 978-1-098-10915-8."

If you feel your use of code examples falls outside fair use or the permission given above, feel free to contact us at *permissions@oreilly.com*.

O'Reilly Online Learning

 For more than 40 years, *O'Reilly Media* has provided technology and business training, knowledge, and insight to help companies succeed.

Our unique network of experts and innovators share their knowledge and expertise through books, articles, and our online learning platform. O'Reilly's online learning platform gives you on-demand access to live training courses, in-depth learning paths, interactive coding environments, and a vast collection of text and video from O'Reilly and 200+ other publishers. For more information, visit *https://oreilly.com*.

How to Contact Us

Please address comments and questions concerning this book to the publisher:

O'Reilly Media, Inc.
1005 Gravenstein Highway North
Sebastopol, CA 95472
800-998-9938 (in the United States or Canada)
707-829-0515 (international or local)
707-829-0104 (fax)

We have a web page for this book, where we list errata, examples, and any additional information. You can access this page at *https://oreil.ly/ansible-3e*.

Email *bookquestions@oreilly.com* to comment or ask technical questions about this book.

For news and information about our books and courses, visit *https://oreilly.com*.

Find us on LinkedIn: *https://linkedin.com/company/oreilly-media*.

Follow us on Twitter: *https://twitter.com/oreillymedia*.

Watch us on YouTube: *https://youtube.com/oreillymedia*.

Acknowledgments

From Lorin

Thanks to Jan-Piet Mens, Matt Jaynes, and John Jarvis for reviewing drafts of the book and providing feedback. Thanks to Isaac Saldana and Mike Rowan at SendGrid for being so supportive of this endeavor. Thanks to Michael DeHaan for creating

Ansible and shepherding the community that sprang up around it, as well as for providing feedback on the book, including an explanation of why he chose to use the name *Ansible*. Thanks to my editor, Brian Anderson, for his endless patience in working with me.

Thanks to Mom and Dad for their unfailing support; my brother Eric, the actual writer in the family; and my two children, Benjamin and Julian. Finally, thanks to my wife, Stacy, for everything.

From René

Thanks to my family, my wife, Simone, for the support and love, my three children— Gil, Sarina, and Léanne—for the joy they brought into my life; to all those people contributing to Ansible, thank you for your work; and a special thanks to Matthias Blaser, who introduced Ansible to me.

From Bas

Thanks to Henk de Jongh for introducing me to O'Reilly books in the early nineties. Thanks to Jordi Clement for introducing me to Ansible. Thanks to all those people contributing to Ansible, thank you for your awesome work. Thanks to the formidable teams that formed me: Antraciet, Integration and Engineering at IMC, iWelcome, CD@GS, Vendora, CDaaS, Spitfire, Colibri, Wilbur, Duck Tape, Purple, ICC. Thanks to Frank Bezema and Werner Dijkerman. Thanks to Jiri Hoogland and Vola Dynamics for supporting open source development. Massive thanks to Ton Kersten and Kerim Satirli! Special thanks to Jan-Piet Mens, Marek Vette, and John Cunniff for reviewing! Thanks to Serge van Ginderachter, Luke Murphy, Robert de Bock, Vincent van der Kussen, Dag Wieers, Arnab Sinha, Anand Buddhef, and all others for their great presentations in the Ansible Benelux Meetup: without them I could not have authored this book. Thanks to Sarah Grey for editing this book. And thanks to my dear family members for all the fun and love.

## CHAPTER 1

Introduction

It's an interesting time to be working in the IT industry. We no longer deliver software to our customers by installing a program on a single machine and calling it a day. Instead, we are all gradually turning into cloud engineers.

We now deploy software applications by stringing together services that run on a distributed set of computing resources and communicate over different networking protocols. A typical application can include web servers, application servers, memory-based caching systems, task queues, message queues, SQL databases, NoSQL datastores, and load balancers.

IT professionals also need to make sure to have the proper redundancies in place, so that when failures happen (and they will), our software systems will handle them gracefully. Then there are the secondary services that we also need to deploy and maintain, such as logging, monitoring, and analytics, as well as third-party services we need to interact with, such as infrastructure-as-a-service (IaaS) endpoints for managing virtual machine instances.[1]

You can wire up these services by hand: spinning up the servers you need, logging into each one, installing packages, editing config files, and so forth, but it's a pain. It's time-consuming, error-prone, and just plain dull to do this kind of work manually, especially around the third or fourth time. And for more complex tasks, like standing up an OpenStack cloud, doing it by hand is madness. There must a better way.

If you're reading this, you're probably already sold on the idea of configuration management and considering adopting Ansible as your configuration management tool.

---

1 For more on building and maintaining these types of distributed systems, check out Thomas A. Limoncelli, Strata R. Chalup, and Christina J. Hogan's *The Practice of Cloud System Administration*, volumes 1 and 2 (Addison-Wesley), and *Designing Data-Intensive Applications* by Martin Kleppman (O'Reilly).

Whether you're a developer deploying your code to production, or you're a systems administrator looking for a better way to automate, I think you'll find Ansible to be an excellent solution to your problem.

A Note About Versions

The example code in this book was tested against several versions of Ansible. Ansible 5.9.0 is the latest version as of this writing; Ansible Tower includes version 2.9.27 in the most recent release. Ansible 2.8 went End of Life with the release of 2.8.20 on April 13, 2021. Expect Ansible to evolve further.

For years the Ansible community has been highly active in creating roles and modules—so active that there are thousands of modules and more than 20,000 roles. The difficulties of managing a project of this scale led creators to reorganize the Ansible content into three parts:

- *Core* components, created by the Ansible team
- *Certified* content, created by Red Hat's business partners
- *Community* content, created by thousands of enthusiasts worldwide

Ansible 2.9 has lots of built-in features, and later versions are more composable. This new setup makes it more easily maintainable as a whole.

The examples provided in this book should work in various versions of Ansible, but version changes in general call for testing, which we will address in Chapter 14.

What's with the Name Ansible?

It's a science-fiction reference. An *ansible* is a fictional communication device that can transfer information faster than the speed of light. Ursula K. Le Guin invented the concept in her book *Rocannon's World* (Ace Books, 1966), and other sci-fi authors have since borrowed the idea, including Orson Scott Card. Ansible cofounder Michael DeHaan took the name Ansible from Card's book *Ender's Game* (Tor, 1985). In that book, the ansible was used to control many remote ships at once, over vast distances. Think of it as a metaphor for controlling remote servers.

Ansible: What Is It Good For?

Ansible is often described as a *configuration management tool* and is typically mentioned in the same breath as Puppet, Chef, and Salt. When IT professionals talk about *configuration management*, we typically mean writing some kind of state description for our servers, then using a tool to enforce that the servers are, indeed, in that state: the right packages are installed, configuration files have the expected values and have the expected permissions, the right services are running, and so on. Like other configuration management tools, Ansible exposes a *domain-specific language* (DSL) that you use to describe the state of your servers.

You can use these tools for software deployment as well. When people talk about *deployment*, they are usually referring to the process of generating binaries or static assets (if necessary) from software written by in-house developers, copying the required files to servers, adding configuration properties and environment variables, and starting services in a particular order. Capistrano and Fabric are two examples of open source deployment tools. Ansible is a great tool for deployment as well as configuration management. Using a single tool for both makes life simpler for the folks responsible for system integration.

Some people talk about the need to orchestrate deployments. *Orchestration* is the process of coordinating deployment when multiple remote servers are involved and things must happen in a specific order. For example, you might need to bring up the database before bringing up the web servers, or take web servers out of the load balancer one at a time to upgrade them without downtime. DeHaan designed Ansible from the ground up to be good at this, and to perform actions on multiple servers. It has a refreshingly simple model for controlling the order in which actions happen.

Finally, you'll hear people talk about provisioning new servers. In the context of public clouds such as Amazon EC2, *provisioning* refers to spinning up new virtual machine instances or cloud-native software as a service (SaaS). Ansible has got you covered here, with modules for talking to clouds including EC2, Azure,[2] Digital Ocean, Google Compute Engine, Linode, and Rackspace,[3] as well as any clouds that support the OpenStack APIs.

 Confusingly, the Vagrant tool, covered later in this chapter, uses the term *provisioner* to refer to a tool that does configuration management. It thus refers to Ansible as a kind of provisioner. Vagrant calls tools that create machines, such as VirtualBox and VMWare, *providers*. Vagrant uses the term *machine* to refer to a virtual machine and *box* to refer to a virtual machine image.

---

2 Yes, Azure supports Linux servers.

3 For example, see "Using Ansible at Scale to Manage a Public Cloud" (*https://oreil.ly/djLsk*), a slide presentation by Jesse Keating, formerly of Rackspace.

How Ansible Works

Figure 1-1 shows a sample use case of Ansible in action. A user we'll call Alice is using Ansible to configure three Ubuntu-based web servers to run NGINX. She has written a script called *webservers.yml*. In Ansible, the equivalent of a script is called a *playbook*. A playbook describes which *hosts* (what Ansible calls remote servers) to configure, and an ordered list of *tasks* to perform on those hosts. In this example, the hosts are web1, web2, and web3, and the tasks are things such as these:

- Install NGINX
- Generate a NGINX configuration file
- Copy over the security certificate
- Start the NGINX service

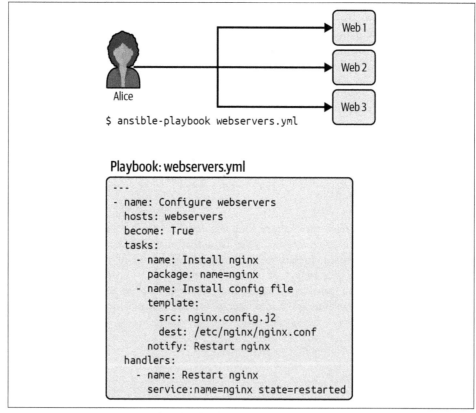

Figure 1-1. Running an Ansible playbook to configure three web servers

In the next chapter, we'll elaborate what's in this playbook; for now, we'll focus on its role in the overall process. Alice executes the playbook by using the `ansible-playbook` command. Alice starts her Ansible playbook by typing first the command and then the name of the playbook on a terminal line:

```
$ ansible-playbook webservers.yml
```

Ansible will make SSH connections in parallel to web1, web2, and web3. It will then execute the first task on the list on all three hosts simultaneously. In this example, the first task is installing the NGINX package, so the task in the playbook would look something like this:

```
- name: Install nginx
  package:
    name: nginx
```

Ansible will do the following:

1. Generate a Python script that installs the NGINX package
2. Copy the script to web1, web2, and web3
3. Execute the script on web1, web2, and web3
4. Wait for the script to complete execution on all hosts

Ansible will then move to the next task in the list and go through these same four steps.

It's important to note the following:

1. Ansible runs each task in parallel across all hosts.
2. Ansible waits until all hosts have completed a task before moving to the next task.
3. Ansible runs the tasks in the order that you specify them.

What's So Great About Ansible?

There are several open source configuration management tools out there to choose from, so why choose Ansible? Here are 21 reasons that drew us to it. In short: Ansible is simple, powerful, and secure.

Simple

Ansible was designed to have a dead simple setup process and a minimal learning curve.

Easy-to-read syntax

Ansible uses the YAML file format and Jinja2 templating, both of which are easy to pick up. Recall that Ansible configuration management scripts are called *playbooks*. Ansible actually builds the playbook syntax on top of YAML, which is a data format language that was designed to be easy for humans to read and write. In a way, YAML is to JSON what Markdown is to HTML.

Easy to audit

You can inspect Ansible playbooks in several ways, like listing all actions and hosts involved. For dry runs, we often use `ansible-playbook --check`. With built-in logging it is easy to see who did what and where. The logging is pluggable and log collectors can easily ingest the logs.

Little to nothing to install on the remote hosts

To manage servers with Ansible, Linux servers need to have SSH and Python installed, while Windows servers need WinRM enabled. On Windows, Ansible uses PowerShell instead of Python, so there is no need to preinstall an agent or any other software on the host.

On the *control machine* (that is, the machine that you use to control remote machines), it is best to install Python 3.8 or later. Depending on the resources you manage with Ansible, you might have external library prerequisites. Check the documentation to see whether a module has specific requirements.

Ansible scales down

The authors of this book use Ansible to manage hundreds of nodes. But what got us hooked is how it scales down. You can use Ansible on very modest hardware, like a Raspberry Pi or an old PC. Using it to configure a single node is easy: simply write a single playbook. Ansible obeys Alan Kay's maxim (*https://oreil.ly/85aCX*): "Simple things should be simple; complex things should be possible."

Easy to share

We do not expect you to reuse Ansible playbooks across different contexts. In Chapter 7, we will discuss roles, which are a way of organizing your playbooks, and Ansible Galaxy, an online repository of these roles.

The primary unit of reuse in the Ansible community nowadays is the *collection*. You can organize your modules, plug-ins, libraries, roles, and even playbooks into a collection and share it on Ansible Galaxy. You can also share internally using Automation Hub, a part of Ansible Tower. Roles can be shared as individual repositories.

In practice, though, every organization sets up its servers a little bit differently, and you are best off writing playbooks for your organization rather than trying to reuse generic ones. We believe the primary value of looking at other people's playbooks is to see how things work, unless you work with a particular product for which the vendor is a certified partner or involved in the Ansible community.

System abstraction

Ansible works with simple *abstractions* of system resources like files, directories, users, groups, services, packages, and web services.

By way of comparison, let's look at how to configure a directory in the shell. You would use these three commands:

```
mkdir -p /etc/skel/.ssh
chown root:root /etc/skel/.ssh
chmod go-wrx /etc/skel/.ssh
```

By contrast, Ansible offers the `file` module as an abstraction, where you define the parameters of the desired state. This one action has the same effect as the three shell commands combined:

```
- name: Ensure .ssh directory in user skeleton
  file:
    path: /etc/skel/.ssh
    mode: '0700'
    owner: root
    group: root
    state: directory
```

With this layer of abstraction, you can use the same configuration management scripts to manage servers running Linux distributions. For example, instead of having to deal with a specific package manager like dnf, yum, or apt, Ansible has a "package" abstraction that you can use instead (just be aware that package names might differ). But you can also use the system-specific abstractions if you prefer.

If you really want to, you can write your Ansible playbooks to take different actions, depending on the variety of operating systems of the remote servers. But Bas, one of the authors of this book, tries to avoid that where he can; he instead focuses on writing playbooks for the systems that are in actual use.

Top to bottom tasks

Books on configuration management often mention the concept of *convergence*, or *eventual consistent state*. Convergence in configuration management is strongly associated with the configuration management system CFEngine (*https://oreil.ly/ngtte*) by Mark Burgess. If a configuration management system is convergent, the system may run multiple times to put a server into its desired state, with each run bringing the server closer to that state.

Eventual consistent state does not really apply to Ansible, since it does not run multiple times to configure servers. Instead, Ansible modules work in such a way that running a playbook a single time should put each server into the desired state.

Powerful

Having Ansible at your disposal can bring huge productivity gains in several areas of systems management. The high-level abstractions Ansible provides (like roles) make it so that you can set up and configure things faster and potentially more securely.

Batteries included

You can use Ansible to execute arbitrary shell commands on your remote servers, but its real power comes from the wide variety of modules available. You use modules to perform *tasks* such as installing a package, restarting a service, or copying a configuration file.

As you will see later, Ansible modules are *declarative*; you use them to describe the state you want the server to be in. For example, you would invoke the user module like this to ensure there is an account named "deploy" in the web group:

```
- name: Ensure deploy user exists
  user:
    name: deploy
    group: web
```

Push-based

Chef and Puppet are configuration management systems that use agents. They are *pull-based* by default. Agents installed on the servers periodically check in with a central service and download configuration information from the service. Making configuration management changes to servers goes something like this:

1. You: make a change to a configuration management script.
2. You: push the change up to a configuration management central service.
3. Agent on server: wakes up after periodic timer fires.
4. Agent on server: connects to configuration management central service.
5. Agent on server: downloads new configuration management scripts.
6. Agent on server: executes configuration management scripts locally that change server state.

In contrast, Ansible is *push-based* by default. Making a change looks like this:

1. You: make a change to a playbook.
2. You: run the new playbook.
3. Ansible: connects to servers and executes modules that change the state of the servers.

As soon as you run the `ansible-playbook` command, Ansible connects to the remote servers and does its thing; this lowers the risk of random servers potentially breaking whenever their scheduled tasks fail to change things successfully. The push-based approach has a significant advantage: you control when the changes happen to the servers. You do not need to wait around for a timer to expire. Each step in a playbook can target one or a group of servers. You get more work done instead of logging into the servers by hand.

Multitier orchestration

Push mode also allows you to use Ansible for *multitier orchestration*, managing distinct groups of machines for an operation like an update. You can orchestrate the monitoring system, the load balancers, the databases, and the web servers with specific instructions so they work in concert. That's very hard to do with a pull-based system.

Masterless

Advocates of the pull-based approach claim that it is superior for scaling to large numbers of servers and for dealing with new servers that can come online anytime. A central configuration management system, however, slowly stops working when thousands of agents pull their configuration at the same time, especially when they need multiple runs to converge. In comparison, Ansible comes with the `ansible-pull` command, which can pull playbooks from a VCS repository like GitHub. Ansible does not need a master, but you can use a central system to run playbooks if you want to.

Pluggable and embeddable

A sizable part of Ansible's functionality comes from the Ansible Plugin System, of which the Lookup and Filter plug-ins are most used. Plug-ins augment Ansible's core functionality with logic and features that are accessible to all modules. Modules introduce new "verbs" to the Ansible language. You can write your own plug-ins (see Chapter 10) and modules (Chapter 12) in Python.

You can integrate Ansible into other products: Kubernetes and Ansible Tower are examples of successful integrations. Ansible Runner "is a tool and python library that helps when interfacing with Ansible directly or as part of another system whether that be through a container image interface, as a standalone tool, or as a Python module that can be imported."[4]

Using the *ansible-runner* library, you can run an Ansible playbook from within a Python script:

```
#!/usr/bin/env python3
import ansible_runner

r = ansible_runner.run(private_data_dir='./playbooks', playbook='playbook.yml')

print("{}: {}".format(r.status, r.rc))
print("Final status:")
print(r.stats)
```

Works with lots of stuff

Ansible modules cater to a wide range of system administration tasks. This list has the categories of the kinds of modules that you can use. These link to the module index (*https://oreil.ly/OXel7*) in the documentation:

- Cloud (*https://oreil.ly/0xeNu*)
- Files (*https://oreil.ly/3cq87*)
- Monitoring (*https://oreil.ly/z6dde*)
- Source Control (*https://oreil.ly/WEMHZ*)
- Clustering (*https://oreil.ly/b31cn*)
- Identity (*https://oreil.ly/39yJA*)
- Net Tools (*https://oreil.ly/Pb137*)
- Storage (*https://oreil.ly/IZBGX*)
- Commands (*https://oreil.ly/wyyJZ*)
- Infrastructure (*https://oreil.ly/XhW90*)
- Network (*https://oreil.ly/UFHZo*)
- System (*https://oreil.ly/mn569*)
- Crypto (*https://oreil.ly/puZGg*)
- Inventory (*https://oreil.ly/zBvdF*)
- Notification (*https://oreil.ly/ulrdH*)
- Utilities (*https://oreil.ly/veSG4*)

---

4 Ansible Runner documentation (*https://oreil.ly/sZwPY*), last accessed June 2, 2022.

- Database (*https://oreil.ly/iEv9l*)
- Messaging (*https://oreil.ly/aTOvP*)
- Packaging (*https://oreil.ly/71GLO*)
- Windows (*https://oreil.ly/c8NwK*)

Really scalable

Large enterprises use Ansible successfully in production with tens of thousands of nodes and have excellent support for environments where servers are dynamically added and removed. Organizations with hundreds of software teams typically use AWX or a combination of Ansible Tower and Automation Hub for auditability, and for security with role-based access controls.

Worried about the scalability of SSH? Ansible uses SSH multiplexing to optimize performance, and there are folks out there who are managing thousands of nodes with Ansible (see Chapter 12 of this book).

Secure

Automation with Ansible helps us to improve system security to security baselines and compliance standards.

Codified knowledge

Your authors like to think of Ansible playbooks as executable documentation. Playbooks are like the README files that used to describe the commands you had to type out to deploy your software, except that these instructions will never go out of date because they are also the code that executes. Product experts can create playbooks that take best practices into account. When novices use such a playbook to install the product, they can be sure they'll get a good result.

Reproducible systems

If you set up your entire system with Ansible, it will pass what Steve Traugott calls the "tenth-floor test" (*https://oreil.ly/AMf1S*): "Can I grab a random machine that's never been backed up and throw it out the tenth-floor window without losing sysadmin work?"

Equivalent environments

Ansible has a clever way to organize content that helps define configuration at the proper level. It is easy to create a setup for distinct development, testing, staging, and production environments. A staging environment is designed to be as similar as possible to the production environment so that developers can detect any problems before changes go live.

Encrypted variables

If you need to store sensitive data such as passwords or tokens, then `ansible-vault` is an effective tool to use. We use it to store encrypted variables in Git. We'll discuss it in detail in Chapter 8.

Secure transport

Ansible simply uses Secure Shell (SSH) for Linux and WinRM for Windows. We typically secure and harden these widely used systems-management protocols with strong configuration and firewall settings.

If you prefer using a pull-based model, Ansible has official support for pull mode, using a tool it ships with called `ansible-pull`. This book won't cover pull mode, but you can read more about it in the official Ansible documentation (*https://docs.ansi ble.com*).

Idempotency

Modules are also *idempotent*. Idempotence is a nice property because it means that it is safe to run an Ansible playbook multiple times against a server. Let's see what that means when we need a user named `deploy`:

```
- name: Ensure deploy user exists
  user:
    name: deploy
    group: web
```

If the `deploy` user does not exist, Ansible will create it. If it does exist, Ansible will not do anything. This is a vast improvement over the homegrown shell script approach, where running the shell script a second time might have a different (and unintended) effect.[5]

No daemons

There is no Ansible agent listening on a port. Therefore, when you use Ansible, there is no extra attack surface. (There is still an attack surface with software supply chain elements like Python libraries and other imported content.)

---

5 If you are interested in what Ansible's original author thinks of the idea of convergence, see Michael DeHaan's Ansible Project newsgroup post "Idempotence, Convergence, and Other Silly Fancy Words We Use Too Often" (*https://oreil.ly/pNSNr*).

What Is Ansible, Inc.'s Relationship to Ansible?

The name *Ansible* refers to both the software and the company that runs the open source project. Michael DeHaan, the creator of Ansible the software, is the former CTO of Ansible the company. To avoid confusion, we refer to the software as Ansible and to the company as Ansible, Inc.

Ansible, Inc. sells training and consulting services for Ansible, as well as a web-based management tool called Ansible Tower, which we cover in Chapter 19. In October 2015, Red Hat bought Ansible, Inc.; IBM bought Red Hat in 2019.

Is Ansible Too Simple?

When Lorin was working on an earlier edition of this book, the editor mentioned that "some folks who use the XYZ configuration management tool call Ansible a for-loop over SSH scripts." If you are considering switching over from another configuration management tool, you might be concerned at this point about whether Ansible is powerful enough to meet your needs.

As you will soon learn, Ansible supplies a lot more functionality than shell scripts. In addition to idempotence, Ansible has excellent support for templating, as well as defining variables at different scopes. Anybody who thinks Ansible is equivalent to working with shell scripts has never had to support a nontrivial program written in shell. We will always choose Ansible over shell scripts for configuration management tasks if given a choice.

What Do I Need to Know?

To be productive with Ansible, you need to be familiar with basic Unix/Linux system administration tasks. Ansible makes it easy to automate your tasks, but it is not the kind of tool that "automagically" does things that you otherwise would not know how to do.

For this book, we have assumed that you are familiar with at least one Linux distribution (such as Ubuntu, RHEL/CentOS, or SUSE), and that you know how to:

- Connect to a remote machine using SSH
- Interact with the Bash command-line shell (pipes and redirection)
- Install packages
- Use the *sudo* command
- Check and set file permissions
- Start and stop services

- Set environment variables
- Write scripts (any language)

If these concepts are all familiar to you, you are good to go with Ansible.

We will not assume you have knowledge of any particular programming language. For instance, you do not need to know Python to use Ansible unless you want to publish your own module.

What Isn't Covered

This book is not an exhaustive treatment of Ansible. The first part is designed to get you working productively in Ansible as quickly as possible. Then it describes how to perform certain tasks that are not obvious from the official documentation.

We don't cover all of Ansible's modules in detail: there are more than 3,500 of them. You can use the `ansible-doc` command-line tool with what you have installed to view the reference documentation and the module index mentioned previously.

Chapter 8 covers only the basic features of Jinja2, the template engine that Ansible uses, primarily because your authors memorize only basic features when we use Jinja2 with Ansible. If you need to use more advanced Jinja2 features in templates, check out the official Jinja2 documentation (*https://oreil.ly/LAXa7*).

Nor do we go into detail about some features of Ansible that are mainly useful when you are running it on an older version of Linux.

Finally, there are features of Ansible we don't cover simply to keep the book a manageable length. We encourage you to check out the official documentation (*https:// docs.ansible.com*) to find out more about these features.

Moving Forward

This introductory chapter covered the basic concepts of Ansible at a general level, including how it communicates with remote servers and how it differs from other configuration management tools. The next chapters discuss how to practice using Ansible.

## CHAPTER 2

Installation and Setup

Ansible is written in Python for use on Linux/macOS/BSD systems. It can target all kinds of systems, and you generally do not need to install anything on the target systems, assuming that the Linux/macOS/BSD systems have Python installed and that Windows machines have PowerShell. So generally you will install Ansible on your workstation. Python 3.8 is recommended on the machine where you run Ansible.

Installing Ansible

All the major Linux distributions package Ansible these days, so if you work on a Linux machine, you can use your native package manager for a casual installation (although this might be an older version of Ansible). If you work on macOS, I recommend using the excellent Homebrew package manager to install Ansible:

```
$ brew install ansible
```

On any Unix/Linux/macOS machine, you can install Ansible using one of the Python package managers. This way you can add Python-based tools and libraries that work for you, provided you add ~/.local/bin to your PATH shell variable. If you want to work with Ansible Tower or AWX, then you should install the same version of ansible-core on your workstation.

```
$ pip3 install --user ansible==2.9.27
```

Using pip3 to install a version above 2.10 (e.g., 5.9.0) installs all standard collections as well. It's still "batteries included."

If you work on multiple projects, you should install Ansible into a Python virtualenv. This lets you avoid interfering with your system Python or cluttering your user environment. Using Python's `venv` module and pip3, you can install just what you need to work on for each project:

```
$ python3 -m venv .venv --prompt A
$ source .venv/bin/activate
(A)
```

During activation of the environment, your shell prompt will change to (A) as a reminder. Enter **deactivate** to leave the virtual environment.

Windows is not officially supported to run Ansible, but you can fully manage Windows systems remotely with Ansible, with PowerShell over WinRM under the hood.[1]

There is a way to run Ansible from a Windows host (that is, to use a Windows-based control machine), and that is to run Ansible within the Windows Subsystem for Linux (WSL2). In practice, this means you'll run Ubuntu next to Windows, on the same machine. WSL2 is a feature that you can enable in Windows 10 Home Edition (and higher). This is not supported by Ansible, so it should not be used for production systems. To install Ansible in WSL2:

```
sudo apt-get update
sudo apt-get install python3-pip git libffi-dev
libssl-dev -y
pip3 install --user ansible
```

Loose Dependencies

Ansible plug-ins and modules might require that you install extra Python libraries. For example, when you want to work with Windows systems and Docker, then you install these two Python libraries:

```
(A) pip3 install pywinrm docker
```

In a way, the Python virtualenv was a precursor to containers: it creates a means to isolate libraries and avoid "dependency hell."

Running Ansible in Containers

`ansible-builder` is a tool that aids in creating execution environments by controlling the execution of Ansible from within a container for single-purpose automation

---

1 To learn why Windows is not supported on the controller, read Matt Davis's blog post "Why No Ansible Controller for Windows?" (*https://oreil.ly/xrtnD*).

workflows. It is based on the directory layout of `ansible-runner`. This is an advanced subject, and outside the scope of this chapter. If you'd like to experiment with it, refer to Chapter 23.

Ansible Development

If you are feeling adventurous and want to use the bleeding-edge version of Ansible, you can grab the development branch from GitHub:

```
$ python3 -m venv .venv --prompt S
$ source .venv/bin/activate
(S) python3 -m pip install --upgrade pip
(S) pip3 install wheel
(S) git clone https://github.com/ansible/ansible.git --recursive
(S) pip3 install -r ansible/requirements.txt
```

If you are running Ansible from the development branch, you need to run these commands each time to set up your environment variables, including your PATH variable, so that your shell knows where the `ansible` and `ansible-playbook` programs are:

```
(S) cd ./ansible
(S) source ./hacking/env-setup
```

Setting Up a Server for Testing

You need to have SSH access and root privileges on a Linux server to follow along with the examples in this book. Fortunately, these days it's easy to get low-cost access to a Linux virtual machine through most public cloud services.

Using Vagrant to Set Up a Test Server

If you prefer not to spend money on a public cloud, install Vagrant on your machine. Vagrant is an excellent open source tool for managing virtual machines. You can use it to boot a Linux virtual machine inside your laptop, which you can use as a test server.

Vagrant is a great environment for testing Ansible playbooks, which is why we'll be using it all along in this book, and why we often use Vagrant for testing our own Ansible playbooks. Vagrant isn't just for testing configuration management scripts; it was originally designed to create repeatable development environments. If you've ever joined a new software team and spent a couple of days discovering what software you had to install on your laptop so you could run a development version of an internal product, you've felt the pain that Vagrant was built to alleviate. Ansible playbooks are a great way to specify how to configure a Vagrant machine, so newcomers on your team can get up and running on day one.

Vagrant needs a hypervisor like VirtualBox installed on your machine. Download VirtualBox first, and then download Vagrant. Vagrant has some built-in support for Ansible that we can take advantage of. This chapter covers Vagrant's support for using Ansible to configure Vagrant machines.

We recommend you create a directory for your Ansible playbooks and related files. In the following example, we've named ours *playbooks*. Directory layout is important for Ansible: if you place files in the right places, the bits and pieces come together.

Run the following commands to create a Vagrant configuration file (Vagrantfile) for an Ubuntu/Focal 64-bit virtual machine image, and boot it:

```
$ mkdir playbooks
$ cd playbooks
$ vagrant init ubuntu/focal64
$ vagrant up
```

 The first time you use Vagrant, it will download the virtual machine image file. This might take a while, depending on your internet connection.

If all goes well, the output should look something like this:

```
$ vagrant up default
Bringing machine 'default' up with 'virtualbox' provider...
==> default: Importing base box 'ubuntu/focal64'...
==> default: Matching MAC address for NAT networking...
==> default: Checking if box 'ubuntu/default64' version is up to date...
==> default: Setting the name of the VM: default
==> default: Clearing any previously set network interfaces...
==> default: Preparing network interfaces based on configuration...
    default: Adapter 1: nat
==> default: Forwarding ports...
    default: 22 (guest) => 2222 (host) (adapter 1)
==> default: Running 'pre-boot' VM customizations...
==> default: Booting VM...
==> default: Waiting for machine to boot. This may take a few minutes...
    default: SSH address: 127.0.0.1:2222
    default: SSH username: vagrant
    default: SSH auth method: private key
==> default: Machine booted and ready!
==> default: Checking for guest additions in VM...
==> default: Setting hostname...
==> default: Configuring and enabling network interfaces...
==> default: Mounting shared folders...
    default: /vagrant => C:/Users/basme/ansiblebook/ch02/playbooks
```

You should be able to log in to your new Ubuntu 20.04 virtual machine by running the following:

```
$ vagrant ssh
```

If this works, you should see a login screen like this:

```
Welcome to Ubuntu 20.04.2 LTS (GNU/Linux 5.4.0-72-generic x86_64)
  * Documentation: https://help.ubuntu.com
  * Management: https://landscape.canonical.com
  * Support: https://ubuntu.com/advantage
  System information as of Sun Apr 18 14:53:23 UTC 2021
  System load: 0.08 Processes: 118
  Usage of /: 3.2% of 38.71GB Users logged in: 0
  Memory usage: 20% IPv4 address for enp0s3: 10.0.2.15
  Swap usage: 0%


1 update can be installed immediately.
0 of these updates are security updates.
To see these additional updates run: apt list --upgradable

vagrant@ubuntu-focal:~$
```

A login with `vagrant ssh` lets you interact with the Bash shell, but Ansible needs to connect to the virtual machine by using the regular SSH client. Tell Vagrant to output its SSH configuration by typing the following:

```
$ vagrant ssh-config
```

On Bas's Windows machine, the output looks like this:

```
Host default
    HostName 127.0.0.1
    User vagrant
    Port 2222
    UserKnownHostsFile /dev/null
    StrictHostKeyChecking no
    PasswordAuthentication no
    IdentityFile C:/Users/basme/.vagrant.d/insecure_private_key
IdentitiesOnly yes
LogLevel FATAL
```

The important lines are shown here:

```
HostName 127.0.0.1
  User vagrant
  Port 2222
  IdentityFile C:/Users/basme/.vagrant.d/insecure_private_key
```

 Starting with version 1.7, Vagrant has changed how it manages private SSH keys: it now generates a new private key for each machine. Earlier versions used the same key, which was in the default location of *$HOME/.vagrant.d/insecure_private_key*. The examples in this book use Vagrant 2.2.

In your case, every field should be the same except for the path of the identity file.

Confirm that you can start an SSH session from the command line by using this information. The SSH command also works with a relative path from the *playbooks* directory:

```
$ ssh vagrant@127.0.0.1 -p 2222 \
    -i .vagrant/machines/default/virtualbox/private_key
```

You should see the Ubuntu login screen. Type **exit** to quit the SSH session.

Telling Ansible About Your Servers

Ansible can manage only the servers it explicitly knows about. You provide Ansible with information about servers by specifying them in an *inventory*. We usually create a directory called *inventory* to hold this information:

```
$ mkdir inventory
```

Each server needs a name that Ansible will use to identify it. You can use the hostname of the server, or you can give it an alias and pass other arguments to tell Ansible how to connect to it. We will give our Vagrant server the alias of testserver.

Create a text file in the *inventory* directory. Name the file *vagrant.ini* if you're using a Vagrant machine as your test server; name it *ec2.ini* if you use machines in Amazon EC2. Be aware that although this inventory file format is called *ini*, it's not strictly an INI file as defined by Microsoft. In that format there are always key-value pairs, which is not the case in an inventory file.

The *.ini* files will serve as an inventory for Ansible. They list the infrastructure that you want to manage under groups, which are denoted in square brackets. If you use Vagrant, your file should look like Example 2-1. The group [webservers] has one host: testserver. Here we see one of the drawbacks of using Vagrant: you need to pass extra *vars* data to Ansible to connect to the group. In most cases, you won't need these variables. On the other hand, if you use staging environments with different security settings, then the inventory is a good place to define these differences.

Example 2-1. inventory/vagrant.ini

```
[webservers]
testserver ansible_port=2222

[webservers:vars]
ansible_host=127.0.0.1
ansible_user=vagrant
ansible_private_key_file=.vagrant/machines/default/virtualbox/private_key
```

If you have an Ubuntu machine on Amazon EC2 with a hostname like *ec2-203-0-113-120.compute-1.amazonaws.com*, then your inventory file will look something like this:

```
[webservers]
testserver ansible_host=ec2-203-0-113-120.compute- 1.amazonaws.com

[webservers:vars]
ansible_user=ec2-user
ansible_private_key_file=/path/to/keyfile.pem
```

 Ansible supports the ssh-agent program, so you don't need to explicitly specify SSH key files in your inventory files. If you log in with your own user ID, then you don't need to specify that either.

We'll use the `ansible` command-line tool to verify that we can use Ansible to connect to the server. You won't use the `ansible` command often; it's mostly used for ad hoc, one-off things.

Let's tell Ansible to connect to the server named testserver described in the inventory file named *vagrant.ini* and invoke the `ping` module:

```
$ ansible testserver -i inventory/vagrant.ini -m ping
```

If your local SSH client has host-key verification enabled, you might see something that looks like this the first time Ansible tries to connect to the server:

```
The authenticity of host '[127.0.0.1]:2222 ([127.0.0.1]:2222)' can't be
established.
ED25519 key fingerprint is SHA256:6l2Lg8/EBqMFstGNPqFtLychVkxRxqdvRhvLlv/Tj1E.
Are you sure you want to continue connecting (yes/no)?
```

You can just type **yes**.

If it succeeds, the output will look like this:

```
testserver | SUCCESS => {
    "ansible_facts": {
        "discovered_interpreter_python": "/usr/bin/python3"
    },
    "changed": false,
    "ping": "pong"
}
```

 If Ansible did not succeed, add the -vvvv flag to see more details about the error:

```
$ ansible testserver -i inventory/vagrant.ini -m ping -vvvv
```

You can see that the module succeeded. The `"changed": false` part of the output tells us that executing the module did not change the state of the server. The `"ping":` `"pong"` output text is specific to the `ping` module.

The `ping` module doesn't do anything other than check that Ansible can start an SSH session with the servers. It's a tool for testing that Ansible can connect to the servers: very useful at the start of a big playbook.

Simplifying with the ansible.cfg File

You had to type a lot to use Ansible to ping your test server. Fortunately, Ansible has ways to organize these sorts of variables, so you don't have to put them all in one place. Right now, we'll add one such mechanism, the *ansible.cfg* file, to set some defaults so we don't need to type as much on the command line.

Where Should I Put My ansible.cfg File?

Ansible looks for an *ansible.cfg* file in the following places, in this order:

- File specified by the `ANSIBLE_CONFIG` environment variable
- *./ansible.cfg* (*ansible.cfg* in the current directory)
- *~/.ansible.cfg* (*.ansible.cfg* in your home directory)
- */etc/ansible/ansible.cfg* (Linux) or */usr/local/etc/ansible/ansible.cfg* (*BSD)

We typically put *ansible.cfg* in the current directory, alongside our playbooks. That way, we can check it into the same version-control repository that our playbooks are in. This also adds the possibility to have a project-based configuration file.

Example 2-2 shows an *ansible.cfg* file that specifies the location of the inventory file (*inventory*) and sets parameters that affect the way Ansible runs, for instance how the output is presented.

Since the user you'll log on to and its SSH private key might depend on the inventory that you use, it is practical to use the *vars* block in the inventory file, rather than in the *ansible.cfg* file, to specify such connection parameter values. Although it is possible to add a private key filename to the *ansible.cfg* or the inventory files, doing so make it less flexible to share your project with multiple users. The alternative is to rely implicitly to your SSH configuration.

Our example *ansible.cfg* configuration also disables SSH host-key checking. This is convenient when dealing with Vagrant machines; otherwise, we need to edit our *~/.ssh/known_hosts* file every time we destroy and re-create a Vagrant machine. However, disabling host-key checking can be a security risk when connecting to other servers over the network.

Example 2-2. ansible.cfg

```
[defaults]
inventory = inventory/vagrant.ini
host_key_checking = False
stdout_callback = yaml
callback_enabled = timer
```

Ansible and Version Control

Ansible uses */etc/ansible/hosts* as the default location for the inventory file. Keeping the inventory in the same directory as the playbooks and so on gives you the possibility of a specific inventory per project instead of just a global one. If you separate your project from your inventory, then it is easier to reuse the project on machines owned by others.

Although we don't cover version control in this book, we strongly recommend you commit to using the Git version-control system to save all changes to your playbooks. If you're a developer, you're already familiar with version-control systems. If you're a systems administrator and aren't using version control yet, Git (*https://git-scm.com*) is a perfect tool for you to really start with *infrastructure as code*!

With your default values set, you can invoke Ansible without passing the -i hostname arguments, like so:

```
$ ansible testserver -m ping
```

We like to use the ansible command-line tool to run arbitrary commands on remote machines, like parallel SSH. You can execute arbitrary commands with the command module. When invoking this module, you also need to pass an argument to the module with the -a flag, which is the command to run.

For example, to check the uptime of your server, you can use this:

```
$ ansible testserver -m command -a uptime
```

The output should look like this:

```
testserver | CHANGED | rc=0 >>
   10:37:28 up 2 days, 14:11, 1 user, load average: 0.00, 0.00, 0.00
```

The command module is so commonly used that it's the default module, so you can omit it:

```
$ ansible testserver -a uptime
```

If your command has spaces, quote it so that the shell passes the entire string as a single argument to Ansible. For example, to view the last ten lines of the */var/log/dmesg* logfile:

```
$ ansible testserver -a "tail /var/log/dmesg"
```

The output from our Vagrant machine looks like this:

```
testserver | CHANGED | rc=0 >>
[ 9.940870] kernel: 14:48:17.642147 main   VBoxService 6.1.16_Ubuntu r140961
(verbosity: 0) linux.amd64 (Dec 17 2020 22:06:23) release log
                    14:48:17.642148 main   Log opened 2021-04-18T14:48:17.642143000Z
[ 9.941331] kernel: 14:48:17.642623 main   OS Product: Linux
[ 9.941419] kernel: 14:48:17.642718 main   OS Release: 5.4.0-72-generic
[ 9.941506] kernel: 14:48:17.642805 main   OS Version: #80-Ubuntu SMP Mon Apr 12
17:35:00 UTC 2021
[ 9.941602] kernel: 14:48:17.642895 main   Executable: /usr/sbin/VBoxService
                    14:48:17.642896 main   Process ID: 751
                    14:48:17.642896 main   Package type: LINUX_64BITS_GENERIC
                    (OSE)
[ 9.942730] kernel: 14:48:17.644030 main   6.1.16_Ubuntu r140961 started.
Verbose level = 0
[ 9.943491] kernel: 14:48:17.644783 main   vbglR3GuestCtrlDetectPeekGetCancelSupport:
Supported (#1)
```

If you need privileged access, pass in the -b or --become flag to tell Ansible to *become* the root user. On Unix/Linux this is commonly done with a tool like *sudo* that needs to be set up. In the Vagrant examples in this book that has been done automatically.

For example, accessing */var/log/syslog* might require elevated privileges:

```
$ ansible testserver -b -a "tail /var/log/syslog"
```

The output looks something like this:

```
testserver | CHANGED | rc=0 >>
Apr 23 10:39:41 ubuntu-focal multipathd[471]: sdb: failed to get udev uid:
Invalid argument
Apr 23 10:39:41 ubuntu-focal multipathd[471]: sdb: failed to get sysfs uid: No
data available
Apr 23 10:39:41 ubuntu-focal multipathd[471]: sdb: failed to get sgio uid: No
data available
Apr 23 10:39:42 ubuntu-focal multipathd[471]: sda: add missing path
Apr 23 10:39:42 ubuntu-focal multipathd[471]: sda: failed to get udev uid:
Invalid argument
Apr 23 10:39:42 ubuntu-focal multipathd[471]: sda: failed to get sysfs uid: No
data available
Apr 23 10:39:42 ubuntu-focal multipathd[471]: sda: failed to get sgio uid: No
data available
Apr 23 10:39:43 ubuntu-focal systemd[1]: session-95.scope: Succeeded.
Apr 23 10:39:44 ubuntu-focal systemd[1]: Started Session 97 of user vagrant.
Apr 23 10:39:44 ubuntu-focal python3[187384]: ansible-command Invoked with
_raw_params=tail /var/log/syslog warn=True _uses_shell=False stdin_add_newline=True
strip_empty_ends=True argv=None chdir=None executable=None creates=None
removes=None stdin=None
```

You can see from this output that Ansible writes to the syslog as it runs.

You are not restricted to the `ping` and `command` modules when using the `ansible` command-line tool: you can use any module that you like. For example, you can install NGINX on Ubuntu by using the following command:

```
$ ansible testserver -b -m package -a name=nginx
```

 If installing NGINX fails for you, you might need to update the package lists. To tell Ansible to do the equivalent of an apt-get update before installing the package, change the argument from `name=nginx` to `name=nginx update_cache=yes`.

You can restart NGINX as follows:

```
$ ansible testserver -b -m service -a "name=nginx
state=restarted"
```

You need the `-b` argument to become the root user because only root can install the NGINX package and restart services.

Kill Your Darlings

We will improve the setup of the test server in this book, so don't become attached to your first virtual machine. Just remove it for now with:

```
$ vagrant destroy -f
```

Convenient Vagrant Configuration Options

Vagrant exposes many configuration options for virtual machines, but there are two that are particularly useful when using Vagrant for testing: setting a specific IP address and enabling agent forwarding.

Port Forwarding and Private IP Addresses

When you create a new Vagrantfile by using the `vagrant init` command, the default networking configuration allows you to reach the Vagrant box only via an SSH port that is forwarded from `localhost`. For the first Vagrant machine that you start, that's port 2222, and each subsequent Vagrant machine you bring up will forward a different port. As a consequence, the only way to access your Vagrant machine in the default configuration is to SSH to `localhost` on port 2222. Vagrant forwards this to port 22 on the Vagrant machine.

This default configuration isn't very useful for testing web-based applications, since the web application will be listening on a port that we can't access.

There are two ways around this. One way is to tell Vagrant to set up another forwarded port. For example, if your web application listens on port 80 inside your Vagrant machine, you can configure Vagrant to forward port 8040 on your local machine to port 80 on the Vagrant machine. Likewise you can forward local port 8443 to port 443 in the guest.

As shown in Figure 2-1, we are going to configure Vagrant so that our local machine forwards browser requests on ports 8080 and 8443 to ports 80 and 443 on the Vagrant machine. This will allow us to access the web server running inside Vagrant at *http://localhost:8080* and *https://localhost:8443*.

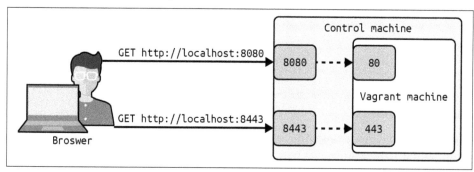

Figure 2-1. Exposing ports on a Vagrant machine

Example 2-3 shows how to configure port forwarding by editing the Vagrantfile.

Example 2-3. Forwarding local port 8000 to Vagrant machine port 80

```
# Vagrantfile
VAGRANTFILE_API_VERSION = "2"

Vagrant.configure(VAGRANTFILE_API_VERSION) do |config|
  # Other config options not shown
  config.vm.network :forwarded_port, host: 8000, guest: 80
  config.vm.network :forwarded_port, host: 8443, guest: 443
end
```

Port forwarding to other machines on the local network also works, so we find it more useful to assign the Vagrant machine its own IP address. That way, interacting with it is more like interacting with a private remote server: you can connect directly to port 80 on the machine's IP rather than connecting to port 8000 on localhost, and you're the only one unless you forward a port as well.

A simpler approach is to assign the machine a private IP. Example 2-4 shows how to assign the IP address *192.168.33.10* to the machine by editing the Vagrantfile.

Example 2-4. Assign a private IP to a Vagrant machine

```
# Vagrantfile
VAGRANTFILE_API_VERSION = "2"

Vagrant.configure(VAGRANTFILE_API_VERSION) do |config|
  # Other config options not shown

  config.vm.network "private_network", ip: "192.168.33.10"
end
```

If we run a web server on port 80 of our Vagrant machine, we can access it at *http://192.168.33.10*.

This configuration uses a Vagrant *private network*. The machine will be accessible only from the machine that runs Vagrant. You won't be able to connect to this IP address from another physical machine, even if it's on the same network as the machine running Vagrant. However, different Vagrant machines can connect to each other.

Check out the Vagrant documentation (*https://oreil.ly/EXvBL*) for more details on the different networking configuration options.

Enabling Agent Forwarding

If you are checking out a remote Git repository over SSH and you need to use agent forwarding, then you must configure your Vagrant machine so that Vagrant enables agent forwarding when it connects to the agent via SSH (see Example 2-5). For more on agent forwarding, see Chapter 20.

Example 2-5. Enabling agent forwarding

```
# Vagrantfile
VAGRANTFILE_API_VERSION = "2"

Vagrant.configure(VAGRANTFILE_API_VERSION) do |config|
  # Other config options not shown
  # enable ssh agent forwarding
  config.ssh.forward_agent = true
end
```

The Docker Provisioner

Sometimes you want to compare containers running on different Linux variants and different container runtimes. Vagrant can create a virtual machine from a box, install Docker or Podman, and run a container image automatically, all in one go:

```
Vagrant.configure("2") do |config|
  config.vm.box = "ubuntu/focal64"
  config.vm.provision "docker" do |d|
    d.run "nginx"
  end
end
```

The Ansible Local Provisioner

Vagrant has external tools called *provisioners* that it uses to configure a virtual machine after it has started up. In addition to Ansible, Vagrant can also provision with shell scripts, Chef, Puppet, Salt, and CFEngine.

Example 2-6 shows a Vagrantfile that has been configured with `ansible_local`, which installs Ansible in the virtual machine and uses it as a provisioner, specifically using the Ansible playbook named *playbook.yml*.

Example 2-6. Vagrantfile

```
VAGRANTFILE_API_VERSION = "2"
Vagrant.configure(VAGRANTFILE_API_VERSION) do |config|
  config.vm.box = "ubuntu/xenial64"
  config.vm.provision "ansible_local" do |ansible|
    ansible.compatibility_mode = "2.0"
    ansible.galaxy_role_file = "roles/requirements.yml"
    ansible.galaxy_roles_path = "roles"
    ansible.playbook = "playbook.yml"
    ansible.verbose = "vv"
  end
end
```

So, you don't need to install Ansible on your machine to use it when you have `config.vm.provision "ansible_local"` in your Vagrantfile; it will be installed and run in the virtual machine. When you use `config.vm.provision "ansible"` in the Vagrantfile, the provisioner does use Ansible on your machine. Adapt the examples in the sample code to your liking.

When the Provisioner Runs

The first time you run `vagrant up`, Vagrant will execute the provisioner and record that the provisioner was run. If you halt the virtual machine and then start it up, Vagrant remembers that it has already run the provisioner and will not run it a second time.

You can force Vagrant to run the provisioner against a running virtual machine as follows:

```
$ vagrant provision
```

You can also reboot a virtual machine and run the provisioner after reboot:

```
$ vagrant reload --provision
```

Similarly, you can start up a halted virtual machine and have Vagrant run the provisioner:

```
$ vagrant up --provision
```

Or you can start up the virtual machine and *not* run the provisioner:

```
$ vagrant up --no-provision
```

We use these commands quite often to run playbooks from the command line, with a tag or a limit.

Vagrant Plug-ins

Vagrant is extensible by a plug-in mechanism. In recent versions you only need to specify which plug-ins you want to use. Let's look at two examples: `vagrant-hostmanager` and `vagrant-vbguest`:

```
config.vagrant.plugins = ["vagrant-hostmanager", "vagrant-vbguest"]
```

Hostmanager

The `vagrant-hostmanager` plug-in helps in addressing multiple virtual machines by hostname. It will change the hostnames and edit */etc/hosts* on the guests, as well as the host at times, depending on the configuration:

```
# manage /etc/hosts
config.hostmanager.enabled = true
config.hostmanager.include_offline = true
config.hostmanager.manage_guest = true
config.hostmanager.manage_host = true
```

VBGuest

The `vagrant-vbguest` plug-in works on VirtualBox and can automatically install or update Guest Additions in your guest virtual machines. Bas usually disables these features on macOS, because file sharing between guests and macOS is not fast enough, and not always reliable. Moreover, file sharing between host and guest does not mimic the way we deploy software, from development to testing, staging, and production environments. But for learning Ansible on Windows it works fine:

```
# update guest additions
if Vagrant.has_plugin?("vagrant-vbguest")
  config.vbguest.auto_update = true
end
```

VirtualBox Customization

You can define properties of your virtual machine and its appearance in VirtualBox. Here is an example:

```
host_config.vm.provider "virtualbox" do |vb|
  vb.name = "web"
  virtualbox.customize ["modifyvm", :id,
      "--audio", "none",
      "--cpus", 2,
      "--memory", 2048,
      "--graphicscontroller", "VMSVGA",
      "--vram", "64"
    ]
end
```

Vagrantfile Is Ruby

It helps to know that a Vagrant 2 file is executed by a Ruby interpreter, if only for syntax highlighting in your editor. You can declare variables, work with control structures and loops, and so on. In the source code that goes with this book, there is a more evolved example (*https://oreil.ly/h1jTF*) of a Vagrantfile that we use to work with 15 different Linux variants as shown in Figure 2-2.

Figure 2-2. Running different Linux distributions in VirtualBox

We use a JSON file for guest configurations with elements like:

```json
[
    {
        "name": "centos8",
        "cpus": 1,
        "distro": "centos",
        "family": "redhat",
        "gui": false,
        "box": "centos/stream8",
        "ip_addr": "192.168.56.6",
        "memory": "1024",
        "no_share": false,
        "app_port": "80",
```

```
            "forwarded_port": "8006"
        },
        {
            "name": "focal",
            "cpus": 1,
            "distro": "ubuntu",
            "family": "debian",
            "gui": false,
            "box": "ubuntu/focal64",
            "ip_addr": "192.168.56.8",
            "memory": "1024",
            "no_share": false,
            "app_port": "80",
            "forwarded_port": "8008"
        }
    ]
```

And in the Vagrantfile, we have a couple of constructs to create one guest by name when we enter, for example:

```
$ vagrant up focal
```

Here is the Vagrantfile:

```
Vagrant.require_version ">= 2.0.0"
# Require JSON module
require 'json'
# Read JSON file with config details
f = JSON.parse(File.read(File.join(File.dirname(__FILE__), 'config.json')))
# Local PATH_SRC for mounting
$PathSrc = ENV['PATH_SRC'] || "."
Vagrant.configure(2) do |config|
  config.vagrant.plugins = ["vagrant-hostmanager", "vagrant-vbguest"]
  # check for updates of the base image
  config.vm.box_check_update = true
  # wait a while longer
  config.vm.boot_timeout = 1200
  # disable update guest additions
  if Vagrant.has_plugin?("vagrant-vbguest")
    config.vbguest.auto_update = false
  end
  # enable ssh agent forwarding
  config.ssh.forward_agent = true
  # use the standard vagrant ssh key
  config.ssh.insert_key = false
  # manage /etc/hosts
  config.hostmanager.enabled = true
  config.hostmanager.include_offline = true
  config.hostmanager.manage_guest = true
  config.hostmanager.manage_host = true
  # Iterate through entries in JSON file
  f.each do |g|
    config.vm.define g['name'] do |s|
      s.vm.box = g['box']
      s.vm.hostname = g['name']
      s.vm.network 'private_network', ip: g['ip_addr']
```

```
        s.vm.network :forwarded_port,
          host: g['forwarded_port'],
          guest: g['app_port']
        # set no_share to false to enable file sharing
        s.vm.synced_folder ".", "/vagrant", disabled: g['no_share']
        s.vm.provider :virtualbox do |virtualbox|
          virtualbox.customize ["modifyvm", :id,
              "--audio", "none",
              "--cpus", g['cpus'],
              "--memory", g['memory'],
              "--graphicscontroller", "VMSVGA",
              "--vram", "64"
          ]
          virtualbox.gui = g['gui']
          virtualbox.name = g['name']
        end
      end
    end
    config.vm.provision "ansible_local" do |ansible|
      ansible.compatibility_mode = "2.0"
      ansible.galaxy_role_file = "roles/requirements.yml"
      ansible.galaxy_roles_path = "roles"
      ansible.playbook = "playbook.yml"
      ansible.verbose = "vv"
    end
  end
```

The properties of each virtual machine are configured in the *config.json* file.

Production Setup

Ansible uses SSH to connect to Linux/macOS/BSD machines, and WinRM to connect to Windows machines. Network devices can be managed over HTTPS or SSH. There is no need for additional software on the target hosts (provided that Linux/macOS/BSD machines have Python, and Windows machines have PowerShell).

Traditional system administrators are cautious when tools are introduced that need system privileges, because typically only the system administrators themselves have these permissions. A common pattern on Unix is to delegate only specific commands to developers using the sudo tool with carefully crafted files in */etc/sudoers.d/*.

This approach does not work with Ansible, nor does a restrictive shell like rbash. Ansible creates temporary directories with random names for various Python scripts, while sudo needs exact commands. The alternative is shifting the focus on the content of changes to version control, in a staging environment, and having a sudoers file for the ansible group like:

```
%ansible    ALL=(ALL) ALL
```

Conclusion

This chapter was an overview of how to get started by installing Ansible and creating a test environment with VirtualBox and Vagrant to learn Ansible. Vagrant supports many other options that aren't covered in this chapter. For more details, see the official Vagrant documentation. A full treatment of Vagrant is beyond the scope of this book. For more information, check out *Vagrant: Up and Running* (O'Reilly), authored by Mitchell Hashimoto, the creator of Vagrant.

## CHAPTER 3

Playbooks: A Beginning

When you start using Ansible, one of the first things you'll do is begin writing playbooks. *Playbook* is the term that Ansible uses for a configuration management script. Let's look at an example: here is a playbook for installing the NGINX web server and configuring it for secure communication.

If you follow along in this chapter, you should end up with the directory tree listed here:

```
.
├── Vagrantfile
├── ansible.cfg
├── files
│   ├── index.html
│   ├── nginx.conf
│   ├── nginx.crt
│   └── nginx.key
├── inventory
│   └── vagrant.ini
├── requirements.txt
├── templates
│   ├── index.html.j2
│   └── nginx.conf.j2
├── webservers-tls.yml
├── webservers.yml
└── webservers2.yml
```

Preliminaries

Modify your Vagrantfile so it looks like this:

```
Vagrant.configure(2) do |config|
  config.vm.box = "ubuntu/focal64"
  config.vm.hostname = "testserver"
  config.vm.network "forwarded_port",
```

```
        id: 'ssh', guest: 22, host: 2202, host_ip: "127.0.0.1", auto_correct: false
    config.vm.network "forwarded_port",
        id: 'http', guest: 80, host: 8080, host_ip: "127.0.0.1"
    config.vm.network "forwarded_port",
        id: 'https', guest: 443, host: 8443, host_ip: "127.0.0.1"
    # disable updating guest additions
    if Vagrant.has_plugin?("vagrant-vbguest")
        config.vbguest.auto_update = false
    end
    config.vm.provider "virtualbox" do |virtualbox|
        virtualbox.name = "ch03"
    end
end
```

This maps port 8080 on your local machine to port 80 of the Vagrant machine, and port 8443 on your local machine to port 443 on the Vagrant machine. Also, it reserves the forwarding port 2202 to this specific virtual machine (VM), as you might still want to run the other from Chapter 1. Once you made these changes, tell Vagrant to implement them by running this command:

```
$ vagrant up
```

You should see output that includes the following:

```
==> default: Forwarding ports...
    default: 22 (guest) => 2202 (host) (adapter 1)
    default: 80 (guest) => 8080 (host) (adapter 1)
    default: 443 (guest) => 8443 (host) (adapter 1)
```

Your test server is up and running now.

A Very Simple Playbook

For our first example playbook, we'll configure a host to run a simple HTTP server. You'll see what happens when we run the playbook in *webservers.yml* (Example 3-1), and then we'll go over the contents of the playbook in detail. This is the simplest playbook to achieve this task, and we will discuss ways to improve it.

Example 3-1. webservers.yml

```
---

- name: Configure webserver with nginx
  hosts: webservers
  become: True
  tasks:
    - name: Ensure nginx is installed
      package: name=nginx update_cache=yes

    - name: Copy nginx config file
      copy:
        src: nginx.conf
```

```
      dest: /etc/nginx/sites-available/default

  - name: Enable configuration
    file: >
      dest=/etc/nginx/sites-enabled/default
      src=/etc/nginx/sites-available/default
      state=link

  - name: Copy index.html
    template: >
      src=index.html.j2
      dest=/usr/share/nginx/html/index.html

  - name: Restart nginx
    service: name=nginx state=restarted
...
```

Specifying an NGINX Config File

This playbook requires an NGINX configuration file.

NGINX ships with a configuration file that works out of the box if you just want to serve static files. But you'll always need to customize this, so we'll overwrite the default configuration file with our own as part of this playbook. As you'll see later, we'll improve the configuration to support TLS. Example 3-2 shows a basic NGINX config file. Put it in *playbooks/files/nginx.conf*.[1]

Example 3-2. nginx.conf

```
server {
        listen 80 default_server;
        listen [::]:80 default_server ipv6only=on;

        root /usr/share/nginx/html;
        index index.html index.htm;

        server_name localhost;

        location / {
                try_files $uri $uri/ =404;
        }
}
```

---

1 Although we call this file *nginx.conf*, it replaces the sites-enabled/default NGINX server block config file, not the main */etc/nginx.conf* config file.

Creating a Web Page

Next, we'll create a simple web page. Ansible has a system to generate the HTML page from a template file. Put the content shown in Example 3-3 in *playbooks/templates/index.html.j2*.

Example 3-3. playbooks/templates/index.html.j2

```
<html>
  <head>
    <title>Welcome to ansible</title>
  </head>
  <body>
  <h1>Nginx, configured by Ansible</h1>
  <p>If you can see this, Ansible successfully installed nginx.</p>

  <p>Running on {{ inventory_hostname }}</p>
  </body>
</html>
```

This template references a special Ansible variable named `inventory_hostname`. When Ansible renders this template, it will replace this variable with the name of the host as it appears in the inventory (see Figure 3-1). Rendered HTML tells a web browser how to display the page.

An Ansible convention is to copy files from a subdirectory named *files*, and to source Jinja2 templates from a subdirectory named *templates*. Ansible searches these directories automatically. We follow this convention throughout the book.

Figure 3-1. Rendered HTML

Creating a Group

Let's create a `webservers` group in our inventory file so that we can refer to this group in our playbook. For now, this group will have only our test server.

The simplest inventory files are in the *.ini* file format. We'll go into this format in detail later in the book. Edit your *playbooks/inventory/vagrant.ini* file to have a [webservers] line above the testserver line, as shown in *playbooks/inventory/ vagrant.ini*. This means that testserver is in the webservers group. The group can have variables, for instance to establish the connection to the servers (vars is a shorthand for variables). Your file should look like Example 3-4.

Example 3-4. playbooks/inventory/vagrant.ini

```
[webservers]
testserver ansible_port=2202

[webservers:vars]
ansible_user = vagrant
ansible_host = 127.0.0.1
ansible_private_key_file = .vagrant/machines/default/virtualbox/private_key
```

You created the *ansible.cfg* file with an inventory entry in Chapter 1, so you don't need to supply the -i command-line argument. You can now check your groups in the inventory with this command:

```
$ ansible-inventory --graph
```

The output should look like this:

```
@all:
  |--@ungrouped:
  |--@webservers:
  |  |--testserver
```

Running the Playbook

The ansible-playbook command executes playbooks. To run the playbook, use this command:

```
$ ansible-playbook webservers.yml
```

Your output should look like Example 3-5.

Example 3-5. Output of ansible-playbook

```
PLAY [Configure webserver with nginx] ****************************************
TASK [Gathering Facts] ******************************************************
ok: [testserver]

TASK [Ensure nginx is installed] ********************************************
changed: [testserver]

TASK [Copy nginx config file] ***********************************************
changed: [testserver]
```

```
TASK [Enable configuration] ***************************************************
ok: [testserver]

TASK [Copy index.html] ********************************************************
changed: [testserver]

TASK [Restart nginx] **********************************************************
changed: [testserver]

PLAY RECAP ********************************************************************
testserver : ok=6 changed=4 unreachable=0 failed=0 skipped=0 rescued=0 ignored=0
Playbook run took 0 days, 0 hours, 0 minutes, 18 seconds
```

If you don't get any errors, you should be able to point your browser to *http://local-host:8080* and see the custom HTML page, as shown in Figure 3-1.[2]

Cowsay

No O'Reilly book with such a cover would be complete without describing cowsay support. If you have the cowsay program installed on your local machine, Ansible output will include a cow in ASCII art like this:

```
< PLAY [Configure webserver with nginx] >
 ----------------------------------------
        \   ^__^
         \  (oo)_____
            (__)\       )\/\
                ||----w |
                ||     ||
```

If you like more animals in your log, then try adding this to your *ansible.cfg* file:

```
[defaults]
cow_selection = random
cowsay_enabled_stencils=cow,bunny,kitty,koala,moose,sheep,tux
```

For a full list of alternate images on your local machine, use:

cowsay -l

If you don't want to see the cows, you can disable it by adding the following to your *ansible.cfg* file:

```
[defaults]
nocows = 1
```

You can disable cowsay by setting the ANSIBLE_NOCOWS environment variable like this:

$ export ANSIBLE_NOCOWS=1

---

2 If you do encounter an error, you might want to skip to Chapter 8 for assistance with debugging.

Playbooks Are YAML

One writes Ansible playbooks in YAML syntax. YAML is a file format very much like JSON, but it's easier for humans to read and write. Before we go over the playbook, let's cover the most important YAML concepts for writing playbooks.

 A valid JSON file is also a valid YAML file. This is because YAML allows strings to be quoted, considers true and false to be valid Booleans, and has inline lists and dictionary syntaxes that are essentially the same as JSON arrays and objects. But don't write your playbooks as JSON—the whole point of YAML is that it's easier for people to read.

Start of Document

YAML has three dashes to mark the beginning of a document. Ansible files have only one YAML document each.

```
---
```

In Ansible playbooks it is customary to start with the three "-" (so that editors can pick up on this). However, if you forget to put those three dashes at the top of your playbook files, Ansible won't complain.

End of File

YAML files may end with three dots, which can be useful to prove completeness. But quite often this practice is skipped.

```
...
```

If you forget to put those three dots at the end of your playbook files, Ansible won't complain.

Comments

Comments start with a hashmark (#) and apply to the end of the line, the same as in shell scripts, Python, and Ruby. Indent comments with the other content.

```
# This is a YAML comment
```

Indentation and Whitespace

Like Python, YAML uses space indentation to reduce the number of interpunction characters. We use two spaces as a standard. For readability, we prefer to add whitespace between each task in a playbook, and between sections in files.

Strings

In general, you don't need to quote YAML strings. Even if there are spaces, you don't need to quote them. For example, this is a string in YAML:

```
this is a lovely sentence
```

The JSON equivalent is as follows:

```
"this is a lovely sentence"
```

In some scenarios in Ansible, you will need to quote strings. It is a good practice just to quote all strings. Double-quoting typically involves the use of variable interpolation or other expressions. Use single quotes for literal values that should not be evaluated, like version numbers and floating point numbers, or strings with reserved characters like colons, brackets, or braces. We'll get to those later.

Never, ever, put Boolean values in quotation marks! Remember this: NO is a string (the country abbreviation of Norway).

Booleans

YAML has a native Boolean type and provides you with a variety of values that evaluate to true or false. For example, these are all Boolean true values in YAML:

```
true, True, TRUE, yes, Yes, YES, on, On, ON
```

JSON only uses:

```
true
```

These are all Boolean false values in YAML:

```
false, False, FALSE, no, No, NO, off, Off, OFF
```

JSON only uses:

```
false
```

Bas uses only lowercase `true` and `false` in Ansible. One reason is that these two are the values that are returned; for example, they are printed in debug when you use any other allowed variant. Because true and false are valid Booleans in JSON too, sticking to these simplifies using dynamic data, because Ansible actions return results as JSON data.

Why Don't You Use True in One Place and Yes in Another?

Sharp-eyed readers might have noticed that *webservers.yml* uses True in one spot in the playbook (to become root) and yes in another (to update the apt cache).

Ansible is flexible in how you use truthy and falsey values in play-books. Strictly speaking, Ansible treats module arguments (e.g., `update_cache=yes`) differently from values elsewhere in playbooks (for example, `become: True`). Values elsewhere are handled by the YAML parser and so use the YAML conventions of truthiness:

1. YAML truthy: true, True, TRUE, yes, Yes, YES, on, On, ON
2. YAML falsey: false, False, FALSE, no, No, NO, off, Off, OFF

Module arguments are passed as strings and use Ansible's internal conventions:

```
module arg truthy: yes, on, 1, true
module arg falsey: no, off, 0, false
```

It is good practice to check all YAML files with a command-line tool called `yamllint`. In its default configuration it will issue this warning:

```
warning truthy value should be one of [false, true] (truthy)
```

To adhere to this "truthy" rule, Bas uses only `true` and `false` (unquoted).

Lists

YAML lists are like arrays in JSON and Ruby, or lists in Python. The YAML specification calls these *sequences*, but we call them *lists* here to be consistent with the official Ansible documentation.

Indent list items and delimit them with hyphens. Lists have a name followed by a colon, as follows:

```
shows:
    - My Fair Lady
    - Oklahoma
    - The Pirates of Penzance
```

This is the JSON equivalent:

```
{
    "shows": [
      "My Fair Lady",
      "Oklahoma",
      "The Pirates of Penzance"
      ]
}
```

As you can see, YAML is easier to read because fewer characters are needed. We don't have to quote the strings in YAML, even though they have spaces in them. YAML also supports an inline format for lists, with comma-separated values in square brackets:

```
shows: [ My Fair Lady , Oklahoma , The Pirates of Penzance ]
```

Dictionaries

YAML dictionaries are like objects in JSON, dictionaries in Python, hashes in Ruby, or associative arrays in PHP. The YAML specification calls them *mappings*, but we call them *dictionaries* here to be consistent with the Ansible documentation. They look like this:

```
address:
  street: Main Street
  appt: 742
  city: Logan
  state: Ohio
```

This is the JSON equivalent:

```
{
  "address": {
    "street": "Main Street",
    "appt": 742,
    "city": "Logan",
    "state": "Ohio"
  }
}
```

YAML also supports an inline format for dictionaries, with comma-separated tuples in braces:

```
address: { street: Main Street, appt: '742', city: Logan, state: Ohio}
```

Multiline Strings

You can format multiline strings with YAML by combining a block style indicator (| or >), a block chomping indicator (+ or –), and even an indentation indicator (1 to 9). For example, when we need a preformatted block, we use the pipe character with a plus sign (|+):

```
---
visiting_address: |+
  Department of Computer Science

  A.V. Williams Building
  University of Maryland
city: College Park
state: Maryland
```

The YAML parser will keep all line breaks as you enter them.

JSON does not support the use of multiline strings. You either need to replace all the line breaks with \n (to encode a newline) or, to encode this in JSON, you would need an array in the address field:

```
{
    "visiting_address": ["Department of Computer Science",
        "A.V. Williams Building",
        "University of Maryland"],
    "city": "College Park",
    "state": "Maryland"
}
```

Pure YAML Instead of String Arguments

When writing playbooks, you'll often find situations where you're passing many arguments to a module. For aesthetics, you might want to break this up across multiple lines in your file. Moreover, you want Ansible to parse the arguments as a YAML dictionary, because you can use yamllint to find typos in YAML that you won't find when you use the string format. This style also has shorter lines, which makes version comparison easier.

Lorin likes this style:

```
- name: Ensure nginx is installed
  package: name=nginx update_cache=true
```

Bas prefers pure-YAML style, because that can be parsed for correctness by yamllint:

```
- name: Ensure nginx is installed
  package:
    name: nginx
    update_cache: true
```

Anatomy of a Playbook

If we apply what we've discussed so far to our playbook, then we have a second version (Example 3-6).

Example 3-6. webservers2.yml

```
---
- name: Configure webserver with nginx
  hosts: webservers
  become: true
  tasks:
    - name: Ensure nginx is installed
      package:
        name: nginx
        update_cache: true

    - name: Copy nginx config file
```

```
    copy:
      src: nginx.conf
      dest: /etc/nginx/sites-available/default

  - name: Enable configuration
    file:
      src: /etc/nginx/sites-available/default
      dest: /etc/nginx/sites-enabled/default
      state: link

  - name: Copy home page template
    template:
      src: index.html.j2
      dest: /usr/share/nginx/html/index.html

  - name: Restart nginx
    service:
      name: nginx
      state: restarted
...
```

Plays

Looking at the YAML, it should be clear that a playbook is a list of dictionaries. Specifically, a playbook is a list of plays. Our example is a list that has only a single play, named Configure webserver with nginx.

Here's the play from our example:

```
- name: Configure webserver with nginx
  hosts: webservers
  become: true

  tasks:
    - name: Ensure nginx is installed
      package:
        name: nginx
        update_cache: true

    - name: Copy nginx config file
      copy:
        src: nginx.conf
        dest: /etc/nginx/sites-available/default

    - name: Enable configuration
      file:
        src: /etc/nginx/sites-available/default
        dest: /etc/nginx/sites-enabled/default
        state: link

    - name: Copy index.html
      template:
        src: index.html.j2
        dest: /usr/share/nginx/html/index.html
```

```
- name: Restart nginx
  service:
    name: nginx
    state: restarted
...
```

Every play must contain the `hosts` variable, and that can be a group like `webservers`, the magic group `all` (all hosts in the inventory), or an expression of a set of hosts to configure. Think of a play as the thing that connects to a group of hosts and a list of things to do on those hosts for you. Sometimes you need to do different things on more groups of hosts, and then you use more plays in a playbook.

In addition to specifying hosts and tasks, plays support optional settings. We'll get into those later, but here are three common ones:

`name:`
   A comment that describes what the play is about. Ansible prints the name when the play starts to run. Start the name with an uppercase letter as a best practice.

`become:`
   If this Boolean variable is true, Ansible will become the `become_user` to run tasks. This is useful when managing Linux servers, since by default you should not log in as the root user. `become` can be specified per task, or per play, as needed, and `become_user` can be used to specify root (the default if omitted) or another user, yet `become` is subject to your system's policies. A *sudoers* file might need to be adjusted to be able to become root.

`vars:`
   A list of variables and values. You'll see this in action later in this chapter.

Tasks

Our example playbook contains one play that has five tasks. Here's the first task of that play:

```
- name: Ensure nginx is installed
  package:
    name: nginx
    update_cache: true
```

In the preceding example, the module name is `package` and the arguments are `name: nginx` and `update_cache: yes`. These arguments tell the `package` module to install the package named `nginx` and to update the package cache (the equivalent of doing an apt-get update on Ubuntu) before installing the package.

The name is optional, but it's good style. Try to name a task with a logical and correct name. Task names serve as good reminders for the intent of the task. (Names will be very useful when somebody is trying to understand your playbook's log, including you in six months.) As you've seen, Ansible will print out the name of a task when it runs. Finally, as you'll see in Chapter 16, you can use the `--start-at-task <task name>` flag to tell `ansible-playbook` to start a playbook in the middle of a play, but you need to reference the task by name.

Arguments for a module can be passed as one string to the `ansible` command with the `-a` flag; the `-m` flag specifies the module:

```
$ ansible webservers -b -m package -a 'name=nginx update_cache=true'
```

However, it's important to understand that in this form, from the Ansible parser's point of view, the arguments are treated as one string, not as a dictionary. In ad hoc commands that's fine, but in playbooks this means that there is more space for bugs to creep in, especially with complex modules with many optional arguments. Bas, for better version control and linting, also prefers to break arguments into multiple lines. Therefore, we always use the YAML syntax, like this:

```
- name: Ensure nginx is installed
  package:
    name: nginx
    update_cache: true
```

Modules

Modules are scripts that come packaged with Ansible and perform some kind of action on a host. That's a pretty generic description, but there is enormous variety among Ansible modules. Recall from Chapter 1 that Ansible executes a task on a host by generating a custom script based on the module name and arguments, and then copies this script to the host and runs it. The modules for Unix/Linux that ship with Ansible are written in Python, and the modules for Windows are written in PowerShell, with a counterpart in Python that contains only the documentation. You can write your own modules in any language.

We use the following modules in this chapter:

package
    Installs or removes packages by using the host's package manager

copy
    Copies a file from the machine where you run Ansible to the web servers

file
    Sets the attribute of a file, symlink, or directory

service
Starts, stops, or restarts a service

template
Generates a file from a template and copies it to the hosts

Viewing Ansible Module Documentation

Ansible ships with the `ansible-doc` command-line tool, which shows documentation about the modules you have installed. Think of it as main pages for Ansible modules. For example, to show the documentation for the `service` module, run this:

```
$ ansible-doc service
```

To find more specific modules related to the Ubuntu apt package manager, try:

```
$ ansible-doc -l | grep ^apt
```

Putting It All Together

To sum up, a playbook contains one or more plays. A play associates an unordered set of hosts with an ordered list of tasks. Each task is associated with exactly one module. Figure 3-2 depicts the relationships between playbooks, plays, hosts, tasks, and modules.

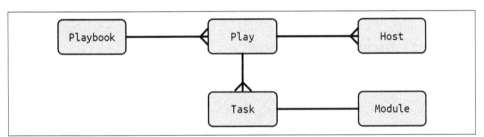

Figure 3-2. Entity-relationship diagram of a playbook

Did Anything Change? Tracking Host State

When you run `ansible-playbook`, Ansible outputs status information for each task it executes in the play.

Looking back at the output in Example 3-5, you might notice that some tasks have the status `changed` and others have the status `ok`. For example, the "Ensure nginx is installed task" has the status `changed`, which appears as yellow on our terminal:

```
TASK: [Ensure nginx is installed] *********************************************
changed: [testserver]
```

The enable configuration, on the other hand, has the status "ok", which appears as green on our terminal:

```
TASK: [Enable configuration] ****************************************************
ok: [testserver]
```

Any Ansible task that runs has the potential to change the state of the host in some way. Ansible modules will first check to see whether the state of the host needs to be changed before taking any action. If the host's state matches the module's arguments, Ansible takes no action on the host and responds with a state of "ok."

On the other hand, if there is a difference between the host's state and the module's arguments, Ansible will change the state of the host and return "changed."

In the example output just shown, the "Ensure nginx is installed" task was changed, which means that before we ran the playbook, the nginx package had not previously been installed on the host. The "Enable configuration" task was unchanged, which meant that there was already a symbolic link on the server that was identical to the one we were creating. This means the playbook has a noop ("no operation": that is, do nothing) that we will remove. Try to run the playbook more often, and verify that the status is "ok" on subsequent runs.

As you'll see later in this chapter, you can use Ansible's state change detection to trigger additional actions using handlers. But, even without using handlers, seeing what changes and where, as the playbook runs, is still a detailed form of feedback.

Getting Fancier: TLS Support

Let's move on to a more complex example. We're going to modify the previous playbook so that our web servers support TLSv1.2. You can find the full playbook in Example 3-9 at the end of this chapter. This section will briefly introduce these Ansible features:

- Variables
- Loops
- Handlers
- Testing
- Validation

TLS versus SSL

You might be familiar with the term SSL (Secure Sockets Layer) rather than TLS (Transport Layer Security) in the context of secure web servers. SSL is a family of protocols that secures the communication between browsers and web servers; this adds the "S" in HTTPS. SSL has evolved over time; the latest variant is TLSv1.3. Although it is common to use the term SSL to refer to the HTTPS secured protocol, in this book, we use TLS.

Generating a TLS Certificate

We will create a TLS certificate. In a production environment, you'd obtain your TLS certificate from a certificate authority. We'll use a self-signed certificate since we can generate it easily for this example. Run this command from the directory *ansiblebook/ch03/playbooks*:

```
$ openssl req -x509 -nodes -days 365 -newkey rsa:2048 \
    -subj /CN=localhost \
    -keyout files/nginx.key -out files/nginx.crt
```

It should generate the files *nginx.key* and *nginx.crt* in the *files* subdirectory of your *playbooks* directory. The certificate has an expiration date of one year from the day you created it.

Variables

The play in our playbook has a new section called vars:. This section defines five variables and assigns a value to each variable:

```
vars:
  tls_dir: /etc/nginx/ssl/
  key_file: nginx.key
  cert_file: nginx.crt
  conf_file: /etc/nginx/sites-available/default
  server_name: localhost
```

In this example, each value is a string (such as */etc/nginx/sites-available/default*), but any valid YAML can be used as the value of a variable. You can use lists and dictionaries in addition to strings and Booleans.

Variables can be used in tasks, as well as in template files. You reference variables by using {{ mustache }} notation. Ansible replaces this {{ mustache }} with the value of the variable named mustache.

Consider this task in the playbook:

```
- name: Manage nginx config template
  template:
    src: nginx.conf.j2
    dest: "{{ conf_file }}"
    mode: '0644'
  notify: Restart nginx
```

Ansible will substitute "`{{ conf_file }}`" with *etc/nginx/sites-available/default* when it executes this task.

Quoting in Ansible Strings

If you reference a variable right after specifying the module, the YAML parser will misinterpret the variable reference as the beginning of an inline dictionary. Consider the following example:

```
- name: Perform some task
  command: {{ myapp }} -a foo
```

Ansible will try to parse the first part of `{{ myapp }} -a foo` as a dictionary instead of a string, and will return an error. In this case, you must quote the arguments:

```
- name: Perform some task
  command: "{{ myapp }} -a foo"
```

A similar problem arises if your argument contains a colon. For example:

```
- name: Show a debug message
  debug:
    msg: The debug module will print a message: neat, eh?
```

The colon in the `msg` argument trips up the YAML parser. To get around this, you need to quote the entire `msg` string. Single and double quotes are both correct; Bas prefers to use double quotes when the string has variables:

```
- name: Show a debug message
  debug:
    msg: "The debug module will print a message: neat, eh?"
```

This will make the YAML parser happy. Ansible supports alternating single and double quotes, so you can do this:

```
- name: Show escaped quotes
  debug:
    msg: '"The module will print escaped quotes: neat, eh?"'

- name: Show quoted quotes
  debug:
    msg: "'The module will print quoted quotes: neat, eh?'"
```

This yields the expected output:

```
TASK [Show escaped quotes] *****************************************************
ok: [localhost] ==> {
    "msg": "\"The module will print escaped quotes: neat, eh?\""
}
TASK [Show quoted quotes] ******************************************************
ok: [localhost] ==> {
    "msg": "'The module will print quoted quotes: neat, eh?'"
}
```

Generating the NGINX Configuration Template

If you've done web programming, you've likely used a template system to generate HTML. A template is just a text file that has special syntax for specifying variables that should be replaced by values. If you've ever received a spam email, it was created using an email template, as shown in Example 3-7.

Example 3-7. An email template

```
Dear {{ name }},
You have {{ random_number }} Bitcoins in your account, please click: {{ phishing_url }}.
```

Ansible's use case isn't HTML pages or emails—it's configuration files. You don't want to hand-edit configuration files if you can avoid it. This is especially true if you have to reuse the same bits of configuration data (say, the IP address of your queue server or your database credentials) across multiple configuration files. It's much better to take the info that's specific to your deployment, record it in one location, and then generate all of the files that need this information from templates.

Ansible uses the Jinja2 template engine to implement templating, just like the excellent web framework Flask does. If you've ever used a templating library such as Mustache, ERB, or Django, Jinja2 will feel very familiar.

NGINX's configuration file needs information about where to find the TLS key and certificate. We're going to use Ansible's templating functionality to define this configuration file so that we can avoid hardcoding values that might change.

In your *playbooks* directory, create a *templates* subdirectory and create the file *templates/nginx.conf.j2*, as shown in Example 3-8.

Example 3-8. templates/nginx.conf.j2

```
server {
        listen 80 default_server;
        listen [::]:80 default_server ipv6only=on;

        listen 443 ssl;
        ssl_protocols TLSv1.2;
        ssl_prefer_server_ciphers on;
        root /usr/share/nginx/html;
```

```
    index index.html;
    server_tokens off;
    add_header X-Frame-Options DENY;
    add_header X-Content-Type-Options nosniff;

    server_name {{ server_name }};
    ssl_certificate {{ tls_dir }}{{ cert_file }};
    ssl_certificate_key {{ tls_dir }}{{ key_file }};

    location / {
        try_files $uri $uri/ =404;
    }
}
```

We use the *.j2* extension to indicate that the file is a Jinja2 template. However, you can use a different extension if you like; Ansible doesn't care.

In our template, we reference four variables. We defined these variables in the playbook:

server_name
> The hostname of the web server (such as *www.example.com*)

cert_file
> The filename of the TLS certificate

key_file
> The filename of the TLS private key

tls_dir
> The directory with the above files

Ansible also uses the Jinja2 template engine to evaluate variables in playbooks. Recall that we saw the {{ conf_file }} syntax in the playbook itself. You can use all of the Jinja2 features in your templates, but we won't cover them in detail here. Check out the Jinja2 Template Designer Documentation (*https://oreil.ly/Je0rA*) for more details. You probably won't need to use those advanced templating features, though. One Jinja2 feature you probably *will* use with Ansible is filters; we'll cover those in a later chapter.

Loop

When you want to run a task with each item from a list, you can use loop. A loop executes the task multiple times, each time replacing item with different values from the specified list:

```
- name: Copy TLS files
  copy:
    src: "{{ item }}"
    dest: "{{ tls_dir }}"
```

```
    mode: '0600'
  loop:
    - "{{ key_file }}"
    - "{{ cert_file }}"
  notify: Restart nginx
```

Handlers

There are two new elements that we haven't discussed yet in our *webservers-tls.yml*
playbook (Example 3-9). There's a handlers section that looks like this:

```
handlers:
  - name: Restart nginx
    service:
      name: nginx
      state: restarted
```

In addition, several of the tasks contain a notify statement. For example:

```
- name: Manage nginx config template
  template:
    src: nginx.conf.j2
    dest: "{{ conf_file }}"
    mode: '0644'
  notify: Restart nginx
```

Handlers are one of the conditional forms that Ansible supports. A *handler* is similar
to a task, but it runs only if it has been notified by a task. A task will fire the
notification if Ansible recognizes that the task has changed the state of the system.

A task notifies a handler by passing the handler's name as the argument. In the
preceding example, the handler's name is `Restart nginx`. For an NGINX server, we'd
need to restart it if any of the following happens:

- The TLS key changes.
- The TLS certificate changes.
- The configuration file changes.
- The contents of the *sites-enabled* directory change.

We put a notify statement on each task to ensure that Ansible restarts NGINX if any
of these conditions are met.

A Few Things to Keep in Mind About Handlers

Handlers usually run at the end of the play after all of the tasks have been run. To
force a notified handler in the middle of a play, we use these two lines of code:

```
- name: Restart nginx
  meta: flush_handlers
```

If a play contains multiple handlers, the handlers always run in the order that they are defined in the handlers section, not the notification order. They run only once, even if they are notified multiple times.

The official Ansible documentation mentions that the only common uses for handlers are reboots and restarting services. Lorin uses them only for restarting services—he thinks it's a pretty small optimization to restart only once on change, since we can always just unconditionally restart the service at the end of the playbook, and restarting a service doesn't usually take very long. But when you restart NGINX, you might affect user sessions; notifying handlers help avoid unnecessary restarts. Bas likes to validate the configuration before restarting, especially if it's a critical service like sshd. He has handlers notifying handlers.

Testing

One pitfall with handlers is that they can be troublesome when debugging a playbook. The problem usually unfolds something like this:

- You run a playbook.
- One of the tasks with a notify on it changes state.
- An error occurs on a subsequent task, stopping Ansible.
- You fix the error in your playbook.
- You run Ansible again.
- None of the tasks reports a state change the second time around, so Ansible doesn't run the handler.

When iterating like this, it is helpful to include a test in the playbook. Ansible has a module called uri that can do an HTTPS request to check if the web server is running and serving the web page:

```
- name: "Test it! https://localhost:8443/index.html"
  delegate_to: localhost
  become: false
  uri:
    url: 'https://localhost:8443/index.html'
    validate_certs: false
    return_content: true
  register: this
  failed_when: "'Running on ' not in this.content"
```

Validation

Ansible is remarkably good at generating meaningful error messages if you forget to put quotes in the right places and end up with invalid YAML; yamllint is very helpful in finding even more issues. In addition, `ansible-lint` is a Python tool that helps you find potential problems in playbooks.

You should also check the Ansible syntax of your playbook before running it. We suggest you check all of your content before running the playbook:

```
$ ansible-playbook --syntax-check webservers-tls.yml
$ ansible-lint webservers-tls.yml
$ yamllint webservers-tls.yml
$ ansible-inventory --host testserver -i inventory/vagrant.ini
$ vagrant validate
```

The Playbook

If you have followed along, your playbook should now look like Example 3-9.

Example 3-9. playbooks/webservers-tls.yml

```
---
- name: Configure webserver with Nginx and TLS
  hosts: webservers
  become: true
  gather_facts: false

  vars:
    tls_dir: /etc/nginx/ssl/
    key_file: nginx.key
    cert_file: nginx.crt
    conf_file: /etc/nginx/sites-available/default
    server_name: localhost

  handlers:
    - name: Restart nginx
      service:
        name: nginx
        state: restarted

  tasks:
    - name: Ensure nginx is installed
      package:
        name: nginx
        update_cache: true
      notify: Restart nginx

    - name: Create directories for TLS certificates
      file:
        path: "{{ tls_dir }}"
        state: directory
        mode: '0750'
      notify: Restart nginx

    - name: Copy TLS files
      copy:
```

```
      src: "{{ item }}"
      dest: "{{ tls_dir }}"
      mode: '0600'
    loop:
      - "{{ key_file }}"
      - "{{ cert_file }}"
    notify: Restart nginx

  - name: Manage nginx config template
    template:
      src: nginx.conf.j2
      dest: "{{ conf_file }}"
      mode: '0644'
    notify: Restart nginx

  - name: Enable configuration
    file:
      src: /etc/nginx/sites-available/default
      dest: /etc/nginx/sites-enabled/default
      state: link

  - name: Install home page
    template:
      src: index.html.j2
      dest: /usr/share/nginx/html/index.html
      mode: '0644'

  - name: Restart nginx
    meta: flush_handlers

  - name: "Test it! https://localhost:8443/index.html"
    delegate_to: localhost
    become: false
    uri:
      url: 'https://localhost:8443/index.html'
      validate_certs: false
      return_content: true
    register: this
    failed_when: "'Running on ' not in this.content"
    tags:
      - test
...
```

Running the Playbook

As before, use the `ansible-playbook` command to run the playbook:

```
$ ansible-playbook webservers-tls.yml
```

The output should look something like this:

```
PLAY [Configure webserver with Nginx and TLS] **********************************

TASK [Ensure nginx is installed] ***********************************************
ok: [testserver]
```

```
TASK [Create directories for TLS certificates] *********************************
changed: [testserver]

TASK [Copy TLS files] *********************************************************
changed: [testserver] => (item=nginx.key)
changed: [testserver] => (item=nginx.crt)

TASK [Manage nginx config template] ******************************************
changed: [testserver]

TASK [Install home page] *****************************************************
ok: [testserver]

RUNNING HANDLER [Restart nginx] **********************************************
changed: [testserver]

TASK [Test it! https://localhost:8443/index.html] ****************************
ok: [testserver]

PLAY RECAP *******************************************************************
testserver : ok=7 changed=4 unreachable=0 failed=0 skipped=0 rescued=0 ignored=0
```

Point your browser to *https://localhost:8443* (don't forget the *s* on *https*). If you're using Chrome, you'll get a ghastly message that says something like, "Your connection is not private" (see Figure 3-3).

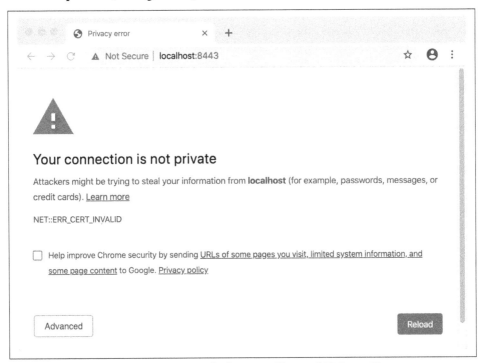

Figure 3-3. Browsers such as Chrome don't trust self-signed TLS certificates

Don't worry, though. We expected that error, since we generated a self-signed TLS certificate: many browsers trust only certificates issued by a certificate authority.

Shebang

When a text file is executable in a Unix-like operating system, then we call it a script. When the first line starts with the two characters #! then the program loader mechanism parses the rest of the file's first line as a script interpreter directive. It will start the script interpreter with the script. We changed the file mode of our playbook (*webservers-tls.yml*) to executable and start the file with the following shebang line. (The # character without ! is just a comment.)

```
#!/usr/bin/env ansible-playbook
# This playbook is executable as a script.
---
```

Conclusion

We've covered a lot in this chapter about the "what" of Ansible, for instance describing what Ansible will do to your hosts. The handlers discussed here are just one form of control flow that Ansible supports. In Chapter 9 you'll learn more about complex playbooks with more loops and running tasks conditionally based on the values of variables. In the next chapter, we'll talk about the "who": in other words, how to describe the hosts against which your playbooks will run.

## CHAPTER 4

Inventory: Describing Your Servers

So far, we've been working with only one server (or *host*, as Ansible calls it). The simplest inventory is a comma-separated list of hostnames, which you can do even without a server:

```
$ ansible all -i 'localhost,' -a date
```

In reality, you're going to be managing multiple hosts. The collection of hosts that Ansible knows about is called the *inventory*. In this chapter, you will learn how to describe a set of hosts as an Ansible inventory by creating an inventory that contains multiple machines.

Your *ansible.cfg* file should look like Example 4-1, which enables all inventory plug-ins explicitly.

Example 4-1. ansible.cfg

```
[defaults]
inventory = inventory

[inventory]
enable_plugins = host_list, script, auto, yaml, ini, toml
```

In this chapter, we will use a directory named *inventory* for the inventory examples. The Ansible inventory is a very flexible object: it can be a file (in several formats), a directory, or an executable, and some executables are bundled as plug-ins. Inventory plug-ins allow us to point at data sources, like your cloud provider, to compile the inventory. An inventory can be stored separately from your playbooks. This means that you can create one inventory directory to use with Ansible on the command line, with hosts running in Vagrant, Amazon EC2, Google Cloud Platform, or Microsoft Azure, or wherever you like!

Serge van Ginderachter is the most knowledgeable person to read on Ansible inventory. See his blog (*https://oreil.ly/tUABr*) for in-depth details.

Inventory/Hosts Files

The default way to describe your hosts in Ansible is to list them in text files, called *inventory hosts files*. The simplest form is just a list of hostnames in a file named *hosts*, as shown in Example 4-2.

Example 4-2. A very simple inventory file

```
frankfurt.example.com
helsinki.example.com
hongkong.example.com
johannesburg.example.com
london.example.com
newyork.example.com
seoul.example.com
sydney.example.com
```

Ansible automatically adds one host to the inventory by default: *localhost*. It understands that localhost refers to your local machine, with which it will interact directly rather than connecting by SSH.

Preliminaries: Multiple Vagrant Machines

To talk about inventory, you'll need to interact with multiple hosts. Let's configure Vagrant to bring up three hosts. We'll unimaginatively call them vagrant1, vagrant2, and vagrant3.

Before you create a new Vagrantfile for this chapter, make sure you destroy your existing virtual machine(s) by running the following:

```
$ vagrant destroy --force
```

If you don't include the --force option, Vagrant will prompt you to confirm that you want to destroy each virtual machine listed in the Vagrantfile.

Next, create a new Vagrantfile that looks like Example 4-3.

Example 4-3. Vagrantfile with three servers

```
VAGRANTFILE_API_VERSION = "2"
Vagrant.configure(VAGRANTFILE_API_VERSION) do |config|
  # Use the same key for each machine
  config.ssh.insert_key = false
```

```
config.vm.define "vagrant1" do |vagrant1|
  vagrant1.vm.box = "ubuntu/focal64"
  vagrant1.vm.network "forwarded_port", guest: 80, host: 8080
  vagrant1.vm.network "forwarded_port", guest: 443, host: 8443
end
config.vm.define "vagrant2" do |vagrant2|
  vagrant2.vm.box = "ubuntu/focal64"
  vagrant2.vm.network "forwarded_port", guest: 80, host: 8081
  vagrant2.vm.network "forwarded_port", guest: 443, host: 8444
end
config.vm.define "vagrant3" do |vagrant3|
  vagrant3.vm.box = "centos/stream8"
  vagrant3.vm.network "forwarded_port", guest: 80, host: 8082
  vagrant3.vm.network "forwarded_port", guest: 443, host: 8445
end
end
```

Vagrant, from version 1.7 on, defaults to using a different SSH key for each host. Example 4-3 contains the line to revert to the earlier behavior of using the same SSH key for each host:

```
config.ssh.insert_key = false
```

Using the same key on each host simplifies our Ansible setup because we can specify a single SSH key in the configuration.

For now, let's assume that each of these servers can potentially be a web server, so Example 4-3 maps ports 80 and 443 inside each Vagrant machine to a port on the local machine.

We should be able to bring up the virtual machines by running the following:

```
$ vagrant up
```

If all goes well, the output should look something like this:

```
Bringing machine 'vagrant1' up with 'virtualbox' provider...
Bringing machine 'vagrant2' up with 'virtualbox' provider...
Bringing machine 'vagrant3' up with 'virtualbox' provider...
...
    vagrant1: 80 (guest) => 8080 (host) (adapter 1)
    vagrant1: 443 (guest) => 8443 (host) (adapter 1)
    vagrant1: 22 (guest) => 2222 (host) (adapter 1)
==> vagrant1: Running 'pre-boot' VM customizations...
==> vagrant1: Booting VM...
==> vagrant1: Waiting for machine to boot. This may take a few minutes...
    vagrant1: SSH address: 127.0.0.1:2222
    vagrant1: SSH username: vagrant
    vagrant1: SSH auth method: private key
==> vagrant1: Machine booted and ready!
==> vagrant1: Checking for guest additions in VM...
==> vagrant1: Mounting shared folders...
    vagrant1: /vagrant => /Users/bas/code/ansible/ansiblebook/ansiblebook/ch03
```

Next, we need to know what ports on the local machine map to the SSH port (22) inside each VM. Recall that we can get that information by running the following:

```
$ vagrant ssh-config
```

The output should look something like this:

```
Host vagrant1
  HostName 127.0.0.1
  User vagrant
  Port 2222
  UserKnownHostsFile /dev/null
  StrictHostKeyChecking no
  PasswordAuthentication no
  IdentityFile /Users/lorin/.vagrant.d/insecure_private_key
  IdentitiesOnly yes
  LogLevel FATAL
Host vagrant2
  HostName 127.0.0.1
  User vagrant
  Port 2200
  UserKnownHostsFile /dev/null
  StrictHostKeyChecking no
  PasswordAuthentication no
  IdentityFile /Users/lorin/.vagrant.d/insecure_private_key
  IdentitiesOnly yes
  LogLevel FATAL
Host vagrant3
  HostName 127.0.0.1
  User vagrant
  Port 2201
  UserKnownHostsFile /dev/null
  StrictHostKeyChecking no
  PasswordAuthentication no
  IdentityFile /Users/lorin/.vagrant.d/insecure_private_key
  IdentitiesOnly yes
  LogLevel FATAL
```

A lot of the `ssh-config` information is repetitive and can be reduced. The information that differs per host is that `vagrant1` uses port 2222, `vagrant2` uses port 2200, and `vagrant3` uses port 2201.

Ansible uses your local SSH client by default, which means that it will understand any aliases that you set up in your SSH config file. Therefore, we use a wildcard alias in the file *~/.ssh/config*:

```
Host vagrant*
  Hostname 127.0.0.1
  User vagrant
  UserKnownHostsFile /dev/null
  StrictHostKeyChecking no
  PasswordAuthentication no
  IdentityFile ~/.vagrant.d/insecure_private_key
  IdentitiesOnly yes
  LogLevel FATAL
```

Modify your *inventory/hosts* file so it looks like this:

```
vagrant1 ansible_port=2222
vagrant2 ansible_port=2200
vagrant3 ansible_port=2201
```

Now, make sure that you can access these machines. For example, to get information about the network interface for `vagrant2`, run the following:

```
$ ansible vagrant2 -a "ip addr show dev enp0s3"
```

Your output should look something like this:

```
vagrant2 | CHANGED | rc=0 >>
2: enp0s3: <BROADCAST,MULTICAST,UP,LOWER_UP> mtu 1500 qdisc fq_codel state UP
group default qlen 1000
    link/ether 02:1e:de:45:2c:c8 brd ff:ff:ff:ff:ff:ff
    inet 10.0.2.15/24 brd 10.0.2.255 scope global dynamic enp0s3
       valid_lft 86178sec preferred_lft 86178sec
    inet6 fe80::1e:deff:fe45:2cc8/64 scope link
       valid_lft forever preferred_lft forever
```

Behavioral Inventory Parameters

To describe our Vagrant machines in the Ansible inventory file, we had to explicitly specify the port (2222, 2200, or 2201) to which Ansible's SSH client should connect. Ansible calls such variables *behavioral inventory parameters*, and there are several of them you can use when you need to override the Ansible defaults for a host (see Table 4-1).

Table 4-1. Behavioral inventory parameters

Name	Default	Description
ansible_host	Name of host	Hostname or IP address to SSH to
ansible_port	22	Port to SSH to
ansible_user	$USER	User to SSH as
ansible_password	*(None)*	Password to use for SSH authentication
ansible_connection	smart	How Ansible will connect to host (see the following section)
ansible_ssh_private_key_file	*(None)*	SSH private key to use for SSH authentication
ansible_shell_type	sh	Shell to use for commands (see the following section)
ansible_python_interpreter	*/usr/bin/python*	Python interpreter on host (see the following section)
ansible_*_interpreter	*(None)*	Like `ansible_python_interpreter` for other languages (see the following section)

For some of these options, the meaning is obvious from the name, but others require more explanation:

ansible_connection

Ansible supports multiple *transports*, which are mechanisms that Ansible uses to connect to the host. The default transport, smart, will check whether the locally installed SSH client supports a feature called ControlPersist. If the SSH client supports ControlPersist, Ansible will use the local SSH client. If not, the smart transport will fall back to using a Python-based SSH client library called *Paramiko*.

ansible_shell_type

Ansible works by making SSH connections to remote machines and then invoking scripts. By default, Ansible assumes that the remote shell is the Bourne shell located at */bin/sh*, and will generate the appropriate command-line parameters that work with that. It creates temporary directories to store these scripts.

Ansible also accepts csh, fish, and (on Windows) powershell as valid values for this parameter. Ansible doesn't work with restricted shells.

ansible_python_interpreter

Ansible needs to know the location of the Python interpreter on the remote machine. You might want to change this to choose a version that works for you. The easiest way to run Ansible under Python 3 is to install it with pip3 and set this:

```
ansible_python_interpreter="/usr/bin/env python3"
```

ansible_*_interpreter

If you are using a custom module that is not written in Python, you can use this parameter to specify the location of the interpreter (such as */usr/bin/ruby*). We'll cover this in Chapter 12.

Changing Behavioral Parameter Defaults

You can override some of the behavioral parameter default values in the inventory file, or you can override them in the defaults section of the *ansible.cfg* file (Table 4-2). Consider where you change these parameters. Are the changes a personal choice, or does the change apply to your whole team? Does a part of your inventory need a different setting? Remember that you can configure SSH preferences in the *~/.ssh/config* file.

Table 4-2. Defaults that can be overridden in ansible.cfg

Behavioral inventory parameter	ansible.cfg option
`ansible_port`	`remote_port`
`ansible_user`	`remote_user`
`ansible_ssh_private_key_file`	`ssh_private_key_file`
`ansible_shell_type`	`executable` (see the following paragraph)

The *ansible.cfg* `executable` config option is not exactly the same as the `ansible_shell_type` behavioral inventory parameter. The executable specifies the full path of the shell to use on the remote machine (for example, */usr/local/bin/fish*). Ansible will look at the base name of this path (in this case *fish*) and use that as the default value for `ansible_shell_type`.

Groups and Groups and Groups

We typically want to perform configuration actions on groups of hosts, rather than on an individual host. Ansible automatically defines a group called `all` (or *), which includes all the hosts in the inventory. For example, we can check whether the clocks on the machines are roughly synchronized by running the following:

```
$ ansible all -a "date"
```

or

```
$ ansible '*' -a "date"
```

The output on Bas's system looks like this:

```
vagrant2 | CHANGED | rc=0 >>
Wed 12 May 2021 01:37:47 PM UTC
vagrant1 | CHANGED | rc=0 >>
Wed 12 May 2021 01:37:47 PM UTC
vagrant3 | CHANGED | rc=0 >>
Wed 12 May 2021 01:37:47 PM UTC
```

We can define our own groups in the inventory hosts file. Ansible uses the *.ini* file format for inventory hosts files; it groups configuration values into sections.

Here's how to specify that our vagrant hosts are in a group called `vagrant`, along with the other example hosts mentioned at the beginning of the chapter:

```
frankfurt.example.com
helsinki.example.com
hongkong.example.com
johannesburg.example.com
london.example.com
newyork.example.com
seoul.example.com
sydney.example.com
```

```
[vagrant]
vagrant1 ansible_port=2222
vagrant2 ansible_port=2200
vagrant3 ansible_port=2201
```

We could alternately list the Vagrant hosts at the top and then also in a group, like this:

```
frankfurt.example.com
helsinki.example.com
hongkong.example.com
johannesburg.example.com
london.example.com
newyork.example.com
seoul.example.com
sydney.example.com
vagrant1 ansible_port=2222
vagrant2 ansible_port=2200
vagrant3 ansible_port=2201

[vagrant]
vagrant1
vagrant2
vagrant3
```

You can use groups in any way that suits you: they can overlap or be nested, however you like. The order does not matter, except for human readability.

Example: Deploying a Django App

Imagine you're responsible for deploying a Django-based web application that processes long-running jobs. The app needs to support the following services:

- The actual Django web app itself, run by a Gunicorn HTTP server
- A NGINX web server, which will sit in front of Gunicorn and serve static assets
- A Celery task queue that will execute long-running jobs on behalf of the web app
- A RabbitMQ message queue that serves as the backend for Celery
- A Postgres database that serves as the persistent store

In later chapters, we will work through a detailed example of deploying this kind of Django-based application, although our example won't use Celery or RabbitMQ. For now, we need to deploy this application into three different environments: production (the real thing), staging (for testing on hosts that our team has shared access to), and Vagrant (for local testing).

When we deploy to production, we want the entire system to respond quickly and reliably, so we do the following:

- Run the web application on multiple hosts for better performance and put a load balancer in front of them
- Run task queue servers on multiple hosts for better performance
- Put Gunicorn, Celery, RabbitMQ, and Postgres all on separate servers
- Use two Postgres hosts: a primary and a replica

Assuming we have one load balancer, three web servers, three task queues, one RabbitMQ server, and two database servers, that's 10 hosts we need to deal with (Figure 4-1).

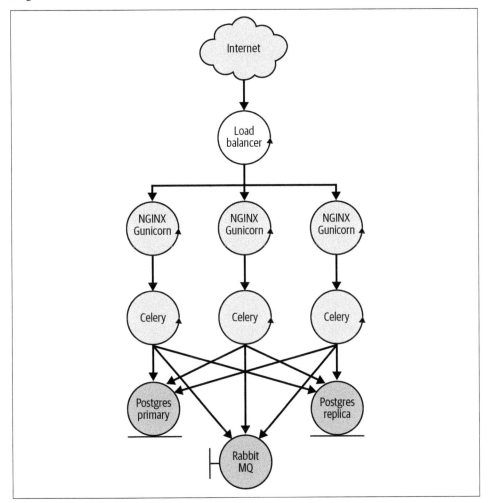

Figure 4-1. Ten hosts for deploying a Django app

For our staging environment, we want to use fewer hosts than we do in production to save costs, since it's going to see a lot less activity than production will. Let's say we decide to use only two hosts for staging; we'll put the web server and task queue on one staging host, and RabbitMQ and Postgres on the other.

For our local Vagrant environment, we decide to use three servers: one for the web app, one for a task queue, and one that will contain RabbitMQ and Postgres.

Example 4-4 shows a sample inventory file that groups servers by environment (production, staging, Vagrant) and by function (web server, task queue, etc.).

Example 4-4. Inventory file for deploying a Django app

```
[production]
frankfurt.example.com
helsinki.example.com
hongkong.example.com
johannesburg.example.com
london.example.com
newyork.example.com
seoul.example.com
sydney.example.com
tokyo.example.com
toronto.example.com

[staging]
amsterdam.example.com
chicago.example.com

[lb]
helsinki.example.com

[web]
amsterdam.example.com
seoul.example.com
sydney.example.com
toronto.example.com
vagrant1

[task]
amsterdam.example.com
hongkong.example.com
johannesburg.example.com
newyork.example.com
vagrant2

[rabbitmq]
chicago.example.com
tokyo.example.com
vagrant3

[db]
chicago.example.com
```

```
frankfurt.example.com
london.example.com
vagrant3
```

We could have first listed all of the servers at the top of the inventory file, without specifying a group, but that isn't necessary, and that would've made this file even longer.

Note that we need to specify the behavioral inventory parameters for the Vagrant instances only once.

Aliases and Ports

We have described our Vagrant hosts like this:

```
[vagrant]
vagrant1 ansible_port=2222
vagrant2 ansible_port=2200
vagrant3 ansible_port=2201
```

The names `vagrant1`, `vagrant2`, and `vagrant3` here are *aliases*. They are not the real hostnames, just useful names for referring to these hosts. Ansible resolves hostnames using the inventory, your SSH config file, */etc/hosts*, and DNS. This flexibility is useful in development but can be a cause of confusion.

Ansible also supports using `<hostname>:<port>` syntax when specifying hosts, so we *could* replace the line that contains `vagrant1` with `127.0.0.1:2222` (Example 4-5).

Example 4-5. This doesn't work

```
[vagrant]
127.0.0.1:2222
127.0.0.1:2200
127.0.0.1:2201
```

However, we can't actually run what you see in Example 4-5. The reason is that Ansible's inventory can associate only a single host with *127.0.0.1*, so the Vagrant group would contain only one host instead of three.

Groups of Groups

Ansible also allows you to define groups that are made up of other groups. For example, since both the web servers and the task queue servers will need Django and its dependencies, it might be useful to define a `django` group that contains both. You would add this to the inventory file:

```
[django:children]
web
task
```

Note that the syntax changes when you are specifying a group of groups, as opposed to a group of hosts. That's so Ansible knows to interpret web and task as groups and not as hosts.

Numbered Hosts (Pets Versus Cattle)

The inventory file you saw back in Example 4-4 looks complex. It describes 15 hosts, which doesn't sound like a large number in this cloudy, scale-out world. However, dealing with 15 hosts in the inventory file can be cumbersome, because each host has a completely different hostname.

Bill Baker of Microsoft came up with the distinction between treating servers as *pets* versus treating them like *cattle*.[1] We give pets distinctive names and treat and care for them as individuals; with cattle, though, we refer to them by identification number and treat them as livestock.

The "cattle" approach to servers is much more scalable, and Ansible supports it well by supporting numeric patterns. For example, if your 20 servers are named *web1.example.com, web2.example.com*, and so on, then you can specify them in the inventory file like this:

```
[web]
web[1:20].example.com
```

If you prefer to have a leading zero (such as *web01.example.com*), specify that in the range, like this:

```
[web]
web[01:20].example.com
```

Ansible also supports using alphabetic characters to specify ranges. If you want to use the convention *web-a.example.com, web-b.example.com*, and so on, for your 20 servers, then you can do this:

```
[web]
web-[a:t].example.com
```

Hosts and Group Variables: Inside the Inventory

Recall how we can specify behavioral inventory parameters for Vagrant hosts:

```
vagrant1 ansible_host=127.0.0.1 ansible_port=2222
vagrant2 ansible_host=127.0.0.1 ansible_port=2200
vagrant3 ansible_host=127.0.0.1 ansible_port=2201
```

---

1 This term has been popularized by Randy Bias of Cloudscaling (*https://oreil.ly/Zsvdf*).

Those parameters are variables that have special meaning to Ansible. We can also define arbitrary variable names and associated values on hosts. For example, we could define a variable named color and set it to a value for each server:

```
amsterdam.example.com color=red
seoul.example.com color=green
sydney.example.com color=blue
toronto.example.com color=purple
```

We could then use this variable in a playbook, just like any other variable. Personally, your authors don't often attach variables to specific hosts. On the other hand, we often associate variables with groups.

Circling back to our Django example, the web application and task queue service need to communicate with RabbitMQ and Postgres. We'll assume that access to the Postgres database is secured both at the network layer (so only the web application and the task queue can reach the database) and by username and password. RabbitMQ is secured only by the network layer.

To set everything up, you can:

- Configure the web servers with the hostname, port, username, password of the primary Postgres server, and name of the database.
- Configure the task queues with the hostname, port, username, password of the primary Postgres server, and the name of the database.
- Configure the web servers with the hostname and port of the RabbitMQ server.
- Configure the task queues with the hostname and port of the RabbitMQ server.
- Configure the primary Postgres server with the hostname, port, and username and password of the replica Postgres server (production only).

This configuration info varies by environment, so it makes sense to define these as group variables on the production, staging, and Vagrant groups. Example 4-6 shows one way to do so in the inventory file. (A better way to store passwords is discussed in Chapter 8).

Example 4-6. Specifying group variables in inventory

```
[all:vars]
ntp_server=ntp.ubuntu.com
[production:vars]
db_primary_host=frankfurt.example.com
db_primary_port=5432
db_replica_host=london.example.com
db_name=widget_production
db_user=widgetuser
db_password=pFmMxcyD;Fc6)6
rabbitmq_host=johannesburg.example.com
```

```
rabbitmq_port=5672
[staging:vars]
db_primary_host=chicago.example.com
db_primary_port=5432
db_name=widget_staging
db_user=widgetuser
db_password=L@4Ryz8cRUXedj
rabbitmq_host=chicago.example.com
rabbitmq_port=5672
[vagrant:vars]
db_primary_host=vagrant3
db_primary_port=5432
db_name=widget_vagrant
db_user=widgetuser
db_password=password
rabbitmq_host=vagrant3
rabbitmq_port=5672
```

Note how the group variables are organized into sections named [<group name>:vars]. Also, we've taken advantage of the all group (which, you'll recall, Ansible creates automatically) to specify variables that don't change across hosts.

Host and Group Variables: In Their Own Files

The inventory file is a reasonable place to put host and group variables if you don't have too many hosts. But as your inventory gets larger, it gets more difficult to manage variables this way. Additionally, even though Ansible variables can hold Booleans, strings, lists, and dictionaries, in an inventory file you can specify only Booleans and strings.

Ansible offers a more scalable approach to keep track of host and group variables: you can create a separate variable file for each host and each group. Ansible expects these variable files to be in YAML format.

It looks for host variable files in a directory called *host_vars* and group variable files in a directory called *group_vars*. Ansible expects these directories to be in either the directory that contains your playbooks or the directory adjacent to your inventory file. When you have both directories, then the first (the playbook directory) has priority.

For example, if Lorin has a directory containing his playbooks at */home/lorin/playbooks/* with an inventory directory and hosts file at */home/lorin/inventory/hosts*, he should put variables for the *amsterdam.example.com* host in the file */home/lorin/inventory/host_vars/amsterdam.example.com* and variables for the production group in the file */home/lorin/inventory/group_vars/production* (shown in Example 4-7).

Example 4-7. group_vars/production

```
---
db_primary_host: frankfurt.example.com
db_primary_port: 5432
db_replica_host: london.example.com
db_name: widget_production
db_user: widgetuser
db_password: 'pFmMxcyD;Fc6)6'
rabbitmq_host: johannesburg.example.com
rabbitmq_port: 5672
...
```

We can also use YAML dictionaries to represent these values, as shown in Example 4-8.

Example 4-8. group_vars/production, with dictionaries

```
---
db:
  user: widgetuser
  password: 'pFmMxcyD;Fc6)6'
  name: widget_production
  primary:
    host: frankfurt.example.com
    port: 5432
  replica:
    host: london.example.com
    port: 5432
rabbitmq:
  host: johannesburg.example.com
  port: 5672
...
```

If we choose YAML dictionaries, we access the variables with dot notation like this:

```
"{{ db.primary.host }}"
```

We can also access the variables in the dictionary like this:

```
"{{ db['primary']['host'] }}"
```

Contrast that to how we would otherwise access them:

```
"{{ db_primary_host }}"
```

If we want to break things out even further, Ansible lets us define *group_vars/production* as a directory instead of a file. We can place multiple YAML files into it that contain variable definitions. For example, we could put database-related variables in one file and the RabbitMQ-related variables in another file, as shown in Examples 4-9 and 4-10.

Example 4-9. group_vars/production/db

```
---
db:
  user: widgetuser
  password: 'pFmMxcyD;Fc6)6'
  name: widget_production
  primary:
    host: frankfurt.example.com
    port: 5432
  replica:
    host: london.example.com
    port: 5432
...
```

Example 4-10. group_vars/production/rabbitmq

```
---
rabbitmq:
  host: johannesburg.example.com
  port: 6379
...
```

It's often better to start simple, rather than splitting variables out across too many files. In larger teams and projects, the value of separate files increases, since many people might need to pull and work in files at the same time.

Dynamic Inventory

Up until this point, we've been explicitly specifying all our hosts in our hosts inventory file. However, you might have a system external to Ansible that keeps track of your hosts. For example, if your hosts run on Amazon EC2, then EC2 tracks information about your hosts for you. You can retrieve this information through EC2's web interface, its Query API, or command-line tools such as `awscli`. Other cloud providers have similar interfaces.

If you're managing your own servers using an automated provisioning system such as Cobbler or Ubuntu Metal as a Service (MAAS), then your system is already keeping track of your servers. Or, maybe you have one of those fancy configuration management databases (CMDBs) where all of this information lives.

You don't want to manually duplicate this information in your hosts file, because eventually that file will not jibe with your external system, which is the true source of information about your hosts. Ansible supports a feature called *dynamic inventory* that allows you to avoid this duplication.

If the inventory file is marked executable, Ansible will assume it is a dynamic inventory script and will execute the file instead of reading it.

To mark a file as executable, use the `chmod +x` command. For example:

```
$ chmod +x vagrant.py
```

Inventory Plug-ins

Ansible comes with several executables that can connect to various cloud systems, provided you install the requirements and set up authentication. These plug-ins typically need a YAML configuration file in the inventory directory, as well as some environment variables or authentication files.

To see the list of available plug-ins:

```
$ ansible-doc -t inventory -l
```

To see plug-in-specific documentation and examples:

```
$ ansible-doc -t inventory <plugin name>
```

Amazon EC2

If you are using Amazon EC2, install the requirements:

```
$ pip3 install boto3 botocore
```

Create a file *inventory/aws_ec2.yml* with, at the very least:

```
plugin: aws_ec2
```

Azure Resource Manager

Install these requirements in a Python virtualenv with Ansible 2.9.xx:

```
$ pip3 install msrest msrestazure
```

Create a file *inventory/azure_rm.yml* with, at the very least:

```
plugin: azure_rm
platform: azure_rm
auth_source: auto
plain_host_names: true
```

The Interface for a Dynamic Inventory Script

An Ansible dynamic inventory script must support two command-line flags:

- `--host=<hostname>` for showing host details
- `--list` for listing groups

Also it should return output in JSON format with a specific structure that Ansible can interpret.

Showing host details

To get the details of the individual host, Ansible will call an inventory script with the `--host=` argument:

```
$ ansible-inventory -i inventory/hosts --host=vagrant2
```

 Ansible includes a script that functions as a dynamic inventory script for the static inventory provided with the `-i` command-line argument: `ansible-inventory`.

The output should contain any host-specific variables, including behavioral parameters, like this:

```
{
    "ansible_host": "127.0.0.1",
    "ansible_port": 2200,
    "ansible_ssh_private_key_file": "~/.vagrant.d/insecure_private_key",
    "ansible_user": "vagrant"
}
```

The output is a single JSON object; the names are variable names, and the values are the variable values.

Listing groups

Dynamic inventory scripts need to be able to list all of the groups and details about the individual hosts. In the GitHub repository (*https://oreil.ly/vseIj*) that accompanies this book, there is an inventory script for the Vagrant hosts called *vagrant.py*. Ansible will call it like this to get a list of all of the groups:

```
$ ./vagrant.py --list
```

In the simplest form the output could look like this:

```
{"vagrant": ["vagrant1", "vagrant2", "vagrant3"]}
```

This output is a single JSON object; the names are Ansible group names, and the values are arrays of hostnames.

As an optimization, the `--list` command can contain the values of the host variables for all of the hosts, which saves Ansible the trouble of making a separate `--host` invocation to retrieve the variables for the individual hosts.

To take advantage of this optimization, the `--list` command should return a key named `_meta` that contains the variables for each host, in this form:

```json
    "_meta": {
        "hostvars": {
            "vagrant1": {
                "ansible_user": "vagrant",
                "ansible_host": "127.0.0.1",
                "ansible_ssh_private_key_file": "~/.vagrant.d/insecure_private_key",
                "ansible_port": "2222"
            },
            "vagrant2": {
                "ansible_user": "vagrant",
                "ansible_host": "127.0.0.1",
                "ansible_ssh_private_key_file": "~/.vagrant.d/insecure_private_key",
                "ansible_port": "2200"
            },
            "vagrant3": {
                "ansible_user": "vagrant",
                "ansible_host": "127.0.0.1",
                "ansible_ssh_private_key_file": "~/.vagrant.d/insecure_private_key",
                "ansible_port": "2201"
            }
        }
    }
```

Writing a Dynamic Inventory Script

One of the handy features of Vagrant is that you can see which machines are currently running by using the `vagrant status` command. Assuming we have a Vagrant file that looks like Example 4-3, if we run `vagrant status`, the output would look like Example 4-11.

Example 4-11. Output of vagrant status

```
$ vagrant status
Current machine states:

vagrant1                  running (virtualbox)
vagrant2                  running (virtualbox)
vagrant3                  running (virtualbox)

This environment represents multiple VMs. The VMs are all listed
above with their current state. For more information about a specific
VM, run 'vagrant status NAME'.
```

Because Vagrant already keeps track of machines for us, there's no need for us to list them in an Ansible inventory file. Instead, we can write a dynamic inventory script that queries Vagrant about which machines are running. Once we've set up a dynamic inventory script for Vagrant, even if we alter our Vagrantfile to run different numbers of Vagrant machines, we won't need to edit an Ansible inventory file.

Let's work through an example of creating a dynamic inventory script that retrieves the details about hosts from Vagrant. Our dynamic inventory script is going to need to invoke the `vagrant status` command. The output shown in Example 4-11 is designed for humans to read. We can get a list of running hosts in a format that is easier for computers to parse with the --machine-readable flag, like so:

```
$ vagrant status --machine-readable
```

The output looks like this:

```
1620831617,vagrant1,metadata,provider,virtualbox
1620831617,vagrant2,metadata,provider,virtualbox
1620831618,vagrant3,metadata,provider,virtualbox
1620831619,vagrant1,provider-name,virtualbox
1620831619,vagrant1,state,running
1620831619,vagrant1,state-human-short,running
1620831619,vagrant1,state-human-long,The VM is running. To stop this
VM%!(VAGRANT_COMMA) you can run `vagrant halt` to\nshut it down
forcefully%!(VAGRANT_COMMA) or you can run `vagrant suspend` to
simply\nsuspend the virtual machine. In either case%!(VAGRANT_COMMA)
to restart it again%!(VAGRANT_COMMA)\nsimply run `vagrant up`.
1620831619,vagrant2,provider-name,virtualbox
1620831619,vagrant2,state,running
1620831619,vagrant2,state-human-short,running
1620831619,vagrant2,state-human-long,The VM is running. To stop this
VM%!(VAGRANT_COMMA) you can run `vagrant halt` to\nshut it down
forcefully%!(VAGRANT_COMMA) or you can run `vagrant suspend` to
simply\nsuspend the virtual machine. In either case%!(VAGRANT_COMMA)
to restart it again%!(VAGRANT_COMMA)\nsimply run `vagrant up`.
1620831620,vagrant3,provider-name,virtualbox
1620831620,vagrant3,state,running
1620831620,vagrant3,state-human-short,running
1620831620,vagrant3,state-human-long,The VM is running. To stop this
VM%!(VAGRANT_COMMA) you can run `vagrant halt` to\nshut it down
forcefully%!(VAGRANT_COMMA) or you can run `vagrant suspend` to
simply\nsuspend the virtual machine. In either case%!(VAGRANT_COMMA)
to restart it again%!(VAGRANT_COMMA)\nsimply run `vagrant up`.
1620831620,,ui,info,Current machine states:\n\nvagrant1
running (virtualbox)\nvagrant2        running (virtualbox)\nvagrant3
running (virtualbox)\n\nThis environment represents multiple VMs. The VMs
are all listed\nabove with their current state. For more information about
a specific\nVM%!(VAGRANT_COMMA) run `vagrant status NAME`
```

To get details about a particular Vagrant machine, say, vagrant2, we would run this:

```
$ vagrant ssh-config vagrant2
```

The output looks like this:

```
Host vagrant2
  HostName 127.0.0.1
  User vagrant
  Port 2200
  UserKnownHostsFile /dev/null
  StrictHostKeyChecking no
  PasswordAuthentication no
  IdentityFile /Users/lorin/.vagrant.d/insecure_private_key
  IdentitiesOnly yes
  LogLevel FATAL
```

Our dynamic inventory script will need to call these commands, parse the outputs, and output the appropriate JSON. We can use the Paramiko library to parse the output of `vagrant ssh-config`. First, install the Python Paramiko library with pip:

```
$ pip3 install --user paramiko
```

Here's an interactive Python session that shows how to use the Paramiko library to do this:

```
$ python3
>>> import io
>>> import subprocess
>>> import paramiko
>>> cmd = ["vagrant", "ssh-config", "vagrant2"]
>>> ssh_config = subprocess.check_output(cmd).decode("utf-8")
>>> config = paramiko.SSHConfig()
>>> config.parse(io.StringIO(ssh_config))
>>> host_config = config.lookup("vagrant2")
>>> print (host_config)
{'hostname': '127.0.0.1', 'user': 'vagrant', 'port': '2200', 'userknownhostsfile':
'/dev/null', 'stricthostkeychecking': 'no', 'passwordauthentication': 'no',
'identityfile': ['/Users/bas/.vagrant.d/insecure_private_key'], 'identitiesonly':
'yes', 'loglevel': 'FATAL'}
```

Example 4-12 shows our complete *vagrant.py* script.

Example 4-12. vagrant.py

```python
#!/usr/bin/env python3
""" Vagrant inventory script """
# Adapted from Mark Mandel's implementation
# https://github.com/markmandel/vagrant_ansible_example

import argparse
import io
import json
import subprocess
import sys

import paramiko


def parse_args():
    """command-line options"""
    parser = argparse.ArgumentParser(description="Vagrant inventory script")
    group = parser.add_mutually_exclusive_group(required=True)
    group.add_argument('--list', action='store_true')
    group.add_argument('--host')
    return parser.parse_args()


def list_running_hosts():
    """vagrant.py --list function"""
    cmd = ["vagrant", "status", "--machine-readable"]
```

```
        status = subprocess.check_output(cmd).rstrip().decode("utf-8")
        hosts = []
        for line in status.splitlines():
            (_, host, key, value) = line.split(',')[:4]
            if key == 'state' and value == 'running':
                hosts.append(host)
        return hosts


def get_host_details(host):
    """vagrant.py --host <hostname> function"""
    cmd = ["vagrant", "ssh-config", host]
    ssh_config = subprocess.check_output(cmd).decode("utf-8")
    config = paramiko.SSHConfig()
    config.parse(io.StringIO(ssh_config))
    host_config = config.lookup(host)
    return {'ansible_host': host_config['hostname'],
            'ansible_port': host_config['port'],
            'ansible_user': host_config['user'],
            'ansible_private_key_file': host_config['identityfile'][0]}


def main():
    """main"""
    args = parse_args()
    if args.list:
        hosts = list_running_hosts()
        json.dump({'vagrant': hosts}, sys.stdout)
    else:
        details = get_host_details(args.host)
        json.dump(details, sys.stdout)


if __name__ == '__main__':
    main()
```

Breaking the Inventory into Multiple Files

If you want to have both a regular inventory file and a dynamic inventory script (or, really, any combination of static and dynamic inventory files), just put them all in the same directory and configure Ansible to use that directory as the inventory. You can do this via the inventory parameter in *ansible.cfg* or by using the -i flag on the command line. Ansible will process all of the files and merge the results into a single inventory.

This means that you can create one inventory directory to use with Ansible on the command line with hosts running in Vagrant, Amazon EC2, Google Cloud Platform, Microsoft Azure, or wherever you need them!

For example, Bas's directory structure looks like this:

inventory/aws_ec2.yml
inventory/azure_rm.yml
inventory/group_vars/vagrant
inventory/group_vars/staging
inventory/group_vars/production
inventory/hosts
inventory/vagrant.py

Adding Entries at Runtime with add_host and group_by

Ansible will let you add hosts and groups to the inventory during the execution of a playbook. This is useful when managing dynamic clusters, such as Redis Sentinel.

add_host

The add_host module adds a host to the inventory; this is useful if you're using Ansible to provision new virtual machine instances inside an infrastructure-as-a-service cloud.

Why Do I Need add_host if I'm Using Dynamic Inventory?

Even if you're using dynamic inventory scripts, the add_host module is useful for scenarios where you start up new virtual machine instances and configure those instances in the same playbook.

If a new host comes online while a playbook is executing, the dynamic inventory script will not pick up this new host. This is because the dynamic inventory script is executed at the beginning of the playbook: if any new hosts are added while the playbook is executing, Ansible won't see them.

We'll cover a cloud computing example that uses the add_host module in Chapter 14.

Invoking the module looks like this:

```
- name: Add the host
  add_host
    name: hostname
    groups: web,staging
    myvar: myval
```

Specifying the list of groups and additional variables is optional.

Here's the `add_host` command in action, bringing up a new Vagrant machine and then configuring the machine:

```
---
- name: Provision a Vagrant machine
  hosts: localhost
  vars:
    box: centos/stream8

  tasks:
    - name: Create a Vagrantfile
      command: "vagrant init {{ box }}"
      args:
        creates: Vagrantfile

    - name: Bring up the vagrant machine
      command: vagrant up
      args:
        creates: .vagrant/machines/default/virtualbox/box_meta

    - name: Add the vagrant machine to the inventory
      add_host:
        name: default
        ansible_host: 127.0.0.1
        ansible_port: 2222
        ansible_user: vagrant
        ansible_private_key_file: >
          .vagrant/machines/default/virtualbox/private_key

- name: Do something to the vagrant machine
  hosts: default
  tasks:
    # The list of tasks would go here
    - name: ping
      ping:
...
```

 The add_host module adds the host only for the duration of the execution of the playbook. It does not modify your inventory file.

When we provision inside our playbooks, we like to split it into two plays. The first play runs against `localhost` and provisions the hosts, and the second play configures the hosts.

Note that we use the `creates: Vagrantfile` argument in this task:

```
- name: Create a Vagrantfile
  command: "vagrant init {{ box }}"
  args:
    creates: Vagrantfile
```

This tells Ansible that if the *Vagrantfile* file is present, there is no need to run the command again. Ensuring that the (potentially nonidempotent) command is run only once is a way of achieving idempotence in a playbook that invokes the command module. The same is done with the vagrant up command module.

group_by

Ansible's group_by module allows you to create new groups while a playbook is executing. Any group you create will be based on the value of a variable that has been set on each host, which Ansible refers to as a *fact*. (Chapter 5 covers facts in more detail.)

If Ansible fact gathering is enabled, Ansible will associate a set of variables with a host. For example, the ansible_machine variable will be i386 for 32-bit x86 machines and x86_64 for 64-bit x86 machines. If Ansible is interacting with a mix of such hosts, we can create i386 and x86_64 groups with the task.

If we'd rather group our hosts by Linux distribution (for example, Ubuntu or CentOS), we can use the ansible_fact.distribution fact:

```
- name: Create groups based on Linux distribution
  group_by:
    key: "{{ ansible_facts.distribution }}"
```

In Example 4-13, we use group_by to create separate groups for our Ubuntu and CentOS hosts, then we use the apt module to install packages onto Ubuntu and the yum module to install packages into CentOS.

Example 4-13. Creating ad hoc groups based on Linux distribution

```
---

- name: Group hosts by distribution
  hosts: all
  gather_facts: true
  tasks:
    - name: Create groups based on distro
      group_by:
        key: "{{ ansible_facts.distribution }}"

- name: Do something to Ubuntu hosts
  hosts: Ubuntu
  become: true
  tasks:
    - name: Install jdk and jre
      apt:
        update_cache: true
        name:
          - openjdk-11-jdk-headless
          - openjdk-11-jre-headless
```

```
- name: Do something else to CentOS hosts
  hosts: CentOS
  become: true
  tasks:
    - name: Install jdk
      yum:
        name:
          - java-11-openjdk-headless
          - java-11-openjdk-devel
```

Conclusion

That about does it for Ansible's inventory. It is a very flexible object that helps describe your infrastructure and the way you want to use it. The inventory can be as simple as one text file or as complex as you can handle.

The next chapter covers how to use variables.

## CHAPTER 5

Variables and Facts

Ansible is not a full-fledged programming language, but it does have several features of one, and one of the most important of these is *variable substitution*, or using the values of variables in strings or in other variables. This chapter presents Ansible's support for variables in more detail, including a certain type of variable that Ansible calls a *fact*.

Defining Variables in Playbooks

The simplest way to define variables is to put a `vars` section in your playbook with the names and values of your variables. Recall from Example 3-9 that we used this approach to define several configuration-related variables, like this:

```
vars:
  tls_dir: /etc/nginx/ssl/
  key_file: nginx.key
  cert_file: nginx.crt
  conf_file: /etc/nginx/sites-available/default
  server_name: localhost
```

Defining Variables in Separate Files

Ansible also allows you to put variables into one or more files, which are then referenced in the playbook using a section called `vars_files`. Let's say you want to take the preceding example and put the variables in a file named *nginx.yml* instead of putting them right in the playbook. You would replace the `vars` section with a `vars_files` that looks like this:

```
vars_files:
  - nginx.yml
```

The *nginx.yml* file would look like Example 5-1.

Example 5-1. nginx.yml

```
key_file: nginx.key
cert_file: nginx.crt
conf_file: /etc/nginx/sites-available/default
server_name: localhost
```

You'll see an example of `vars_files` in action in Chapter 6 when we use it to separate out the variables that hold sensitive information.

Directory Layout

As we discussed in Chapter 4, Ansible also lets you define variables associated with hosts or groups in the inventory. You'll do this in separate directories that live alongside either the inventory hosts file or your playbooks. Files and directories in the subdirectory *group_vars* are matched against the groups defined in the file hosts. Files and directories in the subdirectory *host_vars* are matched against the individual hosts:

```
inventory/
  production/
    hosts
    group_vars/
      webservers.yml
      all.yml
    host_vars/
      hostname.yml
```

Viewing the Values of Variables

For debugging, it's often handy to be able to view the output of a variable. You saw in Chapter 3 how to use the debug module to print out an arbitrary message. You can also use it to output the value of the variable. It works like this:

```
- debug: var=myvarname
```

This shorthand notation, without a name and in pure-YAML style, is practical in development. We'll use this form of the debug module several times in this chapter. We typically remove debug statements before going to production.

Variable Interpolation

When you want to display a debug message with a variable, then you would use a double-quoted string with the variable name embedded in double braces:

```
- name: Display the variable
  debug:
    msg: "The file used was {{ conf_file }}"
```

Variables can be concatenated between the double braces by using the tilde operator
~, as shown here:

```
- name: Concatenate variables
  debug:
    msg: "The URL is https://{{ server_name ~'.'~ domain_name }}/"
```

Registering Variables

Often, you'll need to set the value of a variable based on the result of a task. Remember that each Ansible module returns results in JSON format. To use these results, you create a *registered variable* using the `register` clause when invoking a module. Example 5-2 shows how to capture the output of the `whoami` command to a variable named `login`.

Example 5-2. Capturing the output of a command to a variable

```
- name: Capture output of whoami command
  command: whoami
  register: login
```

To use the `login` variable later, you need to know the type of value to expect. The value of a variable set using the `register` clause is always a dictionary, but the specific keys of the dictionary will be different depending on the module that you use.

Unfortunately, the official Ansible module documentation doesn't contain information about what the return values look like for each module. It does often mention examples that use the `register` clause, which can be helpful. Lorin found that the simplest way to find out what a module returns is to register a variable and then output that variable with the `debug` module.

Let's say we run the playbook shown in Example 5-3.

Example 5-3. whoami.yml

```
---
- name: Show return value of command module
  hosts: fedora
  gather_facts: false
  tasks:
    - name: Capture output of id command
      command: id -un
      register: login

    - debug: var=login
    - debug: msg="Logged in as user {{ login.stdout }}"
...
```

The output of the debug module looks like this:

```
TASK [debug] *********************************************************************
ok: [fedora] ==> {
    "login": {
        "changed": true,                                    ❶
        "cmd": [                                            ❷
            "id",
            "-un"
        ],
        "delta": "0:00:00.002262",
        "end": "2021-05-30 09:25:41.696308",
        "failed": false,
        "rc": 0,                                            ❸
        "start": "2021-05-30 09:25:41.694046",
        "stderr": "",                                       ❹
        "stderr_lines": [],
        "stdout": "vagrant",                                ❺
        "stdout_lines": [                                   ❻
            "vagrant"
        ]
    }
}
```

❶ The changed key is present in the return value of all Ansible modules, and Ansible uses it to determine whether a state change has occurred. For the command and shell modules, this will always be set to true unless overridden with the changed_when clause, which we cover in Chapter 8.

❷ The cmd key contains the invoked command as a list of strings.

❸ The rc key contains the return code. If it is nonzero, Ansible will assume the task failed to execute successfully.

❹ The stderr key contains any text written to standard error, as a single string.

❺ The stdout key contains any text written to standard out, as a single string.

❻ The stdout_lines key contains any text written to split by newline. It is a list, and each element of the list is a line of output.

If you're using the register clause with the command module, you'll likely want access to the stdout key, as shown in Example 5-4.

Example 5-4. Using the output of a command in a task

```
- name: Capture output of id command
  command: id -un
  register: login

- debug: msg="Logged in as user {{ login.stdout }}"
```

Sometimes it's useful to do something with the output of a failed task—for instance, when running a program fails. However, if the task fails, Ansible will stop executing tasks for the failed host. You can use the `ignore_errors` clause, as shown in Example 5-5, so Ansible does not stop on the error. That allows you to print the program's output.

Example 5-5. Ignoring when a module returns an error

```
- name: Run myprog
  command: /opt/myprog
  register: result
  ignore_errors: true

- debug: var=result
```

The `shell` module has the same output structure as the `command` module, but other modules have different keys.

Example 5-6 shows the relevant piece of the output of the `stat` module that collects properties of a file.

Example 5-6. The relevant piece of the `stat` module output

```
TASK [Display result.stat] ************************************************
ok: [ubuntu] ==> {
    "result.stat": {
        "atime": 1622724660.888851,
        "attr_flags": "e",
        "attributes": [
            "extents"
        ],
        "block_size": 4096,
        "blocks": 8,
        "charset": "us-ascii",
        "checksum": "7df51a4a26c00e5b204e547da4647b36d44dbdbf",
        "ctime": 1621374401.1193385,
        "dev": 2049,
        "device_type": 0,
        "executable": false,
        "exists": true,
        "gid": 0,
```

```
                "gr_name": "root",
                "inode": 784,
                "isblk": false,
                "ischr": false,
                "isdir": false,
                "isfifo": false,
                "isgid": false,
                "islnk": false,
                "isreg": true,
                "issock": false,
                "isuid": false,
                "mimetype": "text/plain",
                "mode": "0644",
                "mtime": 1621374219.5709288,
                "nlink": 1,
                "path": "/etc/ssh/sshd_config",
                "pw_name": "root",
                "readable": true,
                "rgrp": true,
                "roth": true,
                "rusr": true,
                "size": 3287,
                "uid": 0,
                "version": "1324051592",
                "wgrp": false,
                "woth": false,
                "writeable": true,
                "wusr": true,
                "xgrp": false,
                "xoth": false,
                "xusr": false
        }
}
```

The results from the stat module tell you everything there is to know about a file.

Accessing Dictionary Keys in a Variable

If a variable contains a dictionary, you can access the keys of the dictionary by using either a dot (.) or a subscript ([]). Example 5-6 has a variable reference that uses dot notation:

```
{{ result.stat }}
```

We could have used subscript notation instead:

```
{{ result['stat'] }}
```

This rule applies to multiple dereferences, so all of the following are equivalent:

```
result['stat']['mode']
result['stat'].mode
result.stat['mode']
result.stat.mode
```

Bas prefers dot notation, unless the key is a string that holds a character that's not allowed as a variable name, such as a dot, space, or hyphen.

A big advantage of subscript notation is that you can use variables in the brackets (these are not quoted):

```
- name: Display result.stat detail
  debug: var=result['stat'][stat_key]
```

Ansible uses Jinja2 to implement variable dereferencing, so for more details on this topic, see the Jinja2 documentation on variables (*https://oreil.ly/8hKiE*).

 If your playbooks use registered variables, make sure you know the content of those variables, both for cases where the module changes the host's state and for when the module doesn't change the host's state. Otherwise, your playbook might fail when it tries to access a key in a registered variable that doesn't exist.

Facts

As you've already seen, when Ansible runs a playbook, before the first task runs, this happens:

```
TASK [Gathering Facts] ********************************************************
ok: [debian]
ok: [fedora]
ok: [ubuntu]
```

When Ansible gathers facts, it connects to the hosts and queries it for all kinds of details about the hosts: CPU architecture, operating system, IP addresses, memory info, disk info, and more. You can access this data in the `ansible_facts` variable. By default, you can also access some Ansible facts as top-level variables with `ansible_` prefix, and they behave just like any other variable. You can disable this behavior using the `INJECT_FACTS_AS_VARS` setting.

Example 5-7 is a playbook that prints out the operating system details of each server.

Example 5-7. Playbook to print operating system details

```
---
- name: 'Ansible facts.'
  hosts: all
  gather_facts: true
  tasks:
    - name: Print out operating system details
      debug:
        msg: >-
          os_family:
          {{ ansible_facts.os_family }},
```

```
        distro:
        {{ ansible_facts.distribution }}
        {{ ansible_facts.distribution_version }},
        kernel:
        {{ ansible_facts.kernel }}
...
```

Here's what the output looks like for virtual machines running Debian, Fedora, and Ubuntu:

```
PLAY [Ansible facts.] ************************************************************
TASK [Gathering Facts] **********************************************************
ok: [debian]
ok: [fedora]
ok: [ubuntu]
TASK [Print out operating system details] ***************************************
ok: [ubuntu] ==> {
    "msg": "os_family: Debian, distro: Ubuntu 20.04, kernel: 5.4.0-73-generic"
}
ok: [fedora] ==> {
    "msg": "os_family: RedHat, distro: Fedora 34, kernel: 5.11.12-300.fc34.x86_64"
}
ok: [debian] ==> {
    "msg": "os_family: Debian, distro: Debian 10, kernel: 4.19.0-16-amd64"
}
PLAY RECAP **********************************************************************
debian : ok=2  changed=0  unreachable=0  failed=0  skipped=0  rescued=0  ignored=0
fedora : ok=2  changed=0  unreachable=0  failed=0  skipped=0  rescued=0  ignored=0
ubuntu : ok=2  changed=0  unreachable=0  failed=0  skipped=0  rescued=0  ignored=0
```

Viewing All Facts Associated with a Server

Ansible implements fact collecting through the use of a special module called the setup module. You don't need to call this module in your playbooks because Ansible does that automatically when it gathers facts. However, you can invoke it manually with the ansible command-line tool, like this:

```
$ ansible ubuntu -m setup
```

When you do this, Ansible will output all of the facts, as shown in Example 5-8.

Example 5-8. Output of setup module

```
ubuntu | SUCCESS => {
    "ansible_facts": {
        "ansible_all_ipv4_addresses": [
            "192.168.4.10",
            "10.0.2.15"
        ],
        "ansible_all_ipv6_addresses": [
            "fe80::a00:27ff:fef1:d47",
            "fe80::a6:4dff:fe77:e100"
```

```
        ],
(many more facts)
```

Note that the returned value is a dictionary whose key is `ansible_facts` and whose value is a dictionary that has the names and values of the actual facts.

Viewing a Subset of Facts

Because Ansible collects so many facts, the `setup` module supports a `filter` parameter that lets you filter by fact name, or by specifying a glob. (A *glob* is what shells use to match file patterns, such as *.txt.) The filter option filters only the first level subkey below `ansible_facts`.

```
$ ansible all -m setup -a 'filter=ansible_all_ipv6_addresses'
```

The output looks like this:

```
debian | SUCCESS => {
    "ansible_facts": {
        "ansible_all_ipv6_addresses": [
            "fe80::a00:27ff:fe8d:c04d",
            "fe80::a00:27ff:fe55:2351"
        ]
    },
    "changed": false
}
fedora | SUCCESS => {
    "ansible_facts": {
        "ansible_all_ipv6_addresses": [
            "fe80::505d:173f:a6fc:3f91",
            "fe80::a00:27ff:fe48:995"
        ]
    },
    "changed": false
}
ubuntu | SUCCESS => {
    "ansible_facts": {
        "ansible_all_ipv6_addresses": [
            "fe80::a00:27ff:fef1:d47",
            "fe80::a6:4dff:fe77:e100"
        ]
    },
    "changed": false
}
```

Using a filter helps with finding the main details of a machine's setup. The filter `ansible_env` collects environment variables on the target hosts.

Any Module Can Return Facts or Info

If you look closely at Example 5-8, you'll see that the output is a dictionary whose key is `ansible_facts`. The use of `ansible_facts` in the return value is an Ansible idiom. If a module returns a dictionary that contains `ansible_facts` as a key, Ansible will create variable names in the environment with those values and associate them with the active host. Modules that return information about objects that are not unique for the host have their name ending in _info.

For modules that return facts, there's no need to register variables, since Ansible creates these variables for you automatically. In Example 5-9, the task uses the service_facts module to retrieve facts about services, then prints out the part about the secure shell daemon. (Note the subscript notation—that's due to the embedded dot.)

Example 5-9. Using the service_facts module to retrieve facts

```
- name: Show a fact returned by a module
  hosts: debian
  gather_facts: false
  tasks:
    - name: Get services facts
      service_facts:

    - debug: var=ansible_facts['services']['sshd.service']
```

The output looks like this:

```
TASK [debug] ****************************************************************
ok: [debian] ==> {
    "ansible_facts['services']['sshd.service']": {
        "name": "sshd.service",
        "source": "systemd",
        "state": "active",
        "status": "enabled"
    }
}
```

Note that we do not need to use the register keyword when invoking service_facts, since the returned values are facts. Several modules that ship with Ansible return facts.

Local Facts

Ansible provides an additional mechanism for associating facts with a host. You can place one or more files on the remote host machine in the */etc/ansible/facts.d* directory. Ansible will recognize the file if it is:

- In *.ini* format
- In JSON format
- An executable that takes no arguments and outputs JSON on the standard output stream

These facts are available as keys of a special variable named `ansible_local`. For instance, Example 5-10 shows a fact file in *.ini* format.

Example 5-10. /etc/ansible/facts.d/example.fact

```
[book]
title=Ansible: Up and Running
authors=Meijer, Hochstein, Moser
publisher=O'Reilly
```

If you copy this file to */etc/ansible/facts.d/example.fact* on the remote host, you can access the contents of the `ansible_local` variable in a playbook:

```
- name: Print ansible_local
  debug: var=ansible_local

- name: Print book title
  debug: msg="The title of the book is {{ ansible_local.example.book.title }}"
```

The output of these tasks looks like this:

```
TASK [Print ansible_local] *****************************************************
ok: [fedora] ==> {
    "ansible_local": {
        "example": {
            "book": {
                "authors": "Meijer, Hochstein, Moser",
                "publisher": "O'Reilly",
                "title": "Ansible: Up and Running"
            }
        }
    }
}
TASK [Print book title] ********************************************************
ok: [fedora] ==> {
    "msg": "The title of the book is Ansible: Up and Running"
}
```

Note the structure of the value in the `ansible_local` variable. Because the fact file is named *example.fact*, the `ansible_local` variable is a dictionary that contains a key named `example`.

Using set_fact to Define a New Variable

Ansible also allows you to set a fact (effectively the same as defining a new variable) in a task by using the `set_fact` module. Lorin often likes to use `set_fact` immediately after `service_facts` to make it simpler to refer to a variable. Example 5-11 demonstrates how to use `set_fact` so that a variable can be referred to as `nginx_state` instead of `ansible_facts.services.nginx.state`.

Example 5-11. Using set_fact to simplify variable reference

```
- name: Set nginx_state
  when: ansible_facts.services.nginx.state is defined
  set_fact:
    nginx_state: "{{ ansible_facts.services.nginx.state }}"
```

Built-In Variables

Ansible defines several variables that are always available in a playbook. Some are shown in Table 5-1. Refer to the online documentation for special magic variables (*https://oreil.ly/hao2l*).

Table 5-1. Built-in variables

Parameter	Description
hostvars	A dict whose keys are Ansible hostnames and values are dicts that map variable names to values
inventory_hostname	The name of the current host as known in the Ansible inventory, might include domain name
inventory_host name_short	Name of the current host as known by Ansible, without the domain name (e.g., myhost)
group_names	A list of all groups that the current host is a member of
groups	A dict whose keys are Ansible group names and values are a list of hostnames that are members of the group. Includes all and ungrouped groups: {"all": [...], "web": [...], "ungrouped": [...]}
ansible_check_mode	A boolean that is true when running in check mode (see "Check Mode")
ansible_play_batch	A list of the inventory hostnames that are active in the current batch (see "Running on a Batch of Hosts at a Time")
ansible_play_hosts	A list of all of the inventory hostnames that are active in the current play
ansible_version	A dict with Ansible version info: {"full": 2.3.1.0", "major": 2, "minor": 3, "revision": 1, "string": "2.3.1.0"}

The hostvars, inventory_hostname, and groups variables merit some additional discussion.

hostvars

In Ansible, variables are scoped by host. It makes sense to talk only about the value of a variable relative to a given host.

The idea that variables are relative to a given host might sound confusing, since Ansible allows you to define variables on a group of hosts. For example, if you define a variable in the vars section of a play, you are defining the variable for the set of hosts in the play. But what Ansible is really doing is creating a copy of that variable for each host in the group.

Sometimes, a task that's running on one host needs the value of a variable defined on another host. Say you need to create a configuration file on web servers that contains the IP address of the *eth1* interface of the database server, and you don't know in advance what this IP address is. This IP address is available as the *ansible_eth1.ipv4.address* fact for the database server.

The solution is to use the `hostvars` variable. This is a dictionary that contains all of the variables defined on all of the hosts, keyed by the hostname as known to Ansible. If Ansible has not yet gathered facts on a host, you will not be able to access its facts by using the `hostvars` variable, unless fact caching is enabled.[1]

Continuing our example, if our database server is *db.example.com*, then we could put the following in a configuration template:

```
{{ hostvars['db.example.com'].ansible_eth1.ipv4.address }}
```

This evaluates to the *ansible_eth1.ipv4.address* fact associated with the host named *db.example.com*.

hostvars Versus host_vars

Please be warned that `hostvars` is computed when you run Ansible, while `host_vars` is a directory that you can use to define variables for a particular system.

inventory_hostname

The `inventory_hostname` is the hostname of the current host, as known by Ansible. If you have defined an alias for a host, this is the alias name. For example, if your inventory contains a line like this:

```
ubuntu ansible_host=192.168.4.10
```

then `inventory_hostname` would be `ubuntu`.

You can output all of the variables associated with the current host with the help of the `hostvars` and `inventory_hostname` variables:

```
- debug: var=hostvars[inventory_hostname]
```

groups

The `groups` variable can be useful when you need to access variables for a group of hosts. Let's say we are configuring a load-balancing host, and our configuration

---

1 See Chapter 11 for information about fact caching.

file needs the IP addresses of all of the servers in our web group. The file template contains a fragment that looks like this:

```
backend web-backend
{% for host in groups.web %}
  server {{ hostvars[host].inventory_hostname }} \
  {{ hostvars[host].ansible_default_ipv4.address }}:80
{% endfor %}
```

The generated file looks like this:

```
backend web-backend
    server georgia.example.com 203.0.113.15:80
    server newhampshire.example.com 203.0.113.25:80
    server newjersey.example.com 203.0.113.38:80
```

With the groups variable you can iterate over hosts in a group in a configuration file template, only by using the group name. You can change the hosts in the group without changing the configuration file template.

Extra Variables on the Command Line

Variables set by passing -e var=value to ansible-playbook have the highest precedence, which means you can use this to override variables that are already defined. Example 5-12 shows how to set the value of the variable named greeting to the value hiya.

Example 5-12. Setting a variable from the command line

```
$ ansible-playbook 4-12-greet.yml -e greeting=hiya
```

Use the ansible-playbook -e variable=value method when you want to use a playbook as you would a shell script that takes a command-line argument. The -e flag effectively allows you to pass a variable with its value. Specify -e multiple times to pass as many variable values as you need.

Example 5-13 shows a playbook that outputs a message specified by a variable.

Example 5-13. Outputting a message specified by a variable

```
---
- name: Pass a message on the command line
  hosts: localhost
  gather_facts: false

  vars:
    greeting: "you didn't specify a message"

  tasks:
    - name: Output a message
```

```
    debug:
      msg: "{{ greeting }}"
...
```

You can invoke it like this:

```
$ ansible-playbook 4-12-greet.yml -e greeting=hiya
```

The output will look like this:

```
PLAY [Pass a message on the command line] ************************************
TASK [Gathering Facts] ******************************************************
ok: [localhost]
TASK [Output a message] *****************************************************
ok: [localhost] ==> {
    "msg": "hiya"
}
PLAY RECAP ******************************************************************
localhost : ok=2  changed=0  unreachable=0  failed=0  skipped=0  rescued=0  ignored=0
```

If you want to put a space in the variable, you need to use quotes like this:

```
$ ansible-playbook greet.yml -e 'greeting="hi there"'
```

You have to put single quotes around the entire `'greeting="hi there"'` so that the shell interprets that as a single argument to pass to Ansible, and you have to put double quotes around `"hi there"` so that Ansible treats that message as a single string.

Ansible also allows you to pass a file containing the variables instead of passing them directly on the command line by passing `@filename.yml` as the argument to `-e`; for example, say you have a file that looks like Example 5-14.

Example 5-14. greetvars.yml

```
greeting: hiya
```

You can pass this file to the command line like this:

```
$ ansible-playbook 5-12-greet.yml -e @5-14-greetvars.yml
```

Example 5-15 shows a simple technique to display any variable given with the `-e` flag on the command line.

Example 5-15. Displaying a variable given with the `-e` flag

```
---
- name: Show any variable during debugging.
  hosts: all
  gather_facts: true
  tasks:
    - debug: var="{{ variable }}"
...
```

Using this technique effectively gives you a "variable variable" that you can use for debugging:

```
$ ansible-playbook 5-15-variable-variable.yml -e variable=ansible_python
```

Precedence

We've covered several ways of defining variables. It is possible to define the same variable multiple times for a host, using different values. Avoid this when you can, but if you can't, then keep in mind Ansible's precedence rules. When the same variable is defined in multiple ways, the precedence rules determine which value wins (or overrides).

Ansible does apply variable precedence,[2] and you might have a use for it. Here is a simple rule of thumb: the closer to the host, the higher the precedence. So group_vars overrules role defaults, and host_vars overrules group_vars. Here is the order of precedence, from least to greatest. The last listed variables override all other variables:

1. command line values (for example, -u my_user; these are not variables)
2. role defaults (defined in *role/defaults/main.yml*)
3. inventory file or script group vars
4. inventory group_vars/all
5. playbook group_vars/all
6. inventory group_vars/*
7. playbook group_vars/*
8. inventory file or script host vars
9. inventory host_vars/*
10. playbook host_vars/*
11. host facts / cached set_facts
12. play vars
13. play vars_prompt
14. play vars_files
15. role vars (defined in *role/vars/main.yml*)
16. block vars (only for tasks in block)
17. task vars (only for the task)

---

2 "Understanding variable precedence," Ansible documentation (*https://oreil.ly/gqsfK*).

18. include_vars

19. set_facts / registered vars

20. role (and include_role) params

21. include params

22. extra vars (for example, `-e "user=my_user"`)

Conclusion

In this chapter, we covered several ways to define and access variables and facts. Separating variables from tasks and creating inventories with the proper values for the variables allows you to create staging environments for your software. Ansible is very powerful in its flexibility to define data at the appropriate level. The next chapter focuses on a realistic example of deploying an application.

## CHAPTER 6

Introducing Mezzanine: Our Test Application

Chapter 3 covered the basics of writing playbooks. But real life is always messier than the introductory chapters of programming books, so in this chapter we're going to work through a complete example of deploying a nontrivial application. In the next chapter we will do the implementation.

Our example application is an open source content management system (CMS) called Mezzanine (*https://oreil.ly/xqgMN*), which is similar in spirit to WordPress. Mezzanine is built on top of Django, the free Python-based framework for writing web applications.

Why Is Deploying to Production Complicated?

Let's take a little detour and talk about the differences between running software in development mode on your laptop versus running the software in production. Mezzanine is a great example of an application that is much easier to run in development mode than it is to deploy. Example 6-1 shows a provisioning script to get Mezzanine running on Ubuntu Focal/64.[1]

Example 6-1. Running Mezzanine in development mode

```
$ sudo apt-get install -y python3-venv
$ python3 -m venv venv
$ source venv/bin/activate
```

---

[1] This installs the Python packages into a virtualenv; the online example provisions a Vagrant VM automatically.

```
$ pip3 install wheel
$ pip3 install mezzanine
$ mezzanine-project myproject
$ cd myproject
$ sed -i 's/ALLOWED_HOSTS = \[\]/ALLOWED_HOSTS = ["*"]/' myproject/settings.py
$ python manage.py migrate
$ python manage.py runserver 0.0.0.0:8000
```

You should eventually see output on the terminal that looks like this:

```
                  .....
            _d^^^^^^^^^b_
         .d''          ``b.
       .p'                `q.
      .d'                   `b.
     .d'                     `b.     * Mezzanine 4.3.1
     ::                       ::     * Django 1.11.29
     ::     M E Z Z A N I N E  ::    * Python 3.8.5
     ::                       ::     * SQLite 3.31.1
     `p.                     .q'     * Linux 5.4.0-74-generic
      `p.                   .q'
       `b.                 .d'
        `q..            ..p'
         ^q........p^
             ''''
Performing system checks...
System check identified no issues (0 silenced).
June 15, 2021 - 19:24:35
Django version 1.11.29, using settings 'myproject.settings'
Starting development server at http://0.0.0.0:8000/
Quit the server with CONTROL-C.
```

If you point your browser to *http://127.0.0.1:8000/*, you should see a web page that looks like Figure 6-1. (This server accepts connections from every IP address; that's what 0.0.0.0 stands for.)

Deploying this application to production is another matter. When you run the mezzanine-project command, Mezzanine will generate a Fabric (*http://www.fab file.org*) deployment script at *myproject/fabfile.py* that you can use to deploy your project to a production server. (Fabric is a Python-based tool that helps automate running tasks via SSH.) The script is almost 700 lines long, and that's not counting the included configuration files that are also involved in deployment.

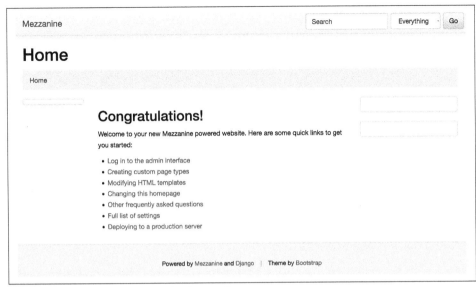

Figure 6-1. Mezzanine after a fresh install

Why is deploying to production so much more complex? We're glad you asked. When run in development, Mezzanine provides the following simplifications (see Figure 6-2):

- The system uses SQLite as the backend database and will create the database file if it doesn't exist.

- The development HTTP server serves up both the static content (images, *.css* files, JavaScript) and the dynamically generated HTML.

- The development HTTP server uses HTTP (insecure), not (secure) HTTPS.

- The development HTTP server process runs in the foreground, taking over your terminal window.

- The hostname for the HTTP server is always 127.0.0.1 (localhost).

Now, let's look at what happens when you deploy to production.

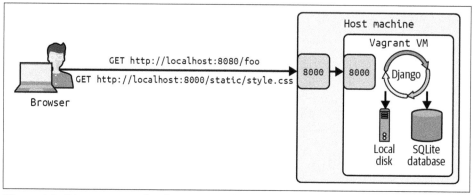

Figure 6-2. Django app in development mode

Postgres: The Database

SQLite is a serverless database. In production, you want to run a server-based database, because those have better support for multiple, concurrent requests, and server-based databases allow us to run multiple HTTP servers for load balancing. This means you need to deploy a database management system, such as MySQL or Postgres. Setting up one of these database servers requires more work. You'll need to do the following:

1. Install the database software.
2. Ensure the database service is running.
3. Create the database inside the database management system.
4. Create a database user who has the appropriate permissions for the database system.
5. Configure the Mezzanine application with the database user credentials and connection information.

Gunicorn: The Application Server

Because Mezzanine is a Django-based application, you can run it using Django's HTTP server, referred to as the *development server* in the Django documentation. Here's what the Django 1.11 docs (*https://oreil.ly/vBIFd*) have to say about the development server:

> Don't use this server in anything resembling a production environment. It's intended only for use while developing. (We're in the business of making Web frameworks, not Web servers.)

Django implements the standard Web Server Gateway Interface (WSGI),[2] so any Python HTTP server that supports WSGI is suitable for running a Django application such as Mezzanine. We'll use Gunicorn, one of the most popular HTTP WSGI servers, which is what the Mezzanine deploy script uses. Also note that Mezzanine uses an insecure version of Django that is no longer supported.

NGINX: The Web Server

Gunicorn will execute our Django application, just like the development server does. However, Gunicorn won't serve any of the static assets associated with the application. *Static assets* are files such as images, *.css* files, and JavaScript files. They are called static because they never change, in contrast with the dynamically generated web pages that Gunicorn serves up.

Although Gunicorn can handle TLS encryption, it's common to configure NGINX to handle the encryption.[3]

We're going to use NGINX as our web server for serving static assets and for handling the TLS encryption, as shown in Figure 6-3.

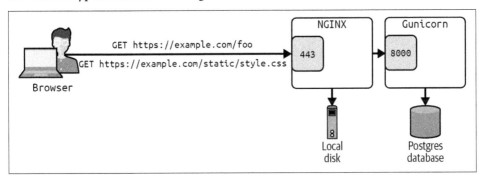

Figure 6-3. NGINX as a reverse proxy

We need to configure NGINX as a *reverse proxy* for Gunicorn. If the request is for a static asset, such as a *.css* file, NGINX will serve that file directly from the local filesystem. Otherwise, NGINX will proxy the request to Gunicorn, by making an HTTP request against the Gunicorn service that is running on the local machine. NGINX uses the URL to determine whether to serve a local file or proxy the request to Gunicorn.

---

2 The WSGI protocol is documented in Python Enhancement Proposal (PEP) 3333 (*https://oreil.ly/yyMcf*).

3 Gunicorn 0.17 added support for TLS encryption. Before that, you had to use a separate application such as NGINX to handle the encryption.

Note that requests to NGINX will be (encrypted) HTTPS, and all requests that NGINX proxies to Gunicorn will be (unencrypted) HTTP.

Supervisor: The Process Manager

When we run in development mode, we run the application server in the foreground of our terminal. If we were to close our terminal, the program would terminate. For a server application, we need it to run as a background process, so it doesn't terminate, even if we close the terminal session we used to start the process.

The colloquial terms for such a process are *daemon* or *service*. We need to run Gunicorn as a daemon, and we'd like to be able to stop it and restart it easily. Numerous service managers can do this job. We're going to use Supervisor because that's what the Mezzanine deployment scripts use.

Conclusion

At this point, you should have a sense of the steps involved in deploying a web application to production. We'll go over how to implement this deployment with Ansible in Chapter 7.

Deploying Mezzanine with Ansible

It's time to write an Ansible playbook, one to deploy Mezzanine to a server. We'll go through it step by step, but if you're the type of person who starts off by reading the last page of a book to see how it ends, you can find the full playbook at the end of this chapter as Example 7-27. It's also available on GitHub. Check out the README file before trying to run it directly.

We have tried to hew as closely as possible to the original scripts that Mezzanine author Stephen McDonald wrote.[1]

Listing Tasks in a Playbook

Before we dive into the guts of our playbook, let's get a high-level view. The `ansible-playbook` command-line tool supports a flag called `--list-tasks`. This flag prints out the names of all the tasks in a playbook. Here's how you use it:

```
$ ansible-playbook --list-tasks mezzanine.yml
```

Example 7-1 shows the output for the *mezzanine.yml* playbook in Example 7-27.

Example 7-1. List of tasks in Mezzanine playbook

```
playbook: mezzanine.yml
  play #1 (web): Deploy mezzanine      TAGS: []
    tasks:
      Install apt packages      TAGS: []
      Create project path       TAGS: []
      Create a logs directory   TAGS: []
      Check out the repository on the host      TAGS: []
```

---

1 Mezzanine no longer ships a fabfile for automatic deployments.

```
Create python3 virtualenv TAGS: []
Copy requirements.txt to home directory   TAGS: []
Install packages listed in requirements.txt      TAGS: []
Create project locale      TAGS: []
Create a DB user  TAGS: []
Create the database        TAGS: []
Ensure config path exists TAGS: []
Create tls certificates    TAGS: []
Remove the default nginx config file       TAGS: []
Set the nginx config file TAGS: []
Enable the nginx config file       TAGS: []
Set the supervisor config file     TAGS: []
Install poll twitter cron job      TAGS: []
Set the gunicorn config file       TAGS: []
Generate the settings file         TAGS: []
Apply migrations to create the database, collect static content   TAGS: []
Set the site id    TAGS: []
Set the admin password     TAGS: []
```

It's a handy way to summarize what a playbook is going to do.

Organization of Deployed Files

As we discussed earlier, Mezzanine is built atop Django. In Django, a web app is called a *project*. We get to choose what to name our project, and we've chosen to name this one *mezzanine_example*.

Our playbook deploys into a Vagrant machine and will deploy the files into the home directory of the Vagrant user's account.

Example 7-2. Directory structure under /home/vagrant

```
.
|---- logs
|---- mezzanine
|    |___ mezzanine_example
|___ .virtualenvs
     |___ mezzanine_example
```

Example 7-2 shows the relevant directories under */home/vagrant*:

- */home/vagrant/mezzanine/mezzanine-example* will contain the source code that will be cloned from a source code repository on GitHub.

- */home/vagrant/.virtualenvs/mezzanine_example* is the virtualenv directory, which means that we're going to install all of the Python packages into that directory.

- */home/vagrant/logs* will contain log files generated by Mezzanine.

Variables and Secret Variables

As you can see in Example 7-3, this playbook defines quite a few variables.

Example 7-3. Defining the variables

```
vars:
  user: "{{ ansible_user }}"
  proj_app: mezzanine_example
  proj_name: "{{ proj_app }}"
  venv_home: "{{ ansible_env.HOME }}/.virtualenvs"
  venv_path: "{{ venv_home }}/{{ proj_name }}"
  proj_path: "{{ ansible_env.HOME }}/mezzanine/{{ proj_name }}"
  settings_path: "{{ proj_path }}/{{ proj_name }}"
  reqs_path: requirements.txt
  manage: "{{ python }} {{ proj_path }}/manage.py"
  live_hostname: 192.168.33.10.nip.io
  domains:
    - 192.168.33.10.nip.io
    - www.192.168.33.10.nip.io
  repo_url: git@github.com:ansiblebook/mezzanine_example.git
  locale: 'en_US.UTF-8'
  # Variables below don't appear in Mezzanine's fabfile.py
  # but I've added them for convenience
  conf_path: /etc/nginx/conf
  tls_enabled: true
  python: "{{ venv_path }}/bin/python"
  database_name: "{{ proj_name }}"
  database_user: "{{ proj_name }}"
  database_host: localhost
  database_port: 5432
  gunicorn_procname: gunicorn_mezzanine

vars_files:
  - secrets.yml
```

We've tried for the most part to use the same variable names that the Mezzanine Fabric script uses. I've also added some extra variables to make things a little clearer. For example, the Fabric scripts directly use `proj_name` as the database name and database username. For clarity, Lorin prefers to define intermediate variables named `database_name` and `database_user` and define these in terms of `proj_name`.

It's worth noting a few things here. First off, we can define one variable in terms of another. For example, we define `venv_path` in terms of `venv_home` and `proj_name`.

Also, we can reference Ansible facts in these variables. For example, `venv_home` is defined in terms of the `ansible_env` fact collected from each host.

Finally, we have specified some of our variables in a separate file, called *secrets.yml*:

```
vars_files:
  - secrets.yml
```

This file contains credentials such as passwords and tokens that need to remain private. The GitHub repository does not actually contain this file. Instead, it contains a file called *secrets.yml.example* that looks like this:

```
db_pass: e79c9761d0b54698a83ff3f93769e309
admin_pass: 46041386be534591ad24902bf72071B
secret_key: b495a05c396843b6b47ac944a72c92ed
nevercache_key: b5d87bb4e17c483093296fa321056bdc

# You need to create a Twitter application at https://dev.twitter.com
# in order to get the credentials required for Mezzanine's
# twitter integration.
## See https://mezzanine.readthedocs.io/en/latest/twitter-integration.html
# for details on Twitter integration
twitter_access_token_key: 80b557a3a8d14cb7a2b91d60398fb8ce
twitter_access_token_secret: 1974cf8419114bdd9d4ea3db7a210d90
twitter_consumer_key: 1f1c627530b34bb58701ac81ac3fad51
twitter_consumer_secret: 36515c2b60ee4ffb9d33d972a7ec350a
```

To use this repo, copy *secrets.yml.example* to *secrets.yml* and edit it so that it contains the credentials specific to your site.

The *secrets.yml* file is included in the *.gitignore* file in the Git repository to prevent someone from accidentally committing these credentials. It's best to avoid committing unencrypted credentials into your version-control repository because of the security risks involved. This is just one possible strategy for maintaining secret credentials. We also could have passed them as environment variables. Another option, which we will describe in Chapter 8, is to commit an encrypted version of the *secrets.yml* file by using ansible-vault functionality.

Installing Multiple Packages

We're going to need to install two types of packages for our Mezzanine deployment: some system-level packages and some Python packages. Because we're going to deploy on Ubuntu, we'll use apt as our package manager for the system packages. We'll use pip to install the Python packages.

System-level packages are generally easier to deal with than Python packages because they're designed specifically to work with the operating system. However, the system package repositories often don't have the newest versions of the Python libraries we need, so we turn to the Python packages to install those. It's a trade-off between stability and running the latest and greatest.

Example 7-4 shows the task we'll use to install the system packages.

Example 7-4. Installing system packages

```
- name: Install apt packages
  become: true
  apt:
    update_cache: true
    cache_valid_time: 3600
    pkg:
      - acl
      - git
      - libjpeg-dev
      - libpq-dev
      - memcached
      - nginx
      - postgresql
      - python3-dev
      - python3-pip
      - python3-venv
      - python3-psycopg2
      - supervisor
```

Because we're installing multiple packages, Ansible will pass the entire list to the apt module, and the module will invoke the apt program only once, passing it the entire list of packages to be installed. The apt module has been designed to handle this list entirely.

Adding the Become Clause to a Task

In the playbook examples you read in Chapter 3, we wanted the whole playbook to run as root, so we added the become: true clause to the play. When we deploy Mezzanine, most of the tasks will be run as the user who is SSHing to the host, rather than root. Therefore, we don't want to run as root for the *entire* play, only for select tasks.

We can accomplish this by adding become: true to the tasks that *do* need to run as root, such as Example 7-4. For auditing purposes, Bas prefers to add become: true right under the - name:.

Updating the apt Cache

Ubuntu maintains a cache with the names of all of the *apt* packages that are available in the Ubuntu package archive. Let's say you try to install the package named *libssl-dev*. We can use the apt-cache program to query the local cache to see what version it knows about:

```
$ apt-cache policy libssl-dev
```

All of the example commands in this subsection are run on the (Ubuntu) remote host, not the control machine.

The output is shown in Example 7-5.

Example 7-5. apt-cache output

```
libssl-dev:
  Installed: (none)
  Candidate: 1.1.1f-1ubuntu2.4
  Version table:
    1.1.1f-1ubuntu2.4 500
       500 http://archive.ubuntu.com/ubuntu focal-updates/main amd64 Packages
    1.1.1f-1ubuntu2.3 500
       500 http://security.ubuntu.com/ubuntu focal-security/main amd64 Packages
    1.1.1f-1ubuntu2 500
       500 http://archive.ubuntu.com/ubuntu focal/main amd64 Packages
```

As you can see, this package is not installed locally. According to the local cache, the latest version is 1.1.1f-1ubuntu2.4. It also tells us the location of the package archive.

In some cases, when the Ubuntu project releases a new version of a package, it removes the old version from the package archive. If the local apt cache of an Ubuntu server hasn't been updated, then it will attempt to install a package that doesn't exist in the package archive.

To continue with our example, let's say we attempt to install the *libssl-dev* package:

```
$ sudo apt-get install libssl-dev
```

If version 1.1.1f-1ubuntu2.4 is no longer available in the package archive, we'll see an error.

On the command line, the way to bring the local apt cache up to date is to run `apt-get update`. When using the apt Ansible module, however, you'll do this update by passing the `update_cache: true` argument when invoking the module, as shown in Example 7-4.

Because updating the cache takes additional time, and because we might be running a playbook multiple times in quick succession to debug it, we can avoid paying the cache update penalty by using the `cache_valid_time` argument to the module. This instructs to update the cache only if it's older than a certain threshold. The example in Example 7-4 uses `cache_valid_time: 3600`, which updates the cache only if it's older than 3,600 seconds (1 hour).

Checking Out the Project Using Git

Although Mezzanine can be used without writing any custom code, one of its strengths is that it is written on top of the Django web application platform, which is great if you know Python. If you just want a CMS, you'll likely just use something like WordPress. But if you're writing a custom application that incorporates CMS functionality, Mezzanine is a good way to go.

As part of the deployment, you need to check out the Git repository that contains your Django applications. In Django terminology, this repository must contain a *project*. We've created a repository on GitHub (*https://oreil.ly/HtoNP*) that contains a Django project with the expected files. That's the project that gets deployed in this playbook.

We created these files using the `mezzanine-project` program that ships with Mezzanine, like this:

```
$ mezzanine-project mezzanine_example
$ chmod +x mezzanine_example/manage.py
```

Note that we don't have any custom Django applications in the repository, just the files that are required for the project. In a real Django deployment, this repository would contain subdirectories with additional Django applications.

Example 7-6 shows how to use the `git` module to check out a Git repository to a remote host.

Example 7-6. Checking out the Git repository

```
- name: Check out the repository on the host
  git:
    repo: "{{ repo_url }}"
    dest: "{{ proj_path }}"
    version: master
    accept_hostkey: true
```

We've made the project repository public so that you can access it, but in general, you'll be checking out private Git repositories over SSH. For this reason, we've set the `repo_url` variable to use the scheme that will clone the repository over SSH:

```
repo_url: git@github.com:ansiblebook/mezzanine_example.git
```

If you're following along at home, to run this playbook, you must have a GitHub account (*https://github.com/signup*). Then, you would:

1. Add your public SSH key (*https://github.com/settings/keys*) to your account

2. Start your SSH agent:
   ```
   $ eval $(ssh-agent)
   ```

3. Once your SSH agent is running, add your key:

```
$ ssh-add <path to the private key>
```

If successful, the following command will output the public key of the SSH you just added:

```
$ ssh-add -L
```

The output should look something like this:

```
ssh-ed25519 AAAAC3NzaC1lZDI1NTE5AAAAIN1/YRlI7Oc+KyM6NFZt7fb7pY+btItKHMLbZhdbwhj2
```

To enable agent forwarding, add the following to your *ansible.cfg*:

```
[ssh_connection]
ssh_args = -o ForwardAgent=yes
```

You can verify that agent forwarding is working by using Ansible to list the known keys:

```
$ ansible web -a "ssh-add -L"
```

You should see the same output as when you run ssh-add -L on your local machine.

Another useful check is to verify that you can reach GitHub's SSH server:

```
$ ansible web -a "ssh -T git@github.com"
```

If successful, the output should look like this:

```
web | FAILED | rc=1 >>
Hi bbaassssiiee! You've successfully authenticated, but GitHub does not provide
shell access.
```

Even though the word FAILED appears in the output (we cannot log in to a bash shell on GitHub), if this message from GitHub appears, then it was successful.

In addition to specifying the repository URL with the repo parameter and the destination path of the repository as the dest parameter, we also pass an additional parameter, accept_hostkey, which is related to *host-key checking*. (We discuss SSH agent forwarding and host-key checking in more detail in Chapter 20.)

Installing Mezzanine and Other Packages into a Virtual Environment

We can install Python packages systemwide as the root user, but it's better practice to install these packages in an isolated environment to avoid polluting the system-level Python packages. In Python, these types of isolated package environments are called virtual environments, or *virtualenvs*. A user can create multiple virtualenvs and can install Python packages into a virtualenv without needing root access. (Remember, we're installing some Python packages to get more recent versions.)

Ansible's `pip` module has support for installing packages into a virtualenv, as well as for creating the virtualenv if it is not available.

Example 7-7 shows how to use `pip` to install a Python 3 virtualenv with the latest package tools.

Example 7-7. Install Python virtualenv

```
- name: Create python3 virtualenv
  pip:
    name:
      - pip
      - wheel
      - setuptools
    state: latest
    virtualenv: "{{ venv_path }}"
    virtualenv_command: /usr/bin/python3 -m venv
```

Example 7-8 shows the two tasks that we use to install Python packages into the virtualenv. A common pattern in Python projects is to specify the package dependencies in a file called *requirements.txt*.

Example 7-8. Install Python packages

```
- name: Copy requirements.txt to home directory
  copy:
    src: requirements.txt
    dest: "{{ reqs_path }}"
    mode: '0644'

- name: install packages listed in requirements.txt
  pip:
    virtualenv: "{{ venv_path }}"
    requirements: "{{ reqs_path }}"
```

Indeed, the repository in our Mezzanine example contains a *requirements.txt* file. It looks like Example 7-9.

Example 7-9. requirements.txt

```
Mezzanine==4.3.1
```

Note that the Mezzanine Python package in *requirements.txt* is pinned to a specific version (4.3.1). That *requirements.txt* file is missing several other Python packages that we need for the deployment, so we explicitly specify these in a *requirements.txt* file in the playbooks directory that we then copy to the host.

Ansible allows you to specify file permissions used by several modules, including `file`, `copy`, and `template`. You can specify the mode as a symbolic mode (for example: `'u+rwx'` or `'u=rw,g=r,o=r'`). For those used to `/usr/bin/chmod`, remember that modes are actually octal numbers. You must either add a leading zero so that Ansible's YAML parser knows it is an octal number (like 0644 or 01777), or quote it (like `'644'` or `'1777'`) so that Ansible receives a string it can convert into a number. If you give Ansible a number without following one of these rules, you will end up with a decimal number, which will have unexpected results. Being explicit with every file's mode, with single quoting and stating absence of special bits (suid, segid) like `'0755'`, is a good practice to avoid ambiguity.

We just take the latest available version of the other dependencies.

Alternately, if you wanted to pin all of the packages, you'd have several options: for example, you could specify all the packages in the *requirements.txt* file, for repeatability. This file contains information about the packages and the dependencies. An example file looks like Example 7-10.

Example 7-10. Example requirements.txt

```
beautifulsoup4==4.9.3
bleach==3.3.0
certifi==2021.5.30
chardet==4.0.0
Django==1.11.29
django-appconf==1.0.4
django-compressor==2.4.1
django-contrib-comments==2.0.0
filebrowser-safe==0.5.0
future==0.18.2
grappelli-safe==0.5.2
gunicorn==20.1.0
idna==2.10
Mezzanine==4.3.1
oauthlib==3.1.1
packaging==21.0
Pillow==8.3.1
pkg-resources==0.0.0
psycopg2==2.9.1
pyparsing==2.4.7
python-memcached==1.59
pytz==2021.1
rcssmin==1.0.6
requests==2.25.1
requests-oauthlib==1.3.0
rjsmin==1.1.0
setproctitle==1.2.2
```

```
six==1.16.0
soupsieve==2.2.1
tzlocal==2.1
urllib3==1.26.6
webencodings==0.5.1
```

If you have an existing virtualenv with the packages installed, you can use the `pip freeze` command to print out a list of installed packages. For example, if your virtualenv is in *~/.virtualenvs/mezzanine_example*, then you can activate your virtualenv and save the packages in the virtualenv into a *requirements.txt* file:

```
$ source .virtualenvs/mezzanine_example/bin/activate
$ pip freeze > requirements.txt
```

Example 7-11 shows how to specify both the package names and their versions in the list. `with_items` passes a list of dictionaries, to dereference the elements with `item.name` and `item.version` when the `pip` module iterates.

Example 7-11. Specifying package names and version

```
- name: Install python packages with pip
  pip:
    virtualenv: "{{ venv_path }}"
    name: "{{ item.name }}"
    version: "{{ item.version }}"
  with_items:
    - {name: mezzanine, version: '4.3.1' }
    - {name: gunicorn, version: '20.1.0' }
    - {name: setproctitle, version: '1.2.2' }
    - {name: psycopg2, version: '2.9.1' }
    - {name: django-compressor, version: '2.4.1' }
    - {name: python-memcached, version: '1.59' }
```

Please note the single quotes around version numbers: this ensures they are treated as literals and are not rounded off in edge cases.

Complex Arguments in Tasks: A Brief Digression

When you invoke a module, you can pass the argument as a string (great for ad hoc use). Taking the pip example from Example 7-11, we could have passed the `pip` module a string as an argument:

```
- name: Install package with pip
  pip: virtualenv={{ venv_path }} name={{ item.name }} version={{ item.version }}
```

If you don't like long lines in your files, you could break up the argument string across multiple lines by using YAML's line folding:

```
- name: Install package with pip
  pip: >
    virtualenv={{ venv_path }}
```

```
    name={{ item.name }}
    version={{ item.version }}
```

Ansible provides a better option for breaking up a module invocation across multiple lines. Instead of passing a string, you can pass a dictionary in which the keys are the variable names. This means you could invoke Example 7-11 like this instead:

```
- name: Install package with pip
  pip:
    virtualenv: "{{ venv_path }}"
    name: "{{ item.name }}"
    version: "{{ item.version }}"
```

The dictionary-based approach to passing arguments is also useful when invoking modules that take a *complex argument*, or an argument to a module that is a list or a dictionary. The uri module, which sends web requests, is a good example. Example 7-12 shows how to call a module that takes a list as an argument for the body parameter.

Example 7-12. Calling a module with complex arguments

```
- name: Login to a form based webpage
  uri:
    url: 'https://your.form.based.auth.example.com/login.php'
    method: POST
    body_format: form-urlencoded
    body:
      name: your_username
      password: 'your_password'
      enter: Sign in
    status_code: 302
  register: login
```

Passing module arguments as dictionaries instead of strings is a practice that can avoid the whitespace bugs that can arise when using optional arguments, and it works really well in version control systems. The big advantage of this type of notation is that this is pure YAML and all YAML parsers and linters understand what you are doing. The notation with the equal sign (=) is considered old-fashioned and is not preferred.

If you want to break your arguments across multiple lines and you aren't passing complex arguments, which form you choose is a matter of taste. Bas generally prefers dictionaries to multiline strings, but in this book we use both forms.

Configuring the Database

When Django runs in development mode, it uses the SQLite backend. This backend will create the database file if the file does not exist.

When using a database management system such as Postgres, we need to first create the user account that owns the database inside Postgres and then create the database. Later, we will configure Mezzanine with the credentials of this user.

Ansible ships with the `postgresql_user` and `postgresql_db` modules for creating users and databases inside Postgres. Example 7-13 shows how we invoke these modules in our playbook.

When creating the database, we specify locale information through the `lc_ctype` and `lc_collate` parameters. We use the `locale_gen` module to ensure that the locale we are using is installed in the operating system.

Example 7-13. Creating the database and database user

```
- name: Create project locale
  become: true
  locale_gen:
    name: "{{ locale }}"

- name: Create a DB user
  become: true
  become_user: postgres
  postgresql_user:
    name: "{{ database_user }}"
    password: "{{ db_pass }}"

- name: Create the database
  become: true
  become_user: postgres
  postgresql_db:
    name: "{{ database_name }}"
    owner: "{{ database_user }}"
    encoding: UTF8
    lc_ctype: "{{ locale }}"
    lc_collate: "{{ locale }}"
    template: template0
```

Note the use of `become: true` and `become_user: postgres` on the last two tasks. When you install Postgres on Ubuntu, the installation process creates a user named `postgres` that has administrative privileges for the Postgres installation. Since the root account does not have administrative privileges in Postgres by default, we need to `become` the Postgres user in the playbook in order to perform administrative tasks, such as creating users and databases.

When we create the database, we set the encoding (UTF8) and locale categories (LC_CTYPE, LC_COLLATE) associated with the database. Because we are setting locale information, we use template0 as the template.[2]

Generating the local_settings.py File from a Template

Django expects to find project-specific settings in a file called *settings.py*. Mezzanine follows the common Django idiom of breaking these settings into two groups:

- Settings that are the same for all deployments (*settings.py*)
- Settings that vary by deployment (*local_settings.py*)

We define the settings that are the same for all deployments in the *settings.py* file in our project repository (*https://oreil.ly/HtoNP*).

The *settings.py* file contains a Python snippet that loads a *local_settings.py* file that contains deployment-specific settings. The *.gitignore* file is configured to ignore the *local_settings.py* file, since developers will commonly create this file and configure it for local development.

As part of our deployment, we need to create a *local_settings.py* file and upload it to the remote host. Example 7-14 shows the Jinja2 template that we use.

Example 7-14. local_settings.py.j2

```
# Make these unique, and don't share it with anybody.
SECRET_KEY = "{{ secret_key }}"
NEVERCACHE_KEY = "{{ nevercache_key }}"
ALLOWED_HOSTS = [{% for domain in domains %}"{{ domain }}",{% endfor %}]

DATABASES = {
    "default": {
        # Ends with "postgresql_psycopg2", "mysql", "sqlite3" or "oracle".
        "ENGINE": "django.db.backends.postgresql_psycopg2",
        # DB name or path to database file if using sqlite3.
        "NAME": "{{ proj_name }}",
        # Not used with sqlite3.
        "USER": "{{ proj_name }}",
        # Not used with sqlite3.
        "PASSWORD": "{{ db_pass }}",
        # Set to empty string for localhost. Not used with sqlite3.
        "HOST": "127.0.0.1",
        # Set to empty string for default. Not used with sqlite3.
        "PORT": "",
    }
}
```

---

2 See the Postgres documentation (*https://oreil.ly/GhjeJ*) for more details about template databases.

```
CACHE_MIDDLEWARE_KEY_PREFIX = "{{ proj_name }}"
CACHES = {
    "default": {
        "BACKEND": "django.core.cache.backends.memcached.MemcachedCache",
        "LOCATION": "127.0.0.1:11211",
    }
}
SESSION_ENGINE = "django.contrib.sessions.backends.cache"
```

Most of this template is straightforward; it uses the {{ variable }} syntax to insert the values of variables such as secret_key, nevercache_key, proj_name, and db_pass. The only nontrivial bit of logic is the line shown in Example 7-15.

Example 7-15. Using a for loop in a Jinja2 template

```
ALLOWED_HOSTS = [{% for domain in domains %}"{{ domain }}",{% endfor %}]
```

If you look back at our variable definition, you'll see we have a variable called domains that's defined like this:

```
domains:
  - 192.168.33.10.nip.io
  - www.192.168.33.10.nip.io
```

Our Mezzanine app is going to respond *only* to requests that are for one of the hostnames listed in the domains variable: *http://192.168.33.10.nip.io* or *http:// www.192.168.33.10.nip.io* in our case. If a request reaches Mezzanine but the host header is something other than those two domains, the site will return "Bad Request (400)."

We want this line in the generated file to look like this:

```
ALLOWED_HOSTS = ["192.168.33.10.nip.io", "www.192.168.33.10.nip.io"]
```

We can achieve this by using a for loop, as shown in Example 7-15. Note that it doesn't do exactly what we want. Instead, it will have a trailing comma, like this:

```
ALLOWED_HOSTS = ["192.168.33.10.nip.io", "www.192.168.33.10.nip.io",]
```

However, Python is perfectly happy with trailing commas in lists, so we can leave it like this.

What's nip.io?

You might have noticed that the domains we are using look a little strange: *192.168.33.10.nip.io* and *www.192.168.33.10.nip.io*. They are domain names, but they have the IP address embedded within them.

When you access a website, you pretty much always point your browser to a domain name, such as *http://www.ansiblebook.com*, instead of an IP address, such as *http://151.101.192.133*. When we write our playbook to deploy Mezzanine to Vagrant, we want to configure the application with the domain name or names by which it should be accessible.

The problem is that we don't have a DNS record that maps to the IP address of our Vagrant box. In this case, that's *192.168.33.10*. There's nothing stopping us from setting up a DNS entry for this. For example, we could create a DNS entry from *mezzanine-internal.ansiblebook.com* that points to *192.168.33.10*.

However, if we want to create a DNS name that resolves to a particular IP address, there's a convenient service called *nip.io*, provided free of charge by Exentrique Solutions, that we can use so that we don't need to create our own DNS records. If *AAA.BBB.CCC.DDD* is an IP address, the DNS entry *AAA.BBB.CCC.DDD.nip.io* will resolve to *AAA.BBB.CCC.DDD*. For example, *192.168.33.10.nip.io* resolves to *192.168.33.10*. In addition, *www.192.168.33.10.nip.io* also resolves to *192.168.33.10*.

I find *nip.io* to be a great tool when I'm deploying web applications to private IP addresses for testing purposes. Alternatively, you can simply add entries to the */etc/hosts* file on your local machine, which also works when you're offline.

Let's examine the Jinja2 for loop syntax. To make things a little easier to read, we'll break it up across multiple lines, like this:

```
ALLOWED_HOSTS = [
{% for domain in domains %}
                "{{ domain }}",
{% endfor %}
                ]
```

The generated config file looks like this, which is still valid Python:

```
ALLOWED_HOSTS = [
                "192.168.33.10.nip.io",
                "www.192.168.33.10.nip.io",
                ]
```

Note that the for loop has to be terminated by an {% endfor %} statement. Furthermore, the for statement and the endfor statement are surrounded by {% %} delimiters, which are different from the {{ }} delimiters that we use for variable substitution.

All variables and facts that have been defined in a playbook are available inside Jinja2 templates, so we never need to explicitly pass variables to templates.

Running django-manage Commands

Django applications use a special script called *manage.py* (*https://oreil.ly/BrUy8*) that performs administrative actions for Django applications such as the following:

- Creating database tables
- Applying database migrations
- Loading fixtures from files into the database
- Dumping fixtures from the database to files
- Copying static assets to the appropriate directory

In addition to the built-in commands that *manage.py* supports, Django applications can add custom commands. Mezzanine adds a custom command called `createdb` that is used to initialize the database and copy the static assets to the appropriate place. The official Fabric scripts do the equivalent of this:

```
$ manage.py createdb --noinput --nodata
```

Ansible ships with a `django_manage` module that invokes `manage.py` commands. We could invoke it like this:

```
- name: Initialize the database
  django_manage:
    command: createdb --noinput --nodata
    app_path: "{{ proj_path }}"
    virtualenv: "{{ venv_path }}"
```

Unfortunately, the custom `createdb` command that Mezzanine adds isn't idempotent. If invoked a second time, it will fail like this:

```
TASK [initialize the database] ********************************************
fatal: [web]: FAILED! => {"changed": false, "cmd": "./manage.py createdb --
noinput --nodata", "msg": "\n:stderr: CommandError: Database already create
d, you probably want the migrate command\n", "path": "/home/vagrant/.virtua
lenvs/mezzanine_example/bin:/usr/local/sbin:/usr/local/bin:/usr/sbin:/usr/b
in:/sbin:/bin:/usr/games:/usr/local/games:/snap/bin", "syspath": ["/tmp/ans
ible_django_manage_payload_4xfy5e7i/ansible_django_manage_payload.zip", "/u
sr/lib/python38.zip", "/usr/lib/python3.8", "/usr/lib/python3.8/lib-dynload
", "/usr/local/lib/python3.8/dist-packages", "/usr/lib/python3/dist-package
s"]}
```

Fortunately, the custom `createdb` command is effectively equivalent to two idempotent built-in `manage.py` commands:

`migrate`
:   Create and update database tables for Django models

`collectstatic`
:   Copy the static assets to the appropriate directories

By invoking these commands, we get an idempotent task:

```
- name: Apply migrations to create the database, collect static content
  django_manage:
    command: "{{ item }}"
    app_path: "{{ proj_path }}"
    virtualenv: "{{ venv_path }}"
  loop:
    - syncdb
    - collectstatic
```

Running Custom Python Scripts in the Context of the Application

To initialize our application, we need to make two changes to our database:

- We need to create a Site model object (*https://oreil.ly/COd8x*) that contains the domain name of our site (in our case, that's *192.168.33.10.nip.io*).
- We need to set the administrator username and password.

Although we could make these changes with raw SQL commands or Django data migrations, the Mezzanine Fabric scripts use Python scripts, so that's how we'll do it.

There are two tricky parts here. The Python scripts need to run in the context of the virtualenv that we've created, and the Python environment needs to be set up properly so that the script will import the *settings.py* file that's in *~/mezzanine/mezzanine_example/mezzanine_example*.

In most cases, if we needed some custom Python code, we'd write a custom Ansible module. However, as far as we know, Ansible doesn't let you execute a module in the context of a virtualenv, so that's out.

We used the `script` module instead. This will copy over a custom script and execute it. Lorin wrote two scripts: one to set the Site record, and the other to set the admin username and password.

You can pass command-line arguments to `script` modules and parse them out, but we decided to pass the arguments as environment variables instead. We didn't want to pass passwords via command-line argument (those show up in the process list when you run the `ps` command), and it's easier to parse out environment variables in the scripts than it is to parse command-line arguments.

 You can set environment variables with an `environment` clause on a task, passing it a dictionary that contains the environment variable names and values. You can add an `environment` clause to any task; it doesn't have to be a `script`.

To run these scripts in the context of the virtualenv, we also needed to set the `path` variable so that the first Python executable in the `path` would be the one inside the virtualenv. Example 7-16 shows how we invoked the two scripts.

Example 7-16. Using the `script` module to invoke custom Python code

```
- name: Set the site id
  script: scripts/setsite.py
  environment:
    PATH: "{{ venv_path }}/bin"
    PROJECT_DIR: "{{ proj_path }}"
    PROJECT_APP: "{{ proj_app }}"
    WEBSITE_DOMAIN: "{{ Uve_hostname }}"

- name: Set the admin password
  script: scripts/setadmin.py
  environment:
    PATH: "{{ venv_path }}/bin"
    PROJECT_DIR: "{{ proj_path }}"
    PROJECT_APP: "{{ proj_app }}"
    ADMIN_PASSWORD: "{{ admin_pass }}"
```

The scripts themselves are shown in Example 7-17 and Example 7-18. You can find them in the *scripts* subdirectory.

Example 7-17. scripts/setsite.py

```
#!/usr/bin/env python3
""" A script to set the site domain """
# Assumes three environment variables
#
# PROJECT_DIR: root directory of the project
# PROJECT_APP: name of the project app
# WEBSITE_DOMAIN: the domain of the site (e.g., www.example.com)
import os
import sys

# Add the project directory to system path
proj_dir = os.path.expanduser(os.environ['PROJECT_DIR'])
sys.path.append(proj_dir)

proj_app = os.environ['PROJECT_APP']
os.environ['DJANGO_SETTINGS_MODULE'] = proj_app + '.settings'
import django
django.setup()
from django.conf import settings
from django.contrib.sites.models import Site
domain = os.environ['WEBSITE_DOMAIN']
Site.objects.filter(id=settings.SITE_ID).update(domain=domain)
Site.objects.get_or_create(domain=domain)
```

Example 7-18. scripts/setadmin.py

```python
#!/usr/bin/env python3
""" A script to set the admin credentials """
# Assumes three environment variables
#
# PROJECT_DIR: root directory of the project
# PROJECT_APP: name of the project app
# ADMIN_PASSWORD: admin user's password

import os
import sys

# Add the project directory to system path
proj_dir = os.path.expanduser(os.environ['PROJECT_DIR'])
sys.path.append(proj_dir)

proj_app = os.environ['PROJECT_APP']
os.environ['DJANGO_SETTINGS_MODULE'] = proj_app + '.settings'
import django
django.setup()
from django.contrib.auth import get_user_model
User = get_user_model()
u, _ = User.objects.get_or_create(username='admin')
u.is_staff = u.is_superuser = True
u.set_password(os.environ['ADMIN_PASSWORD'])
u.save()
```

The environment variable `DJANGO_SETTINGS_MODULE` needs to be set before importing `django`.

Setting Service Configuration Files

Next, we set the configuration file for Gunicorn (our application server), NGINX (our web server), and Supervisor (our process manager), as shown in Example 7-19. The template for the Gunicorn configuration file is shown in Example 7-21, and the template for the Supervisor configuration file is shown in Example 7-22.

Example 7-19. Setting configuration files

```yaml
- name: Set the gunicorn config file
  template:
    src: templates/gunicorn.conf.py.j2
    dest: "{{ proj_path }}/gunicorn.conf.py"
    mode: '0750'

- name: Set the supervisor config file
  become: true
  template:
```

```
    src: templates/supervisor.conf.j2
    dest: /etc/supervisor/conf.d/mezzanine.conf
    mode: '0640'
  notify: Restart supervisor

- name: Set the nginx config file
  become: true
  template:
    src: templates/nginx.conf.j2
    dest: /etc/nginx/sites-available/mezzanine.conf
    mode: '0640'
  notify: Restart nginx
```

In all three cases, we generate the config files by using templates. The Supervisor and NGINX processes are started by root (although they drop down to nonroot users when running), so we need to use become so that we have the appropriate permissions to write their configuration files.

If the Supervisor config file changes, Ansible will notify the restart supervisor handler. If the NGINX config file changes, Ansible will notify the restart nginx handler, as shown in Example 7-20. Notified handlers run after the tasks have been finished.

Example 7-20. Handlers

```
handlers:

  - name: Restart supervisor
    become: true
    supervisorctl:
      name: "{{ gunicorn_procname }}"
      state: restarted

  - name: Restart nginx
    become: true
    service:
      name: nginx
      state: restarted
```

Gunicorn has a Python-based configuration file; we pass in the value of some variables.

Example 7-21. templates/gunicorn.conf.py.j2

```
from multiprocessing import cpu_count

bind = "unix:{{ proj_path }}/gunicorn.sock"
workers = cpu_count() * 2 + 1
errorlog = "/home/{{ user }}/logs/{{ proj_name }}_error.log"
loglevel = "error"
proc_name = "{{ proj_name }}"
```

The Supervisor configuration file also has pretty straightforward variable interpolation.

Example 7-22. templates/supervisor.conf.j2

```
[program:{{ gunicorn_procname }}]
command={{ venv_path }}/bin/gunicorn -c gunicorn.conf.py -p gunicorn.pid \
    {{ proj_app }}.wsgi:application
directory={{ proj_path }}
user={{ user }}
autostart=true
stdout_logfile = /home/{{ user }}/logs/{{ proj_name }}_supervisor
autorestart=true
redirect_stderr=true
environment=LANG="{{ locale }}",LC_ALL="{{ locale }}",LC_LANG="{{ locale }}"
```

The only template that has any template logic (other than variable substitution) is Example 7-23. It has conditional logic to enable TLS if the `tls_enabled` variable is set to `true`. You'll see some `if` statements scattered about the templates that look like this:

```
{% if tls_enabled %}
...
{% endif %}
```

It also uses the `join` Jinja2 filter here:

```
server_name {{ domains|join(", ") }};
```

This code snippet expects the variable `domains` to be a list. It will generate a string with the elements of `domains`, separated by commas. Recall that in our case, the `domains` list is defined as follows:

```
domains:
  - 192.168.33.10.nip.io
  - www.192.168.33.10.nip.io
```

When the template renders, the line looks like this:

```
server_name 192.168.33.10.nip.io, www.192.168.33.10.nip.io;
```

Example 7-23. templates/nginx.conf.j2

```
upstream {{ proj_name }} {
    server unix:{{ proj_path }}/gunicorn.sock fail_timeout=0;
}
server {
    listen 80;
    {% if tls_enabled %}
    listen 443 ssl;
    {% endif %}
    server_name {{ domains|join(", ") }};
    server_tokens off;
```

```
client_max_body_size 10M;
keepalive_timeout    15;
{% if tls_enabled %}
ssl_certificate       conf/{{ proj_name }}.crt;
ssl_certificate_key   conf/{{ proj_name }}.key;
ssl_session_tickets off;
ssl_session_cache     shared:SSL:10m;
ssl_session_timeout  10m;
ssl_protocols TLSv1.3;
ssl_ciphers EECDH+AESGCM:EDH+AESGCM;
ssl_prefer_server_ciphers on;
{% endif %}
location / {
    proxy_redirect      off;
    proxy_set_header    Host                    $host;
    proxy_set_header    X-Real-IP               $remote_addr;
    proxy_set_header    X-Forwarded-For         $proxy_add_x_forwarded_for;
    proxy_set_header    X-Forwarded-Protocol    $scheme;
    proxy_pass          http://{{ proj_name }};
}
location /static/ {
    root            {{ proj_path }};
    access_log      off;
    log_not_found   off;
}
location /robots.txt {
    root            {{ proj_path }}/static;
    access_log      off;
    log_not_found   off;
}
location /favicon.ico {
    root            {{ proj_path }}/static/img;
    access_log      off;
    log_not_found   off;
}
}
```

You can create templates with control structures like if/else and for loops, and Jinja2 templates have lots of features to transform data from your variables, facts, and inventory into configuration files.

Enabling the NGINX Configuration

The convention on Ubuntu with NGINX configuration files is to put your configuration files in */etc/nginx/sites-available* and enable them by creating a symbolic link to */etc/nginx/sites-enabled*. (On Red Hat systems this is */etc/nginx/conf.d*.)

The Mezzanine Fabric scripts just copy the configuration file directly into *sites-enabled*, but we're going to deviate from how Mezzanine does it because it gives us an excuse to use the file module to create a symlink (Example 7-24). We also need to remove the default configuration file that the NGINX package sets up in */etc/nginx/sites-enabled/default*.

Example 7-24. Enabling NGINX configuration

```
- name: Remove the default nginx config file
  become: true
  file:
    path: /etc/nginx/sites-enabled/default
    state: absent
  notify: Restart nginx

- name: Set the nginx config file
  become: true
  template:
    src: templates/nginx.conf.j2
    dest: /etc/nginx/sites-available/mezzanine.conf
    mode: '0640'
  notify: Restart nginx

- name: Enable the nginx config file
  become: true
  file:
    src: /etc/nginx/sites-available/mezzanine.conf
    dest: /etc/nginx/sites-enabled/mezzanine.conf
    state: link
    mode: '0777'
  notify: Restart nginx
```

As shown in Example 7-24, we use the `file` module to create the symlink and to remove the default config file. This module is useful for creating directories, symlinks, and empty files; deleting files, directories, and symlinks; and setting properties such as permissions and ownership.

Installing TLS Certificates

Our playbook defines a variable named `tls_enabled`. If this variable is set to `true`, the playbook will install TLS certificates. In our example, we use self-signed certificates, so the playbook will create the certificate if it doesn't exist. In a production deployment, you would copy an existing TLS certificate that you obtained from a certificate authority.

Example 7-25 shows the two tasks involved in configuring for TLS certificates. We use the `file` module to ensure that the directory that will house the TLS certificates exists.

Example 7-25. Installing TLS certificates

```
- name: Ensure config path exists
  become: true
  file:
    path: "{{ conf_path }}"
    state: directory
```

```
    mode: '0755'

- name: Create tls certificates
  become: true
  command: >
    openssl req -new -x509 -nodes -out {{ proj_name }}.crt
    -keyout {{ proj_name }}.key -subj '/CN={{ domains[0] }}' -days 365
  args:
    chdir: "{{ conf_path }}"
    creates: "{{ conf_path }}/{{ proj_name }}.crt"
  when: tls_enabled
  notify: Restart nginx
```

Note that one task contains this clause:

```
  when: tls_enabled
```

If `tls_enabled` evaluates to `false`, Ansible will skip the task.

Ansible doesn't ship with modules for creating TLS certificates, so we use the `command` module to invoke the `openssl` command in order to create the self-signed certificate. Since the command is very long, we use YAML line-folding syntax, with the ">" character, so that we can break the command across multiple lines.

The `chdir` parameter changes the directory before running the command. The `creates` parameter implements idempotence: Ansible will first check whether the file `{{ conf_path }}/{{ proj_name }}.crt` exists on the host. If it already exists, Ansible will skip this task.

Installing Twitter Cron Job

If you run `manage.py poll_twitter`, Mezzanine will retrieve tweets associated with the configured accounts and show them on the home page. The Fabric scripts that ship with Mezzanine keep these tweets up-to-date by installing a cron job that runs every five minutes.

If we followed the Fabric scripts exactly, we'd copy a cron script into the */etc/cron.d* directory that had the cron job. We could use the `template` module to do this. However, Ansible ships with a `cron` module that allows us to create or delete cron jobs, which we find more elegant. Example 7-26 shows the task that installs the cron job.

Example 7-26. Installing the cron job for polling Twitter

```
- name: Install poll twitter cron job
  cron:
    name: "poll twitter"
    minute: "*/5"
```

```
    user: "{{ user }}"
    job: "{{ manage }} poll_twitter"
```

If you manually SSH to the box, you can see the cron job that gets installed by using
`crontab -l` to list the jobs. Here's what it looks like when we deploy as the Vagrant
user:

```
#Ansible: poll twitter
*/5 * * * * /home/vagrant/.virtualenvs/mezzanine_example/bin/python3 \
/home/vagrant/mezzanine/mezzanine_example/manage.py poll_twitter
```

Notice the comment at the first line. That's how the Ansible module supports deleting
cron jobs by name. For example:

```
- name: Remove cron job
  cron:
    name: "poll twitter"
    state: absent
```

If you were to do this, the `cron` module would look for the comment line that
matches the name and delete the job associated with that comment.

The Full Playbook

Example 7-27 shows the complete playbook in all its glory.

Example 7-27. mezzanine.yml: The complete playbook

```
---
- name: Deploy mezzanine
  hosts: web

  vars:
    user: "{{ ansible_user }}"
    proj_app: 'mezzanine_example'
    proj_name: "{{ proj_app }}"
    venv_home: "{{ ansible_env.HOME }}/.virtualenvs"
    venv_path: "{{ venv_home }}/{{ proj_name }}"
    proj_path: "{{ ansible_env.HOME }}/mezzanine/{{ proj_name }}"
    settings_path: "{{ proj_path }}/{{ proj_name }}"
    reqs_path: '~/requirements.txt'
    manage: "{{ python }} {{ proj_path }}/manage.py"
    live_hostname: 192.168.33.10.nip.io
    domains:
      - 192.168.33.10.nip.io
      - www.192.168.33.10.nip.io
    repo_url: 'git@github.com:ansiblebook/mezzanine_example.git'
    locale: 'en_US.UTF-8'
    # Variables below don't appear in Mezannine's fabfile.py
    # but I've added them for convenience
    conf_path: /etc/nginx/conf
    tls_enabled: true
    python: "{{ venv_path }}/bin/python3"
```

```yaml
    database_name: "{{ proj_name }}"
    database_user: "{{ proj_name }}"
    database_host: localhost
    database_port: 5432
    gunicorn_procname: gunicorn_mezzanine

vars_files:
  - secrets.yml

tasks:
  - name: Install apt packages
    become: true
    apt:
      update_cache: true
      cache_valid_time: 3600
      pkg:
        - acl
        - git
        - libjpeg-dev
        - libpq-dev
        - memcached
        - nginx
        - postgresql
        - python3-dev
        - python3-pip
        - python3-venv
        - python3-psycopg2
        - supervisor

  - name: Create project path
    file:
      path: "{{ proj_path }}"
      state: directory
      mode: '0755'

  - name: Create a logs directory
    file:
      path: "{{ ansible_env.HOME }}/logs"
      state: directory
      mode: '0755'

  - name: Check out the repository on the host
    git:
      repo: "{{ repo_url }}"
      dest: "{{ proj_path }}"
      version: master
      accept_hostkey: true

  - name: Create python3 virtualenv
    pip:
      name:
        - pip
        - wheel
        - setuptools
      state: latest
      virtualenv: "{{ venv_path }}"
```

```
    virtualenv_command: /usr/bin/python3 -m venv

- name: Copy requirements.txt to home directory
  copy:
    src: requirements.txt
    dest: "{{ reqs_path }}"
    mode: '0644'

- name: Install packages listed in requirements.txt
  pip:
    virtualenv: "{{ venv_path }}"
    requirements: "{{ reqs_path }}"

- name: Create project locale
  become: true
  locale_gen:
    name: "{{ locale }}"

- name: Create a DB user
  become: true
  become_user: postgres
  postgresql_user:
    name: "{{ database_user }}"
    password: "{{ db_pass }}"

- name: Create the database
  become: true
  become_user: postgres
  postgresql_db:
    name: "{{ database_name }}"
    owner: "{{ database_user }}"
    encoding: UTF8
    lc_ctype: "{{ locale }}"
    lc_collate: "{{ locale }}"
    template: template0

- name: Ensure config path exists
  become: true
  file:
    path: "{{ conf_path }}"
    state: directory
    mode: '0755'

- name: Create tls certificates
  become: true
  command: >
    openssl req -new -x509 -nodes -out {{ proj_name }}.crt
    -keyout {{ proj_name }}.key -subj '/CN={{ domains[0] }}' -days 365
  args:
    chdir: "{{ conf_path }}"
    creates: "{{ conf_path }}/{{ proj_name }}.crt"
  when: tls_enabled
  notify: Restart nginx

- name: Remove the default nginx config file
  become: true
```

```yaml
      file:
        path: /etc/nginx/sites-enabled/default
        state: absent
      notify: Restart nginx

    - name: Set the nginx config file
      become: true
      template:
        src: templates/nginx.conf.j2
        dest: /etc/nginx/sites-available/mezzanine.conf
        mode: '0640'
      notify: Restart nginx

    - name: Enable the nginx config file
      become: true
      file:
        src: /etc/nginx/sites-available/mezzanine.conf
        dest: /etc/nginx/sites-enabled/mezzanine.conf
        state: link
        mode: '0777'
      notify: Restart nginx

    - name: Set the supervisor config file
      become: true
      template:
        src: templates/supervisor.conf.j2
        dest: /etc/supervisor/conf.d/mezzanine.conf
        mode: '0640'
      notify: Restart supervisor

    - name: Install poll twitter cron job
      cron:
        name: "poll twitter"
        minute: "*/5"
        user: "{{ user }}"
        job: "{{ manage }} poll_twitter"

    - name: Set the gunicorn config file
      template:
        src: templates/gunicorn.conf.py.j2
        dest: "{{ proj_path }}/gunicorn.conf.py"
        mode: '0750'

    - name: Generate the settings file
      template:
        src: templates/local_settings.py.j2
        dest: "{{ settings_path }}/local_settings.py"
        mode: '0750'

    - name: Apply migrations to create the database, collect static content
      django_manage:
        command: "{{ item }}"
        app_path: "{{ proj_path }}"
        virtualenv: "{{ venv_path }}"
      with_items:
        - migrate
```

```
    - collectstatic

  - name: Set the site id
    script: scripts/setsite.py
    environment:
      PATH: "{{ venv_path }}/bin"
      PROJECT_DIR: "{{ proj_path }}"
      PROJECT_APP: "{{ proj_app }}"
      DJANGO_SETTINGS_MODULE: "{{ proj_app }}.settings"
      WEBSITE_DOMAIN: "{{ live_hostname }}"

  - name: Set the admin password
    script: scripts/setadmin.py
    environment:
      PATH: "{{ venv_path }}/bin"
      PROJECT_DIR: "{{ proj_path }}"
      PROJECT_APP: "{{ proj_app }}"
      ADMIN_PASSWORD: "{{ admin_pass }}"

handlers:

  - name: Restart supervisor
    become: true
    supervisorctl:
      name: "{{ gunicorn_procname }}"
      state: restarted

  - name: Restart nginx
    become: true
    service:
      name: nginx
      state: restarted
...
```

Playbooks can become longer than needed, and harder to maintain, when all actions and variables are listed in one file. So this playbook should be considered as a step in your education on Ansible. We'll discuss a better way to structure this in the next chapter.

Running the Playbook Against a Vagrant Machine

The live_hostname and domains variables in our playbook assume that the host we are going to deploy to is accessible at *192.168.33.10*. The Vagrantfile shown in Example 7-28 configures a Vagrant machine with that IP address.

Example 7-28. Vagrantfile

```
Vagrant.configure("2") do |this|
  # Forward ssh-agent for cloning from Github.com
  this.ssh.forward_agent = true
  this.vm.define "web" do |web|
    web.vm.box = "ubuntu/focal64"
```

```
    web.vm.hostname = "web"
    # This IP is used in the playbook
    web.vm.network "private_network", ip: "192.168.33.10"
    web.vm.network "forwarded_port", guest: 80, host: 8000
    web.vm.network "forwarded_port", guest: 443, host: 8443
    web.vm.provider "virtualbox" do |virtualbox|
      virtualbox.name = "web"
    end
  end
  this.vm.provision "ansible" do |ansible|
    ansible.playbook = "mezzanine.yml"
    ansible.verbose = "v"
    ansible.compatibility_mode = "2.0"
    ansible.host_key_checking = false
  end
end
```

Deploying Mezzanine into a new Vagrant machine is fully automated with the provision block:

```
$ vagrant up
```

You can then reach your newly deployed Mezzanine site at any of the following URLs:

- *http://192.168.33.10.nip.io*
- *https://192.168.33.10.nip.io*
- *http://www.192.168.33.10.nip.io*
- *https://www.192.168.33.10.nip.io*

Troubleshooting

You might hit a few speed bumps when trying to run this playbook on your local machine. This section describes how to overcome some common obstacles.

Cannot Check Out Git Repository

You may see the task named "check out the repository on the host" fail with this error:

```
fatal: Could not read from remote repository.
```

A likely fix is to remove a preexisting entry for *192.168.33.10* in your *~/.ssh/known_hosts* file.

Cannot Reach 192.168.33.10.nip.io

Some WiFi routers ship with DNS servers that won't resolve the hostname *192.168.33.10.nip.io*. You can check whether yours does by typing the following on the command line:

```
dig +short 192.168.33.10.nip.io
```

The output should be as follows:

```
192.168.33.10
```

If the output is blank, your DNS server is refusing to resolve *nip.io* hostnames. If this is the case, a workaround is to add the following to your */etc/hosts* file:

```
192.168.33.10 192.168.33.10.nip.io
```

Bad Request (400)

If your browser returns the error "Bad Request (400)," it is likely that you are trying to reach the Mezzanine site by using a hostname or IP address that is not in the ALLOWED_HOSTS list in the Mezzanine configuration file. This list is populated using the domains Ansible variable in the playbook:

```
domains:
  - 192.168.33.10.nip.io
  - www.192.168.33.10.nip.io
```

Conclusion

In this scenario, we've deployed Mezzanine entirely on a single machine. You've now seen what it's like to deploy a real application with Mezzanine.

The next chapter covers some more advanced features of Ansible that didn't come up in our example. We'll show a playbook that deploys across the database and web services on separate hosts, which is common in real-world deployments.

CHAPTER 8

Debugging Ansible Playbooks

Let's face it: mistakes happen. Whether it's a bug in a playbook or a config file on your control machine with the wrong configuration value, eventually something's going to go wrong. In this chapter, we'll review some techniques you can use to help track down those errors.

Humane Error Messages

When an Ansible task fails, the output format isn't very friendly to any human reader trying to debug the problem. Here's an example of an error message generated while working on this book:

```
TASK [mezzanine : check out the repository on the host]
       ************************
fatal: [web]: FAILED! => {"changed": false, "cmd": "/usr/bin/git ls-remote
'' -h refs/heads/master", "msg": "Warning:********@github.com: Permission
denied (publickey).\r\nfatal: Could not read from remote
repository.\n\nPlease make sure you have the correct access rights\nand the
repository exists.", "rc": 128, "stderr": "Warning: Permanently added
'github.com,140.82.121.4' (RSA) to the list of known
hosts.\r\ngit@github.com: Permission denied (publickey).\r\nfatal: Could not
read from remote repository.\n\nPlease make sure you have the correct access
rights\nand the repository exists.\n", "stderr_lines": ["Warning:
Permanently added 'github.com,140.82.121.4' (RSA) to the list of known
hosts.", "git@github.com: Permission denied (publickey).", "fatal: Could not
read from remote repository.", "", "Please make sure you have the correct
access rights", "and the repository exists."], "stdout": "", "stdout_lines":
[]}
```

As mentioned in Chapter 18, the debug callback plug-in makes this output much easier for a human to read:

```
TASK [mezzanine : check out the repository on the host] ************************
fatal: [web]: FAILED! => {
```

```
    "changed": false,
    "cmd": "/usr/bin/git ls-remote '' -h refs/heads/master",
    "rc": 128
}
STDERR:
git@github.com: Permission denied (publickey).
fatal: Could not read from remote repository.
Please make sure you have the correct access rights
and the repository exists.
```

Enable the plug-in by adding the following to the `defaults` section of *ansible.cfg*:

```
[defaults]
stdout_callback = debug
```

Be aware, however, that the debug callback plug-in does not print all the information; the YAML callback plug-in is more verbose than you would expect.

Debugging SSH Issues

Sometimes Ansible fails to make a successful SSH connection with the host. Let's see how it looks if the SSH server is not responding at all:

```
$ ansible web -m ping
web | UNREACHABLE! => {
    "changed": false,
    "msg": "Failed to connect to the host via ssh:
kex_exchange_identification: Connection closed by remote host",
    "unreachable": true
}
```

When this happens, there might be several causes:

- The SSH server is not running at all.
- The SSH server is running on a nonstandard port.
- Something else is running on the port you expect.
- The port might be filtered by the firewall on the host.
- The port might be filtered by another firewall.
- Tcpwrappers is configured, check */etc/hosts.allow* and */etc/hosts.deny*.
- The host runs in a hypervisor with micro-segmetation.

Once you verified on the system console that the SSH server is running on the host, you can try to connect remotely with nc, or even the telnet client to check the banner:

```
$ nc hostname 2222
SSH-2.0-OpenSSH_8.2p1 Ubuntu-4ubuntu0.4
```

Then you can try to connect remotely with the SSH client using the verbose flag for debugging:

```
$ ssh -v user@hostname
```

You can see exactly what arguments Ansible is passing to the underlying SSH client so you can reproduce the problem manually on the command line. It can be handy for debugging to see the exact SSH commands that Ansible invokes:

```
$ ansible web -vvv -m ping
```

Example 8-1 shows parts of the output.

Example 8-1. Example output when three verbose flags are enabled

```
<127.0.0.1> SSH: EXEC ssh -vvv -4 -o PreferredAuthentications=publickey -o
    ForwardAgent=yes -o StrictHostKeyChecking=no -o Port=2200 -o
    'IdentityFile="/Users/bas/.vagrant.d/insecure_private_key"' -o
    KbdInteractiveAuthentication=no -o
    PreferredAuthentications=gssapi-with-mic,gssapi-keyex,hostbased,publickey -o
    PasswordAuthentication=no -o 'User="vagrant"' -o ConnectTimeout=10 127.0.0.1
    '/bin/sh -c '"'"'rm -f -r
    /home/vagrant/.ansible/tmp/ansible-tmp-1633182008.6825979-95820-
    137028099318259/ > /dev/null 2>&1 && sleep 0'"'"''
    <127.0.0.1> (0, b'', b'OpenSSH_8.1p1, LibreSSL 2.7.3\r\ndebug1: Reading
    configuration data /Users/bas/.ssh/config\r\ndebug3: kex names ok:
    [curve25519-sha256,diffie-hellman-group-exchange-sha256]\r\ndebug1: Reading
    configuration data /etc/ssh/ssh_config\r\ndebug1: /etc/ssh/ssh_config line
    20: Applying options for *\r\ndebug1: /etc/ssh/ssh_config line 47: Applying
    options for *\r\ndebug2: resolve_canonicalize: hostname 127.0.0.1 is
    address\r\ndebug1: auto-mux: Trying existing master\r\ndebug2: fd 3 setting
    O_NONBLOCK\r\ndebug2: mux_client_hello_exchange: master version 4\r\ndebug3:
    mux_client_forwards: request forwardings: 0 local, 0 remote\r\ndebug3:
    mux_client_request_session: entering\r\ndebug3: mux_client_request_alive:
    entering\r\ndebug3: mux_client_request_alive: done pid = 95516\r\ndebug3:
    mux_client_request_session: session request sent\r\ndebug3:
    mux_client_read_packet: read header failed: Broken pipe\r\ndebug2: Received
    exit status from master 0\r\n')
web | SUCCESS => {
        "changed": false,
        "invocation": {
            "module_args": {
                "data": "pong"
            }
        },
        "ping": "pong"
}
```

Sometimes you might need to use -vvvv when debugging a connection issue to see an error message that the SSH client is throwing; it's like adding the -v flag for the ssh command that Ansible is using:

```
$ ansible all -vvvv -m ping
```

Example 8-2 shows lots of debug output.

Example 8-2. Example output when four verbose flags are enabled

```
<192.168.56.10> ESTABLISH SSH CONNECTION FOR USER: vagrant
<192.168.56.10> SSH: EXEC ssh -vvv -4 -o PreferredAuthentications=publickey
-o ForwardAgent=yes -o StrictHostKeyChecking=no -o
'IdentityFile="/Users/bas/.vagrant.d/insecure_private_key"' -o
KbdInteractiveAuthentication=no -o
PreferredAuthentications=gssapi-with-mic,gssapi-keyex,hostbased,publickey -o
PasswordAuthentication=no -o 'User="vagrant"' -o ConnectTimeout=10
192.168.56.10 '/bin/sh -c '"'"'/usr/bin/python3 && sleep 0'"'"''
debug1: Reading configuration data /Users/bas/.ssh/config
debug1: Reading configuration data /etc/ssh/ssh_config
debug1: /etc/ssh/ssh_config line 21: include /etc/ssh/ssh_config.d/* matched
no files
debug1: /etc/ssh/ssh_config line 54: Applying options for *
debug1: Authenticator provider $SSH_SK_PROVIDER did not resolve; disabling
debug1: Connecting to 192.168.56.10 [192.168.56.10] port 22.
debug1: fd 3 clearing O_NONBLOCK
debug1: Connection established.
debug1: identity file /Users/bas/.vagrant.d/insecure_private_key type -1
debug1: Local version string SSH-2.0-OpenSSH_8.6
debug1: Remote protocol version 2.0, remote software version OpenSSH_8.2p1
Ubuntu-4ubuntu0.5
debug1: compat_banner: match: OpenSSH_8.2p1 Ubuntu-4ubuntu0.5 pat OpenSSH*
compat 0x04000000
debug1: Authenticating to 192.168.56.10:22 as \'vagrant\'
debug1: SSH2_MSG_KEXINIT sent
debug1: SSH2_MSG_KEXINIT received
debug1: kex: algorithm: curve25519-sha256
debug1: kex: host key algorithm: ssh-ed25519
debug1: kex: server->client cipher: chacha20-poly1305@openssh.com MAC:
<implicit> compression: none
debug1: kex: client->server cipher: chacha20-poly1305@openssh.com MAC:
<implicit> compression: none
debug1: expecting SSH2_MSG_KEX_ECDH_REPLY
debug1: SSH2_MSG_KEX_ECDH_REPLY received
debug1: Server host key: ssh-ed25519
SHA256:BnlxL1InYlrSLQU10HFYzg6ZZkj1boxRSloEsK3bpxA
debug1: Host \'192.168.56.10\' is known and matches the ED25519 host key.
debug1: Found key in /Users/bas/.ssh/known_hosts:57
debug1: rekey out after 134217728 blocks
debug1: SSH2_MSG_NEWKEYS sent
debug1: expecting SSH2_MSG_NEWKEYS
debug1: SSH2_MSG_NEWKEYS received
debug1: rekey in after 134217728 blocks
debug1: Will attempt key: /Users/bas/.vagrant.d/insecure_private_key
explicit
debug1: SSH2_MSG_EXT_INFO received
debug1: kex_input_ext_info:
server-sig-algs=<ssh-ed25519,sk-ssh-ed25519@openssh.com,ssh-rsa,rsa-sha2-256
,rsa-sha2-512,ssh-dss,ecdsa-sha2-nistp256,ecdsa-sha2-nistp384,ecdsa-sha2-
nistp521,sk-ecdsa-sha2-nistp256@openssh.com>
debug1: SSH2_MSG_SERVICE_ACCEPT received
debug1: Authentications that can continue: publickey
debug1: Next authentication method: publickey
```

```
debug1: Trying private key: /Users/bas/.vagrant.d/insecure_private_key
debug1: Authentication succeeded (publickey).
Authenticated to 192.168.56.10 ([192.168.56.10]:22).
debug1: channel 0: new [client-session]
debug1: Requesting no-more-sessions@openssh.com
debug1: Entering interactive session.
debug1: pledge: filesystem full
debug1: client_input_global_request: rtype hostkeys-00@openssh.com
want_reply 0
debug1: client_input_hostkeys: searching /Users/bas/.ssh/known_hosts for
192.168.56.10 / (none)
debug1: client_input_hostkeys: no new or deprecated keys from server
debug1: Remote: /home/vagrant/.ssh/authorized_keys:1: key options:
agent-forwarding port-forwarding pty user-rc x11-forwarding
debug1: Requesting authentication agent forwarding.
debug1: Sending environment.
debug1: channel 0: setting env LC_TERMINAL_VERSION = "3.4.16"
debug1: channel 0: setting env LC_CTYPE = "UTF-8"
debug1: channel 0: setting env LC_TERMINAL = "iTerm2"
debug1: Sending command: /bin/sh -c \'/usr/bin/python3 && sleep 0\'
debug1: client_input_channel_req: channel 0 rtype exit-status reply 0
debug1: channel 0: free: client-session, nchannels 1
Transferred: sent 117208, received 1664 bytes, in 0.4 seconds
Bytes per second: sent 284246.0, received 4035.4
debug1: Exit status 0
')
web | SUCCESS => {
    "changed": false,
    "invocation": {
        "module_args": {
            "data": "pong"
        }
    },
    "ping": "pong"
}
META: ran handlers
META: ran handlers
```

You should know that `"ping"`: `"pong"` means a successful connection was made, even though it is preceded by debug messages.

Common SSH Challenges

Ansible uses SSH to connect to and manage hosts, often with administrative privileges. It is worthwhile to know about its security challenges, which can puzzle casual users at first.

PasswordAuthentication no

`PasswordAuthentication` no greatly improves the security of your servers. By default, Ansible assumes you are using SSH keys to connect to remote machines. Having a SSH key pair is one thing, but the public key needs to be distributed to the machines you want to manage. This is traditionally done with `ssh-copy-id`, but when `PasswordAuthentication` is disabled, an administrator needs to use an account with public keys in place to copy your public key to the servers, preferably with the authorized_key module:

```
- name: Install authorized_keys taken from file
  authorized_key:
    user: "{{ the_user }}"
    state: present
    key: "{{ lookup('file',the_pub_key)  }}"
    key_options: 'no-port-forwarding,from="93.184.216.34"'
    exclusive: true
```

Note that ed25519 public keys are short enough to type in a console if necessary.

SSH as a Different User

You can connect to different hosts with different users. Restrict users from logging in as the root user as much as possible. If you need a particular user per machine, then you can set `ansible_user` in the inventory:

```
[mezzanine]
web ansible_host=192.168.33.10 ansible_user=webmaster
db  ansible_host=192.168.33.11 ansible_user=dba
```

Note that you cannot override that user on the command line, but you can specify a user if it's different:

```
$ ansible-playbook --user vagrant -i inventory/hosts mezzanine.yml
```

You can also use the SSH config file to define the user for each host. Finally, you can set `remote_user:` in the header of a play or on a per task basis.

Host Key Verification Failed

When you try to connect to a machine, you may get an error, such as:

```
$ ansible -m ping web
web | UNREACHABLE! => {
    "changed": false,
    "msg": "Failed to connect to the host via ssh:
@@@@@@@@@@@@@@@@@@@@@@@@@@@@@@@@@@@@@@@@@@@@@@@@@@@@@@@@@@@\r\n@    WARNING:
REMOTE HOST IDENTIFICATION HAS CHANGED!
@\r\n@@@@@@@@@@@@@@@@@@@@@@@@@@@@@@@@@@@@@@@@@@@@@@@@@@@@@@@@@@@\r\nIT IS
POSSIBLE THAT SOMEONE IS DOING SOMETHING NASTY!\r\nSomeone could be
eavesdropping on you right now (man-in-the-middle attack)!\r\nIt is also
possible that a host key has just been changed.\r\nThe fingerprint for the
ED25519 key sent by the remote host
is:\nSHA256:+dX3jRW5eoZ+FzQP9jc6cIALXugh9bftvYvaQig+33c.\r\nPlease contact
your system administrator.\r\nAdd correct host key in
/Users/bas/.ssh/known_hosts to get rid of this message.\r\nOffending ED25519
key in /Users/bas/.ssh/known_hosts:2\r\nED25519 host key for 192.168.56.10
has changed and you have requested strict checking.\r\nHost key verification
```

```
    failed.",
      "unreachable": true
}
```

If that happens, don't disable `StrictHostKeyChecking` in the SSH config. Instead, remove the old host key and add the new key:

```
ssh-keygen -R 192.168.33.10
ssh-keyscan 192.168.33.10 >> ~/.ssh/known_hosts
```

Private Networks

Since Ansible uses the OpenSSH client by default, you can easily use a *bastion host*: a central access point in a DMZ for other hosts in a private network. Here, all hosts in the domain *private.cloud* are accessible through the `ProxyJump bastion` setting in the file *~/.ssh/config*:

```
Host bastion
  Hostname 100.123.123.123
  User bas
  PasswordAuthentication no
Host *.private.cloud
  User bas
  CheckHostIP no
  StrictHostKeyChecking no
  ProxyJump bastion
```

 If you set up the bastion with a VPN, then you don't need SSH on the internet. Tailscale (*https://tailscale.com*) is an easy-to-use VPN based on WireGuard (*https://www.wireguard.com*) that allows traffic from clients via the bastion to other private hosts in a subnet without further configuration on those hosts.

The debug Module

We've used the `debug` module several times in this book. It's Ansible's version of a `print` statement. As shown in Example 8-3, you can use it to print out either the value of a variable or an arbitrary string.

Example 8-3. The debug module in action

```
- debug: var=myvariable
- debug: msg="The value of myvariable is {{ var }}"
```

As we discussed in Chapter 5, you can print out the values of all the variables associated with the current host by invoking the following:

```
  - debug: var=hostvars[inventory_hostname]
```

Playbook Debugger

Ansible 2.5 added support for an interactive debugger. You can use the `debugger` keyword to enable (or disable) the debugger for a specific play, role, block, or task:

```
- name: deploy mezzanine on web
  hosts: web
  debugger: always
  ...
```

If debugging is always enabled like that, Ansible drops into the debugger and you can step though the playbook by entering c (continue):

```
PLAY [deploy mezzanine on web] ************************************************
TASK [mezzanine : install apt packages] **************************************
changed: [web]
[web] TASK: mezzanine : install apt packages (debug)> c
TASK [mezzanine : create a logs directory] ***********************************
changed: [web]
[web] TASK: mezzanine : create a logs directory (debug)> c
```

Table 8-1 shows the seven commands supported by the debugger.

Table 8-1. Debugger commands

Command	Shortcut	Action
`print`	p	Print information about the task
`task.args[key] = value`	no shortcut	Update module arguments
`task_vars[key] = value`	no shortcut	Update task variables (you must update_task next)
`update_task`	u	Re-create a task with updated task variables
`redo`	r	Run the task again
`continue`	c	Continue executing, starting with the next task
`quit`	q	Quit the debugger

Table 8-2 shows the variables supported by the debugger.

Table 8-2. Variables supported by the debugger

Variable	Description
`p task`	The name of the task that failed
`p task.args`	The module arguments
`p result`	The result returned by the failed task
`p vars`	Value of all known variables
`p vars[key]`	Value of one variable

Here's an example interaction with the debugger:

```
TASK [mezzanine : install apt packages ****************************************
ok: [web]
[web] TASK: mezzanine : install apt packages (debug)> p task.args
{'_ansible_check_mode': False,
 '_ansible_debug': False,
 '_ansible_diff': False,
 '_ansible_keep_remote_files': False,
 '_ansible_module_name': 'apt',
 '_ansible_no_log': False,
 '_ansible_remote_tmp': '~/.ansible/tmp',
 '_ansible_selinux_special_fs': ['fuse',
                                 'nfs',
                                 'vboxsf',
                                 'ramfs',
                                 '9p',
                                 'vfat'],
 '_ansible_shell_executable': '/bin/sh',
 '_ansible_socket': None,
 '_ansible_string_conversion_action': 'warn',
 '_ansible_syslog_facility': 'LOG_USER',
 '_ansible_tmpdir': '/home/vagrant/.ansible/tmp/ansible-tmp-1633193380-7157/',
 '_ansible_verbosity': 0,
 '_ansible_version': '2.11.0',
 'cache_valid_time': 3600,
 'pkg': ['git',
         'libjpeg-dev',
         'memcached',
         'python3-dev',
         'python3-pip',
         'python3-venv',
         'supervisor'],
 'update_cache': True}
```

While you'll probably find printing out variables to be its most useful feature, you can also use the debugger to modify variables and arguments to the failed task. See the Ansible playbook debugger docs (*https://oreil.ly/IZSCl*) for more details.

 If you are running legacy playbooks or roles, you may see the debugger enabled as a strategy. This may have been removed in newer versions of Ansible. With the default linear strategy enabled, Ansible halts execution while the debugger is active, then runs the debugged task immediately after you enter the redo command. With the free strategy enabled, however, Ansible does not wait for all hosts and may queue later tasks on one host before a task fails on another host; it does not queue or execute any tasks while the debugger is active. However, all queued tasks remain in the queue and run as soon as you exit the debugger. You can learn more about strategies in the documentation (*https://oreil.ly/bLqah*).

The assert Module

The `assert` module will fail with an error if a specified condition is not met. For example, to fail the playbook if there's no enp0s3 interface:

```
- name: Assert that the enp0s3 ethernet interface exists
  assert:
    that: ansible_enp0s3 is defined
```

When debugging a playbook, it can be helpful to insert assertions so that a failure happens as soon as any assumption you've made is violated.

 Keep in mind that the code in an `assert` statement is Jinja2, not Python. For example, if you want to assert the length of a list, you might be tempted to do this:

```
# Invalid Jinja2, this won't work!
assert:
  that: "len(ports) == 2"
```

Unfortunately, Jinja2 does not support Python's built-in `len` function. Instead, you need to use the Jinja2 `length` filter:

```
assert:
  that: "ports|length == 2"
```

If you want to check on the status of a file on the host's filesystem, it's useful to call the `stat` module first and make an assertion based on the return value of that module:

```
- name: Stat /boot/grub
  stat:
    path: /boot/grub
  register: st

- name: Assert that /boot/grub is a directory
  assert:
    that: st.stat.isdir
```

The `stat` module collects information about the state of a filepath. It returns a dictionary that contains a `stat` field with the values shown in Table 8-3.

Table 8-3. Stat module return values (some platforms might add additional fields)

Field	Description
atime	Last access time of path, in Unix timestamp format
attributes	List of file attributes
charset	Character set or encoding of the file
checksum	Hash value of the file
ctime	Time of last metadata update or creation, in Unix timestamp format
dev	Numeric ID of the device that the inode resides on

Field	Description
executable	Tells you if the invoking user has execute permission on the path
exists	If the destination path actually exists or not
gid	Numeric ID representing the group of the owner
gr_name	Group name of owner
inode	Inode number of the path
isblk	Tells you if the path is a block device
ischr	Tells you if the path is a character device
isdir	Tells you if the path is a directory
isfifo	Tells you if the path is a named pipe
isgid	Tells you if the invoking user's group ID matches the owner's group ID
islnk	Tells you if the path is a symbolic link
isreg	Tells you if the path is a regular file
issock	Tells you if the path is a Unix domain socket
isuid	Tells you if the invoking user's ID matches the owner's ID
lnk_source	Target of the symlink normalized for the remote filesystem
lnk_target	Target of the symlink
mimetype	File magic data or mime-type
mode	Unix permissions as a string, in octal (e.g., "1777")
mtime	Last modification time of path, in Unix timestamp format
nlink	Number of hard links to the file
pw_name	User name of file owner
readable	Tells you if the invoking user has the right to read the path
rgrp	Tells you if the owner's group has read permission
roth	Tells you if others have read permission
rusr	Tells you if the owner has read permission
size	Size in bytes for a plain file, amount of data for some special files
uid	Numeric ID representing the file owner
wgrp	Tells you if the owner's group has write permission
woth	Tells you if others have write permission
writeable	Tells you if the invoking user has the right to write the path
wusr	Tells you if the owner has write permission
xgrp	Tells you if the owner's group has execute permission
xoth	Tells you if others have execute permission
xusr	Tells you if the owner has execute permission

Checking Your Playbook Before Execution

The `ansible-playbook` command supports several flags that allow you to "sanity-check" your playbook before you execute it. They do *not* execute the playbook.

Syntax Check

The --syntax-check flag, shown in Example 8-4, checks that your playbook's syntax is valid.

Example 8-4. Syntax check

```
$ ansible-playbook --syntax-check playbook.yml
```

List Hosts

The --list-hosts flag, shown in Example 8-5, outputs the hosts against which the playbook will run.

Example 8-5. List hosts

```
$ ansible-playbook --list-hosts playbook.yml
```

 Sometimes you get this dreaded warning:

```
[WARNING]: provided hosts list is empty, only localhost
is available. Note that the implicit localhost does not
match 'all'
[WARNING]: Could not match supplied host pattern,
ignoring: db
[WARNING]: Could not match supplied host pattern,
ignoring: web
```

One host must be explicitly specified in your inventory or you'll get this warning, even if your playbook runs against only the local host. If your inventory is initially empty (perhaps because you're using a dynamic inventory script and haven't launched any hosts yet), you can work around this by explicitly adding the groups to your inventory:

```
ansible-playbook --list-hosts -i web,db playbook.yml
```

List Tasks

The --list-tasks flag, shown in Example 8-6, outputs the tasks against which the playbook will run.

Example 8-6. List tasks

```
$ ansible-playbook --list-tasks playbook.yml
```

Recall that we used this flag back in Chapter 7, in Example 7-1, to list the tasks in our first playbook. Again, none of these flags will execute the playbook.

Check Mode

The `-C` and `--check` flags run Ansible in *check mode* (sometimes called a dry run). This tells you whether each task in the playbook will modify the host, but it does not make any changes to the server:

```
$ ansible-playbook -C playbook.yml
$ ansible-playbook --check playbook.yml
```

One of the challenges with using check mode is that later parts of a playbook might succeed only if earlier parts were executed. Running check mode on Example 7-28 yields the error shown in Example 8-7 because this task depended on an earlier task (installing the NGINX program on the host). Another challenge is that the modules used in the playbook should support check mode or else it fails.

Example 8-7. Check mode failing on a correct playbook

```
TASK [nginx : create ssl certificates] ****************************************
fatal: [web]: FAILED! => {
    "changed": false
}
MSG:
Unable to change directory before execution: [Errno 2] No such file or directory:
b'/etc/nginx/conf'
```

See Chapter 19 for more details on how modules implement check mode.

Diff (Show File Changes)

The `-D` and `-diff` flags output differences for any files that are changed on the remote machine. It's a helpful option to use in conjunction with `--check` to show how Ansible would change the file if it were run normally:

```
$ ansible-playbook -D --check playbook.yml
$ ansible-playbook --diff --check playbook.yml
```

If Ansible would modify any files (e.g., using modules such as `copy`, `file`, `template`, and `lineinfile`), it will show the changes in *.diff* format, like this:

```
TASK [mezzanine : create a logs directory] ************************************
--- before
+++ after
@@ -1,4 +1,4 @@
 {
     "path": "/home/vagrant/logs",
-    "state": "absent"
+    "state": "directory"
 }

 changed: [web]
```

Some modules support `diff` as a Boolean telling it to display the diff or not.

Tags

Ansible allows you to add one or more tags to a task, a role, or a play. For example, here's a play that's tagged with `mezzanine` and `nginx`. (Bas prefers to use tags at the role level, because they can be hard to maintain on a task level.)

```
- name: deploy postgres on db
  hosts: db
  debugger: on_failed
  vars_files:
    - secrets.yml
  roles:
    - role: database
      tags: database
      database_name: "{{ mezzanine_proj_name }}"
      database_user: "{{ mezzanine_proj_name }}"

- name: deploy mezzanine on web
  hosts: web
  debugger: always
  vars_files:
    - secrets.yml

  roles:
    - role: mezzanine
      tags: mezzanine
      database_host: "{{ hostvars.db.ansible_enp0s8.ipv4.address }}"
    - role: nginx
      tags: nginx
```

Use the `-t tagnames` or `--tags tagnames` flag to tell Ansible to run only plays and tasks that have certain tags. Use the `--skip-tags tagnames` flag to tell Ansible to skip plays and tasks that have certain tags (see Example 8-8).

Example 8-8. Running or skipping tags

```
$ ansible-playbook -tnxinx playbook.yml
$ ansible-playbook --tags=xinx,database playbook.yml
$ ansible-playbook --skip-tags=mezzanine playbook.yml
```

Limits

Ansible allows you to restrict the set of hosts targeted for a playbook with a `--limit` flag to `ansible-playbook`. You can do a canary release (*https://oreil.ly/seUXz*) this way, but be sure to set it up with an audit trail. The limit flag reduces the run of the playbook to a set of hosts defined by an expression. In the simplest example, it can be a single hostname:

```
$ ansible-playbook -vv --limit db playbook.yml
```

Limits and tags are really useful during development; just be aware that tags are harder to maintain on a large scale. Limits are really useful for testing and rolling out over parts of your infrastructure.

Conclusion

Ansible has several features that help in debugging; if you use them well you can reduce the time it takes to test every change. This is useful when scaling up your playbooks in the coming chapters.

## CHAPTER 9

Roles: Scaling Up Your Playbooks

In Ansible, the *role* is the primary mechanism for breaking a playbook into multiple files. This simplifies writing complex playbooks, and it makes them easier to reuse. Think of a role as something you assign to one or more hosts. For example, you'd assign a database role to the hosts that will function as database servers. One of the things I like about Ansible is how it scales both up and down. Ansible scales down well because simple tasks are easy to implement. It scales up well because it provides mechanisms for decomposing complex jobs into smaller pieces. A role is very structured and doesn't have any site-specific data in it, so it can be shared with others, who can compose their site by combining roles in their own playbooks.

I'm not referring to the number of hosts you're managing, but rather the complexity of the jobs you're trying to automate. This chapter will get you Up and Running with Ansible roles!

Basic Structure of a Role

An Ansible role has a name, such as `database`. Files associated with the database role go in the *roles/database* directory, which contains the following files and directories:

```
defaults/
  main.yml
files/
  pg_hba.conf
handlers/
  main.yml
meta/
  main.yml
tasks/
  main.yml
templates/
  postgres.conf.j2
```

```
vars/
  main.yml
```

Tasks

The *tasks* directory has a *main.yml* file that serves as an entry point for the actions a role does.

Files

Holds files and scripts to be uploaded to hosts.

Templates

Holds Jinja2 template files to be uploaded to hosts.

Handlers

The *handlers* directory has a *main.yml* file that has the actions that respond to change notifications.

Vars

Variables that shouldn't generally be overridden.

Defaults

Default variables that can be overridden.

Meta

Information about the role.

Each individual file is optional; if your role doesn't have any handlers, for example, there's no need to have an empty *handlers/main.yml* file and no reason to commit such a file.

Where Does Ansible Look for My Roles?

Ansible looks for roles in the *roles* directory alongside your playbooks. It also looks for systemwide roles in */etc/ansible/roles*. You can customize the systemwide location of roles by setting the *roles_path* setting in the defaults section of your *ansible.cfg* file, as shown in Example 9-1. This setup separates roles defined in the project from roles installed into the project and has no systemwide location.

Example 9-1. ansible.cfg: Overriding default roles path

```
[defaults]
roles_path = galaxy_roles:roles
```

You can also override this by setting the `ANSIBLE_ROLES_PATH` environment variable.

Example: Deploying Mezzanine with Roles

Let's take our Mezzanine playbook and implement it with Ansible roles. We could create a single role called mezzanine, but instead we're going to break out the deployment of the Postgres database into a separate role called database, and the deployment of NGINX in a separate role as well. This will make it easier to eventually deploy the database on a host separate from the Mezzanine application. It will also separate the concerns related to the web server.

Using Roles in Your Playbooks

Before we get into the details of how to define roles, let's go over how to assign roles to hosts in a playbook. Example 9-2 shows what our playbook looks like for deploying Mezzanine onto a single host, once we have the database, nginx, and mezzanine roles defined.

Example 9-2. mezzanine-single-host.yml

```
---
- name: Deploy mezzanine on vagrant
  hosts: web

  vars_files:
    - secrets.yml

  roles:
    - role: database
      database_name: "{{ mezzanine_proj_name }}"
      database_user: "{{ mezzanine_proj_name }}"
    - role: mezzanine
      database_host: '127.0.0.1'
    - role: nginx
...
```

When we use roles, we usually have a roles section in our playbook. This section expects a list of roles. In our example, our list contains three roles: database, nginx, and mezzanine.

Note that we can pass in variables when invoking the roles. In our example, we passed the database_name and database_user variables for the database role. If these variables have already been defined in the role (either in *vars/main.yml* or *defaults/main.yml*), then the values will be overridden with the variables that were passed in.

If you aren't passing in variables to roles, you can simply specify the names of the role, as we did for nginx in the example.

With the `database`, `nginx`, and `mezzanine` roles defined, writing a playbook that deploys the web application and database services to multiple hosts becomes much simpler. Example 9-3 shows a playbook that deploys the database on the db host and the web service on the web host.

Example 9-3. mezzanine-across-hosts.yml

```
---

- name: Deploy postgres on db
  hosts: db

  vars_files:
    - secrets.yml

  roles:
    - role: database
      database_name: "{{ mezzanine_proj_name }}"
      database_user: "{{ mezzanine_proj_name }}"
- name: Deploy mezzanine on web
  hosts: web

  vars_files:
    - secrets.yml

  roles:
    - role: mezzanine
      database_host: "{{ hostvars.db.ansible_enp0s8.ipv4.address }}"
    - role: nginx
...
```

Note that this playbook contains two separate plays: "Deploy postgres on db" and "Deploy mezzanine on web"; each play affects a different group of hosts in principle, but we have only one machine in each group: a db server and a web server.

Pre-Tasks and Post-Tasks

Sometimes you want to run tasks before or after you invoke your roles. For example, you might want to update the apt cache before you deploy Mezzanine, and you might want to send a notification to a Slack channel after you deploy.

Ansible allows you to define the order in your playbooks:

- A list of tasks that execute before the roles with a `pre_tasks` section
- A list of roles to execute
- A list of tasks that execute after the roles with a `post_tasks` section

Example 9-4 shows an example of using `pre_tasks`, `roles`, and `post_tasks` to deploy Mezzanine.

Example 9-4. Using pre-tasks and post-tasks

```
- name: Deploy mezzanine on web
  hosts: web
  vars_files:
    - secrets.yml

  pre_tasks:
    - name: Update the apt cache
      apt:
        update_cache: yes

  roles:
    - role: mezzanine
      database_host: "{{ hostvars.db.ansible_enp0s8.ipv4.address }}"
    - role: nginx

  post_tasks:
    - name: Notify Slack that the servers have been updated
      delegate_to: localhost
      slack:
        domain: acme.slack.com
        token: "{{ slack_token }}"
        msg: "web server {{ inventory_hostname }} configured."
...
```

But enough about using roles; let's talk about writing them.

A database Role for Deploying the Database

The job of our `database` role will be to install Postgres and create the required database and database user.

Our `database` role is comprised of the following files:

- *roles/database/defaults/main.yml*
- *roles/database/files/pg_hba.conf*
- *roles/database/handlers/main.yml*
- *roles/database/meta/main.yml*
- *roles/database/tasks/main.yml*
- *roles/database/templates/postgresql.conf.j2*
- *roles/database/vars/main.yml*

This role includes two customized Postgres configuration files:

postgresql.conf.j2

Modifies the default `listen_addresses` configuration option so that Postgres will accept connections on any network interface. The default for Postgres is to accept connections only from `localhost`, which doesn't work for us if we want our database to run on a separate host from our web application.

pg_hba.conf

Configures Postgres to authenticate connections over the network by using a username and password.

 These files aren't shown here because they are quite large. You can find them in the code samples on GitHub (*https://oreil.ly/PddOX*) in the *ch07* directory.

Example 9-5 shows the tasks involved in deploying Postgres.

Example 9-5. roles/database/tasks/main.yml

```
---

- name: Install apt packages
  become: true
  apt:
    update_cache: true
    cache_valid_time: 3600
    pkg: "{{ postgres_packages }}"

- name: Copy configuration file
  become: true
  template:
    src: postgresql.conf.j2
    dest: /etc/postgresql/12/main/postgresql.conf
    owner: postgres
    group: postgres
    mode: '0644'
  notify: Restart postgres

- name: Copy client authentication configuration file
  become: true
  copy:
    src: pg_hba.conf
    dest: /etc/postgresql/12/main/pg_hba.conf
    owner: postgres
    group: postgres
    mode: '0640'
  notify: Restart postgres
```

```
- name: Create project locale
  become: true
  locale_gen:
    name: "{{ locale }}"

- name: Create a DB user
  become: true
  become_user: postgres
  postgresql_user:
    name: "{{ database_user }}"
    password: "{{ db_pass }}"

- name: Create the database
  become: true
  become_user: postgres
  postgresql_db:
    name: "{{ database_name }}"
    owner: "{{ database_user }}"
    encoding: UTF8
    lc_ctype: "{{ locale }}"
    lc_collate: "{{ locale }}"
    template: template0
...
```

Example 9-6 shows the handlers file, used when notifying actions trigger a change.

Example 9-6. roles/database/handlers/main.yml

```
---
- name: Restart postgres
  become: true
  service:
    name: postgresql
    state: restarted
...
```

The only thing in vars that we are going to specify is the database port; this is used in the *postgresql.conf.j2* template.

In Example 9-7 we see the list of packages to install, obviously the database itself and the C and Python client libraries, but also acl.

The acl package is needed when both the connection user and the become_user are unprivileged. The module file is written by the connection user, but the file needs to be readable by the become_user. Ansible will use the setfacl command to share the file only with the become_user.

Example 9-7. roles/database/defaults/main.yml

```
---
postgres_packages:
  - acl  # for become_user: postgres
  - libpq-dev
  - postgresql
  - python3-psycopg2
...
```

Note that our list of tasks refers to several variables that we haven't defined anywhere in the role:

- `database_name`

- `database_user`

- `db_pass`

- `locale`

In Examples 9-2 and 9-3, we passed `database_name` and `database_user` when we invoked the database role. We're assuming that `db_pass` is defined in the *secrets.yml* file, which is included in the `vars_files` section. The `locale` variable is likely something that would be the same for every host, and might be used by multiple roles or playbooks, so we defined it in the *group_vars/all* file in the code samples that accompany this book.

Why Are There Two Ways to Define Variables in Roles?

When Ansible first introduced support for roles, there was only one place to define role variables, in *vars/main.yml*. Variables defined in this location have a higher precedence than those defined in the vars section of a play, which meant you couldn't override the variable unless you explicitly passed it as an argument to the role.

Ansible later introduced the notion of default role variables that go in *defaults/main.yml*. This type of variable is defined in a role, but has a low precedence, so it will be overridden if another variable with the same name is defined in the playbook.

If you think you might want to change the value of a variable in a role, use a default variable. If you don't want it to change, use a regular variable.

A mezzanine Role for Deploying Mezzanine

The job of our `mezzanine` role will be to install Mezzanine. This includes installing NGINX as the reverse proxy and Supervisor as the process monitor.

The role is comprised of the following files:

- *roles/mezzanine/files/setadmin.py*
- *roles/mezzanine/files/setsite.py*
- *roles/mezzanine/handlers/main.yml*
- *roles/mezzanine/tasks/django.yml*
- *roles/mezzanine/tasks/main.yml*
- *roles/mezzanine/templates/gunicorn.conf.pyj2*
- *roles/mezzanine/templates/local_settings.py.filters.j2*
- *roles/mezzanine/templates/local_settings.py.j2*
- *roles/mezzanine/templates/supervisor.conf.j2*
- *roles/mezzanine/vars/main.yml*

Example 9-8 shows the variables we've defined for this role. Note that we've prefixed the names of the variables so that they all start with *mezzanine*. It's good practice to do this with role variables because Ansible doesn't have any notion of namespace across roles. This means that variables that are defined in other roles, or elsewhere in a playbook, will be accessible everywhere. This can cause some unexpected behavior if you accidentally use the same variable name in two different roles.

Example 9-8. roles/mezzanine/vars/main.yml

```
---
# vars file for mezzanine
mezzanine_user: "{{ ansible_user }}"
mezzanine_venv_home: "{{ ansible_env.HOME }}/.virtualenvs"
mezzanine_venv_path: "{{ mezzanine_venv_home }}/{{ mezzanine_proj_name }}"
mezzanine_repo_url: git@github.com:ansiblebook/mezzanine_example.git
mezzanine_settings_path: "{{ mezzanine_proj_path }}/{{ mezzanine_proj_name }}"
mezzanine_reqs_path: '~/requirements.txt'
mezzanine_python: "{{ mezzanine_venv_path }}/bin/python"
mezzanine_manage: "{{ mezzanine_python }} {{ mezzanine_proj_path }}/manage.py"
mezzanine_gunicorn_procname: gunicorn_mezzanine
...
```

Because the task list is pretty long, we've decided to break it up across several files. Example 9-9 shows the top-level task file for the `mezzanine` role. It installs the apt packages, and then it uses include statements to invoke two other task files that are in the same directory, shown in Examples 9-10 and 9-11.

Example 9-9. roles/mezzanine/tasks/main.yml

```
---

- name: Install apt packages
  become: true
  apt:
    update_cache: true
    cache_valid_time: 3600
    pkg:
      - git
      - libjpeg-dev
      - memcached
      - python3-dev
      - python3-pip
      - python3-venv
      - supervisor

- include_tasks: setup.yml
- include_tasks: django.yml
...
```

Example 9-10. roles/mezzanine/tasks/setup.yml

```
---
- name: Create a logs directory
  file:
    path: "{{ ansible_env.HOME }}/logs"
    state: directory
    mode: '0755'

- name: Check out the repository on the host
  git:
    repo: "{{ mezzanine_repo_url }}"
    dest: "{{ mezzanine_proj_path }}"
    version: master
    accept_hostkey: true
    update: false
  tags:
    - repo

- name: Create python3 virtualenv
  pip:
    name:
      - pip
      - wheel
      - setuptools
    state: latest
    virtualenv: "{{ mezzanine_venv_path }}"
    virtualenv_command: /usr/bin/python3 -m venv
  tags:
    - skip_ansible_lint

- name: Copy requirements.txt to home directory
  copy:
```

```
    src: requirements.txt
    dest: "{{ mezzanine_reqs_path }}"
    mode: '0644'

- name: Install packages listed in requirements.txt
  pip:
    virtualenv: "{{ mezzanine_venv_path }}"
    requirements: "{{ mezzanine_reqs_path }}"
```

Example 9-11. roles/mezzanine/tasks/django.yml

```
---
- name: Generate the settings file
  template:
    src: templates/local_settings.py.j2
    dest: "{{ mezzanine_settings_path }}/local_settings.py"
    mode: '0750'

- name: Apply migrations to database, collect static content
  django_manage:
    command: "{{ item }}"
    app_path: "{{ mezzanine_proj_path }}"
    virtualenv: "{{ mezzanine_venv_path }}"
  with_items:
    - migrate
    - collectstatic

- name: Set the site id
  script: setsite.py
  environment:
    PATH: "{{ mezzanine_venv_path }}/bin"
    PROJECT_DIR: "{{ mezzanine_proj_path }}"
    PROJECT_APP: "{{ mezzanine_proj_app }}"
    DJANGO_SETTINGS_MODULE: "{{ mezzanine_proj_app }}.settings"
    WEBSITE_DOMAIN: "{{ live_hostname }}"

- name: Set the admin password
  script: setadmin.py
  environment:
    PATH: "{{ mezzanine_venv_path }}/bin"
    PROJECT_DIR: "{{ mezzanine_proj_path }}"
    PROJECT_APP: "{{ mezzanine_proj_app }}"
    ADMIN_PASSWORD: "{{ admin_pass }}"

- name: Set the gunicorn config file
  template:
    src: templates/gunicorn.conf.py.j2
    dest: "{{ mezzanine_proj_path }}/gunicorn.conf.py"
    mode: '0750'

- name: Set the supervisor config file
  become: true
  template:
    src: templates/supervisor.conf.j2
    dest: /etc/supervisor/conf.d/mezzanine.conf
```

```
    mode: '0640'
  notify: Restart supervisor

- name: Install poll twitter cron job
  cron:
    name: "poll twitter"
    minute: "*/5"
    user: "{{ mezzanine_user }}"
    job: "{{ mezzanine_manage }} poll_twitter"
...
```

There's one important caveat when it comes to using the copy, script, or template modules. There is a difference between tasks defined in a role and tasks defined in a regular playbook. When invoking copy or script in a task defined in a role, Ansible will look in this order in these directories for the location of the file to copy or run and will use the first one found. These paths are relative to the directory where you start the top-level playbook from.

- *./roles/role_name/files/*

- *./roles/role_name/*

- *./roles/role_name/tasks/files/*

- *./roles/role_name/tasks/*

- *./files/*

- *./*

Similarly, when invoking template in a task defined in a role, Ansible will first check the *role_name/templates* directory and then the *playbooks/templates* directory for the location of the template to use (along with less obvious directories). This way, roles define default files in their *files/* and *templates/* directories, but you cannot simply override them with files in the *files/* and *templates/* subdirectories of your project.

This means that a task that used to look like this in our playbook:

```
- name: Copy requirements.txt to home directory
  copy:
    src: files/requirements.txt
    dest: "{{ mezzanine_reqs_path }}"
    mode: '0644'
```

now looks like this when invoked from inside a role (note the change of the src parameter):

```
- name: Copy requirements.txt to home directory
  copy:
    src: "{{ files_src_path | default() }}requirements.txt"
    dest: "{{ mezzanine_reqs_path }}"
    mode: '0644'
```

`files_src_path` is a variable path that you can override, but it can be empty as well, for default behavior. Ramon de la Fuente proposed this (*https://oreil.ly/WgI9l*) use of variable paths for files and templates in roles.

Example 9-12 shows the handlers file; handlers run when notified by changes in tasks.

Example 9-12. roles/mezzanine/handlers/main.yml

```
---
- name: Restart supervisor
  become: true
  supervisorctl:
    name: gunicorn_mezzanine
    state: restarted
...
```

We won't show the template files here, since they're basically the same as in the previous chapter, although some of the variable names have changed. Check out the accompanying code samples (*https://oreil.ly/PddOX*) for details.

Creating Role Files and Directories with ansible-galaxy

Ansible ships with another command-line tool we haven't talked about yet: `ansible-galaxy`. Its primary purpose is to download roles that have been shared by the community (*https://galaxy.ansible.com*)—more on that later in the chapter. It can also be used to generate *scaffolding*, an initial set of files and directories involved in a role:

```
$ ansible-galaxy role init --init-path playbooks/roles web
```

The `--init-path` flag tells `ansible-galaxy` the location of your *roles* directory. If you don't specify it, the role files will be created in your current directory. Running the command creates the following files and directories:

```
playbooks
|___ roles
     |___ web
          |— README.md
          |— defaults
          |  |___ main.yml
          |— files
          |— handlers
          |  |___ main.yml
          |— meta
          |  |___ main.yml
          |— tasks
          |  |___ main.yml
          |— templates
          |— tests
          |  |___ inventory
```

```
| |__ test.yml
|__ vars
       |__ main.yml
```

Dependent Roles

Imagine that we have two roles, web and database, that both require an NTP[1] server to be installed on the host. We could specify the installation of the NTP server in both the web and database roles, but that would result in duplication. We could create a separate ntp role, but then we would have to remember that whenever we apply the web or database role to a host, we have to apply the ntp role as well. This would avoid the duplication, but it's error-prone because we might forget to specify the ntp role. What we really want is to have an ntp role that is always applied to a host whenever we apply the web role or the database role.

Ansible supports a feature called *dependent roles* to deal with this scenario. When you define a role, you can specify that it depends on one or more other roles. Ansible will ensure that roles that are specified as dependencies are executed first.

Continuing with our example, let's say that we create an ntp role that configures a host to synchronize its time with an NTP server. Ansible allows us to pass parameters to dependent roles, so let's also assume that we can pass the NTP server as a parameter to that role.

We specify that the web role depends on the ntp role by creating a *roles/web/meta/main.yml* file and listing ntp as a role, with a parameter, as shown in Example 9-13.

Example 9-13. roles/web/meta/main.yml

```
dependencies:
    - { role: ntp, ntp_server=ntp.ubuntu.com }
```

We can also specify multiple dependent roles. For example, if we have a django role for setting up a Django web server, and we want to specify nginx and memcached as dependent roles, then the role metadata file might look like Example 9-14.

Example 9-14. roles/django/meta/main.yml

```
dependencies:
    - { role: web }
    - { role: memcached }
```

---

1 *NTP* stands for *Network Time Protocol*, used for synchronizing clocks.

For details on how Ansible evaluates the role dependencies, check out the official Ansible documentation on role dependencies (*https://oreil.ly/3nJ4K*).

Ansible Galaxy

If you need to deploy an open source software system onto your hosts, chances are some people have already written Ansible roles to do it. Although Ansible does make it easier to write scripts for deploying software, some systems are just plain tricky to deploy.

Whether you want to reuse a role somebody has already written, or you just want to see how someone else solved the problem you're working on, Ansible Galaxy can help you out. *Ansible Galaxy* is an open source repository of Ansible roles contributed by the Ansible community. The roles themselves are stored on GitHub. *https://galaxy.ansible.com* is the central website for Ansible content; `ansible-galaxy` is a command-line interface (CLI) tool.

Web Interface

You can explore the available roles on the Ansible Galaxy site (*https://galaxy.ansible.com*). Galaxy supports free text searching, filtering, and browsing by category or contributor.

Command-Line Interface

The `ansible-galaxy` command-line tool allows you to download roles from Ansible Galaxy, or to create a standard directory structure for an `ansible-role`.

Installing a role

Let's say I want to install a role named `ntp`, written by GitHub user *oefenweb* (Mischa ter Smitten, one of the most active authors on Ansible Galaxy). This is a role that will configure a host to synchronize its clock with an NTP server.

You can install the role with the `ansible-galaxy install` command:

```
$ ansible-galaxy install oefenweb.ntp
```

The `ansible-galaxy` program will install roles to the first directory in *roles_path* by default (see "Where Does Ansible Look for My Roles?" on page 160), but you can override this path with the `-p` flag (the directory is created if needed).

The output should look something like this:

```
Starting galaxy role install process
- downloading role 'ntp', owned by oefenweb
- downloading role from https://github.com/Oefenweb/ansible-ntp/archive/v1.1.33.
tar.gz
```

```
- extracting oefenweb.ntp to ./galaxy_roles/oefenweb.ntp
- oefenweb.ntp (v1.1.33) was installed successfully
```

The `ansible-galaxy` tool will install the role files to *galaxy_roles/oefenweb.ntp*.

Ansible will install some metadata about the installation to the file *./galaxy_roles/oefenweb.ntp/meta/.galaxy_install_info*. On Bas' machine, that file contains the following:

```
install_date: Tue Jul 20 12:13:44 2021
version: v1.1.33
```

 The `oefenweb.ntp` role has a specific version number, so the version will be listed. Some roles will not have a specific version number and will be listed with their default branch in Git, like main.

Listing installed roles

You can list installed roles as follows:

```
$ ansible-galaxy list
```

The output is based on the `galaxy_info` key in *meta/main.yml*, which should look similar to the following:

```
# /Users/bas/ansiblebook/ch07/playbooks/galaxy_roles
- oefenweb.ntp, v1.1.33
# /Users/bas/ansiblebook/ch07/playbooks/roles
- database, (unknown version)
- web, (unknown version)
```

Uninstalling a role

You can remove a role with the `remove` command:

```
$ ansible-galaxy remove oefenweb.ntp
```

Role Requirements in Practice

It is common practice to list dependencies in a file called *requirements.yml* in the *roles* directory, located at *<project-top-level-directory>/roles/requirements.yml*. If this file is found when using AWX/Ansible Tower, then `ansible-galaxy` installs the listed roles automatically. This file allows you to reference Galaxy roles, or roles within other repositories, which can be checked out in conjunction with your own project. The addition of this Ansible Galaxy support eliminates the need to create Git submodules for achieving this result.

In the following code snippet the first source is a dependency on the `oefenweb.ntp` role (downloads are counted by Galaxy when specifying `src` in this way). The second example does a direct download from GitHub of a `docker` role written by Jeff Geerling (well known in the Ansible community for his book *Ansible for DevOps*, 2nd ed. [LeanPub], and many roles on Galaxy). The third example downloads from an on-premises Git repo. The `name` parameter in *requirements.yml* can be used to rename roles after downloading.

```
---

- src: oefenweb.ntp

- src: https://github.com/geerlingguy/ansible-role-docker.git
  scm: git
  version: '4.0.0'
  name: geerlingguy.docker

- src: https://tools.example.intra/bitbucket/scm/ansible/install-nginx.git
  scm: git
  version: master
  name: web
...
```

Contributing Your Own Role

See "Contributing Content" (*https://oreil.ly/lfLle*) on the Ansible Galaxy website for details on how to contribute a role to the community. Because the roles are hosted on GitHub, you need to have a GitHub account to contribute.

Conclusion

At this point, you should have an understanding of how to use roles, how to write your own roles, and how to download roles written by others. Roles are a great way to organize your playbooks. We use them all the time, and we highly recommend them. If you find that a particular resource that you work on has no role on Galaxy, then consider uploading!

## CHAPTER 10

Complex Playbooks

In the preceding chapter, we went over a fully functional Ansible playbook for deploying the Mezzanine CMS. That example used some common Ansible features, but it didn't cover all of them. This chapter touches on those other features, which makes it a bit of a grab bag.

Dealing with Badly Behaved Commands

Recall that in Chapter 7, we avoided invoking the custom `createdb manage.py` command, shown in Example 10-1, because the call wasn't idempotent.

Example 10-1. Calling `django manage.py createdb`

```
- name: Initialize the database
  django_manage:
    command: createdb --noinput --nodata
    app_path: "{{ proj_path }}"
    virtualenv: "{{ venv_path }}"
```

We got around this problem by invoking several `django manage.py` commands that were idempotent, and that did the equivalent of `createdb`. But what if we didn't have a module that could invoke equivalent commands? The answer is to use `changed_when` and `failed_when` clauses to change how Ansible detects that a task has changed state or failed.

Let's make sure you understand the output of this command the first and second times it's run.

Recall from Chapter 5 that to capture the output of a failed task, you add a `register` clause to save the output to a variable and a `failed_when: false` clause so that the execution doesn't stop even if the module returns failure. Then you add a debug task to print out the variable, and finally a `fail` clause so that the playbook stops executing, as shown in Example 10-2.

Example 10-2. Viewing the output of a task

```
- name: Initialize the database
  django_manage:
    command: createdb --noinput --nodata
    app_path: "{{ proj_path }}"
    virtualenv: "{{ venv_path }}"
  failed_when: false
  register: result

- debug: var=result

- fail:
```

The output of the playbook, when invoked another time, is shown in Example 10-3.

Example 10-3. Returned values when database has already been created

```
TASK [debug] ************************************************************
ok: [web] ==> {
    "result": {
        "changed": false,
        "cmd": "./manage.py createdb --noinput --nodata",
        "failed": false,
        "failed_when_result": false,
        "msg": "\n:stderr: CommandError: Database already created, you probably want
the migrate command\n",
        "path": "/home/vagrant/.virtualenvs/mezzanine_example/bin:/usr/local/sbin:/
usr/local/bin:/usr/sbin:/usr/bin:/sbin:/bin:/usr/games:/usr/local/
games:/snap/bin",
        "syspath": [
            "/tmp/ansible_django_manage_payload_hb62e1ie/ansible_django_manage_pay
load.zip",
            "/usr/lib/python38.zip",
            "/usr/lib/python3.8",
            "/usr/lib/python3.8/lib-dynload",
            "/usr/local/lib/python3.8/dist-packages",
            "/usr/lib/python3/dist-packages"
        ]
    }
}
```

This is what happens when the task has been run multiple times. To see what happens the *first* time, drop the database and then have the playbook re-create it. The simplest way to do that is to run an Ansible ad hoc task that drops the database:

```
$ ansible web -b --become-user postgres -m postgresql_db \
    -a "name=mezzanine_example state=absent"
```

Now when we run the playbook again, we get the output in Example 10-4.

Example 10-4. Returned values when invoked the first time

```
TASK [debug] **********************************************************
ok: [web] ==> {
    "result": {
        "app_path": "/home/vagrant/mezzanine/mezzanine_example",
        "changed": false,
        "cmd": "./manage.py createdb --noinput --nodata",
        "failed": false,
        "failed_when_result": false,
        "out": "Operations to perform:\n  Apply all migrations: admin, auth, blog,
        conf, contenttypes, core, django_comments, forms, galleries, generic, pages,
        redirects, sessions, sites, twitter\nRunning migrations:\n  Applying
        contenttypes.0001_initial... OK\n  Applying auth.0001_initial... OK\n
        Applying admin.0001_initial... OK\n  Applying
        admin.0002_logentry_remove_auto_add... OK\n  Applying
        contenttypes.0002_remove_content_type_name... OK\n  Applying
        auth.0002_alter_permission_name_max_length... OK\n  Applying
        auth.0003_alter_user_email_max_length... OK\n  Applying
        auth.0004_alter_user_username_opts... OK\n  Applying
        auth.0005_alter_user_last_login_null... OK\n  Applying
        auth.0006_require_contenttypes_0002... OK\n  Applying
        auth.0007_alter_validators_add_error_messages... OK\n  Applying
        auth.0008_alter_user_username_max_length... OK\n  Applying
        sites.0001_initial... OK\n  Applying blog.0001_initial... OK\n  Applying
        blog.0002_auto_20150527_1555... OK\n  Applying blog.0003_auto_20170411_0504...
        OK\n  Applying conf.0001_initial... OK\n  Applying core.0001_initial... OK\n
        Applying core.0002_auto_20150414_2140... OK\n  Applying
        django_comments.0001_initial... OK\n  Applying
        django_comments.0002_update_user_email_field_length... OK\n  Applying
        django_comments.0003_add_submit_date_index... OK\n
        Applying pages.0001_initial... OK\n  Applying forms.0001_initial... OK\n
        Applying forms.0002_auto_20141227_0224... OK\n  Applying forms.0003_emailfield...
        OK\n  Applying forms.0004_auto_20150517_0510... OK\n  Applying
        forms.0005_auto_20151026_1600... OK\n  Applying forms.0006_auto_20170425_2225...
        OK\n  Applying galleries.0001_initial... OK\n  Applying
        galleries.0002_auto_20141227_0224... OK\n  Applying generic.0001_initial... OK\n
        Applying generic.0002_auto_20141227_0224... OK\n  Applying
        generic.0003_auto_20170411_0504... OK\n  Applying pages.0002_auto_20141227_0224...
        OK\n  Applying pages.0003_auto_20150527_1555... OK\n  Applying
        pages.0004_auto_20170411_0504... OK\n  Applying redirects.0001_initial... OK\n
        Applying sessions.0001_initial... OK\n  Applying sites.0002_alter_domain_unique...
        OK\n  Applying twitter.0001_initial... OK\n\nCreating default site record: web
        ...\n\nInstalled 2 object(s) from 1 fixture(s)\n",
        "pythonpath": null,
        "settings": null,
        "virtualenv": "/home/vagrant/.virtualenvs/mezzanine_example"
    }
}
```

Note that changed is set to `false` even though it did, indeed, change the state of the database. That's because the `django_manage` module always returns `"changed"`: `false` when it runs commands that the module doesn't know about.

We can add a `changed_when` clause that looks for `"Creating tables"` in the `out` return value, as shown in Example 10-5.

Example 10-5. First attempt at adding changed_when

```
- name: Initialize the database
  django_manage:
    command: createdb --noinput --nodata
    app_path: "{{ proj_path }}"
    virtualenv: "{{ venv_path }}"
  register: result
  changed_when: '"Creating tables" in result.out'
```

The problem with this approach is that, if we look back at Example 10-3, we see that there is no `out` variable. Instead, there's a `msg` variable. If we executed the playbook, we would get the following (not terribly helpful) error the second time:

```
TASK: [Initialize the database] ********************************************
fatal: [default] => error while evaluating conditional: "Creating tables" in
result.out
```

Instead, we need to ensure that Ansible evaluates `result.out` only if that variable is defined. One way is to explicitly check whether the variable is defined:

```
changed_when: result.out is defined and "Creating tables" in result.out
```

Alternatively, we could provide a default value for `result.out` if it doesn't exist by using the Jinja2 `default` filter:

```
changed_when: '"Creating tables" in result.out|default("")'
```

The final idempotent task is shown in Example 10-6.

Example 10-6. Idempotent manage.py created

```
- name: Initialize the database
  django_manage:
    command: createdb --noinput --nodata
    app_path: "{{ proj_path }}"
    virtualenv: "{{ venv_path }}"
  register: result
  changed_when: '"Creating tables" in result.out|default("")'
```

Filters

Filters are a feature of the Jinja2 templating engine. Since Ansible uses Jinja2 for evaluating variables as well as for templates, you can use filters inside `{{ double curly braces }}` in your playbooks and your template files. Using filters resembles using Unix pipes, whereby a variable is piped through a filter. Jinja2 ships with a set of built-in filters (*https://oreil.ly/7svtE*). In addition, Ansible ships with its own filters (*https://oreil.ly/DlvWZ*) to augment the Jinja2 filters.

We'll cover a few sample filters here, but check out the official Jinja2 and Ansible docs for a complete list of the available filters.

The default Filter

The `default` filter is a useful one. Here's an example of this filter in action:

```
host: "{{ database_host | default('localhost') }}"
```

If the variable `database_host` is defined, the braces will evaluate to the value of that variable. If the variable `database_host` is not defined, the braces will evaluate to the string `localhost`. Some filters take arguments, some don't.

Filters for Registered Variables

Let's say we want to run a task and print out its output, even if the task fails. However, if the task does fail, we want Ansible to fail for that host after printing the output. Example 10-7 shows how to use the `failed` filter in the argument to the `failed_when` clause.

Example 10-7. Using the `failed` filter

```
- name: Run myprog
  command: /opt/myprog
  register: result
  ignore_errors: true

- debug: var=result

- debug:
    msg: "Stop running the playbook if myprog failed"
  failed_when: result|failed

# more tasks here
```

Table 10-1 shows a list of filters you can use on registered variables to check the status.

Table 10-1. Task return value filters

Name	Description
failed	True if the value was registered by a task that failed
changed	True if the value was registered by a task changed
success	True if the value was registered by a task that succeeded
skipped	True if the value was registered by a task that was skipped

Filters That Apply to Filepaths

Table 10-2 shows filters that are useful when a variable holds the path to a file on the control machine's filesystem.

Table 10-2. Filepath filters

Name	Description
basename	Base name of filepath
dirname	Directory of filepath
expanduser	Filepath with ~ replaced by home directory
realpath	Canonical path of filepath, resolves symbolic links

Consider this playbook fragment:

```
vars:
  homepage: /usr/share/nginx/html/index.html

tasks:
  - name: Copy home page
    copy:
      src: files/index.html
      dest: "{{ homepage }}"
```

Note that it references *index.html* twice: once in the definition of the homepage variable, and a second time to specify the path to the file on the control machine.

The basename filter extracts the *index.html* part of the filename from the full path, allowing us to write the playbook without repeating the filename:[1]

```
vars:
  homepage: /usr/share/nginx/html/index.html

tasks:

  - name: Copy home page
    copy:
      src: "files/{{ homepage | basename }}"
      dest: "{{ homepage }}"
```

---

1 Thanks to John Jarvis for this tip.

Writing Your Own Filter

Recall that in our Mezzanine example, we generated the *local_settings.py* file from a template, and a line in the generated file looks like Example 10-8.

Example 10-8. Line from local_settings.py generated by template

```
ALLOWED_HOSTS = ["www.example.com", "example.com"]
```

We used a variable named `domains` that had a list of the hostnames. We originally used a `for` loop in our template to generate this line, but a filter would be an even more elegant approach.

There is a built-in Jinja2 filter called `join` that will join a list of strings with a delimiter such as a comma. Unfortunately, it doesn't quite give us what we want. If we did this in the template:

```
    ALLOWED_HOSTS = [{{ domains|join(", ") }}]
```

We would end up with the strings unquoted in our file, as shown in Example 10-9.

Example 10-9. Strings incorrectly unquoted

```
ALLOWED_HOSTS = [www.example.com, example.com]
```

If we had a Jinja2 filter that quoted the strings in the list, as shown in Example 10-10, then the template would generate the output depicted in Example 10-8.

Example 10-10. Using a filter to quote the strings in the list

```
ALLOWED_HOSTS = [{{ domains|surround_by_quotes|join(", ") }}]
```

Unfortunately, there's no existing `surround_by_quotes` filter that does what we want. However, we can write it ourselves.In fact, Hanfei Sun covered this very topic on Stack Overflow (*https://oreil.ly/Y5kqL*).

Ansible will look for custom filters in the *filter_plugins* directory, relative to the directory containing your playbooks.

Example 10-11 shows what the filter implementation looks like.

Example 10-11. filter_plugins/surround_by_quotes.py

```
''' https://stackoverflow.com/a/68610557/571517 '''
class FilterModule():
    ''' FilterModule class must have a method named filters '''
    @staticmethod
    def surround_by_quotes(a_list):
```

```
        ''' implements surround_by_quotes for each list element '''
        return ['"%s"' % an_element for an_element in a_list]
    def filters(self):
        ''' returns a dictionary that maps filter names to
        callables implementing the filter '''
        return {'surround_by_quotes': self.surround_by_quotes}
```

The surround_by_quotes function defines the Jinja2 filter. The FilterModule class defines a filters method that returns a dictionary with the name of the filter function and the function itself. The FilterModule class is Ansible-specific code that makes the Jinja2 filter available to Ansible.

You can also place filter plug-ins in the *~/.ansible/plugins/filter* directory or the */usr/share/ansible/plugins/filter* directory, or you can specify by setting the ANSIBLE_FILTER_PLUGINS environment variable to the directory where your plug-ins are located.

More examples and documentation of filter plug-ins are available on GitHub (*https://oreil.ly/hGzbQ*).

Lookups

In an ideal world, all of your configuration information would be stored as Ansible variables in all the various places where Ansible lets you define variables (like the vars section of your playbooks, files loaded by vars_files, or files in the *host_vars* or *group_vars* directories discussed in Chapter 3).

Alas, the world is a messy place, and sometimes a piece of configuration data you need lives somewhere else. Maybe it's in a text file or a *.csv* file, and you don't want to just copy the data into an Ansible variable file because having to maintain two copies of the same data would violate the DRY[2] principle. Or maybe the data isn't maintained as a file at all, but in a key-value storage service such as Redis. Ansible has a feature called *lookups* that allows you to read in configuration data from various sources and then use that data in your playbooks and template.

Ansible supports a collection of lookups for retrieving data from diverse sources. To list the lookups in your installed Ansible, try:

```
$ ansible-doc -t lookup -l
```

The ansible.builtin lookups are shown in Table 10-3.

---

2 Don't Repeat Yourself, a term popularized by *The Pragmatic Programmer: From Journeyman to Master* (Addison-Wesley), which is a fantastic book.

Table 10-3. ansible.builtin lookups

Name	Description
config	Look up current Ansible configuration values
csvfile	Entry in a *.csv* file
dict	Returns key/value pair items from dictionaries
dnstxt	DNS TXT record
env	Environment variable
file	Contents of a file
fileglob	List files matching a pattern
first_found	Return first file found from list
indexed_items	Rewrites lists to return "indexed items"
ini	Read data from a INI file
inventory_hostnames	List of inventory hosts matching a host pattern
items	List of items
lines	Read lines from command
list	Simply returns what it is given
nested	Composes a list with nested elements of other lists
password	Retrieve or generate a random password, stored in a file
pipe	Output of locally executed command
random_choice	Return random element from list
redis	Redis key lookup
sequence	Generate a list based on a number sequence
subelements	Traverse nested key from a list of dictionaries
template	Jinja2 template after evaluation
together	Merges lists into synchronized list
unvault	Read vaulted file(s) contents
url	Return contents from URL
varnames	Look up matching variable names
vars	Look up templated value of variables

To learn how to use any lookup, run:

```
$ ansible-doc -t lookup <plugin name>
```

All Ansible lookup plug-ins execute on the control machine, not the remote host.

You invoke lookups by calling the lookup function with two arguments. The first is a string with the name of the lookup, and the second is a string that contains one or more arguments to pass to the lookup. For example, we call the file lookup like this:

```
lookup('file', '/path/to/file.txt')
```

You can invoke lookups in your playbooks between {{ braces }} or put them in templates.

In the next sections, we provide only a few examples of the many lookups available. The Ansible documentation (*https://oreil.ly/tnCmt*) supplies more details.

file

Let's say you have a text file on your control machine that has a public SSH key that you want to copy to a remote server. Example 10-12 shows how to use the file lookup to read the contents of a file and pass that as a parameter to the authorized_key module.[3]

Example 10-12. Using the file lookup

```
- name: Add my public key for SSH
  authorized_key:
      user: vagrant
      key: "{{ lookup('file', item) }}"
  with_first_found:
      - ~/.ssh/id_ed25519.pub
      - ~/.ssh/id_rsa.pub
      - ~/.ssh/id_ecdsa.pub
```

You can invoke lookups in templates as well. If we want to use the same lookup to create an *authorized_keys* file that contains the contents of a public-key file and options, we could create a Jinja2 template that invokes the lookup (Example 10-13), and then call the template module in our playbook, as shown in Example 10-14.

Example 10-13. authorized_keys.j2

```
from="10.0.2.2" {{ lookup('file', '~/.ssh/id_ed25519.pub') }}
```

Example 10-14. Task to generate authorized_keys

```
- name: Copy authorized_keys template
  template:
    src: authorized_keys.j2
    dest: /home/vagrant/.ssh/authorized_keys
    owner: vagrant
    group: vagrant
    mode: '0600'
```

---

3 Run ansible-doc authorized_key to learn how this module helps protect your SSH configuration.

pipe

The `pipe` lookup invokes an external program on the control machine and evaluates to the program's output on standard out. For example, to install the default public key for the Vagrant user, we could use this `pipe` lookup. Every vagrant install comes with the same *insecure_private_key* file, so every developer can use Vagrant boxes. The public key can be derived from it with a command that we define as a variable (to avoid a line-length warning):

```
- name: Add default public key for vagrant user
  authorized_key:
    user: vagrant
    key: "{{ lookup('pipe', pubkey_cmd ) }}"
  vars:
    pubkey_cmd: 'ssh-keygen -y -f ~/.vagrant.d/insecure_private_key'
```

env

The `env` lookup retrieves the value of an environment variable set on the control machine. For example, we could use the lookup like this:

```
- name: Get the current shell
  debug: msg="{{ lookup('env', 'SHELL') }}"
```

Since Bas uses the bash shell, the output looks like this when he runs it:

```
TASK: [Get the current shell] **************************************************
ok: [web] ==> {
    "msg": "/bin/bash"
}
```

password

The `password` lookup evaluates to a random password, and it will also write the password to a file specified in the argument. For example, if we want to create a user named `deploy` with a random password and write that password to *pw.txt* on the control machine, we can do this:

```
- name: Create deploy user, save random password in pw.txt
  become: true
  user:
    name: deploy
    password: "{{ lookup('password', 'pw.txt encrypt=sha512_crypt') }}"
```

template

The `template` lookup lets you specify a Jinja2 template file, then returns the result of evaluating the template. Say we have a template that looks like Example 10-15.

Example 10-15. message.j2

```
This host runs {{ ansible_facts.distribution }}
```

If we define a task like this:

```
- name: Output message from template
  debug:
    msg: "{{ lookup('template', 'message.j2') }}"
```

then we'll see output that looks like this:

```
TASK: [Output message from template] ****************************************
ok: [web] ==> {
    "msg": "This host runs Ubuntu\n"
}
```

csvfile

The `csvfile` lookup reads an entry from a *.csv* file. Assume Lorin has a *.csv* file that looks like Example 10-16.

Example 10-16. users.csv

```
username,email
lorin,lorin@ansiblebook.com
john,john@example.com
sue,sue@example.org
```

If he wants to extract Sue's email address by using the `csvfile` lookup plug-in, he would invoke the lookup plug-in like this:

```
lookup('csvfile', 'sue file=users.csv delimiter=, col=1')
```

The `csvfile` lookup is a good example of a lookup that takes multiple arguments. Here, four arguments are being passed to the plug-in:

- sue
- file=users.csv
- delimiter=,
- col=1

You don't specify a name for the first argument to a lookup plug-in, but you do specify names for the additional arguments. In the case of `csvfile`, the first argument is an entry that must appear exactly once in column 0 (the first column, 0-indexed) of the table.

The other arguments specify the name of the *.csv* file, the delimiter, and which column should be returned. In our example, we want to do three things:

- Look in the file named *users.csv* and locate where the fields are delimited by commas.
- Look up the row where the value in the first column is sue.
- Return the value in the second column (column 1, indexed by 0). This evaluates to *sue@example.org*.

If the username we want to look up is stored in a variable named username, we could construct the argument string by using the + sign to concatenate the username string with the rest of the argument string:

```
lookup('csvfile', username + ' file=users.csv delimiter=, col=1')
```

dig

If you're reading this book, you probably know what the Domain Name System (DNS) does, but just in case you don't: DNS is the service that translates hostnames, such as *ansiblebook.com*, to IP addresses, such as *64.98.145.30*.

> The dig module requires that you install the *dnspython* Python package on the Ansible controller.

DNS works by associating one or more records with a hostname. The most common types of DNS records are *A* records and *CNAME* records, which associate a hostname with an IP address (an A record) or specify that a hostname is an alias for another hostname (a CNAME record).

The DNS protocol supports another type called a *TXT* record: an arbitrary string that you can attach to a hostname so that anybody can retrieve it by using a DNS client.

For example, Lorin owns the domain *ansiblebook.com*, so he can create TXT records associated with any hostnames in that domain.[4] He associated a TXT record with the *ansiblebook.com* hostname that contains the ISBN number for this book. You can look up the TXT record by using the dig command-line tool, as shown in Example 10-17.

---

4 DNS service providers typically have web interfaces to let you perform DNS-related tasks such as creating TXT records.

Example 10-17. Using the dig tool to look up a TXT record

```
$ dig +short ansiblebook.com TXT
"isbn=978-1098109158"
```

The dig lookup queries the DNS server for records associated with the host. We create a task in a playbook to query the TXT records:

```
- name: Look up TXT record
  debug:
    msg: "{{ lookup('dnstxt', 'ansiblebook.com', 'qtype=TXT') }}"
```

And the output will look like this:

```
TASK: [Look up TXT record] ********************************************
ok: [myserver] ==> {
    "msg": "isbn=978-1098109158"
}
```

For more information on the dig lookup plug-in:

```
$ ansible-doc -t lookup dig
```

redis

Redis is a popular key-value store, commonly used as a cache, as well as a data store for job queue services such as Sidekiq. You can use the redis lookup to retrieve the value of a list of keys. The list must be expressed as a string, as the module does the equivalent of calling the Redis GET command. This lookup is configured differently than most others because it supports looking up lists of variable length.

> The redis module requires that you install the *redis* Python package on the control machine.

For example, let's say that we have a Redis server running on our control machine. We set the key weather to the value sunny and the key temp to 25 by doing something like this:

```
$ redis-cli SET weather sunny
$ redis-cli SET temp 25
```

We define a task in our playbook that invokes the redis lookup:

```
- name: Look up values in Redis
  debug:
    msg: "{{ lookup('redis', 'weather','temp') }}"
```

The output will look like this:

```
TASK: [Look up values in Redis] ************************************************
ok: [localhost] ==> {
    "msg": "sunny,25"
}
```

The module will default to *redis://localhost:6379* if the host and port aren't specified. We should invoke the module with environment variables if we need another server for this task:

```
- name: Look up values in Redis
  environment:
    ANSIBLE_REDIS_HOST: redis1.example.com
    ANSIBLE_REDIS_PORT: 6379
  debug:
    msg: "{{ lookup('redis', 'weather','temp' ) }}"
```

You can also configure Redis in *ansible.cfg*:

```
[lookup_redis]
host: redis2.example.com
port: 6666
```

Redis can be configured as a cluster.

Writing Your Own Lookup Plug-in

You can also write your own lookup plug-in if you need functionality that is not provided by the existing plug-ins. Writing custom lookup plug-ins is out of scope for this book, but if you're really interested, we suggest that you take a look at the source code (*https://oreil.ly/DbSU4*) for the lookup plug-ins that ship with Ansible.

Once you've written your lookup plug-in, place it in one of the following directories:

- The *lookup_plugins* directory next to your playbook
- *~/.ansible/plugins/lookup*
- */usr/share/ansible/plugins/lookup*
- The directory specified in your ANSIBLE_LOOKUP_PLUGINS environment variable

More Complicated Loops

Up until this point, whenever we've written a task that iterates over a list of items, we've used the with_items clause to specify that list. Although this is the most common way to do a loop, Ansible supports other mechanisms for iteration. For instance, you can use the until keyword to retry a task until it succeeds:

```
- name: Unarchive maven
  unarchive:
    src: "{{ maven_url }}"
    dest: "{{ maven_location }}"
    copy: false
```

```
    mode: '0755'
  register: maven_download
  until: maven_download is success
  retries: 5
  delay: 3
```

The keyword `loop` is equivalent to `with_items`, and the list should be a uniform list, not a list with various data (not a mixed list with scalars, arrays, and dicts). You can do all kinds of things with `loop`! The official documentation (*https://oreil.ly/bgbdX*) covers these quite thoroughly, so we'll show examples from just a few of them to give you a sense of how they work and when to use them. Here is one from a more complicated loop:

```
- name: Iterate with loop
  debug:
    msg: "KPI: {{ item.kpi }} prio: {{ i + 1 }} goto: {{ item.dept }}"
  loop:
    - kpi: availability
      dept: operations
    - kpi: performance
      dept: development
    - kpi: security
      dept: security
  loop_control:
    index_var: i
    pause: 3
```

You can pass a list directly to most packaging modules, such as `apt`, `yum`, and `pack age`. Older playbooks might still have `with_items`, but that is no longer needed. Nowadays we use:

```
- name: Install packages
  become: true
  package:
    name: "{{ list_of_packages }}"
    state: present
```

With Lookup Plug-in

It's good to know that `with_items` relies on a lookup plug-in; `items` is just one of the lookups. Table 10-4 provides a summary of the available constructs for looping with a lookup plug-in. You can even hook up your own lookup plug-in to iterate.

Table 10-4. Looping constructs

Name	Input	Looping strategy
with_items	List	Loop over list elements
with_lines	Command to execute	Loop over lines in command output
with_fileglob	Glob	Loop over filenames
with_first_found	List of paths	First file in input that exists

Name	Input	Looping strategy
with_dict	Dictionary	Loop over dictionary elements
with_flattened	List of lists	Loop over flattened list
with_indexed_items	List	Single iteration
with_nested	List	Nested loop
with_random_choice	List	Single iteration
with_sequence	Sequence of integers	Loop over sequence
with_subelements	List of dictionaries	Nested loop
with_together	List of lists	Loop over zipped list
with_inventory_hostnames	Host pattern	Loop over matching hosts

Let's go over a few of the most important constructs.

with_lines

The with_lines looping construct lets you run an arbitrary command on your control machine and iterate over the output, one line at a time.

Imagine you have a file that has a list of names. You want your computer to pronounce their names. Imagine a file like this:

```
Ronald Linn Rivest
Adi Shamir
Leonard Max Adleman
Whitfield Diffie
Martin Hellman
```

Example 10-18 shows how to use with_lines to read a file and iterate over its contents line by line.

Example 10-18. Using with_lines as a loop

```
- name: Iterate over lines in a file
  say:
    msg: "{{ item }}"
  with_lines:
    - cat files/turing.txt
```

with_fileglob

The with_fileglob construct is useful for iterating over a set of files on the control machine.

Example 10-19 shows how to iterate over files that end in *.pub* in the */var/keys* directory, as well as a *keys* directory next to your playbook. It then uses the file lookup plug-in to extract the contents of the file, which are passed to the authorized_key module.

Example 10-19. Using `with_fileglob` to add keys

```
- name: Add public keys to account
  become: true
  authorized_key:
    user: deploy
    key: "{{ lookup('file', item) }}"
  with_fileglob:
    - /var/keys/*.pub
    - keys/*.pub
```

with_dict

The `with_dict` construct lets you iterate over a dictionary instead of a list. When you use this looping construct, each `item` loop variable is a dictionary with two properties:

key
> One of the keys in the dictionary

value
> The value in the dictionary that corresponds to *key*

For example, if our host has an `enp0s8` interface, there will be an Ansible fact named `ansible_enp0s8`. It will have a key named `ipv4` that contains a dictionary that looks something like this:

```
{
  "address": "192.168.33.10",
  "broadcast": "192.168.33.255",
  "netmask": "255.255.255.0",
  "network": "192.168.33.0"
}
```

We could iterate over this dictionary and print out the entries one at a time:

```
- name: Iterate over ansible_enp0s8
  debug:
    msg: "{{ item.key }}={{ item.value }}"
  with_dict: "{{ ansible_enp0s8.ipv4 }}"
```

The output looks like this:

```
TASK [Iterate over ansible_enp0s8] ********************************************
ok: [web] => (item={'key': 'address', 'value': '192.168.33.10'}) => {
    "msg": "address=192.168.33.10"
}
ok: [web] => (item={'key': 'broadcast', 'value': '192.168.33.255'}) => {
    "msg": "broadcast=192.168.33.255"
}
ok: [web] => (item={'key': 'netmask', 'value': '255.255.255.0'}) => {
    "msg": "netmask=255.255.255.0"
}
ok: [web] => (item={'key': 'network', 'value': '192.168.33.0'}) => {
```

```
      "msg": "network=192.168.33.0"
  }
```

Iterating over a dictionary often helps reduce the amount of code.

Looping Constructs as Lookup Plug-ins

Ansible implements looping constructs as lookup plug-ins. You just slap a `with` onto the beginning of a lookup plug-in to use it in its loop form. For example, we can rewrite Example 10-12 by using the `with_file` form in Example 10-20.

Example 10-20. Using the `file` lookup as a loop

```
- name: Add my public key for SSH
  authorized_key:
    user: vagrant
    key: "{{ item }}"
    key_options: 'from="10.0.2.2"'
    exclusive: true
  with_file: '~/.ssh/id_ed25519.pub'
```

Typically, we use a lookup plug-in as a looping construct only if it returns a list, which is how we were able to separate out the plug-ins into Table 10-3 (return strings) and Table 10-4 (return lists).

Loop Controls

Ansible provides users with more control over loop handling than most programming languages, but that does not mean you should use all the variants. Try to keep it as simple as possible.

Setting the Variable Name

The `loop_var` control allows us to give the iteration variable a different name than the default name, `item`, as shown in Example 10-21.

*Example 10-21. Use *user* as loop variable*

```
- name: Add users
  become: true
  user:
    name: "{{ user.name }}"
  with_items:
    - { name: gil }
    - { name: sarina }
    - { name: leanne }
  loop_control:
    loop_var: user
```

Although in Example 10-21 `loop_var` provides only a cosmetic improvement, it can be essential for more advanced loops.

In Example 10-22, we would like to loop over multiple tasks at once. One way to achieve that is to use `include` with `with_items`.

However, the *vhosts.yml* file that is going to be included may also contain `with_items` in some tasks. This would produce a conflict, because the default `loop_var` `item` is used for *both* loops at the same time. To prevent a naming collision, we specify a different name for `loop_var` in the outer loop.

Example 10-22. Use vhost as loop variable

```
- name: Run a set of tasks in one loop
  include: vhosts.yml
  with_items:
    - { domain: www1.example.com }
    - { domain: www2.example.com }
    - { domain: www3.example.com }
  loop_control:
    loop_var: vhost
```

In the included task file *vhosts.yml* (Example 10-23), we can now use the default `loop_var` name `item`, as we used to do.

Example 10-23. Included file can contain a loop

```
- name: Create nginx directories
  file:
    path: "/var/www/html/{{ vhost.domain }}/{{ item }}"
  state: directory
  with_items:
    - logs
    - public_http
    - public_https
    - includes

- name: Create nginx vhost config
  template:
    src: "{{ vhost.domain }}.j2"
    dest: /etc/nginx/conf.d/{{ vhost.domain }}.conf
```

We keep the default loop variable in the inner loop.

Labeling the Output

The `label` control was added in Ansible 2.2 and provides some control over how the loop output will be shown to the user during execution.

The following example contains an ordinary list of dictionaries:

```
- name: Create nginx vhost configs
  become: true
  template:
    src: "{{ item.domain }}.conf.j2"
    dest: "/etc/nginx/conf.d/{{ item.domain }}.conf"
    mode: '0640'
  with_items:
    - { domain: www1.example.com, tls_enabled: true }
    - { domain: www2.example.com, tls_enabled: false }
    - { domain: www3.example.com, tls_enabled: false,
        aliases: [ edge2.www.example.com, eu.www.example.com ] }
```

By default, Ansible prints the entire dictionary in the output. For larger dictionaries, the output can be difficult to read without a `loop_control` clause that specifies a label:

```
TASK [Create nginx vhost configs] ********************************************
changed: [web] => (item={'domain': 'www1.example.com', 'tls_enabled': True})
changed: [web] => (item={'domain': 'www2.example.com', 'tls_enabled': False})
changed: [web] => (item={'domain': 'www3.example.com', 'tls_enabled': False,
'aliases': ['edge2.www.example.com', 'eu.www.example.com']})
```

Since we are interested only in the domain names, we can simply add a `label` in the `loop_control` clause describing what should be printed when we iterate over the items:

```
- name: Create nginx vhost configs
  become: true
  template:
    src: "{{ item.domain }}.conf.j2"
    dest: "/etc/nginx/conf.d/{{ item.domain }}.conf"
    mode: '0640'
  with_items:
    - { domain: www1.example.com, tls_enabled: true }
    - { domain: www2.example.com, tls_enabled: false }
    - { domain: www3.example.com, tls_enabled: false,
        aliases: [ edge2.www.example.com, eu.www.example.com ] }
  loop_control:
    label: "for domain {{ item.domain }}"
```

This results in much more readable output:

```
TASK [Create nginx vhost configs] ********************************************
ok: [web] => (item=for domain www1.example.com)
ok: [web] => (item=for domain www2.example.com)
ok: [web] => (item=for domain www3.example.com)
```

 Keep in mind that running in verbose mode (using -v) will show the full dictionary; don't use `label` to hide your passwords from log output! Set `no_log: true` on the task instead.

Imports and Includes

The `import_*` feature allows you to include tasks, or even whole roles, in the tasks section of a play through the use of the keywords `import_tasks` and `import_role`. When *importing* files in other playbooks statically, Ansible runs the plays and tasks in each imported playbook in the order they are listed, just as if they had been defined directly in the main playbook.

The `include_*` features allow you to dynamically include tasks, vars, or even whole roles by the use of the keywords `include_tasks`, `include_vars`, and `include_role`. This is often used in roles to separate or even group tasks and task arguments to each task in the included file. Included roles and tasks may—or may not—run, depending on the results of other tasks in the playbook. When a loop is used with `include_tasks` or `include_role`, the included tasks or role will be executed once for each item in the loop.

 Please note that the bare `include` keyword is deprecated in favor of the keywords `include_tasks`, `include_vars`, and `include_role`.

Let's consider an example. Example 10-24 contains two tasks of a play that share an identical `become` argument, a `when` condition, and a `tag`.

Example 10-24. Identical arguments

```
- name: Install nginx
  become: true
  when: ansible_os_family == 'RedHat'
  package:
    name: nginx
  tags:
    - nginx

- name: Ensure nginx is running
  become: yes
  when: ansible_os_family == 'RedHat'
  service:
    name: nginx
    state: started
    enabled: yes
  tags:
    -nginx
```

When we separate these two tasks in a file as in Example 10-25 and use `include_tasks`, as in Example 10-26, we can simplify the play by adding the task arguments only to the `include_tasks`.

Example 10-25. Separate tasks into a different file

```
- name: Install nginx
  package:
    name: nginx

- name: Ensure nginx is running
  service:
    name: nginx
    state: started
    enabled: yes
```

Example 10-26. Using an include for the tasks file applying the arguments in common

```
- include_tasks: nginx_include.yml
  become: yes
  when: ansible_os_family == 'RedHat'
  tags: nginx
```

Dynamic Includes

A common pattern in roles is to define tasks specific to a particular operating system into separate task files. Depending on the number of operating systems supported by the role, this can lead to a lot of boilerplate for the `include_tasks`:

```
- include_tasks: Redhat.yml
  when: ansible_os_family == 'Redhat'

- include_tasks: Debian.yml
  when: ansible_os_family == 'Debian'
```

Since version 2.0, Ansible has allowed users to include a file dynamically by using variable substitution. This is called a *dynamic include*:

```
- name: Play platform specific actions
  include_tasks: "{{ ansible_os_family }}.yml"
```

However, there is a drawback to using dynamic includes. If Ansible does not have enough information to populate the variables that determine which file will be included, `ansible-playbook --list-tasks` might not list the tasks. For example, fact variables (see Chapter 5) are not populated when the `--list-tasks` argument is used.

Role Includes

The `include_role` clause differs from the `import_role` clause, which statically imports all parts of the role. By contrast, `include_role` allows us to select what parts of a role to include and use, as well as where in the play:

```
- name: Install nginx
  yum:
    pkg: nginx

- name: Install php
  include_role:
    name: php

- name: Configure nginx
  template:
    src: nginx.conf.j2
    dest: /etc/nginx/nginx.conf
```

> The `include_role` clause makes the handlers available as well, so you can notify about a restart, for instance.

Role Flow Control

You can use separate task files in an Ansible role's tasks directory for the separate use cases it supports. The *main.yml* tasks file will use `include_tasks` for each use case. However, the `include_role` clause can run parts of roles with `tasks_from`. Imagine that in a role dependency that runs before the main role, a file task changes the owner of a file—but the system user now designated as the owner does not yet exist. It will be created later, in the main role, during a package installation:

```
- name: Install nginx
  yum:
    pkg: nginx

- name: Install php
  include_role:
    name: php
    tasks_from: install

- name: Configure nginx
  template:
    src: nginx.conf.j2
    dest: /etc/nginx/nginx.conf

- name: Configure php
  include_role:
    name: php
    tasks_from: configure
```

1. Include and run *install.yml* from the php role.

2. Include and run *configure.yml* from the php role.

Blocks

Much like the `include_*` clauses, the `block` clause provides a mechanism for grouping tasks. It allows you to set conditions or arguments for all tasks within a block at once:

```
- block:
  - name: Install nginx
    package:
      name: nginx

  - name: Ensure nginx is running
    service:
      name: nginx
      state: started
      enabled: yes

  become: yes
  when: "ansible_os_family == 'RedHat'
```

 Unlike the `include` clause, however, looping over a `block` clause is not currently supported.

Next, let's look at an even more interesting application for the `block` clause: error handling.

Error Handling with Blocks

Dealing with error scenarios has always been a challenge. Historically, Ansible has been error-agnostic, in the sense that errors and failures may occur on a host. Ansible's default error-handling behavior is to take a host out of the play if a task fails but continue the play as long as there are hosts remaining that haven't encountered errors.

In combination with the `serial` and `max_fail_percentage` clause, Ansible gives users some control over when a play must be declared failed. With the `block` clause, as shown in Example 10-27, it advances error handling a bit further and lets us automate recovery and roll back tasks in case of a failure.

Example 10-27. app-upgrade.yml

```
- block:       ❶
    - debug: msg="You will see a failed tasks right after this"

    - name: Returns 1
      command: /usr/bin/false

    - debug: msg="You never see this message"
  rescue:      ❷
    - debug: msg="You see this message in case of failure in the block"

  always:      ❸
    - debug: msg="This will be always executed"
```

❶   block starts the construct.

❷   rescue lists tasks to be executed in case of a failure in the block clause.

❸   always lists tasks to execute either way.

If you have some programming experience, the way error handling is implemented may remind you of the try-except-finally paradigm—and it works much the same way as in this Python division function:

```
def division(x, y):
    try:
        result = x / y
    except ZeroDivisionError:
        print("division by zero!")
    else:
        print("result is", result)
    finally:
        print("executing finally clause")
```

To demonstrate how upgrades always work, René starts with a daily chore: upgrading an application. The application is distributed in a cluster of virtual machines (VMs) and deployed on an IaaS cloud (Apache CloudStack (*https://oreil.ly/zIDUh*)). Cloud-Stack provides the functionality to snapshot a VM. Simplified, the playbook looks like this:

1. Take VM out of the load balancer.

2. Create a VM snapshot before the app upgrade.

3. Upgrade the application.

4. Run smoke tests.

5. Roll back when something goes wrong.

6. Move VM back to the load balancer.

7. Clean up and remove the VM snapshot.

Let's put these tasks into a playbook (Example 10-28). Note that they are still simplified and not yet runnable.

Example 10-28. app-upgrade.yml

```
---

- hosts: app-servers
  serial: 1
  tasks:
    - name: Take VM out of the load balancer
    - name: Create a VM snapshot before the app upgrade
    - block:
        - name: Upgrade the application
        - name: Run smoke tests
      rescue:
        - name: Revert a VM to the snapshot after a failed upgrade
      always:
        - name: Re-add webserver to the loadbalancer
        - name: Remove a VM snapshot
..
```

In this playbook, we will most certainly end up with a running VM as a member of a load-balancer cluster, even if the upgrade fails. No downtime due to failure!

> The tasks under the `always` clause will be executed, even if an error occurs in the `rescue` clause! Be careful what you put in the `always` clause.

If all we want to do is get upgraded VMs back to the load-balancer cluster, the play will look a bit different (Example 10-29).

Example 10-29. app-upgrade.yml

```
---
- hosts: app-servers
  serial: 1

  tasks:

    - name: Take VM out of the load balancer

    - name: Create a VM snapshot before the app upgrade

    - block:
        - name: Upgrade the application
```

```
  - name: Run smoke tests

rescue:
  - name: Revert a VM to the snapshot after a failed upgrade

  - name: Re-add webserver to the loadbalancer
  - name: Remove a VM snapshot
...
```

In this example, we removed the `always` clause and put the two tasks at the end of the play. This ensures that the two tasks will be executed *only* if the rescue goes through. As a result, only upgraded VMs go back to the load balancer.

The final playbook is shown in full in Example 10-30.

Example 10-30. Error-agnostic application-upgrade playbook

```
---
- hosts: app-servers
  serial: 1
  tasks:

  - name: Take app server out of the load balancer
    delegate_to: localhost
    cs_loadbalancer_rule_member:
      name: balance_http
      vm: "{{ inventory_hostname_short }}"
      state: absent

  - name: Create a VM snapshot before an upgrade
    delegate_to: localhost
    cs_vmsnapshot:
      name: Snapshot before upgrade
      vm: "{{ inventory_hostname_short }}"
      snapshot_memory: true

  - block:
      - name: Upgrade the application
        script: upgrade-app.sh
      - name: Run smoke tests
        script: smoke-tests.sh
    rescue:
      - name: Revert the VM to a snapshot after a failed upgrade
        delegate_to: localhost
        cs_vmsnapshot:
          name: Snapshot before upgrade
          vm: "{{ inventory_hostname_short }}"
          state: revert

  - name: Re-add app server to the loadbalancer
    delegate_to: localhost
    cs_loadbalancer_rule_member:
      name: balance_http
      vm: "{{ inventory_hostname_short }}"
```

```
    state: present

- name: Remove a VM snapshot after successful upgrade or successful rollback
  delegate_to: localhost
  cs_vmsnapshot:
    name: Snapshot before upgrade
    vm: "{{ inventory_hostname_short }}"
    state: absent
...
```

On day two we should look into the failed VMs.

Encrypting Sensitive Data with ansible-vault

The Mezzanine playbook requires access to sensitive information, such as database and administrator passwords. We dealt with this in Chapter 6 by putting all of the sensitive information in a separate file called *secrets.yml* and making sure that we didn't check this file into our version-control repository.

Ansible provides an alternative solution: instead of keeping the *secrets.yml* file out of version control, we can commit an encrypted file. That way, even if our version-control repository is compromised, the attacker can't access to the contents of the file unless they also have the password used for the encryption.

The `ansible-vault` command-line tool allows us to create and edit an encrypted file that `ansible-playbook` will recognize and decrypt automatically, given the password.

Encryption at Rest

This tool ensures the data is encrypted at rest (i.e, on disk) only. It is your own responsibility to set `no_log: true` on tasks that use this data.

We can encrypt an existing file like this:

```
$ ansible-vault encrypt secrets.yml
```

Alternately, we can create a new encrypted file in the special directory *group_vars/all/* next to our playbook. Bas stores global variables in *group_vars/all/vars.yml* and secrets in *group_vars/all/vault* (without extension, to not confuse linters and editors).

```
$ mkdir -p group_vars/all/
$ ansible-vault create group_vars/all/vault
```

`ansible-vault` prompts for a password, and will then launch a text editor so that you can work in the file. It launches the editor specified in the $EDITOR environment variable. If that variable is not defined in your shell's profile (export EDITOR=code), it defaults to `vim`.

Example 10-31 shows an example of the contents of a file encrypted using `ansible-vault`.

Example 10-31. Partial contents of file encrypted with `ansible-vault`

```
$ANSIBLE_VAULT;1.1;AES256
38626635666338393730353966303331643566646561363838333832623138613931363835363963
36383965386264333937633861366362353261396336666640a34343761356461663531653237363 5
...
35373564313132356663363363334613637633263336653736343632324666636335653038656261646 3
35343436313638613837386661336636663832333938666532303931346434386433
```

Use the `vars_files` section of a play to reference a file encrypted with `ansible-vault` the same way you would access a regular file: you don't need to change Example 7-28 at all when you encrypt the *secrets.yml* file.

`ansible-playbook` needs to prompt us for the password of the encrypted file, or it will simply error out. Do so by using the `--ask-vault-pass` argument:

```
$ ansible-playbook --ask-vault-pass playbook.yml
```

You can also store the password in a text file and tell `ansible-playbook` its location by using the `ANSIBLE_VAULT_PASSWORD_FILE` environment variable or the `--vault-password-file` argument:

```
$ ansible-playbook playbook.yml --vault-password-file ~/password.txt
```

If the argument to `--vault-password-file` has the executable bit set, Ansible will execute it and use the contents of `standard` out as the vault password. This allows you to use a script to supply the password to Ansible.

Table 10-5 shows the available `ansible-vault` commands.

Table 10-5. `ansible-vault` commands

Command	Description
ansible-vault encrypt *file.yml*	Encrypt the plain-text *file.yml* file
ansible-vault decrypt *file.yml*	Decrypt the encrypted *file.yml* file
ansible-vault view *file.yml*	Print the contents of the encrypted *file.yml* file
ansible-vault create *file.yml*	Create a new encrypted *file.yml* file
ansible-vault edit *file.yml*	Edit an encrypted *file.yml* file
ansible-vault rekey *file.yml*	Change the password on an encrypted *file.yml* file

Multiple Vaults with Different Passwords

One password might be sufficient for a small team, but you might want to segretate concerns by having different passwords for the production environment. In version 2.4, support was introduced to have a separate vault-ID for a particular encrypted file. Such a vault identity is like the name for the specific password; for example, the vault-ID "dev" is for the development environment, and the vault-ID "prod" is for the production environment.

In *ansible.fcg* under [defaults] we create a reference for the vault-IDs and their corresponding vault password file (these files should exist):

```
[defaults]
vault_identity_list = dev@~/.vault_dev, prod@~/.vault_prod
```

When we encrypt the production variables with the vault-ID prod:

```
ansible-vault encrypt --encrypt-vault-id=prod group_vars/prod/vault
```

Then we notice the vault-ID in the header of the encrypted file:

```
$ANSIBLE_VAULT;1.2;AES256;prod
```

Conclusion

Ansible has lots of features that help everyone work with corner cases in flexible ways, whether it is handling errors, data inputs and transformation, iteration, exceptions, or sensitive data. This chapter introduced some complex features of Ansible— you might want to revisit it if you actually need them. The next chapter is more helpful for beginners.

## CHAPTER 11

Customizing Hosts, Runs, and Handlers

Sometimes Ansible's default behaviors don't quite fit your use case. In this chapter, we cover Ansible features that provide customization by controlling which hosts to run against, and how tasks and handlers are run.

Patterns for Specifying Hosts

So far, the `host` parameter in our plays has specified a single host or group, like this:

```
hosts: web
```

Instead of specifying a single host or group, though, you can also specify a *pattern*. You've already seen the `all` pattern, which will run a play against all known hosts:

```
hosts: all
```

You can specify a union of two groups with a colon; this example specifies all dev and staging machines:

```
hosts: dev:staging
```

You can specify an intersection by using a colon and ampersand. For example, to specify all of the database servers in your staging environment, you might do this:

```
hosts: staging:&database
```

Table 11-1 shows the patterns that Ansible supports. Note that the regular-expression pattern *always* starts with a tilde.

Table 11-1. Supported patterns

Action	Example usage
All hosts	`all`
All hosts	`*`
Union	`dev:staging`
Intersection	`staging:&database`
Exclusion	`dev:!queue`
Wildcard	`*.example.com`
Range of numbered servers	`web[5:10]`
Regular expression	`~web\d+\.example\.(com|org)`

Ansible supports multiple combinations of patterns:

```
hosts: dev:staging:&database:!queue
```

Limiting Which Hosts Run

A *limit* targets a playbook to a subset of all potential hosts. Use either the `-l` or the `--limit` flag, as shown in Example 11-1 with a pattern of choice.

Example 11-1. Limiting which hosts run

```
$ ansible-playbook -l <pattern> playbook.yml
```

```
$ ansible-playbook --limit <pattern> playbook.yml
```

You can use the pattern syntax to specify arbitrary combinations of hosts. For example:

```
$ ansible-playbook -l 'staging:&database' playbook.yml
```

Running a Task on the Control Machine

Sometimes you want to run a particular task on the control machine instead of on the remote host. To support this, Ansible provides the `delegate_to: localhost` clause for tasks.

In most organizations you cannot access the internet directly from servers, but you might be able to download, using a proxy, on your laptop. If so, then you can delegate downloading to your laptop:

```
- name: Download goss binary
  delegate_to: localhost
  connection: local
  become: false
  get_url:
```

```
    url: "https://oreil.ly/RuRsL"
    dest: "~/Downloads/goss"
    mode: '0755'
  ignore_errors: true
```

Bas uses `ignore_errors: true` because if this action fails, we need shadow IT[1] to get that file into the *Downloads* directory. Goss is a very comprehensive server-validation tool based on a YAML specification.

Manually Gathering Facts

If it's possible that the SSH server wasn't yet running when you started the playbook, you need to turn off explicit fact gathering; otherwise, Ansible will try to SSH to the host to gather facts before running the first tasks. Because you still need access to facts (recall that we use the `ansible_env` fact in the playbook), you can explicitly invoke the `setup` module to get Ansible to gather facts, as shown in Example 11-2.

Example 11-2. Waiting for SSH server to come up

```
---
- name: Chapter 9 playbook
  hosts: web
  gather_facts: false
  become: false
  tasks:
    - name: Wait for web ssh daemon to be running
      wait_for:
        port: 22
        host: "{{ inventory_hostname }}"
        search_regex: OpenSSH

    - name: Gather facts
      setup:
...
```

Retrieving an IP Address from the Host

In our playbook, several of the hostnames we use are derived from the IP address of the web server:

```
live_hostname: 192.168.33.10.xip.io
domains:
  - 192.168.33.10.xip.io
  - www.192.168.33.10.xip.io
```

---

1 *Shadow IT* refers to practices that people resort to when the (central) IT department limits or restricts access to code from the internet. For instance, you can uuencode binaries into Microsoft Word documents that you mail to yourself.

What if we want to use the same scheme but not hardcode the IP addresses into the variables? That way, if the IP address of the web server changes, we don't have to change our playbook.

Ansible retrieves the IP addresses of each host and stores that information in `ansible_facts`. Each network interface has an associated Ansible fact. For example, details about network interface `eth0` are stored in the `ansible_eth0` fact (see Example 11-4).

Example 11-4. ansible_eth0 fact

```
"ansible_eth0": {
    "active": true,
    "device": "eth0",
    "ipv4": {
        "address": "10.0.2.15",
        "broadcast": "10.0.2.255",
        "netmask": "255.255.255.0",
        "network": "10.0.2.0"
    },
    "ipv6": [
        {
            "address": "fe80::5054:ff:fe4d:77d3",
            "prefix": "64",
            "scope": "link"
        }
    ],
    "macaddress": "52:54:00:4d:77:d3",
    "module": "e1000",
    "mtu": 1500,
    "promisc": false,
    "speed": 1000,
    "type": "ether"
}
```

Our Vagrant box has two interfaces, `eth0` and `eth1`. The `eth0` interface is a private interface whose IP address (*10.0.2.15*) we cannot reach. The `eth1` interface is the one that has the IP address we've assigned in our Vagrantfile (*192.168.33.10*).

We can define our variables like this:

```
live_hostname: "{{ ansible_facts.eth1.ipv4.address }}.xip.io"
domains:
  - "{{ ansible_facts.eth1.ipv4.address }}.xip.io"
  - "www.{{ ansible_facts.eth1.ipv4.address }}.xip.io"
```

Running a Task on a Machine Other than the Host

Sometimes you want to run a task that's associated with a host, but you want to execute the task on a different server. You can use the `delegate_to` clause to run the task on a different host.

Two common use cases are as follows:

- Enabling host-based alerts with an alerting system, such as Nagios
- Adding a host to a load balancer, such as HAProxy

For example, imagine we want to enable Nagios alerts for all of the hosts in our web group. Assume we have an entry in our inventory named *nagios.example.com* that is running Nagios. Example 11-5 shows an example that uses `delegate_to`.

Example 11-5. Using `delegate_to` with Nagios

```
- name: Enable alerts for web servers
  hosts: web
  tasks:
    - name: enable alerts
      delegate_to: nagios.example.com
      nagios:
        action: enable_alerts
        service: web
        host: "{{ inventory_hostname }}"
```

In this example, Ansible would execute the `nagios` task on *nagios.example.com*, but the `inventory_hostname` variable referenced in the play would evaluate to the web host.

For a more detailed example that uses `delegate_to`, see the *lamp_haproxy/rolling_update.yml* example in the Ansible project's examples GitHub repo (*https://oreil.ly/XtkLO*).

Running on One Host at a Time

By default, Ansible runs each task in parallel across all hosts. Sometimes you want to run your task on one host at a time. The canonical example is when upgrading application servers that are behind a load balancer. Typically, you take the application server out of the load balancer, upgrade it, and put it back. But you don't want to take *all* of your application servers out of the load balancer, or your service will become unavailable.

You can use the `serial` clause on a play to tell Ansible to restrict the number of hosts on which a play runs. Example 11-6 removes hosts one at a time from an Amazon EC2 elastic load balancer, upgrades the system packages, and then puts them back. (We cover Amazon EC2 in more detail in Chapter 14.)

Example 11-6. Removing hosts from load balancer and upgrading packages

```
---
- name: Upgrade packages on servers behind load balancer
  hosts: myhosts
  serial: 1
  tasks:
    - name: Get the ec2 instance id and elastic load balancer id
      ec2_facts:

    - name: Take the host out of the elastic load balancer
      delegate_to: localhost
      ec2_elb:
        instance_id: "{{ ansible_ec2_instance_id }}"
        state: absent

    - name: Upgrade packages
      apt:
        update_cache: true
        upgrade: true

    - name: Put the host back in the elastic load balancer
      delegate_to: localhost
      ec2_elb:
        instance_id: "{{ ansible_ec2_instance_id }}"
        state: present
        ec2_elbs: "{{ item }}"
      with_items: ec2_elbs
...
```

In our example, we pass 1 as the argument to the `serial` clause, telling Ansible to run on only one host at a time. If we had passed 2, Ansible would have run two hosts at a time.

Normally, when a task fails, Ansible stops running tasks against the host that fails but continues to run them against other hosts. In the load-balancing scenario, you might want Ansible to fail the entire play before all hosts have failed a task. Otherwise, you might end up with no hosts left inside your load balancer (you have taken each host out of the load balancer and they all fail).

You can use a `max_fail_percentage` clause along with the `serial` clause to specify the maximum percentage of failed hosts before Ansible fails the entire play. A maximum fail percentage of 25% is shown here:

```
- name: Upgrade packages on servers behind load balancer
  hosts: myhosts
  serial: 1
  max_fail_percentage: 25
  tasks:
    # tasks go here
```

If we have four hosts behind the load balancer and one fails a task, then Ansible will keep executing the play, because this doesn't exceed the 25% threshold. However, if a second host fails a task, Ansible will fail the entire play. If you want Ansible to fail if any of the hosts fail a task, set the `max_fail_percentage` to 0.

Running on a Batch of Hosts at a Time

You can also pass `serial` a percentage value instead of a fixed number. Ansible will apply this percentage to the total number of hosts per play to determine the number of hosts per batch, as shown in Example 11-7.

Example 11-7. Using a percentage value as a `serial`

```
- name: Upgrade 50% of web servers
  hosts: myhosts
  serial: 50%
  tasks:
    # tasks go here
```

We can get even more sophisticated. For example, you might want to run the play on one host first, to verify that it works as expected, and then run it on a larger number of hosts in subsequent runs. A possible use case would be managing a large logical cluster of independent hosts: for example, 30 hosts of a content delivery network (CDN).

Since version 2.2, Ansible has let users specify a list of `serials` (number or percentage) to achieve this behavior, as shown in Example 11-8.

Example 11-8. Using a list of `serials`

```
- name: Configure CDN servers
  hosts: cdn
  serial:
    - 1
    - 30%
  tasks:
    # tasks go here
```

Ansible will restrict the number of hosts on each run to the next available `serial` item unless the end of the list has been reached or there are no hosts left. This means that the last `serial` will be kept and applied to each batch run as long as there are hosts left in the play.

In the preceding play, with 30 CDN hosts, Ansible would run against one host on the first batch run, and on each subsequent batch run it would run against at most 30% of the hosts (for instance, 1, 9, 9, 9, and 2).

Running Only Once

Sometimes you might want a task to run only once, even if there are multiple hosts. For example, perhaps you have multiple application servers running behind the load balancer and you want to run a database migration, but you need to run the migration on only one application server.

You can use the `run_once` clause to tell Ansible to run the command only once:

```
- name: Run the database migrations
  command: /opt/run_migrations
  run_once: true
```

This can be particularly useful when using `delegate_to: localhost`, if your playbook involves multiple hosts and you want to run the local task only once:

```
- name: Run the task locally, only once
  delegate_to: localhost
  command /opt/my-custom-command
  run_once: true
```

Limiting Which Tasks Run

Sometimes you don't want Ansible to run every single task in your playbook, particularly when you're first writing and debugging it. Ansible provides several command-line options that let you control which tasks run.

step

The `--step` flag has Ansible prompt you before running each task, like this:

```
$ ansible-playbook --step playbook.yml
Perform task: Install packages (y/n/c):
```

You can choose to execute the task (y), skip it (n), or continue running the rest of the playbook without Ansible prompting you (c).

start-at-task

The `--start-at-task taskname` flag tells Ansible to start running the playbook at the specified task, instead of at the beginning. This can be handy if one of your tasks fails because of a bug and you want to rerun your playbook starting at the task you just fixed.

Running Tags

Ansible allows you to add one or more tags to a task, a role, or a play. Use the `-t tagnames` or `--tags tag1,tag2` flag to tell Ansible to run only plays, roles, and tasks that have certain tags (Example 11-9).

Example 11-9. Tagging tasks

```
---
- name: Strategies
  hosts: strategies
  connection: local
  gather_facts: false

  tasks:

    - name: First task
      command: sleep "{{ sleep_seconds }}"
      changed_when: false
      tags:
        - first

    - name: Second task
      command: sleep "{{ sleep_seconds }}"
      changed_when: false
      tags:
        - second

    - name: Third task
      command: sleep "{{ sleep_seconds }}"
      changed_when: false
      tags:
        - third
...
```

When we run this playbook with the argument `--tags first`, the output looks as in Example 11-10.

Example 11-10. Run only the first tag

```
$ ./playbook.yml --tags first
PLAY [Strategies] *************************************************************
PLAY [Strategies] *************************************************************
TASK [First task] *************************************************************
ok: [one]
ok: [two]
ok: [three]
PLAY RECAP *******************************************************************
one    : ok=1  changed=0  unreachable=0  failed=0  skipped=0  rescued=0  ignored=0
three  : ok=1  changed=0  unreachable=0  failed=0  skipped=0  rescued=0  ignored=0
two    : ok=1  changed=0  unreachable=0  failed=0  skipped=0  rescued=0  ignored=0
```

"Tagging all the things" is one way to get granular control over your playbooks.

Skipping Tags

Use the `--skip-tags tagnames` flag to tell Ansible to skip plays, roles, and tasks that have certain tags.

Running Strategies

The `strategy` clause on a play level gives you additional control over how Ansible behaves per task for all hosts.

The default behavior we are already familiar with is the `linear` strategy, in which Ansible executes one task on all hosts and waits until it has completed (or failed) on all hosts before executing the next task on all hosts. As a result, a task takes as much time as the slowest host takes to complete the task.

Let's create a play to demonstrate the `strategy` feature (Example 11-9). We create a minimalistic `hosts` file (Example 11-11), which contains three hosts, each containing the variable `sleep_seconds` with a different value in seconds.

Example 11-11. Inventory group with three hosts having a different value for
`sleep_seconds`

```
[strategies]
one    sleep_seconds=1
two    sleep_seconds=6
three  sleep_seconds=10
```

Linear

The playbook in Example 11-12, which we execute locally by using `connection: local`, has a play with three identical tasks. In each task, we execute `sleep` with the time specified in `sleep_seconds`.

Example 11-12. Playbook in `linear` strategy

```
---
- name: Strategies
  hosts: strategies
  connection: local
  gather_facts: false

  tasks:

    - name: First task
      command: sleep "{{ sleep_seconds }}"
      changed_when: false

    - name: Second task
```

```
    command: sleep "{{ sleep_seconds }}"
    changed_when: false

  - name: Third task
    command: sleep "{{ sleep_seconds }}"
    changed_when: false
...
```

Running the playbook in the default `strategy` as `linear` results in the output shown in Example 11-13.

Example 11-13. Result of the `linear` strategy run

```
$ ./playbook.yml -l strategies
PLAY [Strategies] ************************************************************
TASK [First task] ***********************************************************
Sunday 08 August 2021  16:35:43 +0200 (0:00:00.016)      0:00:00.016 *********
ok: [one]
ok: [two]
ok: [three]
TASK [Second task] **********************************************************
Sunday 08 August 2021  16:35:54 +0200 (0:00:10.357)      0:00:10.373 *********
ok: [one]
ok: [two]
ok: [three]
TASK [Third task] ***********************************************************
Sunday 08 August 2021  16:36:04 +0200 (0:00:10.254)      0:00:20.628 *********
ok: [one]
ok: [two]
ok: [three]
PLAY RECAP ******************************************************************
one    : ok=3  changed=0  unreachable=0  failed=0  skipped=0  rescued=0  ignored=0
three  : ok=3  changed=0  unreachable=0  failed=0  skipped=0  rescued=0  ignored=0
two    : ok=3  changed=0  unreachable=0  failed=0  skipped=0  rescued=0  ignored=0
Sunday 08 August 2021  16:36:14 +0200 (0:00:10.256)      0:00:30.884 *********
===========================================================================
First task ------------------------------------------------------- 10.36s
Third task ------------------------------------------------------- 10.26s
Second task ------------------------------------------------------ 10.25s
```

We get the familiar ordered output. Note the identical order of task results: host `one` is always the quickest (as it sleeps the least) and host `three` is the slowest (as it sleeps the most).

Free

Another strategy available in Ansible is the `free` strategy. In contrast to `linear`, Ansible will not wait for results of the task to execute on all hosts. Instead, if a host completes one task, Ansible will execute the next task on that host.

Depending on the hardware resources and network latency, one host may have executed the tasks faster than other hosts located at the end of the world. As a result, some hosts will already be configured, while others are still in the middle of the play.

If we change the playbook to the free strategy, the output changes (Example 11-14).

Example 11-14. Playbook in free strategy

```
---
- name: Strategies
  hosts: strategies
  connection: local
  strategy: free
  gather_facts: false

  tasks:

    - name: First task
      command: sleep "{{ sleep_seconds }}"
      changed_when: false

    - name: Second task
      command: sleep "{{ sleep_seconds }}"
      changed_when: false

    - name: Third task
      command: sleep "{{ sleep_seconds }}"
      changed_when: false
...
```

Note that we changed the strategy to free on the third line of this play. As the output in Example 11-15 shows, host one is already finished before host three has even finished its first task.

Example 11-15. Results of running the playbook with the free strategy

```
$ ./playbook.yml -l strategies
PLAY [Strategies] ************************************************************
Sunday 08 August 2021  16:40:35 +0200 (0:00:00.020)       0:00:00.020 ********
Sunday 08 August 2021  16:40:35 +0200 (0:00:00.008)       0:00:00.028 ********
Sunday 08 August 2021  16:40:35 +0200 (0:00:00.006)       0:00:00.035 ********
TASK [First task] ***********************************************************
ok: [one]
Sunday 08 August 2021  16:40:37 +0200 (0:00:01.342)       0:00:01.377 ********
TASK [Second task] **********************************************************
ok: [one]
Sunday 08 August 2021  16:40:38 +0200 (0:00:01.225)       0:00:02.603 ********
TASK [Third task] ***********************************************************
ok: [one]
TASK [First task] ***********************************************************
ok: [two]
Sunday 08 August 2021  16:40:42 +0200 (0:00:03.769)       0:00:06.372 ********
```

```
ok: [three]
Sunday 08 August 2021  16:40:46 +0200 (0:00:04.004)        0:00:10.377 *********
TASK [Second task] ************************************************************
ok: [two]
Sunday 08 August 2021  16:40:48 +0200 (0:00:02.229)        0:00:12.606 *********
TASK [Third task] *************************************************************
ok: [two]
TASK [Second task] ************************************************************
ok: [three]
Sunday 08 August 2021  16:40:56 +0200 (0:00:07.998)        0:00:20.604 *********
TASK [Third task] *************************************************************
ok: [three]
PLAY RECAP ********************************************************************
one    : ok=3  changed=0  unreachable=0  failed=0  skipped=0  rescued=0  ignored=0
three  : ok=3  changed=0  unreachable=0  failed=0  skipped=0  rescued=0  ignored=0
two    : ok=3  changed=0  unreachable=0  failed=0  skipped=0  rescued=0  ignored=0
Sunday 08 August 2021  16:41:06 +0200 (0:00:10.236)        0:00:30.841 *********
===============================================================================
Third task --------------------------------------------------------- 10.24s
Second task -------------------------------------------------------- 2.23s
First task --------------------------------------------------------- 1.34s
```

To add timing information to the logging, we added a line to the *ansible.cfg* file (callbacks are discussed in the next chapter):

```
callback_whitelist = profile_tasks  ;
```

`callback_whitelist` will be normalized to `callback_enabled`.

Like many core parts in Ansible, `strategy` is implemented as a new type of plug-in.

Advanced Handlers

When Ansible's default behavior for handlers doesn't quite fit your particular use case, you can gain tighter control over when your handlers fire. This subsection describes how.

Handlers in Pre- and Post-Tasks

When we covered handlers, you learned that they are usually executed after all tasks once, and only when they get notified. But keep in mind there are not only `tasks` but `pre_tasks` and `post_tasks`.

Each `tasks` section in a playbook is handled separately; any handler notified in `pre_tasks`, `tasks`, or `post_tasks` is executed at the end of each section. As a result, it is possible to execute one handler several times in one play, as shown in Example 11-16.

Example 11-16. handlers.yml

```
---
- name: Chapter 9 advanced handlers
  hosts: localhost

  handlers:
    - name: Print message
      command: echo handler executed

  pre_tasks:
    - name: Echo pre tasks
      command: echo pre tasks
      notify: Print message

  tasks:
    - name: Echo tasks
      command: echo tasks
      notify: Print message

  post_tasks:
    - name: Post tasks
      command: echo post tasks
      notify: Print message
```

When we run the playbook, we see the results in Example 11-17.

Example 11-17. handlers.yml output

```
$ ./handlers.yml
PLAY [Chapter 9 advanced handlers] *****************************************
TASK [Gathering Facts] ****************************************************
ok: [localhost]
TASK [Echo pre tasks] ****************************************************
changed: [localhost]
RUNNING HANDLER [Print message] ******************************************
changed: [localhost]
TASK [Echo tasks] ********************************************************
changed: [localhost]
RUNNING HANDLER [Print message] ******************************************
changed: [localhost]
TASK [Post tasks] ********************************************************
changed: [localhost]
RUNNING HANDLER [Print message] ******************************************
changed: [localhost]
PLAY RECAP ***************************************************************
localhost : ok=7  changed=6  unreachable=0  failed=0  skipped=0  rescued=0  ignored=0
```

In a play there are more sections to notify handlers.

Flush Handlers

You may be wondering why we wrote that handlers *usually* execute after all tasks. We say *usually* because this is the default. However, Ansible lets us control the execution point of the handlers with the help of a special module called `meta`.

In Example 11-18, we see a part of a play in which we use `meta` with `flush_handlers` in the middle of the tasks. We do this for a reason: we want to run a *smoke test* and validate a health check URL, returning OK if the application is in a healthy state. But validating the healthy state before the services restart would not make sense.

Example 11-18. Smoke test for the home page

```
- name: Install home page
  template:
    src: index.html.j2
    dest: /usr/share/nginx/html/index.html
    mode: '0644'
  notify: Restart nginx

- name: Restart nginx
  meta: flush_handlers

- name: "Test it! https://localhost:8443/index.html"
  delegate_to: localhost
  become: false
  uri:
    url: 'https://localhost:8443/index.html'
    validate_certs: false
    return_content: true
  register: this
  failed_when: "'Running on ' not in this.content"
  tags:
    - test
```

With `flush_handlers` we force notified handlers to run in the middle of this play.

Meta Commands

Meta commands can influence Ansible's internal execution or state; they can be used anywhere in your playbook. One example is the command `flush_handlers` that we just discussed, another is `refresh_inventory` to reload the inventory (ensure it's not cached). `clear_facts` and `clear_host_errors` are options not often needed. If you need more flow control `meta` offers:

- `end_batch` ends the current batch when using `serial`
- `end_host` ends tasks for the current host without failing
- `end_play` ends the play without failure

Handlers Notifying Handlers

In the handlers file of the role *roles/nginx/tasks/main.yml* we run a configuration check before reloading the configuration of restarting NGINX (Example 11-19). This prevents downtime when the new configuration is incorrect.

Example 11-19. Checking the configuration before the service restarts

```
---
- name: Restart nginx
  debug:
    msg: "checking config first"
  changed_when: true
  notify:
    - Check nginx configuration
    - Restart nginx - after config check

- name: Reload nginx
  debug:
    msg: "checking config first"
  changed_when: true
  notify:
    - Check nginx configuration
    - Reload nginx - after config check

- name: Check nginx configuration
  command: "nginx -t"
  register: result
  changed_when: "result.rc != 0"
  check_mode: false

- name: Restart nginx - after config check
  service:
    name: nginx
    state: restarted

- name: Reload nginx - after config check
  service:
    name: nginx
    state: reloaded
```

You can notify a list of handlers; they will execute in the order of the list.

Handlers Listen

Before Ansible 2.2, there was only one way to notify a handler: by calling notify on the handler's name. This is simple and works well for most use cases.

Before we go into detail about how the handler's listen feature can simplify your playbooks and roles, take a look at Example 11-20.

Example 11-20. `listen` feature for handlers

```
---
- hosts: mailservers
  tasks:

    - name: Copy postfix config file
      copy:
        src: main.conf
        dest: /etc/postfix/main.cnf
        mode: '0640'
      notify: Postfix config changed

  handlers:
    - name: Restart postfix
      service:
        name: postfix
        state: restarted
      listen: Postfix config changed
...
```

The `listen` clause defines what we'll call an *event*, on which one or more handlers can listen. This decouples the task notification key from the handler's name. To notify more handlers of the same event, we just let them listen; they will also get notified.

 The scope of all handlers is on the play level. We cannot notify across plays, with or without handlers listening.

The SSL Case for the listen Feature

The real benefit of the `listen` feature for handlers is related to roles and role dependencies. One of the most obvious use cases we have come across is managing SSL certificates for different services.

Because developers use SSL heavily in our hosts and across projects, it makes sense to make an `ssl` role. It is a simple role whose only purpose is to copy our SSL certificates and keys to the remote host. It does this in a few tasks, as in *roles/ssl/tasks/main.yml* in Example 11-21, and it is prepared to run on Red Hat–based Linux operating systems because it has the appropriate paths set in the variables file *roles/ssl/vars/RedHat.yml* (Example 11-22).

Example 11-21. Role tasks in the `ssl` role

```
---

- name: Include OS specific variables
  include_vars: "{{ ansible_os_family }}.yml"

- name: Copy SSL certs
  copy:
    src: "{{ item }}"
    dest: {{ ssl_certs_path }}/
    owner: root
    group: root
    mode: '0644'
  loop: "{{ ssl_certs }}"

- name: Copy SSL keys
  copy:
    src: "{{ item }}"
    dest: "{{ ssl_keys_path }}/"
    owner: root
    group: root
    mode: '0640'
  with_items: "{{ ssl_keys }}"
  no_log: true
...
```

Example 11-22. Variables for Red Hat–based systems

```
---
ssl_certs_path: /etc/pki/tls/certs
ssl_keys_path: /etc/pki/tls/private
...
```

In the definition of the role defaults in Example 11-23, we have empty lists of SSL certificates and keys, so no certificates and keys will be handled. We have options for overwriting these defaults to make the role copy the files.

Example 11-23. Defaults of the `ssl` role

```
---
ssl_certs: []
ssl_keys: []
...
```

At this point, we can use the `ssl` role in other roles as a *dependency*, just as we do in Example 11-24 for an `nginx` role by modifying the file *roles/nginx/meta/main.yml*. Every role dependency will run before the parent role. This means in our case that the `ssl` role tasks will be executed before the `nginx` role tasks. As a result, the SSL certificates and keys are already in place and usable within the nginx role (that is, in the *vhost* config).

Example 11-24. The nginx role depends on ssl

```
---
dependencies:
  - role: ssl
...
```

Logically, the dependency would be one way: the nginx role depends on the ssl role, as shown in Figure 11-1.

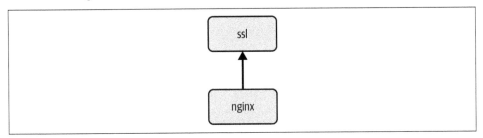

Figure 11-1. One-way dependency

Our nginx role would, of course, handle all aspects of the NGINX web server. This role has tasks in *roles/nginx/tasks/main.yml* for templating the NGINX config and restarting the NGINX service by notifying the appropriate handler by its name (Example 11-25).

Example 11-25. Tasks in the nginx role

```
- name: Configure nginx
  template:
    src: nginx.conf.j2
    dest: /etc/nginx/nginx.conf
  notify: Restart nginx
```

The last line notifies the handler to restart the NGINX web server.

As you would expect, the corresponding handler for the nginx role in *roles/nginx/handlers/main.yml* looks like Example 11-26.

Example 11-26. Handlers in the nginx role

```
- name: Restart nginx
  service:
    name: nginx
    state: restarted
```

That's it, right?

Not quite. The SSL certificates need to be replaced occasionally. And when that happens, every service consuming an SSL certificate must be restarted to make use of the new certificate.

So how should we do that? Notify to `restart nginx` in the `ssl` role, I hear you say? OK, let's try it.

We edit *roles/ssl/tasks/main.yml* of our `ssl` role to append the `notify` clause for restarting NGINX to the tasks of copying the certificates and keys (Example 11-27).

Example 11-27. Append `notify` to the tasks to restart NGINX

```
---

- name: Include OS specific variables
  include_vars: "{{ ansible_os_family }}.yml"

- name: Copy SSL certs
  copy:
    src: "{{ item }}"
    dest: {{ ssl_certs_path }}/
    owner: root
    group: root
    mode: '0644'
  with_items: "{{ ssl_certs }}"
  notify: Restart nginx

- name: Copy SSL keys
  copy:
    src: "{{ item }}"
    dest: "{{ ssl_keys_path }}/"
    owner: root
    group: root
    mode: '0644'
  with_items: "{{ ssl_keys }}"
  no_log: true
  notify: Restart nginx
...
```

Great, that works. But wait! We've just added a new dependency to our `ssl` role: the `nginx` role (Figure 11-2).

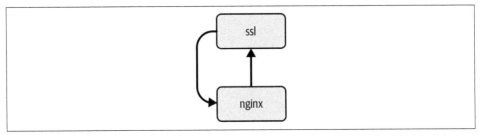

Figure 11-2. The `nginx` *role depends on the* `ssl` *role, and the* `ssl` *role depends on the* `nginx` *role*

What are the consequences of this? If we use the `ssl` role for other roles as a dependency the way we use it for `nginx` (that is, for `postfix`, `dovecot`, or `ldap`, to name just a few possibilities), Ansible will complain about notifying an undefined handler, because `restart nginx` will not be defined within these roles.

 Ansible version 1.9 complained about notifying undefined handlers. This behavior was seen as a regression bug and reimplemented in version 2.2. However, you can configure it in *ansible.cfg* with `error_on_missing_handler`. The default is `error_on_miss ing_handler = True`.

What's more, we would need to add more handler names to be notified for every additional role where we use the `ssl` role as a dependency. This simply wouldn't scale well.

This is where `listen` comes into the game! Instead of notifying a handler's name in the `ssl` role, we notify an *event*—for example, `ssl_certs_changed`, as in Example 11-28.

Example 11-28. Notify an event to `listen` *in handlers*

```
---
- name: Include OS specific variables
  include_vars: "{{ ansible_os_family }}.yml"

- name: Copy SSL certs
  copy:
    src: "{{ item }}"
    dest: "{{ ssl_certs_path }}/"
    owner: root
    group: root
    mode: '0644'
  with_items: "{{ ssl_certs }}"
  notify: ssl_certs_changed
```

```
- name: Copy SSL keys
  copy:
    src: "{{ item }}"
    dest: "{{ ssl_keys_path }}/"
    owner: root
    group: root
    mode: '0644'
  with_items: "{{ ssl_keys }}"
  no_log: true
  notify: ssl_certs_changed
...
```

Ansible will still complain about notifying an undefined handler, but making it happy again is as simple as adding a no-op handler to the ssl role (Example 11-29).

Example 11-29. Add a no-op handler to the ssl role to listen to the event

```
---
- name: SSL certs changed
  debug:
    msg: SSL changed event triggered
  listen: ssl_certs_changed
...
```

Back to our nginx role, where we want to react to the ssl_certs_changed event and restart the NGINX service when a certificate has been replaced. Because we already have an appropriate handler that does the job, we simply append the listen clause to the corresponding handler, as in Example 11-30.

Example 11-30. Append the listen clause to the existing handler in the nginx role

```
---
- name: restart nginx
  debug:
    msg: "checking config first"
  changed_when: true
  notify:
    - check nginx configuration
    - restart nginx - after config check
  listen: Ssl_certs_changed
...
```

Let's look back to our dependency graph (Figure 11-3). Things looks a bit different. We restored the one-way dependency and can reuse the ssl role in other roles, just as we use it in the nginx role.

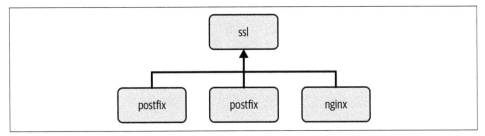

Figure 11-3. Use the ssl role in other roles

Role creators on Ansible Galaxy should consider using the listen feature and event notifications in Ansible roles where it makes sense.

Conclusion

Well, you made it! By now you know how Ansible basically works. The rest of the book is dedicated to specific use cases for Ansible, and ways to extend and secure IT automation.

## CHAPTER 12

Managing Windows Hosts

Ansible is sometimes called "SSH configuration management on steroids." Historically, Ansible has had a strong association with Unix and Linux, and we saw evidence of this in things like variable naming (`ansible_ssh_host`, `ansible_ssh_connection`, and `sudo`, for example). However, Ansible has had built-in support for various connection mechanisms since its early days.

Supporting unfamiliar operating systems—as Windows is to Linux—was a matter of not only figuring out how to connect to Windows but also making internal naming more operating-system generic (e.g., renaming variables `ansible_ssh_host` to `ansible_host`, and `sudo` to `become`).

Windows module contributions have lagged a bit compared to the Linux community's contributions. If you are interested in using Ansible to manage Windows systems, follow the blog posts (*https://oreil.ly/s3zeS*) of Jordan Borean, the Windows specialist on the Ansible Core team. He created the VirtualBox image we'll use in this chapter.

Connection to Windows

To add Windows support, Ansible did not depart from its path by adding an agent on Windows—and in our opinion, this was a great decision. Introducing a new agent that listens on the network would introduce a new attack surface. Instead, Ansible uses the integrated Windows Remote Management (WinRM) functionality, a SOAP-based protocol over HTTPS created by Microsoft.

WinRM is the first dependency, and you should install the WinRM Python library in a virtualenv on the control host (authentication to Active Directory requires Kerberos):

```
$ python3 -mvenv py3
source py3/bin/activate
```

```
pip3 install --upgrade pip
pip3 install wheel
pip3 install pywinrm[kerberos]
```

By default, Ansible will try to connect by SSH to a remote machine, which is why we must tell it in advance to change the connection mechanism. Usually, the idea here is to put all Windows hosts into an inventory group. The particular group name you choose doesn't matter, but we use the same group names for development and production in separate inventory files, while development uses the *vagrant.ini* file that defines the Vagrant/VirtualBox development environment described in this chapter:

```
[windows]
windows2022 ansible_host=127.0.0.1
```

We then add the connection variables to the inventory file (hosts). If you have more environments, it makes sense to set connection variables in a particular inventory because security requirements, like certificate validation, might differ:

```
[windows:vars]
ansible_user=vagrant
ansible_password=vagrant
ansible_connection=winrm
ansible_port=45986
ansible_winrm_server_cert_validation=ignore
ansible_winrm_scheme=https
ansible_become_method=runas
ansible_become_user=SYSTEM
```

The SOAP-based protocol relies on HTTP in this case. By default, Ansible attempts to set up a secured HTTP (HTTPS) connection on port 5986 unless the `ansible_port` is configured to 5985.

PowerShell

PowerShell on Microsoft Windows is a powerful command-line interface and scripting language built on top of the .NET framework. It supplies full management access from the local environment and through remote access. Ansible modules for Windows are all written in PowerShell as PowerShell scripts.

 In 2016, Microsoft made PowerShell open source under the MIT license. The source and binary packages for recent versions of macOS, Ubuntu, and CentOS are available on GitHub (*https:// oreil.ly/PbQOt*). As of early 2022, the stable version of PowerShell is 7.1.3.

Ansible expects at least PowerShell version 3 to be present on the remote machine. PowerShell 3 is available for Microsoft Windows 7 SP1, Microsoft Windows Server

2008 SP1, and later versions of these. To see the version of PowerShell you have installed, run the following command in a PowerShell console:

```
$PSVersionTable
```

You should see output that looks like Figure 12-1.

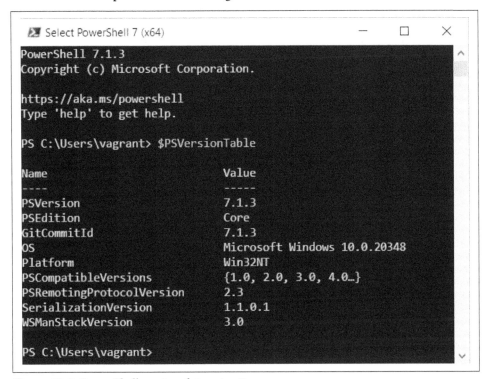

Figure 12-1. PowerShell version determination

The control machine, from which we run Ansible, is not required to have PowerShell installed!

However, there were bugs in version 3; use the latest patches from Microsoft if you must stick with version 3 for any reason. To simplify the process of installation, upgrade, setup, and configuring PowerShell for Windows, Ansible provides a script (*https://oreil.ly/shpIC*). For development purposes this is fine, but for production you will need to improve its security.

To get started on your own Windows machine, run the code in Example 12-1 in PowerShell, and you are ready to go. The script won't break anything if you run it multiple times. You *don't* need to run the script if you are using the example source code that comes with this chapter.

Example 12-1. Setting up Windows for Ansible

```
[Net.ServicePointManager]::SecurityProtocol = [Net.SecurityProtocolType]::Tls12
$url = "https://gist.github.com/bbaassssiiee/9b4b4156cba717548650b0e115344337"
$file = "$env:temp\ConfigureRemotingForAnsible.ps1"
(New-Object -TypeName System.Net.WebClient).DownloadFile($url, $file)
powershell.exe -ExecutionPolicy ByPass -File $file
```

To test the connection configuration, try a simple ping via win_ping to the Windows host. Like the Ansible ping on Linux, this is not an ICMP ping; it is a test for establishing an Ansible connection:

```
$ ansible windows -i inventory -m win_ping
```

If you get an error like the one in Example 12-2, you must either get a valid public TLS/SSL certificate or add a trust chain for an existing internal certificate authority.

Example 12-2. Error resulting from an invalid certificate

```
$ ansible windows -i inventory -m win_ping
windows2022 | UNREACHABLE! => {
  "changed": false,
  "msg": "ssl: HTTPSConnectionPool(host='127.0.0.1', port=45986): Max
retries exceeded with url: /wsman (Caused by
SSLError(SSLCertVerificationError(1, '[SSL: CERTIFICATE_VERIFY_FAILED]
certificate verify failed: self signed certificate (_ssl.c:1131)')))",
  "unreachable": true
}
```

To disable TLS/SSL certificate validation (at your own risk), use:

```
ansible_winrm_server_cert_validation: ignore
```

If you see output that looks like Example 12-3, you have successfully tested the connection.

Example 12-3. Result of a working connection

```
$ ansible -m win_ping -i hosts windows
windows2022 | SUCCESS => {
    "changed": false,
    "ping": "pong"
}
```

The online documentation has more information about connecting with WinRM (*https://oreil.ly/ghlAM*).

Windows Modules

With Ansible's native Windows support out of the box, you can:

- Gather facts on Windows hosts
- Install and uninstall MSIs
- Enable and disable Windows features
- Start, stop, and manage Windows services
- Create and manage local users and groups
- Manage Windows packages via the Chocolatey package manager
- Manage and install Windows updates
- Fetch files from remote sites
- Push and execute any PowerShell scripts you write

Modules for Windows are prefixed with win_, except for the setup module, which works both on Linux and Windows. Here is a simple example to create a directory:

```
- name: Manage tools directory
  win_file:
    path: 'C:/Tools'
    state: directory
```

The online documentation (*https://oreil.ly/bgg0u*) lists common use cases for managing Windows with Ansible.

Our Java Development Machine

Now that we have a Windows machine, let's create a playbook to show the usage of Windows modules. The machine will be provisioned with software for Java programming: not the latest version, but you'll get the idea. Chocolatey is an open source package manager for Windows. Its choco command can install and update many packages, made available online (*https://chocolatey.org*). The Ansible module win_chocolatey can be used in a comparable way as the package module on Linux, except that it is also capable of installing Chocolatey on the Windows machine if it is not present:

```
- name: Use Chocolatey
  win_chocolatey:
    name: "chocolatey"
    state: present
```

Let's create a simple playbook, shown in Example 12-4, in which we install software and do some configuration.

Example 12-4. Playbook for Windows

```yaml
---
- name: Setup machine for Java development
  hosts: windows
  gather_facts: false
  vars:
  pre_tasks:
    - name: Verifying connectivity
      win_ping:
  roles:
    - role: win_config
      tags: config
    - role: win_choco
      tags: choco
    - role: win_vscode
      tags: vscode
    - role: java_developer
      tags: java
    - role: win_updates
      tags: updates
...
```

The playbook in Example 12-4 doesn't look much different from what we would have implemented for Linux.

> It is a widespread practice to create roles for several operating systems. The *tasks/main.yml* file of such a role looks like this:
>
> ```yaml
> ---
> # multi-platform tasks file
> - name: install software on Linux
>   include_tasks: linux.yml
>   when:
>     - ansible_facts.os_family != 'Windows'
>     - ansible_facts.os_family != 'Darwin'
>   tags:
>     - linux
>
> - name: install software on MacOS
>   include_tasks: macos.yml
>   when:
>     - ansible_facts.os_family == 'Darwin'
>   tags:
>     - mac
>
> - name: install software on Windows
>   include_tasks: windows.yml
>   when: ansible_facts.os_family == 'Windows'
>   tags:
>     - windows
> ...
> ```

Adding a Local User

In this part of the chapter, we are going to create a user and a group on Windows. You might think that this is a solved problem: just use Microsoft Active Directory, right? However, being able to run Windows anywhere in the cloud without relying on a directory service can be helpful for some use cases.

In Example 12-5, we are going to create a group named `developers` and a user, just to show the modules. In a more production-like Ansible project, the users and groups would be defined in `group_vars` with dictionaries to loop over, and the password would be an encrypted variable, but for better readability we'll keep this quite simple.

Example 12-5. Manage local groups and users on Windows

```
- name: Ensure group developers
  win_group:
    name: developers

- name: Ensure ansible user exists
  win_user:
    name: ansible
    password: '%4UJ[nLbQz*:BJ%9gV|x'
    groups: developers
    password_expired: true
    groups_action: add
```

Note that the `password_expired` parameter is set to `true`. This means that the user needs to define a new password next time they log on.

The `win_user`'s default behavior of groups is `replace`: the user will be removed from any other group they are already a member of. We change the default to `add` to prevent any removal. However, we can overwrite the behavior per user.

Windows Features

Windows has features that you can disable or enable. Run `Get-WindowsFeature` in PowerShell to get the full list and make a list of the ones you want to remove named `windows_features_remove`:

```
    - name: Manage Features
      win_feature:
        name: "{{ item }}"
        state: absent
      loop: "{{ windows_features_remove }}"

    - name: Manage IIS Web-Server with sub features and management tools
      win_feature:
        name: Web-Server
        state: present
```

```
    include_sub_features: true
    include_management_tools: true
  register: win_iis_feature

- name: Reboot if installing Web-Server feature requires it
  win_reboot:
  when: win_iis_feature.reboot_required
```

Windows reboots are often needed; `win_feature` has a return value for that.

Installing Software with Chocolatey

To ensure that we can maintain the installed software, we'll create two lists. Once that is done, we can use this *tasks/main.yml* file in a role:

```
- name: Use Chocolatey
  win_chocolatey:
    name: "chocolatey"
    state: present

- name: Ensure absense of some packages
  win_chocolatey:
    name: "{{ uninstall_choco_packages }}"
    state: absent
    force: true

- name: Ensure other packages are present
  win_chocolatey:
    name: "{{ install_choco_packages }}"
    state: present
```

For smaller packages this works fine, but sometimes the internet does not work as we wish. To make the installation of Visual Studio Code more robust, we've added a `win_stat` check and `retries`:

```
- name: Check for vscode
  win_stat:
    path: 'C:\Program Files\Microsoft VS Code\Code.exe'
  register: vscode

- name: Install VSCode
  when: not vscode.stat.exists|bool
  win_chocolatey:
    name: "{{ vscode_distribution }}"
    state: present
  register: download_vscode
  until: download_vscode is succeeded
  retries: 10
  delay: 2

- name: Install vscode extensions
  win_chocolatey:
    name: "{{ item }}"
    state: present
```

```
    with_items: "{{ vscode_extensions }}"
    retries: 10
    delay: 2
```

Configuration of Java

It is by now clear that you can use Chocolatey to install software, but in the case of good old Java 8, we need to configure a bit more:

```
- name: Install Java8
  win_chocolatey:
    name: "{{ jdk_package }}"
    state: present

- name: Set Java_home
  win_environment:
    state: present
    name: JAVA_HOME
    value: "{{ win_java_home }}"
    level: machine

- name: Add Java to path
  win_path:
    elements:
      - "{{ win_java_path }}"
```

The takeaway here is that you can configure environment variables on Windows as well as the PATH.

Updating Windows

One of an administrator's daily hassles is installing software security updates. It is one of these tasks no administrator really likes—it's important and necessary, but boring. It can also cause a lot of trouble if the update goes wrong. Therefore, we recommend you disable automated installation of security updates in your operating system settings and test updates before you run them in production environments.

Ansible helps to automate software installation with simple tasks, as shown in Example 12-6. The machine also reboots afterward if necessary. Finally, it informs all users to log out before the system goes down.

Example 12-6. Windows updates

```
- name: Install critical and security updates
  win_updates:
    category_names:
      - CriticalUpdates
      - SecurityUpdates
    state: installed
  register: update_result
```

```
- name: Reboot if required
  win_reboot:
    when: update_result.reboot_required
```

Ansible makes managing Microsoft Windows hosts almost as simple as managing Linux and Unix.

Conclusion

Microsoft's WinRM works well, even though its execution speed is not as fast as with SSH. The Ansible modules for Windows are very usable and not divergent from the other modules. The community around them is still small. Nevertheless, Ansible is the simplest tool for orchestrating IT across operating systems.

## CHAPTER 13

Ansible and Containers

The Docker project has taken the IT world by storm since it was introduced in 2013. We can't think of another technology that was so quickly embraced by the community. This chapter covers how Ansible relates to container images.

What Is a Container?

In hardware virtualization, a program called the *hypervisor* virtualizes an entire physical machine, including a virtualized CPU, memory, and devices such as disks and network interfaces. Because the entire machine is virtualized, hardware virtualization is flexible. You can run an entirely different operating system in the guest computer than in the host computer (for example, a Windows Server 2016 guest inside a Red Hat Enterprise Linux host), and you can suspend and resume a virtual machine just as you can a physical machine. This flexibility brings with it extra overhead needed to virtualize the hardware.

Containers are sometimes referred to as *operating system virtualization* to distinguish them from *hardware virtualization* technologies. With operating system virtualization (containers), the guest processes are isolated from the host by the operating system. The guest processes run on the same kernel as the host. The host operating system ensures that the guest processes are fully isolated from the host.

Containerization is a form of virtualization. When you use virtualization to run processes in a guest operating system, these guest processes have no visibility into the host operating system that runs on the physical hardware. Guest processes cannot access physical resources directly, even if they are provided with the illusion that they have root access.

When running a Linux-based container program such as Docker, the guest processes also must be Linux programs. However, the overhead is much lower than that of hardware virtualization because you are running only a single operating system. Processes start up much more quickly inside containers than inside virtual machines.

Docker, Inc. (Docker's creator—I'll use the "Inc." here to distinguish the company name from the product name) created more than just containers, however: Docker is known as the platform where containers are a building block. To use an analogy, containers are to Docker what virtual machines are to a hypervisor such as VMWare or VirtualBox. The other two major pieces Docker, Inc. created are its image format and the Docker API.

To illustrate, let's compare container images to virtual machine images. *A container image* holds a filesystem with an installed operating system, along with metadata. One major difference from virtual machine images is that container images are layered. To create a new container image, you customize an existing one by adding, changing, and removing files. The new container image will contain a reference to the original container image, as well as the filesystem differences between the two. The layered approach means that container images are smaller than traditional virtual machine images, so they're faster to transfer over the internet than virtual machine images are. The Docker project hosts (*https://hub.docker.com*) a *registry* (that is, a repository) of publicly available images.

Docker also has a remote API that enables third-party tools to interact with Docker. Ansible's docker_* modules use the Docker remote API. You can use these Ansible modules to manage containers on the Docker platform. You can manage the whole software life cycle with Ansible, the OS, the container runtimes, the tools, the registry, the containers, all of it.

Kubernetes

Containers running on Kubernetes are typically not orchestrated using Ansible from a control host, although the k8s module (*https://oreil.ly/yRVOx*) can be used for that purpose. The Kubernetes Operator SDK offers three other ways to manage Kubernetes resources: Go Operators, Helm Charts, and Ansible Operators. Helm Charts are most popular in the community. I won't go into detail about Kubernetes and Ansible. If you are interested in Ansible and Kubernetes, Jeff Geerling is currently writing the book *Ansible for Kubernetes*. *Kubernetes Operators* by Jason Dobies and Joshua Wood (O'Reilly) covers operators in depth.

If you are looking for a public cloud for trying out containers, Red Hat operates an OpenShift-based cloud platform called OpenShift Online (*https://oreil.ly/t6XgM*), and Google provides a trial of its Google Kubernetes Engine (*https://oreil.ly/hCSNm*).

Both platforms are also open source, so if you manage your own hardware, you can deploy either OpenShift or Kubernetes on them. If you want to deploy on another platform, read this blog post about a Vagrant setup (*https://oreil.ly/b0aKF*). You can use Kubespray (*https://oreil.ly/M2jiC*) for other setups.

You should know that serious production systems often rely on using Kubernetes combined with bare-metal or virtual machines for storage or specific software; for example, see the documentation for installing wire-server (*https://oreil.ly/rMZYp*). Ansible is useful for gluing pieces together in such infrastructures, in a common language.

Docker Application Life Cycle

Here's what the typical life cycle of a container-based application looks like:

1. Pull container base image from registry.
2. Customize container image on your local machine.
3. Push container image up from your local machine to the registry.
4. Pull container image down to your remote hosts from the registry.
5. Run containers on the remote hosts, passing in any configuration information to the containers on startup.

You typically create your container image on your local machine or a continuous integration system that supports creating container images, such as GitLab or Jenkins. Once you've created your image, you need to store it somewhere that will be convenient for downloading onto your remote hosts.

Registries

Container images typically reside in a *registry*. The Docker project runs a registry called *Docker Hub*, which can host both public and private container images. The Docker command-line tools there have built-in support for pushing images up to a registry and for pulling images down from a registry. Red Hat runs a registry called Quay (*https://quay.io*). You can host registries on-premises using Sonatype Nexus (*https://oreil.ly/IvZ9G*). Public cloud providers can host private registries for your organization as well.

Once your container image is in the registry, you connect to a remote host, pull down the container image, and then run the container. Note that if you try to run a container whose image isn't on the host, Docker will automatically pull down the image from the registry, so you do not need to explicitly issue a command to do so.

Ansible and Docker

When you use Ansible to create container images and start the containers on the remote hosts, the application life cycle looks like this:

1. Write Ansible playbooks for creating container images.
2. Run the playbooks to create container images on your local machine.
3. Push container images up from your local machine to the registry.
4. Write Ansible playbooks to pull container images down to remote hosts and run them, passing in configuration information.
5. Run Ansible playbooks to start up the containers.

Connecting to the Docker Daemon

All the Ansible Docker modules communicate with the Docker daemon. If you are running on Linux or on macOS using Docker Desktop, all modules should work without passing other arguments.

If you are running on macOS using Boot2Docker or Docker Machine, or for other cases where the machine that executes the module is not the same machine running the Docker daemon, you may need to pass extra information to the modules so they can reach the Docker daemon. Table 13-1 lists these options, which can be passed as either module arguments or environment variables. See the `docker_container` module documentation for more details.

Table 13-1. Docker connection options

Module argument	Environment variable	Default
docker_host	DOCKER_HOST	unix://var/run/docker.sock
tls_hostname	DOCKER_TLS_HOSTNAME	localhost
api_version	DOCKER_API_VERSION	auto
cert_path	DOCKER_CERT_PATH	(None)
ssl_version	DOCKER_SSL_VERSION	(None)
tls	DOCKER_TLS	no
tls_verify	DOCKER_TLS_VERIFY	no
timeout	DOCKER_TIMEOUT	60 (seconds)

Example Application: Ghost

In this chapter, we're going to switch from Mezzanine to Ghost as our example application. Ghost is an open source blogging platform, like WordPress. The Ghost project has an official Docker container that we'll be using.

What we'll cover in this chapter:

- Running a Ghost container on your local machine
- Running a Ghost container fronted by an NGINX container with SSL configured
- Pushing a custom NGINX image to a registry
- Deploying our Ghost and NGINX containers to a remote machine

Running a Docker Container on Our Local Machine

The `docker_container` module starts and stops Docker containers, implementing some of the functionality of the `docker` command-line tool such as the `run`, `kill`, and `rm` commands.

Assuming you have Docker installed locally, the following invocation will download the Ghost image from the Docker registry and execute it locally. It will map port 2368 inside the container to 8000 on your machine, so you can access Ghost at *http://localhost:8000*:

```
$ ansible localhost -m docker_container -a "name=test-ghost image=ghost \
  ports=8000:2368"
```

The first time you run this, it may take minutes for Docker to download the image. If it succeeds, this `docker ps` command will show relevant details of the running container:

```
$ docker ps --format "table {{.ID }} {{.Image}} {{.Ports}}"
CONTAINER ID IMAGE PORTS
ff728315015e ghost 0.0.0.0:8000->2368/tcp
```

To stop and remove the container, run:

```
$ ansible localhost -m docker_container -a "name=test-ghost state=absent"
```

The `docker_container` module supports many options: if you can pass an argument by using the `docker` command-line tool, you're likely to find an equivalent possibility on the module.

Building an Image from a Dockerfile

The official way to create your own container images is by writing special text files called *Dockerfiles*, which resemble shell scripts. The stock Ghost image works great on its own, but if you want to ensure that access is secure, you'll need to front it with a web server configured for TLS.

The NGINX project puts out a stock NGINX image, but you'll need to configure it to function as a frontend for Ghost and to enable TLS, like we did in Chapter 7 for Mezzanine. Example 13-1 shows the Dockerfile for this.

Example 13-1. Dockerfile

```
FROM nginx
RUN rm /etc/nginx/conf.d/default.conf
COPY ghost.conf /etc/nginx/conf.d/ghost.conf
```

Example 13-2 shows the NGINX configuration for being a frontend for Ghost. The main difference between this one and the one for Mezzanine is that in this case NGINX is communicating with Ghost by using a TCP socket (port 2368), while with Mezzanine the communication was over a Unix domain socket.

The other difference is that the path holding the TLS files is */certs*.

Example 13-2. ghost.conf

```
server {
    listen 80 default_server;
    listen [::]:80 default_server;
    server_name _;
    return 301 https://$host$request_uri;
}
server {
    listen 443 ssl;
    client_max_body_size 10M;
    keepalive_timeout    15;
    ssl_certificate      /certs/nginx.crt;
    ssl_certificate_key  /certs/nginx.key;
    ssl_session_cache    shared:SSL:10m;
    ssl_session_timeout  10m;
    ssl_protocols TLSv1.3;
    ssl_ciphers EECDH+AESGCM:EDH+AESGCM;
    ssl_prefer_server_ciphers on;
    location / {
        proxy_pass          http://ghost:2368;
        proxy_set_header    X-Real-IP $remote_addr;
        proxy_set_header    Host      $http_host;
        proxy_set_header X-Forwarded-Proto https;
        proxy_set_header X-Forwarded-For $proxy_add_x_forwarded_for;
    }
}
```

This configuration assumes that NGINX can reach the Ghost server via the hostname ghost. When you deploy these containers, ensure that this is the case; otherwise, the NGINX container will not be able to reach the Ghost container.

Assuming you put the Dockerfile and *nginx.conf* file in a directory named *nginx*, this task will create an image named *ansiblebook/nginx-ghost*. We used the prefix *ansiblebook/* since we pushed to the *ansiblebook/nginx-ghost* Docker Hub repository, but you should use the prefix that corresponds to your username on the Docker site (*https://hub.docker.com*):

```
- name: Create Nginx image
  docker_image:
    build:
      path: ./nginx
    source: build
    name: ansiblebook/nginx-ghost
    state: present
    force_source: "{{ force_source | default(false) }}"
    tag:  "{{ tag | default('latest') }}"
```

You can confirm this with the docker images command:

```
$ docker images
REPOSITORY                TAG      IMAGE ID       CREATED         SIZE
ansiblebook/nginx-ghost   latest   e8d39f3e9e57   6 minutes ago   133MB
ghost                     latest   e8bc5f42fe28   3 days ago      450MB
nginx                     latest   87a94228f133   3 weeks ago     133MB
```

Note that invoking the docker_image module to build an image will have no effect if an image with that name already exists, even if you've updated the Dockerfile. If you've updated the Dockerfile and want to rebuild, set the force_source: true option with an extra variable:

```
$ ansible-playbook build.yml -e force_source=true
```

In general, though, it's a clever idea to add a tag option with a version number as an extra variable and increment this each time you do a new build. The docker_image module will then build the new image without needing to be forced. The tag latest is the default, but it's not really useful for specific versioning.

```
$ ansible-playbook build.yml -e tag=v2
```

Pushing Our Image to the Docker Registry

We'll use a separate playbook to publish our image to Docker Hub (Example 13-3). Note that you must invoke the docker_login module to log in to the registry before you can push the image. The docker_login and docker_image modules both default to Docker Hub as the registry.

Example 13-3. publish.yml

```
---
- name: Publish image to docker hub
  hosts: localhost
  gather_facts: false

  vars_prompt:
    - name: username
      prompt: Enter Docker Registry username
    - name: password
      prompt: Enter Docker Registry password
      private: true
```

```
    tasks:

      - name: Authenticate with repository
        docker_login:
          username: "{{ username }}"
          password: "{{ password }}"
        tags:
          - login

      - name: Push image up
        docker_image:
          name: "ansiblebook/nginx-ghost"
          push: true
          source: local
          state: present
        tags:
          - push
```

If you wish to use a different registry, specify a `registry_url` option to `docker_login` and prefix the image name with the hostname and port (if not using the standard HTTP/HTTPS port) of the registry. Example 13-4 shows how the tasks change when using a registry at *http://reg.example.com*.

Example 13-4. publish.yml with custom registry

```
    tasks:
      - name: Authenticate with repository
        docker_login:
          registry_url: https://reg.example.com
          username: "{{ username }}"
          password: "{{ password }}"
        tags:
          - login

      - name: Push image up
        docker_image:
          name: reg.example.com/ansiblebook/nginx-ghost
          push: true
          source: local
          state: present
        tags:
          - push
```

Note that the playbook for creating the image will also need to change to reflect the new name of the image: *reg.example.com/ansiblebook/nginx-ghost*.

Orchestrating Multiple Containers on Our Local Machine

It's common to run multiple Docker containers and wire them up together. During development, you typically run all these containers together on your local machine;

in production, they are usually hosted on different machines. Applications are often deployed to a Kubernetes cluster, while databases often run on dedicated machines.

For local development, where all containers run on the same machine, the Docker project has a tool called *Docker Compose* that makes it simpler to bring containers up and wire them together. You use the `docker_compose` Ansible module to control Docker Compose—that is, to bring the services up or down.

Example 13-5 shows a *docker-compose.yml* file that will start up NGINX and Ghost. The file assumes there's a directory that has the TLS certificate files.

Example 13-5. docker-compose.yml

```
version: '2'
services:
  nginx:
    image: ansiblebook/nginx-ghost
    ports:
      - "8000:80"
      - "8443:443"
    volumes:
      - ${PWD}/certs:/certs
    links:
      - ghost
  ghost:
    image: ghost
```

Example 13-6 shows a playbook that creates the custom NGINX image file, creates self-signed certificates, and then starts up the services specified in Example 13-5.

Example 13-6. ghost.yml

```
---
- name: Run Ghost locally
  hosts: localhost
  gather_facts: false
  tasks:

    - name: Create Nginx image
      docker_image:
        build:
          path: ./nginx
        source: build
        name: bbaassssiiee/nginx-ghost
        state: present
        force_source: "{{ force_source | default(false) }}"
        tag: "{{ tag | default('v1') }}"

    - name: Create certs
      command: >
        openssl req -new -x509 -nodes
```

```
      -out certs/nginx.crt -keyout certs/nginx.key
      -subj '/CN=localhost' -days 365
    args:
      creates: certs/nginx.crt

  - name: Bring up services
    docker_compose:
      project_src: .
      state: present
...
```

`docker_compose` is an interesting module for application developers. Once the application matures to be deployed in production, the runtime requirements often lead to the use of Kubernetes.

Querying Local Images

The `docker_image_info` module allows you to query the metadata on a locally stored image. Example 13-7 shows an example of a playbook that uses this module to query the Ghost image for the exposed port and volumes.

Example 13-7. image-info.yml

```
---
- name: Get exposed ports and volumes
  hosts: localhost
  gather_facts: false
  vars:
    image: ghost
  tasks:

    - name: Get image info
      docker_image_info:
        name: ghost
      register: ghost

    - name: Extract ports
      set_fact:
        ports: "{{ ghost.images[0].Config.ExposedPorts.keys() }}"

    - name: We expect only one port to be exposed
      assert:
        that: "ports|length == 1"

    - name: Output exposed port
      debug:
        msg: "Exposed port: {{ ports[0] }}"

    - name: Extract volumes
      set_fact:
        volumes: "{{ ghost.images[0].Config.Volumes.keys() }}"
```

```
    - name: Output volumes
      debug:
        msg: "Volume: {{ item }}"
      with_items: "{{ volumes }}"
...
```

The output looks like this:

```
$ ansible-playbook image-info.yml
PLAY [Get exposed ports and volumes] ****************************************
TASK [Get image info] *******************************************************
ok: [localhost]
TASK [Extract ports] ********************************************************
ok: [localhost]
TASK [We expect only one port to be exposed] ********************************
ok: [localhost] ==> {
    "changed": false,
    "msg": "All assertions passed"
}
TASK [Output exposed port] **************************************************
ok: [localhost] ==> {
    "msg": "Exposed port: 2368/tcp"
}
TASK [Extract volumes] ******************************************************
ok: [localhost]
TASK [Output volumes] *******************************************************
ok: [localhost] => (item=/var/lib/ghost/content) => {
    "msg": "Volume: /var/lib/ghost/content"
}
```

Use the docker_image_info module to log important details about your images.

Deploying the Dockerized Application

By default, Ghost uses SQLite as its database backend; however, for deployment in this chapter, we're going to use MySQL.

We're going to provision two separate machines with Vagrant. One machine (ghost) will run Docker to run the Ghost and NGINX containers, and the other machine (mysql) will run the MySQL server as a persistent store for the Ghost data.

This example assumes the following variables are defined somewhere where they are in scope for the frontend and backend machines, such as in the *group_vars/all* file:

- database_name=ghost
- database_user=ghost
- database_password=mysupersecretpassword

Provisioning MySQL

To provision the MySQL machine, we install a couple of packages (Example 13-8).

Example 13-8. MySQL provisioning

```
- name: Provision database machine
  hosts: mysql
  become: true
  gather_facts: false
  tasks:

    - name: Install packages for mysql
      apt:
        update_cache: true
        cache_valid_time: 3600
        name:
          - mysql-server
          - python3-pip
        state: present

    - name: Install requirements
      pip:
        name: PyMySQL
        state: present
        executable: /usr/bin/pip3
```

Deploying the Ghost Database

To deploy the Ghost database we need to create a database and database user that can connect from another machine. This means we need to reconfigure MySQL's `bind-address` so it listens to the network, then restart MySQL with a handler so it only restarts if that configuration changes (Example 13-9).

Example 13-9. Deploy database

```
- name: Deploy database
  hosts: database
  become: true
  gather_facts: false

  handlers:
    - name: Restart Mysql
      systemd:
        name: mysql
        state: restarted
  tasks:

    - name: Listen
      lineinfile:
        path: /etc/mysql/mysql.conf.d/mysqld.cnf
        regexp: '^bind-address'
```

```
      line: 'bind-address          = 0.0.0.0'
      state: present
    notify: Restart Mysql

  - name: Create database
    mysql_db:
      name: "{{ database_name }}"
      state: present
      login_unix_socket: /var/run/mysqld/mysqld.sock

  - name: Create database user
    mysql_user:
      name: "{{ database_user }}"
      password: "{{ database_password }}"
      priv: '{{ database_name }}.*:ALL'
      host: '%'
      state: present
      login_unix_socket: /var/run/mysqld/mysqld.sock
```

In this example, we listen to 0.0.0.0 and the user can connect from any machine (not the most secure setup).

Frontend

The frontend deployment is more complex since we have two containers to deploy: Ghost and NGINX. We also need to wire them up and pass configuration information to the Ghost container so it can access the MySQL database.

We're going to use Docker networks to enable the NGINX container to connect to the Ghost container. Using Docker networks, we'll create a custom Docker network and attach containers to it. The containers can access each other by using the container names as hostnames.

Creating a Docker network is simple:

```
  - name: Create network
    docker_network:
      name: "{{ net_name }}"
```

It makes more sense to use a variable for the network name, since we'll need to reference it for each container we bring up. Example 13-10 illustrates how our playbook will start.

Example 13-10. Deploy Ghost

```
- name: Deploy Ghost
  hosts: ghost
  become: true
  gather_facts: false

  vars:
    url: "https://{{ inventory_hostname }}"
```

```
    database_host: "{{ groups['database'][0] }}"
    data_dir: /data/ghostdata
    certs_dir: /data/certs
    net_name: ghostnet

  tasks:
    - name: Create network
      docker_network:
        name: "{{ net_name }}"
```

Note that this playbook assumes there's a group named `database` that has a single host; it uses this information to populate the `database_host` variable.

Frontend: Ghost

We need to configure Ghost to connect to the MySQL database, as well as to run in production mode, by passing the `production` flag to the `npm start` command. We pass this configuration to the container in environment variables. We also want to ensure that the persistent files that it generates are written to a volume mount.

Here's the part of the playbook that creates the directory that will hold the persistent data. It also starts up the container, connected to the `ghostnet` network (Example 13-11).

Example 13-11. Ghost container

```
- name: Create ghostdata directory
  file:
    path: "{{ data_dir }}"
    state: directory
    mode: '0750'

- name: Start ghost container
  docker_container:
    name: ghost
    image: ghost
    container_default_behavior: compatibility
    network_mode: host
    networks:
      - name: "{{ net_name }}"
    volumes:
      - "{{ data_dir }}:/var/lib/ghost/content"
    env:
      database__client: mysql
      database__connection__host: "{{ database_host }}"
      database__connection__user: "{{ database_user }}"
      database__connection__password: "{{ database_password }}"
      database__connection__database: "{{ database_name }}"
      url: "https://{{ inventory_hostname }}"
      NODE_ENV: production
```

Note that we don't need to publish any ports here, since only the NGINX container will communicate with the Ghost container.

Frontend: NGINX

We hardwired the NGINX container's configuration into it when we created the *ansiblebook/nginx-ghost* image: it is configured to connect to ghost:2368.

However, we do need to copy the TLS certificates. As in earlier examples, we'll just generate self-signed certificates (Example 13-12).

Example 13-12. NGINX container

```
- name: Create certs directory
  file:
    path: "{{ certs_dir }}"
    state: directory
    mode: '0750'

- name: Generate tls certs
  command: >
    openssl req -new -x509 -nodes
    -out "{{ certs_dir }}/nginx.crt"
    -keyout "{{ certs_dir }}/nginx.key"
    -subj "/CN={{ ansible_host }}" -days 90
  args:
    creates: certs/nginx.crt

- name: Start nginx container
  docker_container:
    name: nginx_ghost
    image: bbaassssiiee/nginx-ghost
    container_default_behavior: compatibility
    network_mode: "{{ net_name }}"
    networks:
      - name: "{{ net_name }}"
    pull: true
    ports:
      - "0.0.0.0:80:80"
      - "0.0.0.0:443:443"
    volumes:
      - "{{ certs_dir }}:/certs"
```

Only use self-signed certificates for a short time, while developing on your internal network. As soon as others depend on the web service, get a certificate signed by a certificate authority.

Cleaning Out Containers

Ansible makes it easy to stop and remove containers, which is useful when you're developing and testing deployment scripts. Example 13-13 is a playbook that cleans up the ghost host.

Example 13-13. Container cleanup

```
---
- name: Remove all Ghost containers and networks
  hosts: ghost
  become: true
  gather_facts: false
  tasks:

    - name: Remove containers
      docker_container:
        name: "{{ item }}"
        state: absent
        container_default_behavior: compatibility
      loop:
        - nginx_ghost
        - ghost

    - name: Remove network
      docker_network:
        name: ghostnet
        state: absent
```

docker_container also has a cleanup Boolean parameter, which ensures the container is removed after each run.

Conclusion

Docker has clearly proven that it has staying power. In this chapter, we covered how to manage container images, containers, and networks with Ansible modules.

## CHAPTER 14

Quality Assurance with Molecule

If you want to develop a role, then you need test infrastructure. Using disposable Docker containers is a perfect fit for testing with multiple distributions, or versions, of Linux without touching the machines others use.

Molecule is a Python testing framework for Ansible roles. Using it, you can test multiple instances, operating systems, and distributions. You can use a couple of test frameworks and as many testing scenarios as you need. Molecule is extensible in its support for various virtualization platforms, using a type of plug-in called a *driver*. A driver, for a provider, is a Python library that is used to manage test hosts (that is, to create and destroy them).

Molecule encourages an approach that results in consistently developed roles that are well-written and easily understood and maintained. Developed as open source on GitHub since 2015 by @retr0h, Molecule is now community-maintained as part of the Ansible by Red Hat project.

Installation and Setup

Molecule depends on Python version 3.6 or greater and Ansible version 2.8 or greater. Depending on your operating system, you might need to install additional packages. Ansible is not a direct dependency but is called as a command-line tool.

For Red Hat, the command is:

```
# yum install -y gcc python3-pip python3-devel openssl-devel python3-libselinux
```

For Ubuntu, use:

```
# apt install -y python3-pip libssl-dev
```

After installing the required dependencies, you can install Molecule with pip. We recommend you install it in a Python virtual environment (*https://oreil.ly/wtQ6p*). It is important to isolate Molecule and its Python dependencies from the system Python packages. This can save time and energy when managing Python packaging issues.

Configuring Molecule Drivers

Molecule comes with only the driver named `delegated`. If you want to have Molecule manage instances in containers, hypervisors, or the cloud, then you need to install a driver plug-in and its dependencies. Several driver plug-ins depend on `pyyaml>=5.1,<6`.

Drivers are installed with pip just like other Python dependencies. Ansible dependencies are nowadays bundled as Collections (more about Collections in the next chapter). To install the Collection you'll need, use the following:

```
$ ansible-galaxy collection install <collection_name>
```

Molecule can be extended for specific cloud enviroments, so it is possible to create an ephemeral test infrastructure.

Table 14-1 provides a list of Molecule drivers and their dependencies.

Table 14-1. Molecule drivers

Driver plug-in	Public cloud	Private cloud	Containers	Python dependencies	Ansible collection
molecule-alicloud	√			ansible_alicloud ansible_alicloud_module_utils	
molecule-azure	√				
molecule-containers			√	molecule-docker molecule-podman	
molecule-docker			√	docker	community.docker
molecule-digitalocean	√				
molecule-ec2	√			boto3	
molecule-gce	√				google.cloud community.crypto
molecule-hetznercloud	√				
molecule-libvirt					
molecule-linode					
molecule-lxd			√		
molecule-openstack		√		openstacksdk	
molecule-podman			√		containers.podman
molecule-vagrant				python-vagrant	
molecule-vmware		√		pyvmomi	

Creating an Ansible Role

You can create a role with:

```
$ ansible-galaxy role init my_role
```

This creates the following files in the directory *my_role*:

```
my_role/
├── README.md
├── defaults
│   └── main.yml
├── files
├── handlers
│   └── main.yml
├── meta
│   └── main.yml
├── tasks
│   └── main.yml
├── templates
├── tests
│   ├── inventory
│   └── test.yml
└── vars
    └── main.yml
```

To initialize Molecule in an existing role, or add a scenario, you would use:

```
$ molecule init scenario -r <role_name> --driver-name docker s_name
```

`molecule init` extends `ansible-galaxy role init` by creating a directory tree for a role with additional files, for testing with Molecule. The following command should get you started running Molecule:

```
$ molecule init role my_new_role --driver-name docker
```

This creates the following files in the directory *my_new_role*:

```
├── README.md
├── defaults
│   └── main.yml
├── files
├── handlers
│   └── main.yml
├── meta
│   └── main.yml
├── molecule
│   └── default
│       ├── converge.yml
│       ├── molecule.yml
│       └── verify.yml
├── tasks
│   └── main.yml
├── templates
├── tests
│   ├── inventory
```

```
|   └── test.yml
└── vars
    └── main.yml
```

Scenarios

In the above example, you see a subdirectory named *default*. This is a first scenario where you can use the `molecule test` command to check the syntax, run linters, run a playbook with the role, run it again to check idempotence, and run a verification check. This all happens using a CentOS 8 container in Docker.

You can add scenarios when, for instance, you would like to test with Ubuntu or Debian. Each scenario can be used independent of the other with the following flag:

```
$ molecule test -s <scenario_name>
```

Desired State

Bas often adds a scenario for localhost when he creates a role that installs software. Using the commands `molecule converge` (to install) and `molecule cleanup` (to uninstall), Bas can test the desired states. A role's *tasks* directory contents could be:

- *absent.yml*
- *main.yml*
- *present.yml*

main.yml is simply an entry point from which the absent and present files are referenced, depending on the `desired_state` variable:

```
---
- name: "Desired state is {{ desired_state }}"
  include_tasks: "{{ desired_state }}.yml"
...
```

Configuring Scenarios in Molecule

The file *molecule/s_name/molecule.yml* is used to configure Molecule and the driver used in a scenario.

Let's look at three example configurations that we find useful. The minimal example (Example 14-1) uses localhost for testing with the `delegated` driver. The only thing you need to do is make sure that you can log in with SSH. You can use the `delegated` driver with existing inventory.

Example 14-1. delegated driver

```
---
dependency:
  name: galaxy
  options:
    role-file: requirements.yml
    requirements-file: collections.yml
driver:
  name: delegated
lint: |
  set -e
  yamllint .
  ansible-lint
platforms:
  - name: localhost
provisioner:
  name: ansible
verifier:
  name: ansible
```

Note that Molecule can install roles and collections in the dependency phase of its operation, as shown in Example 14-1. If you work on-premises, you can set options to ignore certificates; however, don't do that when using proper certificates.

Managing Virtual Machines

Molecule works great with containers, but in some scenarios, like when targeting Windows machines, we like to use a virtual machine. Data scientists working with Python often use Conda as a package manager for Python and other libraries. To test a role for installing Miniconda (*https://oreil.ly/YU8KJ*) on various operating systems, you can create a scenario for Windows with a separate *molecule.yml* file.

Example 14-2 uses the `vagrant` driver to launch a Windows VM in VirtualBox.

Example 14-2. Windows machine in Vagrant VirtualBox

```
---
driver:
  name: vagrant
  provider:
    name: virtualbox
lint: |
  set -e
  yamllint .
  ansible-lint
platforms:
  - name: WindowsServer2016
    box: jborean93/WindowsServer2016
    memory: 4069
    cpus: 2
```

```
    groups:
      - windows
provisioner:
  name: ansible
  inventory:
    host_vars:
      WindowsServer2016:
        ansible_user: vagrant
        ansible_password: vagrant
        ansible_port: 55986
        ansible_host: 127.0.0.1
        ansible_connection: winrm
        ansible_winrm_scheme: https
        ansible_winrm_server_cert_validation: ignore
verifier:
  name: ansible
```

The VirtualBox image in this example was created by Jordan Borean, who has blogged about the process of creating it with Packer (*https://oreil.ly/CXzzg*).

Managing Containers

Molecule can create a network for containers in Docker that allows us to evaluate cluster setups. Redis is an open source, in-memory data structure store, used as a database, cache, and message broker. Redis provides data structures such as strings, hashes, lists, sets, sorted sets with range queries, bitmaps, hyperlogs, geospatial indexes, and streams. It works great for large-scale applications, and as a cache for Ansible facts. Example 14-3 uses the docker driver to simulate a Redis Sentinel cluster running on CentOS 7 as illustrated in Figure 14-1.

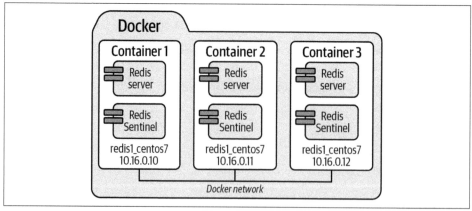

Figure 14-1. Using the docker driver to simulate a Redis Sentinel cluster on CentOS 7

Such a cluster runs multiple instances of Redis that watch each other; if the main instance goes down, another one can be elected to take the lead.

Example 14-3. Redis cluster with Docker

```
---
dependency:
  name: galaxy
driver:
  name: docker
lint: |
  set -e
  yamllint .
  ansible-lint
platforms:
  - name: redis1_centos7
    image: milcom/centos7-systemd
    privileged: true
    groups:
      - redis_server
      - redis_sentinel
    docker_networks:
      - name: 'redis'
        ipam_config:
          - subnet: '10.16.0.0/24'
    networks:
      - name: "redis"
        ipv4_address: '10.16.0.10'
  - name: redis2_centos7
    image: milcom/centos7-systemd
    privileged: true
    groups:
      - redis_server
      - redis_sentinel
    docker_networks:
      - name: 'redis'
        ipam_config:
          - subnet: '10.16.0.0/24'
    networks:
      - name: "redis"
        ipv4_address: '10.16.0.11'
  - name: redis3_centos7
    image: milcom/centos7-systemd
    privileged: true
    groups:
      - redis_server
      - redis_sentinel
    docker_networks:
      - name: 'redis'
        ipam_config:
          - subnet: '10.16.0.0/24'
    networks:
      - name: "redis"
        ipv4_address: '10.16.0.12'
provisioner:
  name: ansible
verifier:
  name: ansible
```

If you run `molecule converge` from the role's directory, you can watch the cluster being created in Docker and the Redis software being installed and configured.

Molecule Commands

Molecule is a command with subcommands, each of which performs part of the quality assurance. Table 14-2 lists the purpose of each command.

Table 14-2. Molecule subcommands

Command	Purpose
check	Use the provisioner to perform a dry run (destroy, dependency, create, prepare, converge).
cleanup	Use the provisioner to clean up any changes made to external systems during the stages of testing.
converge	Use the provisioner to configure instances (dependency, create, prepare, converge).
create	Use the provisioner to start the instances.
dependency	Manage the role's dependencies.
destroy	Use the provisioner to destroy the instances.
drivers	List drivers.
idempotence	Use the provisioner to configure the instances and parse the output to determine idempotence.
init	Initialize a new role or scenario.
lint	Lint the role (dependency, lint).
list	List status of instances.
login	Log in to one instance.
matrix	List matrix of steps used to test instances.
prepare	Use the provisioner to prepare the instances into a particular starting state.
reset	Reset molecule temporary folders.
side-effect	Use the provisioner to perform side effects on the instances.
syntax	Use the provisioner to syntax-check the role.
test	Runs a matrix of tests
verify	Run automated tests against instances.

We usually start by running `molecule converge` several times to get the Ansible role just right. Converge runs the *converge.yml* playbook that `molecule init` created. If there is a pre-condition for the role, like another role to run first, then it makes sense to create a *prepare.yml* playbook to save time during development. When using the `delegated` driver, create a *cleanup.yml* playbook. You can call these extra playbooks with `molecule prepare` and `molecule cleanup`, respectively.

Linting

Linting is the process of running a program that will analyze code for potential errors, before running the code. Ansible content can be analyzed on several levels:

---

the `ansible-playbook` command has a `--syntax-check` option, and there are other programs that look at the YAML formatting, the application of best practices, and good code style. Molecule can run all these linters in one go. If you are into code quality and verification, this configuration for `molecule lint` is quite useful:

```
lint: |
  set -e
  yamllint .
  ansible-lint
  ansible-later
```

YAMLlint

YAMLlint checks YAML files (*https://oreil.ly/2rhid*) not only for syntax validity but also for weirdness like key repetition and cosmetic problems such as line length, trailing spaces, indentation, etc. YAMLlint helps in creating uniform YAML files, and that is very useful when you share code. We typically create a config file named *.yamllint* for it so it works well with the other linters (Example 14-4).

Example 14-4. YAMLlint config file (.yamllint)

```
---
extends: default
rules:
  braces:
    max-spaces-inside: 1
    level: error
  document-start: enable
  document-end: enable
  key-duplicates: enable
  line-length: disable
  new-line-at-end-of-file: enable
  new-lines:
    type: unix
  trailing-spaces: enable
  truthy: enable
...
```

You can enable or disable these rules. We recommend at least adhering to YAMLlint's default settings.

ansible-lint

`ansible-lint` was created by Will Thames as a static analysis tool for Ansible. It checks playbooks for practices and behavior that can potentially be improved. It uses a directory with rules (*https://oreil.ly/WtN09*) implemented as Python scripts. You can even program an extra directory with rules yourself if you want to check certain behavior.

To check a playbook you use the ansible-lint command with the playbook's filename as argument. To run Example 14-5, you would run:

```
$ ansible-lint lintme.yml
```

Example 14-5. lintme.yml

```
---
- name: Run ansible-lint with the roles
  hosts: all
  gather_facts: true
  become: yes
  roles:
    - ssh
    - miniconda
    - redis
```

When we run `ansible-lint` with Example 14-5, the following output is shown:

```
WARNING  Listing 3 violation(s) that are fatal
yaml: truthy value should be one of [false, true] (yaml[truthy])
lintme.yml:6

yaml: missing document end "..." (yaml[document-end])
lintme.yml:14

yaml: too many blank lines (3> 0) (yaml[empty-lines])
lintme.yml:14

You can skip specific rules by adding them to your configuration file:
# .config/ansible-lint.yml
skip_list:
  - yaml  # Violations reported by yamllint.

Finished with 3 failure(s), 0 warning(s) on 22 files.
```

Usually it is a good idea to fix any issue that arises: this makes your Ansible code more easily maintainable.[1] `ansible-lint` is maintained by the Ansible community on GitHub.

ansible-later

`ansible-later` is another best-practice scanner for Ansible roles and playbooks; it was forked from `ansible-review`, which was another project (abandoned) by Will Thames. The nice thing about it is that it helps to enforce code-style guidelines (*https://oreil.ly/Yq7nq*). This will make Ansible roles more readable for all maintainers and can reduce troubleshooting time. `ansible-later` complements YAMLlint and

---

1 Alternatively, you can maintain a skip_list: in a file named *.ansible-lint*.

ansible-lint when configured for compatibility with a file named *.later.yml* in the top-level directory (Example 14-6).

Example 14-6. ansible-later config file (.later.yml)

```
---
ansible:
  # Add the name of used custom Ansible modules.
  custom_modules: []
  # List of yamllint compatible literal bools (ANSIBLE0014)
  literal-bools:
    - "true"
    - "false"
...
```

Verifiers

Verifiers are tools used to assert the success of running the role in a playbook. While we know that each module of Ansible has been tested, the outcome of a role is not guaranteed. It is good practice to automate tests that validate the outcome. There are three verifiers available for use with Molecule:

Ansible
    The default verifier

Goss
    A third-party verifier based on YAML specifications

TestInfra
    A Python test framework

The Goss and TestInfra verifiers use the files from the *tests* subdirectory of a molecule scenario, *test_default.yaml* for Goss and *test_default.py* for TestInfra.

Ansible

You can use a playbook named *verify.yml* to verify the results of the converge and idempotence steps once they have finished. Just use Ansible modules like `wait_for`, `package_facts`, `service_facts`, `uri`, and `assert` to test the outcomes. To do so, use:

```
$ molecule verify
```

Goss

You can do server validation quickly and easily with Goss, a YAML-based program (*https://oreil.ly/QTJ4H*) published by Ahmed Elsabbahy. To see what Goss can verify, let's look at the *test_sshd.yml* file for SSH, shown in Example 14-7. This checks if the

SSH service is running, if it is enabled after reboot, if it listens on TCP port 22, what the properties of the host key are, and so on.

Example 14-7. Goss file for SSH server

```
---
file:
  /etc/ssh/ssh_host_ed25519_key.pub:
    exists: true
    mode: '0644'
    owner: root
    group: root
    filetype: file
    contains:
      - 'ssh-ed25519 '
port:
  tcp:22:
    listening: true
    ip:
      - 0.0.0.0
service:
  sshd:
    enabled: true
    running: true
user:
  sshd:
    exists: true
    uid: 74
    gid: 74
    groups:
      - sshd
    home: /var/empty/sshd
    shell: /sbin/nologin
group:
  sshd:
    exists: true
process:
  sshd:
    running: true
```

If you run Goss to validate the server settings with this file on the command line, it will look like this:

```
$ /usr/local/bin/goss -g /tmp/molecule/goss/test_sshd.yml v -f tap
1..18
ok 1 - Group: sshd: exists: matches expectation: [true]
ok 2 - File: /etc/ssh/ssh_host_ed25519_key.pub: exists: matches expectation:
[true]
ok 3 - File: /etc/ssh/ssh_host_ed25519_key.pub: mode: matches expectation:
["0644"]
ok 4 - File: /etc/ssh/ssh_host_ed25519_key.pub: owner: matches expectation:
["root"]
ok 5 - File: /etc/ssh/ssh_host_ed25519_key.pub: group: matches expectation:
["root"]
```

```
ok 6 - File: /etc/ssh/ssh_host_ed25519_key.pub: filetype: matches expectation:
["file"]
ok 7 - File: /etc/ssh/ssh_host_ed25519_key.pub: contains: all expectations found:
[ssh-ed25519 ]
ok 8 - Process: sshd: running: matches expectation: [true]
ok 9 - User: sshd: exists: matches expectation: [true]
ok 10 - User: sshd: uid: matches expectation: [74]
ok 11 - User: sshd: gid: matches expectation: [74]
ok 12 - User: sshd: home: matches expectation: ["/var/empty/sshd"]
ok 13 - User: sshd: groups: matches expectation: [["sshd"]]
ok 14 - User: sshd: shell: matches expectation: ["/sbin/nologin"]
ok 15 - Port: tcp:22: listening: matches expectation: [true]
ok 16 - Port: tcp:22: ip: matches expectation: [["0.0.0.0"]]
ok 17 - Service: sshd: enabled: matches expectation: [true]
ok 18 - Service: sshd: running: matches expectation: [true]
```

To integrate Goss with Molecule, install `molecule-goss` with pip and create a scenario:

```
$ molecule init scenario -r ssh \
    --driver-name docker \
    --verifier-name goss goss
```

Create the Goss YAML files in the *molecule/goss/tests/* subdirectory of your role. It's a quick, powerful way to introduce automated testing to operations.

TestInfra

If you have advanced testing requirements, it's helpful to have a Python-based test framework. With TestInfra, you can write unit tests in Python to verify the actual state of your Ansible-configured servers. TestInfra aspires to be the Python equivalent of the Ruby-based ServerSpec, which gained popularity as a test framework for systems managed with Puppet.

To use TestInfra as a verifier, install it first:

```
$ pip install pytest-testinfra
```

Create a scenario:

```
$ molecule init scenario -r ssh \
    --driver-name docker \
    --verifier-name testinfra testinfra
```

To create a test suite in TestInfra for an SSH server, create a file named *molecule/testinfra/tests/test_default.py* and add the code from Example 14-8. After importing libraries, it calls upon the Molecule inventory to get `testinfra_hosts`.

Each host in turn is tested for the presence of the `openssh-server` package, the `sshd` service, the file with the ed25519 host key, and the proper user and group.

Example 14-8. TestInfra file for SSH server

```
import os
import testinfra.utils.ansible_runner

testinfra_hosts = testinfra.utils.ansible_runner.AnsibleRunner(
    os.environ["MOLECULE_INVENTORY_FILE"]
).get_hosts("all")


def test_sshd_is_installed(host):
    sshd = host.package("openssh-server")
    assert sshd.is_installed


def test_sshd_running_and_enabled(host):
    sshd = host.service("sshd")
    assert sshd.is_running
    assert sshd.is_enabled


def test_sshd_config_file(host):
    sshd_config = host.file("/etc/ssh/ssh_host_ed25519_key.pub")
    assert sshd_config.contains("ssh-ed25519 ")
    assert sshd_config.user == "root"
    assert sshd_config.group == "root"
    assert sshd_config.mode == 0o644


def test_ssh_user(host):
    assert host.user("sshd").exists


def test_ssh_group(host):
    assert host.group("ssh").exists
```

As you might imagine, you'll have lots of possibilities for verifying your servers if you have Python available. TestInfra reduces the work by offering tests for the common cases.

Conclusion

If you're an Ansible user, Molecule is a terrific addition to your toolbox. It can help you develop roles that are consistent, tested, well-written, and easily understood and maintained.

CHAPTER 15
Collections

Collections are a distribution format for Ansible content. A typical collection addresses a set of related use cases. For example, the cisco.ios collection automates management of Cisco iOS devices. Ansible Content Collections, which we'll simply refer to as collections for the rest of the chapter, represent the new standard of distributing, maintaining, and consuming automation. You can think of collections as a package format for Ansible content. By combining multiple types of Ansible content (playbooks, roles, modules, and plug-ins), collections greatly improve flexibility and scalability.

Traditionally, module creators have had to wait for their modules to be marked for inclusion in an upcoming Ansible release or else add them to roles, which made consumption and management more difficult. Now that the Ansible project has decoupled Ansible executables from most of the content, high-quality Ansible releases can be delivered more quickly and asynchronously from collection releases.

Shipping modules in Ansible Collections, along with roles and documentation, removes a barrier to entry, so creators can move as fast as the demand for their collection. This means vendors can roll out and automate new functionalities for existing or new products and services, independent of the release of Ansible.

Anyone can create a collection and publish it to Ansible Galaxy or to a private Automation Hub instance. Red Hat partners can publish certified collections to the Red Hat Automation Hub, part of the Red Hat Ansible Automation Platform—the release of which means Ansible Content Collections are now fully supported.

Confession

Up until this point in the book, Bas has written every module name as a single word to ease your learning curve. This did not take namespaces into account. Namespaces are used to distinguish owners/maintainers and their collections. It makes sense to use the *fully qualified collection name* (FQCN) in playbooks, since module names become so specific that we can look them up (try googling "group" versus "ansible.builtin.group").

Instead of using only a module, like so:

```
- name: create group members
  group:
    name: members
```

We use the `namespace.collection.module` notation:

```
- name: create group members
  ansible.builtin.group:
    name: members
```

For `ansible.builtin` this might look odd, but when using collections it becomes essential to avoiding name collisions.

The `collections` keyword lets you define a list of collections that your role or playbook should search for unqualified module and action names. So you can use the collections keyword, then refer to modules and action plug-ins by their short-form names throughout that role or playbook:

```
# myrole/meta/main.yml
collections:
  - my_namespace.first_collection:version
```

You can install a collection next to a full Ansible install and override the bundled collection with the version you installed.

Installing Collections

You can find and download collections through the website Ansible Galaxy and with the `ansible-galaxy` command. By default, `ansible-galaxy collection install` uses *https://galaxy.ansible.com* as the Galaxy server, but you can store roles and collections in private Git repositories just as well:

```
$ ansible-galaxy collection install my_namespace.my_collection
```

You can use a *requirements.yml* file that lists recommended security-related collections and roles as input for the `ansible-galaxy` command:

```
$ ansible-galaxy install -r requirements.yml
```

By default, this will install the collections in a "global" way, in a subdirectory in your home directory:

$HOME/.ansible/collections/ansible_collections

Configure `collections_paths` in *ansible.cfg* to install elsewhere. A *collections* directory, next to the *playbook.yml*, is a good place in a project structure.

Example 15-1 shows the format for a `requirements.yml` file with two lists: one for the roles and the other for the collections.

Example 15-1. requirements.yml

```
---
roles:
  - src: leonallen22.ansible_role_keybase
    name: keybase
  - src: https://github.com/dockpack/base_tailscale.git
    name: tailscale
collections:
  - check_point.gaia
  - check_point.mgmt
  - cyberark.conjur
  - cyberark.pas
  - fortinet.fortios
  - ibm.isam
  - junipernetworks.junos
  - paloaltonetworks.panos
...
```

Listing Collections

The first thing to do after installing collections is to see which collections you installed separately and which came bundled with your installed Ansible:

```
$ ansible-galaxy collection list
```

The list has more than a hundred entries, but Ansible does have *"batteries included."* To list the modules included in a collection, run:

```
$ ansible-doc -l namespace.collection
```

Ansible collections extend what you can do. If you find this overwhelming, consider installing just `ansible-core` and the collections you really need.

Using Collections in a Playbook

Collections can package and distribute playbooks, roles, modules, and plug-ins. When you depend on modules from collections that you install, it makes sense to start using the FQCN for modules in your playbooks: for example, instead of writing file, you'd write `ansible.builtin.file`. Also, for clarity, when you use custom collections, use the `collections` keyword at the top of the playbook to declare the ones you use (Example 15-2).

Example 15-2. Collections playbook

```
---
- name: Collections playbook
  hosts: all
  collections:
    - our_namespace.her_collection
  tasks:
    - name: Using her module from her collection
      her_module:
        option1: value

    - name: Using her role from her collection
      import_role:
        name: her_role

    - name: Using lookup and filter plug-ins from her collection
      debug:
        msg: '{{ lookup("her_lookup", "param1") | her_filter }}'

    - name: Create directory
      become: true
      become_user: root
      ansible.builtin.file:
        path: /etc/my_software
        state: directory
        mode: '0755'
...
```

Collections actually allow us to extend Ansible with "new words in the language," and we can choose to run `ansible-core` only with the collections that we really need.

Developing a Collection

Collections have a simple, predictable data structure with a straightforward defini-tion. The `ansible-galaxy` command-line utility has been updated to manage collec-tions, providing much of the same functionality as has always been used to manage, create, and consume roles. For example, `ansible-galaxy collection init` can be used to create a starting point for a new user-created collection:

```
$ ansible-galaxy collection init a_namespace.the_bundle
```

When I create a collection named the_bundle under the namespace ansiblebook, this directory structure is created:

```
ansiblebook/
└── the_bundle
    ├── README.md
    ├── docs
    ├── galaxy.yml
    ├── plugins
    │   └── README.md
    └── roles
```

The metadata for the collection is stored in the file *galaxy.yml* (Example 15-3). This includes links to the repository, its documentation, and the issue tracker. The tags are search terms for *https://galaxy.ansible.com*. build_ignore is used to filter files from the artifact.

Example 15-3. Example galaxy.yml

```
namespace: community
name: postgresql
version: 2.1.3
readme: README.md
authors:
  - Ansible PostgreSQL community
description: null
license_file: COPYING
tags:
  - database
  - postgres
  - postgresql
repository: https://github.com/ansible-collections/community.postgresql
documentation: https://docs.ansible.com/ansible/latest/collections/community/postgresql
homepage: https://github.com/ansible-collections/community.postgresql
issues: https://github.com/ansible-collections/community.postgresql/issues
build_ignore:
  - .gitignore
  - changelogs/.plugin-cache.yaml
  - '*.tar.gz'
```

Refer to the developer guide for distributing collections (*https://oreil.ly/zo08v*) for full information on the requirements and distribution process.

To distribute your collection and allow others to use it, you can publish your collection on one or more distribution servers. Distribution servers include Ansible Galaxy, Red Hat Automation Hub (content by certified Red Hat partners), and a privately hosted Automation Hub (see Chapter 23).

Collections distribution is based on tarballs instead of source code, as is usual for roles on Ansible Galaxy (*https://galaxy.ansible.com*). The *tag.gz* format is more suitable for use on-premises. The tarball is created from the collection with this command:

```
$ ansible-galaxy collection build
```

Verify the installation locally and test it:

```
$ ansible-galaxy collection install \
    a_namespace-the_bundle-1.0.0.tar.gz \
    -p ./collections
```

Now you can finally publish the collection:

```
$ ansible-galaxy collection publish path/to/a_namespace-the_bundle-1.0.0.tar.gz
```

Conclusion

Collections have been a great step forward in the maturity of the Ansible project. The project's vision of Ansible coming with "batteries included" turned out not to be maintainable over time with thousands of developers. We believe that having proper namespaces and segregation of duties, with vendors taking part in Red Hat's ecosystem and enough room for community innovation, will bring back users' trust in Ansible for critical IT automation. If you manage your dependencies well—your collections, roles, and Python libraries—then you can automate with confidence.

## CHAPTER 16

Creating Images

Creating Images with Packer

Packer is a tool that helps create machine images for multiple platforms from a single source. Both virtual machine images and container images can be constructed with Packer.

A Dockerfile lets you package your application into a single image that's easy to deploy in different environments (yet on a container platform only), which is why the Docker project has embraced the metaphor of the shipping container. Its remote API simplifies the automation of software systems that run on top of Docker, but one should be aware of the security challenges of such an API.

For simple container images the standard Dockerfile works just fine. However, when you start to create more complex images, you'll quickly miss the power that Ansible provides. Fortunately, you can use Ansible playbooks as a *provisioner* for HashiCorp Packer (*https://oreil.ly/Fktch*). Using a playbook with roles helps reduce the complexity.

The workflows in this chapter are useful when you want to postpone the choice of where and how you run your applications; with one source, you can create images for several cloud providers as well as for containers. Also you can reduce you cloud bills because you can combine online use in the cloud with local development in Vagrant VirtualBox.

Vagrant VirtualBox VM

The first example is a Packer definition to create a RHEL 8 image for Vagrant/Virtual-Box, or a *box* as VirtualBox calls it.

Build the image with:

```
$ packer build rhel8.pkr.hcl
```

This Packer file defines variables for the ISO image used in the Kickstart, the properties of the virtual machine used to build the image, and the steps of provisioning (Example 16-1). The installation of Red Hat Linux variants is based on Kickstart: when starting the machine, a boot command requests a Kickstart configuration over HTTP. This Kickstart configuration is input for the Red Hat installer, named Anaconda.

Example 16-1. rhel8.pkr.hcl

```
variable "iso_url1" {
  type    = string
  default = "file:///Users/Shared/rhel-8.4-x86_64-dvd.iso"
}
variable "iso_url2" {
  type    = string
  default = "https://developers.redhat.com/content-gateway/file/rhel-8.4-x86_64-dvd.iso"
}
variable "iso_checksum" {
  type    = string
  default = "sha256:48f955712454c32718dcde858dea5aca574376a1d7a4b0ed6908ac0b85597811"
}
source "virtualbox-iso" "rhel8" {
  boot_command            = [
   "<tab> text inst.ks=http://{{ .HTTPIP }}:{{ .HTTPPort }}/
  ks.cfg<enter><wait>"
   ]
  boot_wait               = "5s"
  cpus                    = 2
  disk_size               = 65536
  gfx_controller          = "vmsvga"
  gfx_efi_resolution      = "1920x1080"
  gfx_vram_size           = "128"
  guest_os_type           = "RedHat_64"
  guest_additions_mode    = "upload"
  hard_drive_interface    = "sata"
  headless                = true
  http_directory          = "kickstart"
  iso_checksum            = "${var.iso_checksum}"
  iso_urls                = ["${var.iso_url1}", "${var.iso_url2}"]
  memory                  = 4096
  nested_virt             = true
  shutdown_command        = "echo 'vagrant' | sudo -S /sbin/halt -h -p"
  ssh_password            = "vagrant"
  ssh_username            = "root"
  ssh_wait_timeout        = "10000s"
  rtc_time_base           = "UTC"
  virtualbox_version_file = ".vbox_version"
  vrdp_bind_address       = "0.0.0.0"
  vrdp_port_min           = "5900"
```

```
    vrdp_port_max        = "5900"
    vm_name              = "RedHat-EL8"
}
build {
  sources = ["source.virtualbox-iso.rhel8"]
  provisioner "shell" {
    execute_command = "echo 'vagrant' | {{ .Vars }} sudo -S -E bash '{{ .Path }}'"
    scripts         = ["scripts/vagrant.sh", "scripts/cleanup.sh"]
  }
  provisioner "ansible" {
    playbook_file = "./packer-playbook.yml"
  }
  post-processors {
    post-processor "vagrant" {
      keep_input_artifact  = true
      compression_level    = 9
      output               = "output-rhel8/rhel8.box"
      vagrantfile_template = "Vagrantfile.template"
    }
  }
}
```

When the Anaconda installer finishes, the virtual machine reboots and Packer starts provisioning by running the scripts and eventually *packer-playbook.yml* with the provisioner "ansible". This runs from your machine.

Individual developers can register and manage 16 RHEL 8 systems for free (*https://oreil.ly/Z8HUI*). Since this is subscription-based, you need to define three environment variables with your login (RH_USER) and password (RH_PASS) for Red Hat and optionally a Pool ID (*https://oreil.ly/DuyQ8*) (RH_POOL). You can do that in a shell before running Packer. This playbook in Example 16-2 registers the virtual machine and installs container tools.

Example 16-2. packer-playbook.yml

```
---
- hosts: all:!localhost
  become: true
  gather_facts: false
  tasks:

    - name: Register RHEL 8
      redhat_subscription:
        state: present
        username: "{{ lookup('env','RH_USER') }}"
        password: "{{ lookup('env','RH_PASS') }}"
        pool_ids: "{{ lookup('env','RH_POOL') }}"
        syspurpose:
          role: "Red Hat Enterprise Server"
          usage: "Development/Test"
          service_level_agreement: "Self-Support"
```

```
- name: Install packages
  yum:
    name: "{{ item }}"
    state: present
  loop:
    - podman
    - skopeo
...
```

When the build finishes successfully, you can add the box file as a template for Vagrant/VirtualBox:

```
$ vagrant box add --force --name RedHat-EL8 output-rhel8/rhel8.box
```

The sample code for this chapter includes a Vagrantfile that you can use to bring up a virtual machine named rhel8 based on that template:

```
$ vagrant up rhel8
```

Once it launches, you can connect to it with Remote Desktop as the Vagrant user on:

```
rdp://localhost:5900
```

Launch Visual Studio Code to see what was installed.

Combining Packer and Vagrant

For developing images with Packer, it makes sense to make use of Vagrant. You can use a Vagrantfile to prototype new features that you eventually add to the cloud images. A playbook running against a local virtual machine will finish quicker than a full Packer run, allowing you to develop faster. Packer runs in one go and will destroy any resources it created on failure. Having Vagrant on the side adds the possibility for more incremental development. This Vagrantfile launches a virtual machine with a box called "centos/7":

```
Vagrant.configure("2") do |config|
  config.vm.box = "centos/7"
  config.vm.box_check_update = true
  if Vagrant.has_plugin?("vagrant-vbguest")
    config.vbguest.auto_update = false
  end
  config.vm.graceful_halt_timeout=15
  config.ssh.insert_key = false
  config.ssh.forward_agent = true
  config.vm.provider "virtualbox" do |virtualbox|
    virtualbox.gui = false
    virtualbox.customize ["modifyvm", :id, "--memory", 2048]
    virtualbox.customize ["modifyvm", :id, "--vram", "64"]
  end
  config.vm.define :bastion do |host_config|
    host_config.vm.box = "centos/7"
    host_config.vm.hostname = "bastion"
    host_config.vm.network "private_network", ip: "192.168.56.20"
    host_config.vm.network "forwarded_port", id: 'ssh', guest: 22, host: 2220
```

```
      host_config.vm.synced_folder ".", "/vagrant", disabled: true
      host_config.vm.provider "virtualbox" do |vb|
        vb.name = "bastion"
        vb.customize ["modifyvm", :id, "--memory", 2048]
        vb.customize ["modifyvm", :id, "--vram", "64"]
      end
    end
    config.vm.provision :ansible do |ansible|
      ansible.compatibility_mode = "2.0"
      # Disable default limit to connect to all the servers
      ansible.limit = "all"
      ansible.galaxy_role_file = "ansible/roles/requirements.yml"
      ansible.galaxy_roles_path = "ansible/roles"
      ansible.inventory_path = "ansible/inventories/vagrant.ini"
      ansible.playbook = "ansible/playbook.yml"
      ansible.verbose = ""
    end
  end
```

Vagrant can configure many aspects of the Ansible provisioner; everything can happen automatically, but you can also run parts of the playbook with tags, log in to inspect, etc.

Cloud Images

Packer can create virtual machine images for the major cloud providers (AWS EC2, Azure, Digital Ocean, GCP, Hetzner Cloud, Oracle) and for hypervisors (OpenStack, Hyper-V, Proxmox, VMWare, VirtualBox, QEMU). Packer allows you to postpone decisions about deploying your applications and unifies lots of the differences in a common interface.

These cloud providers and technologies work with both Ansible and Packer:

Alicloud ECS	Amazon EC2	Azure	CloudStack	Digital Ocean
Docker	Google Cloud Platform	Hetzner Cloud	HuaweiCloud	Hyper-V
Kamatera	Linode	LXC	LXD	OpenStack
Oracle	Parallels	ProfitBricks	Proxmox	QEMU
Scaleway	Vagrant	VirtualBox	VMware	Vultr

Google Cloud Platform

Getting started with Google Cloud Platform (GCP) is straightforward. Sign in (*https://oreil.ly/4hLD4*), create a project in the Compute Engine, and copy the project ID (the name with a number appended). Create an environment variable with that project ID:

```
export GCP_PROJECT_ID=myproject-332421
```

Select a default and zone on the settings page (*https://oreil.ly/zTvzc*) for your project and create a pair of environment variables:

```
export CLOUDSDK_COMPUTE_REGION=europe-west4
export CLOUDSDK_COMPUTE_ZONE=europe-west4-b
```

The examples in *ansiblebook/ch16/cloud* are based on `ansible-roles` in the *requirements.yml* file. To install these roles, run:

```
cd ansible && ansible-galaxy install -f -p roles -r roles/requirements.yml
```

This Packer file (Example 16-3) defines variables for GCP, the base image used in the install, the name of the resulting image, the properties of the virtual machine used to build the image, and the steps in provisioning. The machine type used to create the image is unrelated to the machine that is instantiated from that image. We use powerful machines to create complex images, at the same cost, but the job is done quickly.

Example 16-3. gcp.pkr.hcl

```
variable "gcp_project_id" {
  type        = string
  default     = "${env("GCP_PROJECT_ID")}"
  description = "Create a project and use the project-id"
}
variable "gcp_region" {
  type        = string
  default     = "${env("CLOUDSDK_COMPUTE_REGION")}"
  description = "https://console.cloud.google.com/compute/settings"
}
variable "gcp_zone" {
  type        = string
  default     = "${env("CLOUDSDK_COMPUTE_ZONE")}"
  description = "https://console.cloud.google.com/compute/settings"
}
variable "gcp_centos_image" {
  type        = string
  default     = "centos-7-v20211105"
  description = ""
}
variable "image" {
  type        = string
  default     = "centos7"
  description = "Name of the image when created"
}
source "googlecompute" "gcp_image" {
  disk_size     = "30"
  image_family  = "centos-7"
  image_name    = "${var.image}"
  machine_type  = "e2-standard-2"
  project_id    = "${var.gcp_project_id}"
  region        = "${var.gcp_region}"
  source_image  = "${var.gcp_centos_image}"
```

```
  ssh_username  = "centos"
  state_timeout = "20m"
  zone          = "${var.gcp_zone}"
}
build {
  sources = ["googlecompute.gcp_image"]
  provisioner "shell" {
    execute_command = "{{ .Vars }} sudo -S -E bash '{{ .Path }}'"
    scripts         = ["scripts/ansible.sh"]
  }
  provisioner "ansible-local" {
    extra_arguments = ["--extra-vars \"image=${var.image}\""]
    playbook_dir    = "./ansible"
    playbook_file   = "ansible/packer.yml"
  }
  provisioner "shell" {
    execute_command = "{{ .Vars }} /usr/bin/sudo -S -E bash '{{ .Path }}'"
    script          = "scripts/cleanup.sh"
  }
}
```

First, the provisioner "shell" runs a script to install Ansible on the virtual machine. This can then be used as provisioner "ansible-local". Effectively, the whole directory where the Packer file is stored is uploaded to the virtual machine running in GCP, so be cautious when creating boxes in that same directory.

Azure

To get started with Azure, sign in (*https://portal.azure.com*) and search for your Subscription ID. Create an environment variable with it:

```
export ARM_SUBSCRIPTION_ID=xxxxxxxx-xxxx-xxxx-xxxx-xxxxxxxxxxxx
```

Before you can create images, you need to create two other things first: a resource group and a storage account. You also need to decide on which location (*https://oreil.ly/UOXYU*) to use to host them.

The Packer file (Example 16-4) to create a virtual machine image is similar to the one for GCP, but it needs more details and other variables.

Example 16-4. azure.pkr.hcl

```
variable "arm_subscription_id" {
  type        = string
  default     = "${env("ARM_SUBSCRIPTION_ID")}"
  description = "https://www.packer.io/docs/builders/azure/arm"
}
variable "arm_location" {
  type        = string
  default     = "westeurope"
  description = "https://azure.microsoft.com/en-us/global-infrastructure/geographies/"
}
```

```
variable "arm_resource_group" {
  type        = string
  default     = "${env("ARM_RESOURCE_GROUP")}"
  description = "make arm-resourcegroup in Makefile"
}
variable "arm_storage_account" {
  type        = string
  default     = "${env("ARM_STORAGE_ACCOUNT")}"
  description = "make arm-storageaccount in Makefile"
}
variable "image" {
  type        = string
  default     = "centos7"
  description = "Name of the image when created"
}
source "azure-arm" "arm_image" {
  azure_tags = {
    product = "${var.image}"
  }
  image_offer                         = "CentOS"
  image_publisher                     = "OpenLogic"
  image_sku                           = "7.7"
  location                            = "${var.arm_location}"
  managed_image_name                  = "${var.image}"
  managed_image_resource_group_name   = "${var.arm_resource_group}"
  os_disk_size_gb                     = "30"
  os_type                             = "Linux"
  subscription_id                     = "${var.arm_subscription_id}"
  vm_size                             = "Standard_D8_v3"
}
build {
  sources = ["source.azure-arm.arm_image"]
  provisioner "shell" {
    execute_command = "{{ .Vars }} sudo -S -E bash '{{ .Path }}'"
    scripts         = ["scripts/ansible.sh"]
  }
  provisioner "ansible-local" {
    extra_arguments = ["--extra-vars \"image=${var.image}\""]
    playbook_dir    = "./ansible"
    playbook_file   = "ansible/packer.yml"
  }
  provisioner "shell" {
    execute_command = "{{ .Vars }} /usr/bin/sudo -S -E bash '{{ .Path }}'"
    script          = "scripts/cleanup.sh"
  }
  provisioner "shell" {
    execute_command = "chmod +x {{ .Path }}; {{ .Vars }} sudo -E sh '{{ .Path }}'"
    inline = [
      "/usr/sbin/waagent -force -deprovision+user",
      "sync"
    ]
    inline_shebang = "/bin/sh -x"
  }
}
```

The provisioning extends the one for GCP by running the waagent at the end. This cleans the VM from users and SSH keys so that the image can safely be used in a new virtual machine instance.

Amazon EC2

To get started with EC2, the infrastructure as a service part of Amazon's cloud offering, log in (*https://aws.amazon.com/console*) and set up Identity and Access Management. We assume you know how to use the environment variables AWS_ACCESS_KEY_ID, AWS_SECRET_ACCESS_KEY, and AWS_REGION. More information on Amazon's cloud infrastructure is given in the next chapter.

The Packer template (Example 16-5) is similar to the other cloud image templates, yet it needs a region-specific base image in the variable aws_centos_image.

Example 16-5. aws.pkr.hcl

```
variable "aws_region" {
  type        = string
  default     = "${env("AWS_REGION")}"
  description = "https://docs.aws.amazon.com/general/latest/gr/rande.html"
}

variable "aws_centos_image" {
  type        = string
  default     = "ami-0e8286b71b81c3cc1"
  description = "https://docs.aws.amazon.com/AWSEC2/latest/UserGuide/AMIs.html"
}

variable "image" {
  type        = string
  default     = "centos7"
  description = "Name of the image when created"
}

locals { timestamp = regex_replace(timestamp(), "[- TZ:]", "") }

source "amazon-ebs" "aws_image" {
  ami_name      = "${var.image}-${local.timestamp}"
  instance_type = "t2.micro"
  region        = "${var.aws_region}"
  source_ami    = "${var.aws_centos_image}"
  ssh_username  = "centos"
  tags = {
    Name = "${var.image}"
  }
}

build {
  sources = ["source.amazon-ebs.aws_image"]
```

```
provisioner "shell" {
  execute_command = "{{ .Vars }} sudo -S -E bash '{{ .Path }}'"
  scripts         = ["scripts/ansible.sh"]
}

provisioner "ansible-local" {
  extra_arguments = ["--extra-vars \"image=${var.image}\""]
  playbook_dir    = "./ansible"
  playbook_file   = "ansible/playbook.yml"
}

provisioner "shell" {
  execute_command = "{{ .Vars }} /usr/bin/sudo -S -E bash '{{ .Path }}'"
  script          = "scripts/cleanup.sh"
}

}
```

The Playbook

The images are based on CentOS 7, a well-known distribution that can be used as a bastion host or as a VPN:

```
---
- hosts: all:127.0.0.1
  gather_facts: true
  become: true
  vars:
    net_allow:
      - '10.1.0.0/16'
      - '192.168.56.0/24'
    roles:
      - {role: common, tags: common}
      - {role: epel, tags: epel}
      - {role: ansible-auditd, tags: auditd}
      - {role: nettime, tags: nettime}
      - {role: rsyslog, tags: syslog}
      - {role: crontab, tags: crontab}
      - {role: keybase, tags: keybase}
      - {role: gpg_agent, tags: gpg}
      - {role: tailscale, tags: tailscale}
...
```

Virtual machines in the cloud need to be secured, so we run a couple of roles to set up security, auditing, and time synchronization. Then we configure the SSH settings and install extra software for encryption and VPN.

Docker Image: GCC 11

The last example in this chapter is using Packer to create a complex container image for GCC. GCC is used to create Linux and compile native software for it. Your Linux distribution came bundled with a version of GCC so you can compile C/C++

source code. GCC is under active development, and newer versions of the compilers typically create faster binaries of the same source code than older versions, due to advances in optimization technology. In short, if you want the fastest programs, use the latest compiler; if needed, compile GCC 11 yourself, because it is not bundled yet.

To compile GCC and use it for C++ programming on CentOS/RHEL 7, you need to install some other packages, tools, and libraries. For instance, Boost is a well-known set of libraries for C++ programming; CMake is a build tool that is widely used. The Red Hat Developer Toolset (DTS) bundles lots of other tools required by developers.

Let's assume you want to configure the versions and options in a playbook that requires other roles (which Bas has published on Ansible Galaxy). You can specify such requirements in a file named *requirements.yml* in a directory named *roles*:

```
---
- src: dockpack.base_gcc
  name: base_gcc
  version: '1.3.2'
- src: dockpack.compile_gcc
  name: compile_gcc
  version: 'v1.0.5'
- src: dockpack.base_cmake
  name: base_cmake
  version: '1.3.1'
- src: dockpack.base_boost
  name: base_boost
  version: '2.1.9'
- src: dockpack.base_python
  name: base_python
  version: 'v1.1.2'
```

The playbook sets the variables and the order of installation (Example 16-6). To compile the source code for GCC 11 you need GCC, a kind of a chicken-and-egg problem. We will install Developer Toolset 10 from Software Collections (*https://oreil.ly/6EzPZ*) on CentOS 7 to have the latest release of GCC, and we'll also install Python and CMake before compiling GCC. Once we compile GCC, we can compile Boost with it.

Example 16-6. docker-playbook.yml

```
---
- hosts: all:!localhost
  gather_facts: true
  vars:
    # Install Software Collections?
    collections_enabled: true
    # Devtoolset to compile with
    DTSVER: 10
    # C++ compiler to compile
    GCCVER: '11.2.0'
    dependencies_url_signed: false
```

```
  # Boost version to compile
  boost_version: 1.66.0
  boost_cflags: '-fPIC -fno-rtti'
  boost_cxxflags: '-fPIC -fno-rtti'
  boost_properties: "link=static threading=multi runtime-link=shared"
 roles:
  - role: base_python
  - role: base_cmake
  - role: base_gcc
  - role: compile_gcc
  - role: base_boost
...
```

Packer's behavior is determined by a template, which consists of a series of declarations and commands for Packer to follow. This template, *gcc.pkr.hcl* (Example 16-7), tells Packer what plug-ins (builders, provisioners, post-processors) to use, how to configure each of those plug-ins, and what order to run them in.

Example 16-7. gcc.pkr.hcl

```
packer {
  required_plugins {
    docker = {
      version = ">= 0.0.7"
      source = "github.com/hashicorp/docker"
    }
  }
}
source "docker" "gcc" {
  changes    = ["CMD [\"/bin/bash\"]", "ENTRYPOINT [\"\"]"]
  commit = true
  image  = "centos:7"
  run_command = [
    "-d",
    "-i",
    "-t",
    "--network=host",
    "--entrypoint=/bin/sh",
    "--", "{{ .Image }}"
  ]
}
build {
  name    = "docker-gcc"
  sources = [
    "source.docker.gcc"
  ]
  provisioner "shell" {
    inline = ["yum -y install sudo"]
  }
  provisioner "ansible" {
    playbook_file = "./playbooks/docker-playbook.yml"
    galaxy_file   = "./roles/requirements.yml"
  }
```

```
  post-processors {
    post-processor "docker-tag" {
        repository =  "localhost/gcc11-centos7"
        tags = ["0.1"]
      }
  }
}
```

To create the container image, run the Packer build:

```
$ packer build gcc.pkr.hcl
```

Please note that this will take hours to complete.

Conclusion

We know that Docker images can become complex when created with Dockerfiles. Packer and Ansible, however, provide a clean separation of concerns that allows us to rethink what we do with our software at any time. Packer, Vagrant, and Ansible are a fantastic combination for creating base images for infrastructure as a service, in the cloud, and on-premises. If you work in a large organization, you can create base images that others can build upon.

## CHAPTER 17

Cloud Infrastructure

Ansible has several features that make working with public and private clouds much easier. A cloud can be seen as a layered platform where the user can create resources to run software applications.[1] Users can dynamically allocate or programmatically remove cloud infrastructure—including compute, networking, and storage resources—which is called *infrastructure as a service* (*IaaS*).

An IaaS cloud service enables users to provision (create) new servers. All IaaS clouds are *self-service*, meaning that the user interacts directly with a software service rather than, say, filing a ticket with the IT department. Most IaaS clouds offer three types of interfaces to allow users to interact with the system:

- Web interface
- Command-line interface
- REST API

In the case of EC2, the web interface is called the AWS Management Console (*https://oreil.ly/b443M*), and the command-line interface is called (unimaginatively) the AWS Command-Line Interface (*https://oreil.ly/tm9Rx*). The REST API is documented at Amazon (*http://amzn.to/1F7g6yA*).

IaaS clouds typically use virtual machines to implement the servers, although you can build an IaaS cloud by using *bare-metal servers* (where users run directly on the

---

1 The National Institute of Standards and Technology (NIST) has a pretty good definition of cloud computing in "The NIST Definition of Cloud Computing" (*https://oreil.ly/Y1hnY*).

hardware rather than inside a virtual machine) or containers. Most IaaS clouds let you do more than just start up and tear down servers. In particular, they typically let you provision storage so you can attach and detach disks to and from your servers. This type of storage is commonly referred to as *block storage*. They also offer networking features, so you can define network topologies that describe how your servers are interconnected, as well as firewall rules or security groups that restrict networking to and from your servers.

The next layer in a cloud consists of specific innovations developed by cloud service providers and application runtimes like container clusters, application servers, serverless environments, operating systems, and databases. This layer is called *platform as a service (PaaS)*. You manage your applications and data; the platform manages the rest. PaaS allows distinctive features that are a point of competition among cloud providers, especially since competing over cost-efficiency in IaaS is a race to the bottom. However, the Kubernetes container platform, a common platform in any cloud, has seen the greatest interest.

Any app that runs in the cloud has many layers, but when only one is visible to the cloud customer (or their customers) it is *software as a service (SaaS)*. They just use the software, unaware of the servers' whereabouts.

What Is Cloud Provisioning?

We'll be precise about what we mean by provisioning. To start, here's a typical user interaction with an IaaS cloud:

User
> I want five servers, each one with two CPUs, 4 GB of memory, and 100 GB of storage, running Ubuntu 20.04.

Service
> Request received. Your request number is 432789.

User
> What's the current status of request 432789?

Service
> Your servers are ready to go, at IP addresses *203.0.113.5*, *203.0.113.13*, *203.0.113.49*, *203.0.113.124*, and *203.0.113.209*.

User
> I'm done with the servers associated with request 432789.

Service
> Request received. The servers will be terminated.

Provisioning is the process of creating the resources needed to configure and run software.

The professional way to create resources in a cloud is using its API in one way or another, called *infrastructure as code*. There are some generic cloud APIs and vendor-specific APIs, and as programmers do, there are abstractions that let us combine some of these APIs. You can create a *declarative* model of the desired state of the resources, have the tool compare that to the current state, and act accordingly; or you can *imperatively* code the actions required to achieve one desired state. Starting from scratch, either method will need to describe the resources and their properties. The imperative coder needs to know more about the order of the stack's creation: network, subnet, security group, network interface, disk, virtual machine image, virtual machine. The declarative coder only needs to know the interdependencies. HashiCorp Terraform is a declarative tool for provisioning, whereas Ansible is more imperative: it can define one state in an idempotent way. These two methods differ when you want to change the infrastructure as well as when the infrastructure changes state by other means than the provisioning tool.

Could you simply provision any other version of the infrastructure? Ansible modules are not required to be inversible, but with some extra effort we can make our playbooks idempotent and *undoable*, that is, using a desired state variable to allow us to remove the resources:

```
state: "{{ desired_state }}"
```

But even if we implement the undo/redo pattern, Ansible has no state that it uses to plan changes, like Terraform does. Ansible inventories can be versioned with idempotent, desired-state provisioning playbooks in similar amounts of code, due to the length of the object property descriptions. The amount of Ansible code increases when, to make changes, you need to query the state of the infrastructure.

Ansible ships with modules for many other cloud services, including Microsoft Azure, Alibaba, Cloudscale, Digital Ocean, Google Compute Engine, Hetzner, Oracle Cloud, IBM Cloud, Rackspace, and Vultr, as well as private clouds built using oVirt, OpenStack, CloudStack, Proxmox, and VMWare vSphere.

When you install Ansible, most of the capabilities are provided by bundled collections, which might not be the very latest version. When you use a specific cloud service, then it makes sense to install the collection for it. If you can't find the vendor in Table 17-1, then look into the documentation for the community.general collection (*https://oreil.ly/HHKMk*), which has lots of functionality. In general, if the vendor has not published a collection yet, you will need to install the required Python library for the cloud of your choice.

Table 17-1. Cloud service collections and Python libraries

Cloud	Collection	Python library
Amazon Web Services (*https://oreil.ly/1T1Rp*)	amazon.aws	boto3
Alibaba Cloud Compute Services (*https://oreil.ly/9YoAD*)		footmark
Cloudscale.ch (*https://oreil.ly/k3iCE*)	cloudscale_ch.cloud	
CloudStack (*https://oreil.ly/AdPO8*)	ngine_io.cloudstack	cs
Digital Ocean (*https://oreil.ly/Nhbkq*)	community.digitalocean	
Google Cloud (*https://oreil.ly/TqTn9*)	google.cloud	google-auth requests
Hetzner Cloud (*https://oreil.ly/bh4Pw*)	hetzner.hcloud	hcloud-python
IBM Cloud (*https://oreil.ly/R11XU*)	ibm.cloudcollection	
Microsoft Azure (*https://oreil.ly/B4nmQ*)	azure.azcollection	ansible[azure]
Openstack (*https://oreil.ly/VGkRE*)	openstack.cloud	
Oracle Cloud Infrastructure (*https://oreil.ly/Si7nX*)	oracle.oci	oci
Ovirt (*https://www.ovirt.org*)	ovirt.ovirt	
Packet.net (*https://oreil.ly/8PYcX*)		packet-python
Rackspace (*https://oreil.ly/ycnze*)	openstack.cloud	
Scaleway (*https://oreil.ly/Yf8Of*)	community.general	
Vultr (*https://www.vultr.com*)	ngine_io.vultr	

Amazon EC2

This chapter focuses on Amazon Elastic Compute Cloud (EC2) because it's the most popular cloud service. However, many of the concepts should transfer to other clouds supported by Ansible. Ansible supports EC2 in two ways:

- A dynamic inventory plug-in for automatically populating your Ansible inventory, instead of manually specifying your servers
- Modules that perform actions on EC2, such as creating new servers

This chapter covers both the EC2 dynamic inventory plug-in and the bundled EC2 modules.

Ansible has more than a hundred modules that relate to EC2 as well as to other features offered by Amazon Web Services (AWS). We have space to cover only a few of them here, so we will focus on the basics.

Terminology

EC2 exposes many concepts. We'll explain these concepts as they come up in this chapter, but there are three terms we'd like to cover up front: *instance*, *Amazon Machine Image*, and *tags*.

Instance

EC2's documentation uses the term *instance* to refer to a virtual machine, and we use that terminology in this chapter. Keep in mind that an EC2 instance is a *host* from Ansible's perspective.

EC2 documentation (*http://amzn.to/1Fw5S8l*) interchangeably uses the terms *creating instances*, *launching instances*, and *running instances* to describe the process of bringing up a new instance. However, *starting instances* means something different— starting up an instance that had previously been put in the stopped state.

Amazon Machine Image

An *Amazon Machine Image* (AMI) is a virtual machine image that has a filesystem with an operating system installed on it. When you create an instance on EC2, you choose which operating system you want your instance to run by specifying the AMI that EC2 will use to create the instance.

Each AMI has an associated identifier string, called an *AMI ID*, which starts with `ami-` and then has hexadecimal characters—for example, `ami-1234567890abcdef0`. Prior to January 2016, the IDs assigned to newly created AMIs used eight characters after the hyphen (for example, `ami-1a2b3c4d`). Between January 2016 and June 2018, Amazon was in the process of changing the IDs of all these resource types to use 17 characters after the hyphen. Depending on when your account was created, you might have resources with short IDs, though any new resources of these types receive the longer IDs.

Tags

EC2 lets you annotate your instances (and other entities such as AMIs, volumes, and security groups) with custom metadata that it calls *tags*. Tags are just key-value pairs of strings. For example, we could annotate an instance with the following tags:

```
Name=Staging database
env=staging
type=database
```

If you've ever given your EC2 instance a name in the AWS Management Console, you've used tags without even knowing it. EC2 implements instance names as tags; the key is `Name`, and the value is whatever name you gave the instance. Other than that, there's nothing special about the Name tag, and you can also configure the management console to show the values of other tags.

Tags don't have to be unique, so you can have one hundred instances that all have the same tag. Because Ansible's EC2 modules often use tags to identify resources and implement idempotence, they will come up several times in this chapter.

 It's good practice to add meaningful tags to all your EC2 resources, since they function as a form of documentation.

Specifying Credentials

When you make requests against Amazon EC2, you need to specify credentials. If you've used the Amazon web console, you've used your username and password to log in. However, all the bits of Ansible that interact with EC2 talk to the EC2 API. The API does not use a username and password for credentials. Instead, it uses two strings: an *access key ID* and a *secret access key*.

These strings typically look like this:

- Sample EC2 access key ID: `AKIAIOSFODNN7EXAMPLE`
- Sample EC2 secret access key: `wJalrXUtnFEMI/K7MDENG/bPxRfiCYEXAMPLEKEY`

You can obtain these credentials through the *Identity and Access Management (IAM)* service. Using this service, you can create different IAM users with different permissions. Once you have created an IAM user, you can generate the access key ID and secret access key for that user.

When you are calling EC2-related modules, you can pass these strings as module arguments. For the dynamic inventory plug-in, you can specify the credentials in the *aws_ec2.yml* file (discussed in the next section). However, both the EC2 modules and the dynamic inventory plug-in also allow you to specify these credentials as environment variables. You can also use something called *IAM roles (https://oreil.ly/2oll2)* if your control machine is itself an Amazon EC2 instance.

Environment Variables

Although Ansible does allow you to pass credentials explicitly as arguments to modules, it also supports setting EC2 credentials as environment variables. Example 17-1 shows how to set these environment variables.

Example 17-1. Setting EC2 environment variables

```
# Don't forget to replace these values with your actual credentials!
export AWS_ACCESS_KEY_ID=AKIAIOSFODNN7EXAMPLE
export AWS_SECRET_ACCESS_KEY=wJatrXUtnFEMI/K7MDENG/bPxRfiCYEXAMPLEKEY
export AWS_DEFAULT_REGION=us-west-2
```

Bas recommends using environment variables for AWS_ACCESS_KEY_ID and AWS_SECRET_ACCESS_KEY, because this allows you to use EC2-related modules and inventory plug-ins without putting your credentials in any of your Ansible-related files.

Bas exports the variables in a file named *.env.rc*, which is encrypted with ansible-vault. The file is loaded when the session starts. Bas uses Zsh, so in this case, that file is *~/.zshrc*. If you're running Bash, you might want to put it in your *-/.bash_profile* file. If you're using a shell other than Bash or Zsh, you're probably knowledgeable enough to know which dotfile to modify to set these environment variables:

```
export ANSIBLE_VAULT_PASSWORD_FILE=~/.apw_exe
$(ansible-vault view ~/.ec2.rc)
```

The ANSIBLE_VAULT_PASSWORD_FILE is an executable that is used to decrypt yet another file that has the password. Bas uses GNU Privacy Guard (GPG), the open source variant of PGP:

```
#!/bin/sh
exec gpg -q -d ${HOME}/vault_pw.gpg
```

GPG ensures there is no sensitive data unencrypted at rest: in other words, there is no plain-text file with the vault password. GPG Agent removes the burden of typing the password all the time.

Once you have set these credentials in your environment variables, you can invoke the Ansible EC2 modules on your control machine and use the dynamic inventory.

Configuration Files

An insecure alternative to using environment variables is to place your EC2 credentials in a configuration file. As discussed in the next section, Ansible uses the Python Boto3 library, so it supports Boto3's conventions for maintaining credentials in a Boto configuration file. We don't cover the format here; for more information, check out the Boto3 config documentation (*https://oreil.ly/FtqeK*).

Prerequisite: Boto3 Python Library

All the Ansible EC2 functionality requires you to install the Python Boto3 library as a Python system package on the control machine. To do so, use this command:[2]

```
# python3 -m venv --system-site-packages /usr/local
# source /usr/local/bin/activate
(local) # pip3 install boto3
```

If you already have instances running on EC2, you can verify that Boto3 is installed properly and that your credentials are correct by interacting with the Python command line, as shown in Example 17-2.

Example 17-2. Testing out Boto3 and credentials

```
$ python3
Python 3.6.8 (default, Sep  9 2021, 07:49:02)
[GCC 8.5.0 20210514 (Red Hat 8.5.0-3)] on linux
Type "help", "copyright", "credits" or "license" for more information.
>>> import boto3
>>> ec2 = boto3.client("ec2")
>>> regions = [region["RegionName"] for region in ec2.describe_regions()["Regions"]]
>>> for r in regions:
...     print(f"  - {r}")
...
  - eu-north-1
  - ap-south-1
  - eu-west-3
  - eu-west-2
  - eu-west-1
  - ap-northeast-3
  - ap-northeast-2
  - ap-northeast-1
  - sa-east-1
  - ca-central-1
  - ap-southeast-1
  - ap-southeast-2
  - eu-central-1
  - us-east-1
  - us-east-2
  - us-west-1
  - us-west-2
>>>
```

When you explore the modules installed with Ansible, then you might stumble upon legacy modules that require the Boto library for Python 2, for instance the `ec2` module maintained by the Ansible Core Team (not by Amazon):

---

2 You might need to use sudo or activate another virtualenv to install this package, depending on how you installed Ansible.

```
fatal: [localhost]: FAILED! => changed=false
  msg: boto required for this module
```

In such cases, you should ensure that the playbook uses the fully qualified module names, prefixed with `amazon.aws`.

Dynamic Inventory

If your servers live on EC2, you don't want to keep a separate copy of these servers in an Ansible inventory file, because that file is going to go stale as you spin up new servers and tear down old ones. It's much simpler to track your EC2 servers by taking advantage of Ansible's support for a dynamic inventory plug-in to pull information about hosts directly from EC2.

This plug-in is part of the `amazon.aws` collection (*https://oreil.ly/OpS3x*) (version 2.2.0). You might already have this collection installed if you installed the Ansible package. To check which version is installed, run:

```
$ ansible-galaxy collection list|grep amazon.aws
```

To install the latest version of the collection, use:

```
$ ansible-galaxy collection install amazon.aws
```

Previously, we had a *playbooks/inventory/hosts* file that served as our inventory. Now, we're going to use a *playbooks/inventory* directory. We'll place a file named *aws_ec2.yml* into that directory.

Example 17-3 shows an example of a simple EC2 inventory.

Example 17-3. EC2 dynamic inventory

```
---
# Minimal example using environment variables
# Fetch all hosts in eu-central-1
plugin: amazon.aws.aws_ec2
regions:
  - eu-north-1
  - ap-south-1
  - eu-west-1
  - ap-northeast-1
  - sa-east-1
  - ca-central-1
  - ap-southeast-1
  - eu-central-1
  - us-east-1
  - us-west-1
# Ignores 403 errors rather than failing
strict_permissions: false
...
```

If you've set up your environment variables as described in the previous section, you should be able to confirm that the inventory is working by running the following:

```
$ ansible-inventory --list|jq -r .aws_ec2
```

The command should output information about your EC2 instances. The structure should look something like this:

```
{
  "hosts": [
    "ec2-203-0-113-75.eu-central-1.compute.amazonaws.com"
  ]
}
```

Inventory Caching

When Ansible executes the EC2 inventory plug-in, the script has to make requests against one or more EC2 endpoints to retrieve this information. Because this can take time, the script can cache the information the first time it is invoked by writing to local cache: on subsequent calls, the dynamic inventory script will use the cached information until the cache expires.

You can modify this behavior by editing the cache configuration options in the Ansible configuration file *ansible.cfg*. The cache timeout defaults to 300 seconds (5 minutes). If you want caching for an hour, you can set it to 3,600 (Example 17-4).

Example 17-4. ansible.cfg

```
[defaults]
fact_caching = jsonfile
fact_caching_connection = /tmp/ansible_fact_cache
fact_caching_timeout = 3600

[inventory]
cache = true
cache_plugin = jsonfile
cache_timeout = 3600
```

Listing the inventory should be faster in the next hour after you do this. Ansible will cache inventory details in the fact cache. You can verify that the cache has been created:

```
$ ls /tmp/ansible_fact_cache/
ansible_inventory_amazon.aws.aws_ec2_6b737s_3206c
```

 If you create or destroy instances, the EC2 dynamic inventory script will not reflect these changes unless the cache expires or you manually remove the cache.

Other Configuration Options

The *aws_ec2.yml* file includes configuration options that control the behavior of the dynamic inventory script. Because the parameters are well-documented (*https://oreil.ly/FGx2h*), we won't cover those options in detail here.

Defining Dynamic Groups with Tags

Recall that the dynamic inventory script automatically creates groups based on qualities such as instance type, security group, key pair, and tags. EC2 tags are the most convenient way of creating Ansible groups because you can define them however you like.

When using the inventory plug-in, you can configure extra inventory structure based on the metadata returned by AWS. For example, you might use keyed_groups to create groups from instance tags:

```
plugin: aws_ec2
keyed_groups:
  - prefix: tag
    key: tags
```

Ansible will automatically create a group called tag_type_web that contains all of the servers tagged with a name of type and a value of web.

EC2 allows you to apply multiple tags to an instance. For example, if you have separate staging and production environments, you can tag your production web servers like this:

```
env=production
type=web
```

Now you can refer to production machines as tag_env_production and your web servers as tag_type_web. If you want to refer to your production web servers, use the Ansible intersection syntax, like this:

```
hosts: tag_env_production:&tag_type_web
```

Applying Tags to Existing Resources

Ideally, you'll tag your EC2 instances as soon as you create them. However, if you're using Ansible to manage existing EC2 instances, you will likely already have instances running that you need to tag. Ansible has an ec2_tag module that allows you to do so.

For example, if you want to tag an instance with env=production and type=web, you can do it in a simple playbook, as shown in Example 17-5.

Example 17-5. Adding EC2 tags to instances

```
---
- name: Add tags to existing instances
  hosts: localhost
  vars:
    web_production:
      - i-1234567890abcdef0
      - i-1234567890abcdef1
    web_staging:
      - i-abcdef01234567890
      - i-33333333333333333
  tasks:
    - name: Tag production webservers
      ec2_tag:
        resource: "{{ item }}"
        region: "{{ lookup('env','AWS_REGION') }}"
        args:
          tags: {type: web, env: production}
      loop: "{{ web_production }}"

    - name: Tag staging webservers
      ec2_tag:
        resource: "{{ item }}"
        region: "{{ lookup('env','AWS_REGION') }}"
        args:
          tags: {type: web, env: staging}
      loop: "{{ web_staging }}"
...
```

This example uses the inline syntax for YAML dictionaries when specifying the tags ({type: web, env: production}) to make the playbook more compact, but the regular YAML dictionary syntax would work as well:

```
tags:
  type: web
  env: production
```

Nicer Group Names

Personally, Lorin doesn't like the name tag_type_web for a group. He prefers to just call it web.

To change that name, we need to add a new file to the *playbooks/inventory* directory that will have information about groups. This is just a traditional Ansible inventory file, which we'll call *playbooks/inventory/hosts* (see Example 17-6).

Example 17-6. playbooks/inventory/hosts

```
[web:children]
tag_type_web
[tag_type_web]
```

Once you do this, you can refer to web as a group in your Ansible plays.

 The aws_ec2 inventory plug-in has many other features for fine-grained control over your inventory. Example 17-3 is just enough to get started. For more information refer to the aws_ec2 inventory plug-in documentation (*https://oreil.ly/nP8px*).

Virtual Private Clouds

When Amazon first launched EC2 back in 2006, all of the EC2 instances were effectively connected to the same flat network.[3] Every EC2 instance had a private IP address and a public IP address. In 2009, Amazon introduced a feature called *Virtual Private Cloud* (VPC). VPC allows users to control how their instances are networked together and whether they will be publicly accessible from the internet or isolated. Amazon uses the term *VPC* to describe the virtual networks that users can create inside EC2. Think of a VPC as an isolated network. When you create a VPC, you specify an IP address range. It must be a subset of one of the private address ranges (*10.0.0.0/8, 172.16.0.0/12,* or *192.168.0.0/16*).

You carve your VPC into subnets, which have IP ranges that are subsets of the IP range of your entire VPC. In Example 17-14, the VPC has the IP range *10.0.0.0/16*, and you'll associate two subnets: *10.0.0.0/24* and *10.0.10.0/24*.

When you launch an instance, you assign it to a subnet in a VPC. You can configure your subnets so that your instances get either public or private IP addresses. EC2 also allows you to define routing tables for routing traffic between your subnets and to create internet gateways for routing traffic from your subnets to the internet.

Configuring networking is a complex topic that's (way) outside the scope of this book. For more info, check out Amazon's EC2 documentation on VPC (*http://amzn.to/1Fw89Af*).

Configuring ansible.cfg for Use with ec2

When Lorin is using Ansible to configure EC2 instances, he adds the following lines to his *ansible.cfg file*:

```
[defaults]
remote_user = ec2-user
host_key_checking = False
```

---

3 Amazon's internal network is divided into subnets, but users do not have any control over how instances are allocated to subnets.

Depending on the images you use, you need to SSH as a particular user, in this case ec2-user, but it could also be ubuntu or centos. Lorin also turns off host-key checking, since he doesn't know in advance what the host keys are for new instances.[4]

Launching New Instances

The amazon.aws.ec2_instance module allows you to launch new instances on EC2. It's one of the most complex Ansible modules because it supports so many arguments.

Example 17-7 shows a simple playbook for launching an Ubuntu 20.04 EC2 instance.

Example 17-7. Action to create an EC2 instance

```
- name: Configure and start EC2 instance
  amazon.aws.ec2_instance:
    name: 'web1'
    image_id: 'ami-0e8286b71b81c3cc1'
    instance_type: 't2.micro'
    key_name: 'ec2key'
    region: "{{ lookup('env', 'AWS_REGION') }}"
    security_group: "{{ security_group }}"
    network:
      assign_public_ip: true
    tags:
      type: web
      env: production
    volumes:
      - device_name: /dev/sda1
        ebs:
          volume_size: 16
          delete_on_termination: true
    wait: true
    register: ec2
```

Let's go over what these parameters mean.

The image_id parameter in Example 17-7 refers to the AMI ID, which you must always specify. As described earlier in the chapter, an image is basically a filesystem that contains an installed operating system. The example just used, ami-0e8286b71b81c3cc1, refers to an image that has the 64-bit version of CentOS 7 installed on it.

The instance_type parameter describes the number of CPU cores and the amount of memory and storage your instance will have. EC2 doesn't let you choose arbitrary

---

4 From Lorin: It's possible to retrieve the host key by querying EC2 for the instance console output, but I must admit that I never bother doing this because I've never gotten around to writing a proper script that parses out the host key from the console output.

combinations of cores, memory, and storage. Instead, Amazon defines a collection of instance types.[5] Example 17-7 uses the *t2.micro* instance type. This is a 64-bit instance type with one core, 1 GB of RAM, and EBS-based storage (more on that later).

The key_name parameter refers to a registered SSH key pair. Amazon uses SSH key pairs to provide users with access to their servers. Before you start your first server, you must either create a new SSH key pair or upload the public key of a key pair that you have previously created. Either way, you must register your SSH key pair under a name.

The regions parameter refers to the location of the data center where the instance will be hosted. In this example we look up the value for the environment variable AWS_REGION.

The security_group parameter refers to a list of firewall rules associated with an instance. Such security groups determine the kinds of inbound and outbound network connections that are allowed, like for a web server to listen on TCP ports 80 and 443, and for Ansible to use SSH on TCP port 22.

Under network we specified that we'd like a public IP address on the internet.

The tags parameter associates metadata with the instance in the form of EC2 tags, which are key-value pairs. In the preceding example, we set the following tags:

```
tags:
  Name: ansiblebook
  type: web
  env: production
```

 Invoking the amazon.aws.ec2_instance module from the command line is a simple way to terminate an instance, assuming you know the instance ID:

```
$ ansible localhost -m amazon.aws.ec2_instance -a \
'instance_id=i-01176c6682556a360' \
-a state=absent'
```

EC2 Key Pairs

In Example 17-7, we assumed that Amazon already knew about an SSH key pair named mykey. Let's see how you can use Ansible to register your key pair.

---

5 There's also a handy (unofficial) website (*https://oreil.ly/ztoCB*) that provides a single table with all of the available EC2 instance types.

Creating a New Key

First you create a secure key pair by using a passphrase on a keypair of type ed25519, with brute-force protection:

```
$ ssh-keygen -t ed25519 -a 100 -C '' -f ~/.ssh/ec2-user
```

The public key is saved in the file *~/.ssh/ec2-user.pub*. This file will have just one line, like:

```
ssh-ed25519 AAAAC3NzaC1lZDI1NTE5AAAAIOvcnUtQI2wd4GwfOL4RckmwTinG1Zw7ia96EpVObs9x
```

Uploading Your Public Key

If you have an SSH key pair, you should only upload the public key to Amazon to register the key pair. The private key is not to be shared with anyone, and you should not log the public key you use, either. Privacy and security matter.

```
---
- name: Register SSH keypair
  hosts: localhost
  gather_facts: false
  tasks:
    - name: Upload public key
      amazon.aws.ec2_key:
        name: ec2key
        key_material: "{{ item }}"
        state: present
        force: true
      no_log: true
      with_file:
        - ~/.ssh/ec2key.pub
...
```

Security Groups

Example 17-7 assumes that the security group my_security_group already exists. We can use the amazon.aws.ec2_group module to ensure that we have this security group before we use it.

Security groups are like firewall rules: you specify who may connect to the machine and how. In Example 17-8, we specify the security group as allowing anybody on the internet to connect to ports 80 and 443. For this example, we allow anybody on the internet to connect on port 22, but you might want to restrict that to known addresses. We allow outbound HTTP and HTTPS connections to the internet, because we need them enabled to download packages from the internet. A safer alternative would be to allow access to a repository or filtering proxy server.

Example 17-8. Security groups

```
- name: Configure SSH security group
  amazon.aws.ec2_group:
    name: my_security_group
    description: SSH and Web Access
    rules:
      - proto: tcp
        from_port: 22
        to_port: 22
        cidr_ip: '0.0.0.0/0'
      - proto: tcp
        from_port: 80
        to_port: 80
        cidr_ip: 0.0.0.0/0
      - proto: tcp
        from_port: 443
        to_port: 443
        cidr_ip: 0.0.0.0/0
    rules_egress:
      - proto: tcp
        from_port: 443
        to_port: 443
        cidr_ip: 0.0.0.0/0
      - proto: tcp
        from_port: 80
        to_port: 80
        cidr_ip: 0.0.0.0/0
```

If you haven't used security groups before, the parameters to the rules dictionary bear some explanation. Table 17-2 supplies a quick summary of the parameters for security group connection rules.

Table 17-2. Security group rule parameters

Parameter	Description
proto	IP protocol (tcp, udp, icmp) or all to allow all protocols and ports
cidr_ip	Subnet of IP addresses that are allowed to connect, using CIDR notation
from_port	The first port in the range of permitted ports
to_port	The last port in the range of permitted ports

Permitted IP Addresses

Security groups allow you to restrict which IP addresses may connect to an instance. You specify a subnet by using classless interdomain routing (CIDR) notation. An example of a subnet specified with CIDR notation is *203.0.113.0/24*,[6] which means

---

6 This example happens to correspond to a special IP address range named TEST-NET-3, which is reserved for examples. It's the *example.com* of IP subnets.

that the first 24 bits of the IP address must match the first 24 bits of *203.0.113.0*. People sometimes just say "/24" to refer to the size of a CIDR that ends in */24*.

A */24* is a nice value because it corresponds to the first three octets of the address, namely 203.0.113.[7] What this means is that any IP address that starts with *203.0.113* is in the subnet, that is, any IP address in the range *203.0.113.0* to *203.0.113.255*. Be aware that addresses 0 and 255 are not allowed for hosts.

If you specify *0.0.0.0/0*, any IP address may connect.

Security Group Ports

One of the things that we find confusing about EC2 security groups is the `from port` and `to port` notation. EC2 allows you to specify a range of ports that you may use. For example, you could allow TCP connections on any port from 5900 to 5999 by specifying the following:

```
- proto: tcp
  from_port: 5900
  to_port: 5999
  cidr_ip: 0.0.0.0/0
```

However, we find the from/to notation confusing because we almost never specify a range of ports.[8] Instead, I usually want to enable nonconsecutive ports, such as 80 and 443. Therefore, in almost every case, the `from_port` and `to_port` parameters are going to be the same.

The `amazon.aws.ec2_group` module has other parameters. Check out its documentation for more details.

Getting the Latest AMI

In Example 17-7, we explicitly specified a CentOS AMI like this:

```
image_id: ami-0e8286b71b81c3cc1
```

However, suppose you want to launch the latest Ubuntu 20.04 image instead: you wouldn't want to hardcode the AMI like this. That's because Canonical (the company that runs the Ubuntu project) frequently makes minor updates to Ubuntu, and every time it does, it generates a new AMI. Just because `ami-0d527b8c289b4af7f` corresponded to the latest release of Ubuntu 20.04 yesterday doesn't mean it will correspond to the latest release of Ubuntu 20.04 tomorrow.

---

7 Subnets that are /8, /16, and /24 make splendid examples because the math is much easier than, say, /17 or /23.

8 Sharp observers might have noticed that ports 5900–5999 are commonly used by the VNC remote desktop protocol, one of the few applications where specifying a range of ports makes sense.

The `amazon.aws` collection has a module called `ec2_ami_info` that will retrieve a list of AMIs based on filter criteria, such as the architecture, name of the image, and so forth. Example 17-9 shows how to use this to find an AMI identifier for the latest version of 64-bit Ubuntu Focal 20.04 running for an EBS-backed instance that uses SSDs. You could use the same means to create an instance with the latest AMI.

Example 17-9. Retrieving the latest Ubuntu AMI

```
---
- name: Find latest Ubuntu image on Amazon EC2
  hosts: localhost
  gather_facts: false
  tasks:
    - name: Gather information on Ubuntu AMIs published by Canonical
      amazon.aws.ec2_ami_info:
        owners: 099720109477
        filters:
          name: "ubuntu/images/hvm-ssd/ubuntu-focal-20.04-*"
          architecture: "x86_64"
          root-device-type: "ebs"
          virtualization-type: "hvm"
          state: "available"
      register: ec2_ami_info

    - name: Sort the list of AMIs by date for the latest image
      set_fact:
        latest_ami: |
          {{ ec2_ami_info.images | sort(attribute='creation_date') | last }}
    - name: Display the latest AMI ID
      debug:
        var: latest_ami.image_id
...
```

Here we needed to know the naming convention that Ubuntu uses for images. Its image names always end with a date stamp: for example, *ubuntu/images/hvm-ssd/ubuntu-focal-20.04-amd64-server-20211129*. The `name` filter for the `ec2_ami_info` module permits specifying * as a glob.

The task registers the list of AMIs, so the way to get the most recent image is to sort on creation date and use just the very last AMI.

> Each distribution uses its own naming strategy for AMIs, so if you want to deploy an AMI from a distribution other than Ubuntu, you'll need to do some research to figure out the appropriate search string.

Create a New Instance and Add It to a Group

Sometimes Lorin likes to write a single playbook that launches an instance and then runs a playbook against that instance.

Unfortunately, before you've run the playbook, the host doesn't exist yet. Disabling caching on the dynamic inventory script won't help here, because Ansible invokes the dynamic inventory script only at the beginning of playbook execution—which is before the host exists.

You can add a task that uses the `add_host` module to add the instance to a group, as shown in Example 17-10.

Example 17-10. Adding an instance to groups

```
- name: Create an ubuntu instance on Amazon EC2
  hosts: localhost
  gather_facts: false
  tasks:
    - name: Configure and start EC2 instance
      amazon.aws.ec2_instance:
        name: 'web1'
        image_id: "{{ latest_ami.image_id }}"
        instance_type: "{{ instance_type }}"
        key_name: "{{ key_name }}"
        security_group: "{{ security_group }}"
        network:
          assign_public_ip: true
        tags: {type: web, env: production}
        volumes:
          - device_name: /dev/sda1
            ebs:
            volume_size: 16
            delete_on_termination: true
        wait: true
      register: ec2

    - name: Add the instances to the web and production groups
      add_host:
        hostname: "{{ item.public_dns_name }}"
        groupname:
          - web
          - production
      loop: "{{ ec2.instances }}"
    - name: Configure Web Server
      hosts: web:&production
      become: true
      gather_facts: true
      remote_user: ubuntu
      roles:
        - webserver
```

Returned Information

The `amazon.aws.ec2_instance` module returns a dictionary with lots of information about the instances launched. To read the documentation, run this command for your installed collection instead of Googling:

```
$ ansible-doc amazon.aws.ec2_instance
```

Waiting for the Server to Come Up

While IaaS clouds like EC2 are remarkable feats of technology, creating new instances still requires some time. You can't run a playbook against an EC2 instance immediately after you submit a request to create it. Instead, you need to wait for the EC2 instance to come up. You should also be aware that an instance consists of multiple parts, each created in turn. So you have to wait, but how?

The `ec2` module supports a `wait` parameter. If it's set to yes, the `ec2` task will not return until the instance has transitioned to the running state.

Unfortunately, waiting for the instance to be in the running state isn't enough to ensure that you can execute a playbook against a host. You still need to wait until the instance has advanced far enough in the boot process that the SSH server has started and is accepting incoming connections.

The `wait_for` module is designed for this kind of scenario. Here's how you would use the `ec2` and `wait_for` modules in concert to start an instance and then wait until the instance is ready to receive SSH connections:

```
- name: Wait for EC2 instance to be ready
  wait_for:
    host: "{{ item.public_dns_name }}"
    port: 22
    search_regex: OpenSSH
    delay: 60
  loop: "{{ ec2.instances }}"
  register: wait
```

This invocation of `wait_for` uses the `search_regex` argument to look for the string `OpenSSH` after connecting to the host. This `regex` takes advantage of the fact that a fully functioning SSH server will return a string that looks something like Example 17-11 when an SSH client first connects.

Example 17-11. Initial response of an SSH server running on Ubuntu

```
SSH-2.0-OpenSSH_8.2p1 Ubuntu-4ubuntu0.3
```

You could invoke the `wait_for` module just to check if port 22 is listening for incoming connections. However, sometimes an SSH server has gotten far enough along in the startup process that it is listening on port 22 but is not fully functional yet. You'll use a delay of one minute because the public DNS name takes extra time. Waiting for the initial response ensures that the `wait_for` module will return only when the SSH server has fully started up.

Putting It All Together

Example 17-12 shows the playbook that creates an EC2 instance and configures it as a web server. This playbook is idempotent, so you can safely run it multiple times, and it will create a new instance only if it isn't created yet.

Example 17-12. ec2-example.yml: complete EC2 playbook

```
---
- name: Provision Ubuntu Web Server on Amazon EC2
  hosts: localhost
  gather_facts: false
  vars:
    instance_type: t2.micro
    key_name: ec2key
    aws_region: "{{ lookup('env', 'AWS_REGION') }}"
    security_group: my_security_group
  tasks:
    - name: Upload public key ec2key.pub
      amazon.aws.ec2_key:
        name: "{{ key_name }}"
        key_material: "{{ item }}"
        state: present
        force: true
      no_log: true
      with_file:
        - ~/.ssh/ec2key.pub

    - name: Configure my_security_group
      amazon.aws.ec2_group:
        name: "{{ security_group }}"
        region: "{{ aws_region }}"
        description: SSH and Web Access
        rules:
          - proto: tcp
            from_port: 22
            to_port: 22
            cidr_ip: '0.0.0.0/0'
          - proto: tcp
            from_port: 80
            to_port: 80
            cidr_ip: 0.0.0.0/0
          - proto: tcp
            from_port: 443
            to_port: 443
            cidr_ip: 0.0.0.0/0
        rules_egress:
```

```
              - proto: tcp
                from_port: 443
                to_port: 443
                cidr_ip: 0.0.0.0/0
              - proto: tcp
                from_port: 80
                to_port: 80
                cidr_ip: 0.0.0.0/0

    - name: Gather information on Ubuntu AMIs published by Canonical
      amazon.aws.ec2_ami_info:
        region: "{{ aws_region }}"
        owners: 099720109477
        filters:
          name: "ubuntu/images/hvm-ssd/ubuntu-focal-20.04-*"
          architecture: "x86_64"
          root-device-type: "ebs"
          virtualization-type: "hvm"
          state: "available"
      register: ec2_ami_info

    - name: Sort the list of AMIs by date for the latest image
      set_fact:
        latest_ami: |
          {{ ec2_ami_info.images | sort(attribute='creation_date') | last }}

    - name: Configure and start EC2 instance
      amazon.aws.ec2_instance:
        region: "{{ aws_region }}"
        name: 'web1'
        image_id: "{{ latest_ami.image_id }}"
        instance_type: "{{ instance_type }}"
        key_name: "{{ key_name }}"
        security_group: "{{ security_group }}"
        network:
          assign_public_ip: true
        tags:
          type: web
          env: production
        volumes:
          - device_name: /dev/sda1
            ebs:
              volume_size: 16
              delete_on_termination: true
        wait: true
      register: ec2

    - name: Wait for EC2 instance to be ready
      wait_for:
        host: "{{ item.public_dns_name }}"
        port: 22
        search_regex: OpenSSH
        delay: 30
      loop: "{{ ec2.instances }}"
      register: wait
```

```
  - name: Add the instances to the web and production groups
    add_host:
      hostname: "{{ item.public_dns_name }}"
      groupname:
        - web
        - production
    loop: "{{ ec2.instances }}"

- name: Configure Web Server
  hosts: web:&production
  become: true
  gather_facts: true
  remote_user: ubuntu
  roles:
    - ssh
    - webserver
...
```

The roles in this example can be found on GitHub (*https://oreil.ly/2hAPe*).

Specifying a Virtual Private Cloud

So far, we've been launching our instances into the default VPC. Ansible also allows us to create new VPCs and launch instances into them.

Example 17-13 shows how to create a VPC with an internet gateway, two subnets, and a routing table that routes outbound connections using the internet gateway.

Example 17-13. create-vpc.yml: creating a VPC

```
---
- name: Create a Virtual Private Cloud (VPC)
  hosts: localhost
  gather_facts: false
  vars:
    aws_region: "{{ lookup('env', 'AWS_REGION') }}"
  tasks:
    - name: Create a vpc
      amazon.aws.ec2_vpc_net:
        region: "{{ aws_region }}"
        name: "Book example"
        cidr_block: 10.0.0.0/16
        tags:
          env: production
      register: result

    - name: Set vpc_id as fact
      set_fact:
        vpc_id: "{{ result.vpc.id }}"

    - name: Add gateway
      amazon.aws.ec2_vpc_igw:
        region: "{{ aws_region }}"
```

```
      vpc_id: "{{ vpc_id }}"

  - name: Create web subnet
    amazon.aws.ec2_vpc_subnet:
      region: "{{ aws_region }}"
      vpc_id: "{{ vpc_id }}"
      cidr: 10.0.0.0/24
      tags:
        env: production
        tier: web

  - name: Create db subnet
    amazon.aws.ec2_vpc_subnet:
      region: "{{ aws_region }}"
      vpc_id: "{{ vpc_id }}"
      cidr: 10.0.1.0/24
      tags:
        env: production
        tier: db

  - name: Set routes
    amazon.aws.ec2_vpc_route_table:
      region: "{{ aws_region }}"
      vpc_id: "{{ vpc_id }}"
      tags:
        purpose: permit-outbound
      subnets:
        - 10.0.0.0/24
        - 10.0.1.0/24
      routes:
        - dest: 0.0.0.0/0
          gateway_id: igw
...
```

Each of these commands is idempotent, but the idempotence-checking mechanism differs slightly per module, as shown in Table 17-3.

Table 17-3. Idempotence-checking logic for some VPC modules

Module	Idempotence check
ec2_vpc_net	Name and CIDR options
ec2_vpc_igw	An internet gateway exists
ec2_vpc_subnet	vpc_id and CIDR options
ec2_vpc_route_table	vpc_id and tags[a]

[a] If the lookup option is set to id, the idempotence check will use the route_table_id option instead of tags.

If multiple entities match the idempotence check, Ansible will fail the module.

If you don't specify tags to the `ec2_vpc_route_table`, it will create a new route table each time you execute the module.

Admittedly, Example 17-12 is a simple example from a networking perspective, as we've defined just two subnets: one subnet that's routable to the internet, and another that's not routable to the internet. We should have some security groups for routing traffic from the web subnet to the database, from the internet to the web subnet, SSH access to the restricted subnet where we are, and the outbound rules to install packages. Example 17-14 shows an example of creating such security groups.

Example 17-14. EC2 security groups

```
---
- name: Create EC2 Security Groups
  hosts: localhost
  vars:
    aws_region: "{{ lookup('env', 'AWS_REGION') }}"
    database_port: 5432
    cidrs:
      web: 10.0.0.0/24
      db: 10.0.1.0/24
      ssh: 203.0.113.0/24
  tasks:
    - name: DB security group
      amazon.aws.ec2_group:
        name: db
        region: "{{ aws_region }}"
        description: allow database access for web servers
        vpc_id: "{{ vpc_id }}"
        rules:
          - proto: tcp
            from_port: "{{ database_port }}"
            to_port: "{{ database_port }}"
            cidr_ip: "{{ cidrs.web }}"

    - name: Web security group
      amazon.aws.ec2_group:
        name: web
        region: "{{ aws_region }}"
        description: allow http and https access to web servers
        vpc_id: "{{ vpc_id }}"
        rules:
          - proto: tcp
            from_port: 80
            to_port: 80
            cidr_ip: 0.0.0.0/0
          - proto: tcp
            from_port: 443
            to_port: 443
```

```
        cidr_ip: 0.0.0.0/0

  - name: SSH security group
    amazon.aws.ec2_group:
      name: ssh
      region: "{{ aws_region }}"
      description: allow ssh access
      vpc_id: "{{ vpc_id }}"
      rules:
        - proto: tcp
          from_port: 22
          to_port: 22
          cidr_ip: "{{ cidrs.ssh }}"

  - name: Outbound security group
    amazon.aws.ec2_group:
      name: outbound
      description: allow outbound connections to the internet
      region: "{{ aws_region }}"
      vpc_id: "{{ vpc_id }}"
      rules_egress:
        - proto: all
          cidr_ip: 0.0.0.0/0
...
```

Please note that the `vpc_id` should be a cached fact or an extra variable on the command line.

Dynamic Inventory and VPC

When using a VPC, you often will place some instances inside a private subnet that is not routable from the internet. When you do this, no public IP address is associated with the instance.

In such cases, you might want to run Ansible from an instance inside your VPC. The Ansible dynamic inventory script is smart enough that it will return internal IP addresses for VPC instances that don't have public IP addresses.

Conclusion

Ansible supports even more of EC2, as well as other AWS services. Using Ansible with EC2 is a large enough topic that you could write a whole book about it. In fact, Yan Kurniawan wrote that book: *Ansible for AWS* (Packt, 2016). After digesting this chapter, you should have enough knowledge under your belt to pick up the other modules without difficulty.

## CHAPTER 18

Callback Plug-ins

Ansible supports a feature called *callback plug-ins* that can perform custom actions in response to Ansible events, such as a play starting or a task completing on a host. You can use a callback plug-in to do things such as send a Slack message or write an entry to a remote logging server. In fact, the output you see in your terminal when you execute an Ansible playbook is implemented as a callback plug-in.

Ansible supports three kinds of callback plug-ins:

- *Stdout plug-ins*
- *Notification plug-ins*
- *Aggregate plug-ins*

Stdout plug-ins control the format of the output displayed to the terminal. Ansible's implementation makes no distinction between notification and aggregate plug-ins, which can perform a variety of actions.

Stdout Plug-ins

Only a single stdout plug-in can be active at a time. You specify a stdout callback by setting the `stdout_callback` parameter in the `defaults` section of *ansible.cfg*. For example, here is how to select the `yaml` plug-in, which makes the logging more readable:

```
[defaults]
stdout_callback = yaml
```

You can use `ansible-doc -t callback -l` to see the list of plug-ins available in the version you installed. Some `stdout_callback` plug-ins that Bas finds interesting are listed in Table 18-1.

Table 18-1. Stdout plug-ins

Name	Description	Python requirement
ara	ARA Records Ansible	*ara[server]*
debug	Formatted stdout/stderr display	
default	Default Ansible screen output	
dense	Overwrite output instead of scrolling	
json	JSON output	
minimal	Show task results with minimal formatting	
null	Don't display this to screen	
oneline	Like minimal, but on a single line	

 `actionable` has been removed in Ansible 2.11. Use the `default` callback plug-in with the `display_skipped_hosts = false` and `display_ok_hosts = false` options.

ARA

ARA Records Ansible (ARA, another recursive acronym) is more than just a callback plug-in. It provides reporting by saving detailed and granular results of `ansible` and `ansible-playbook` commands wherever you run them (Figure 18-1). If your whole team uses ARA everyone can see what is going on!

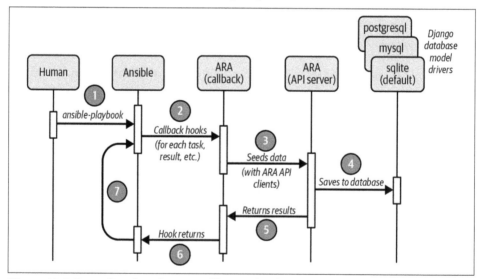

Figure 18-1. Recording data from Ansible to a database by ARA

In the simplest setup it simply records into an SQLite file, but you can also run a Django site to view with a browser, an API, or the CLI client (*https://oreil.ly/RCqcF*). Install ARA with the Python that you use for Ansible:

```
$ pip3 install --user "ara[server]"
$ export ANSIBLE_CALLBACK_PLUGINS="$(python3 -m ara.setup.callback_plugins)"
# ... run playbooks or ad-hoc ...
$ ara-manage runserver
```

Read more about it at in the ARA documentation (*https://oreil.ly/1q40c*).

debug

The debug plug-in makes it easier to read stdout (normal output of commands) and stderr (error output of commands) returned by tasks, which can be helpful for debugging. The default plug-in can make it difficult to read the output:

```
TASK [Clone repository] ********************************************************
fatal: [one]: FAILED! => {"changed": false, "cmd": "/usr/bin/git clone --origin
origin '' /tmp/mezzanine_example", "msg": "Cloning into '/tmp/mezzanine_example'...
\n/private/tmp/mezzanine_example/.git: Permission denied", "rc": 1, "stderr":
"Cloning into '/tmp/mezzanine_example'...\n/private/tmp/mezzanine_example/.git:
Permission denied\n", "stderr_lines": ["Cloning into '/tmp/mezzanine_example'...",
"/private/tmp/mezzanine_example/.git: Permission denied"], "stdout": "",
"stdout_lines": []}
```

With the debug plug-in, the formatting is much easier to read:

```
TASK [Clone repository] ********************************************************
fatal: [one]: FAILED! => {
    "changed": false,
    "cmd": "/usr/bin/git clone --origin origin '' /tmp/mezzanine_example",
    "rc": 1
}
STDERR:
Cloning into '/tmp/mezzanine_example'...
/private/tmp/mezzanine_example/.git: Permission denied
MSG:
Cloning into '/tmp/mezzanine_example'...
/private/tmp/mezzanine_example/.git: Permission denied
```

default

If you do not configure stdout_callback the default plug-in formats a task like this:

```
TASK [Clone repository] ********************************************************
changed: [one]
```

dense

The dense plug-in (new in Ansible 2.3) always shows two lines of output. It overwrites the existing lines rather than scrolling:

```
PLAY 1: LOCAL
task 1: one
```

json

The `json` plug-in generates machine-readable JSON as output. This is useful if you want to process the Ansible output by using a script. Note that this callback will not generate output until the entire playbook has finished executing. The JSON output is too verbose to show here.

minimal

The `minimal` plug-in does very little processing of the result Ansible returns from an event. For example, the `default` plug-in formats a task like this:

```
TASK [Clone repository] ************************************************
changed: [one]
```

However, the `minimal` plug-in outputs this:

```
one | CHANGED => {
    "after": "2c19a94be566058e4430c46b75e3ce9d17c25f56",
    "before": null,
    "changed": true
}
```

null

The `null` plug-in shows no output at all.

oneline

The `oneline` plug-in is similar to minimal, but it prints output on a single line (shown in the print book on multiple lines because the text doesn't fit on one line in the book):

```
one | CHANGED => {"after": "2c19a94be566058e4430c46b75e3ce9d17c25f56","before": ...
```

Notification and Aggregate Plug-ins

Other plug-ins perform a variety of actions, such as recording execution time or sending a Slack notification. Table 18-2 lists them.

Unlike stdout plug-ins, you can enable multiple other plug-ins at the same time. Enable the other plug-ins you want in *ansible.cfg* by setting `callback_whitelist` to a comma-separated list; for example:

```
[defaults]
callback_whitelist = mail, slack
```

`callback_whitelist` will be normalized to `callback_enabled`.

Many of these plug-ins have configuration options, which are set via environment variables or in *ansible.cfg*. Bas prefers setting these options in *ansible.cfg* so as to not clutter the environment variables. Additionally, *ansible.cfg* can be stored in source control so users/developers can share these settings.

To look up a particular callback plug-in's options, try:

```
$ ansible-doc -t callback plugin
```

Table 18-2. Other plug-ins

Name	Description	Python requirement
foreman	Send notifications to Foreman	*requests*
jabber	Send notifications to Jabber	*xmpppy*
junit	Write JUnit-formatted XML file	*junit_xml*
log_plays	Log playbook results per hosts	
logentries	Send notifications to Logentries	*certifi flatdict*
logstash	Send results to Logstash	*logstash*
mail	Send email when tasks fail	
nrdp	Post task result to a Nagios server	
say	Notify using software speech synthesizer	
profile_roles	Adds timing information to roles	
profile_tasks	Adds time information to tasks	
slack	Send notifications to Slack	*prettytable*
splunk	Sends task result events to Splunk	
timer	Adds time to play stats	

Python Requirements

Many plug-ins need one or two Python libraries installed on the Ansible control host. Table 18-2 lists the plug-ins and their requirements. Install them in the Python that you use for Ansible, for instance, the prettytable Python library for Slack:

```
$ pip3 install prettytable
```

foreman

The `foreman` plug-in sends notifications to Foreman (*http://theforeman.org*). Table 18-3 lists the config items under the group [`callback_foreman`] in *ansible.cfg* used to configure this plug-in.

Table 18-3. foreman plug-in environment variables

Environment var	Description	Default
url	URL to the Foreman server.	*http://localhost:3000*
client_cert	X509 certificate to authenticate to Foreman if HTTPS is used.	/etc/foreman/client_cert.pem
client_key	The corresponding private key.	/etc/foreman/client_key.pem
verify_certs	Tells Ansible whether to verify the Foreman certificate. Can be set to 1 to verify SSL certificates using the installed CAs or to a path pointing to a CA bundle. Set to 0 to disable certificate checking.	1

jabber

The `jabber` plug-in sends notifications to Jabber (*http://jabber.org*). Note that there are no default values for any of the configuration options for the `jabber` plug-in. These options are set as environment variables exclusively, as listed in Table 18-4.

Table 18-4. jabber plug-in environment variables

Environment var	Description
JABBER_SERV	Hostname of Jabber server
JABBER_USER	Jabber username for auth
JABBER_PASS	Jabber password auth
JABBER_TO	Jabber user to send the notification to

junit

The `junit` plug-in writes the results of a playbook execution to an XML file in JUnit format. It is configured by using the environment variables listed in Table 18-5. The plug-in uses the conventions in Table 18-6 for generating the XML report.

Table 18-5. junit plug-in environment variables

Environment var	Description	Default
JUNIT_OUTPUT_DIR	Destination directory for files	~/.ansible.log
JUNIT_TASK_CLASS	Configure output: one class per YAML file	false
JUNIT_FAIL_ON_CHANGE	Consider any tasks reporting "changed" as a JUnit test failure	false
JUNIT_FAIL_ON_IGNORE	Consider failed tasks as a JUnit test failure even if ignore_on_error is set	false
JUNIT_HIDE_TASK_ARGUMENTS	Hide the arguments for a task	false
JUNIT_INCLUDE_SETUP_TASKS_IN_REPORT	Should the setup tasks be included in the final report	true

Table 18-6. JUnit report

Ansible task output	JUnit report
ok	pass
failed with EXPECTED FAILURE in the task name	pass
failed due to an exception	error
failed for other reasons	failure
skipped	skipped

log_plays

The log_plays plug-in logs the results to log files in log_folder, one log file per host.

logentries

The logentries plug-in will generate JSON objects and send them to Logentries (*http://logentries.com*) via TCP for auditing/debugging purposes. The plug-in's config items can be put under a group [callback_logentries] in *ansible.cfg* and are listed in Table 18-7.

Table 18-7. logentries plug-in config items

Logentries config item	Description	Default
token	Logentries token	*(None)*
api	Hostname of Logentries endpoint	data.logentries.com
port	Logentries port	80
tls_port	Logentries TLS port	443
use_tls	Use TLS with Logentries	false
flatten	Flatten results	false

logstash

The logstash plug-in will report facts and task events to Logstash (*https://oreil.ly/uajyQ*). The plug-in's config items can be put under a group [callback_logstash] in *ansible.cfg*; they're listed in Table 18-8.

Table 18-8. logstash plug-in config items

Logstash config item	Description	Default
format_version	Logging format	v1
server	Logstash server hostname	localhost
port	Logstash server port	5000
pre_command	Executes command before run and result put to ansible_pre_command_output field	null
type	Message type	ansible

mail

The mail plug-in sends an email whenever a task fails on a host. The plug-in's config items can be put under a group [callback_mail] in *ansible.cfg*; they're listed in Table 18-9.

Table 18-9. mail plug-in environment variables

Environment var	Description	Default
bcc	BCC'd recipient	null
cc	CC'd recipient	null
mta	Mail transfer agent	localhost
mtaport	Mail transfer agent port	25
sender	Mail sender	null
to	Mail recipient	root

profile_roles

This callback module aggregates profiling information for Ansible roles.

profile_tasks

The profile_tasks plug-in generates a summary of the execution time of individual tasks and total execution time for the playbook:

```
Wednesday 11 August 2021  23:00:43 +0200 (0:00:00.910)      0:01:26.498 ******
===============================================================================
Install apt packages ----------------------------------------------- 83.50s
Gathering Facts ---------------------------------------------------- 1.46s
Check out the repository on the host ------------------------------- 0.91s
Create project path ------------------------------------------------ 0.40s
Create a logs directory -------------------------------------------- 0.21s
```

The plug-in also outputs execution time info as the tasks are running, displaying the following:

- Date and time that the task started
- Execution time of previous task, shown in parentheses
- Cumulative execution time for this play

Here's an example of that output:

```
TASK [Create project path] *************************************************
Wednesday 11 August 2021  23:00:42 +0200 (0:01:23.500)        0:01:24.975
changed: [web] ==> {"changed": true, "gid": 1000, "group": "vagrant", "mode":
"0755", "owner": "vagrant", "path": "/home/vagrant/mezzanine/mezzanine_example",
"size": 4096, "state": "directory", "uid": 1000}
```

Table 18-10 lists the environment variables used for configuration.

Table 18-10. profile-tasks plug-in environment variables

Environment var	Description	Default
PROFILE_TASKS_SORT_ORDER	Sort output (ascending, none)	none
PROFILE_TASKS_TASK_OUTPUT_LIMIT	Number of tasks to show, or all	20

say

The say plug-in uses the say or espeak program to speak about play events. The say plug-in has no configuration options. The say module has a voice parameter.

Note that osx_say was renamed say in version 2.8.

slack

The slack plug-in sends notifications to a Slack (*http://slack.com*) channel during playbook execution. The plug-in's config items can be put under a group [call back_slack] in *ansible.cfg*. The variables are listed in Table 18-11.

Table 18-11. slack plug-in environment variables

Config item	Description	Default
webhook_url	Slack webhook URL	*(None)*
channel	Slack room to post in	#ansible
username	Username to post as	ansible
validate_certs	Validate the SSL certificate of the Slack server	true

splunk

This callback plug-in will send task results as JSON-formatted events to a Splunk HTTP collector. The plug-in's config items can be put under a group [call back_mail] in *ansible.cfg* and are listed in Table 18-12.

Table 18-12. splunk plugin environment variables

Config item	Description	Default
authtoken	Token to authenticate the connection to the Splunk HTTP collector	*null*
include_milliseconds	Whether to include milliseconds as part of the generated timestamp field	false
url	URL to the Splunk HTTP collector source	ansible
validate_certs	Validate the SSL certificate of the Splunk server	true

timer

The `timer` plug-in simply adds total play duration to your statistics:

```
Playbook run took 0 days, 0 hours, 2 minutes, 16 seconds
```

You're generally better off using the `profile_tasks` plug-in instead, which also shows execution time per task.

Conclusion

Ansible's callback plug-ins provide many ways to integrate reporting into the communication channels that organizations use. This adds value because Ansible can be used to compose solutions in various domains in harmony with other tools.

## CHAPTER 19

Custom Modules

Sometimes you want to perform a task that is too complex for the command or shell modules, and there is no existing module that does what you want. In that case, you might want to write your own module.

You can think of modules as the "verbs" of the Ansible "language"—without them, the YAML would not do anything. Ansible modules are programmed in Python for Linux/BSD/Unix machines and in PowerShell for Windows machines, but in principle they can be written in any language. Figure 19-1 shows the major components of Ansible: projects witplaybooks, inventory, and modules.

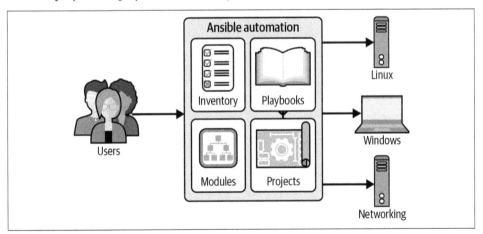

Figure 19-1. Modules

Example: Checking That You Can Reach a Remote Server

Let's say you want to check that you can connect to a remote server on a particular port. If you can't, you want Ansible to treat that as an error and stop running the play.

 The custom module we will develop in this chapter is basically a simpler version of the wait_for module.

Using the Script Module Instead of Writing Your Own

Recall that back in Chapter 7, in Example 7-13, we used the script module to execute custom scripts on remote hosts. Sometimes it's simpler to use the script module than to write a full-blown Ansible module.

Lorin likes putting these types of scripts in a *scripts* folder along with his playbooks. For example, we could create a script file called *playbooks/scripts/can_reach.sh* that accepts as arguments the name of a host, the port to connect to, and how long it should try to connect before timing out:

```
$ ./can_reach.sh www.example.com 80 1
```

We can create a shell script to call netcat as shown in Example 19-1.

Example 19-1. can_reach.sh

```
#!/bin/bash -eu
host="$1"
port="$2"
timeout="$3"
nc -z -w "$timeout" "$host" "$port"
```

We can then invoke this:

```
- name: Run my custom script
  script: scripts/can_reach.sh www.google.com 80 1
```

Keep in mind that your script will execute on the remote hosts, just like Ansible modules do. Therefore, any program your script requires must have been installed previously on the remote hosts (like nc in Example 19-1). The example Vagrantfile for this chapter provisions everything required with vagrant up, so you can play it with the *playbook.yml*.

You can write your script in pure Perl if Perl is installed on the remote hosts. The first line of the script will invoke the Perl interpreter, as in Example 19-2.[1]

Example 19-2. can_reach.pl

```perl
#!/usr/bin/perl
use strict;
use English qw( -no_match_vars );    # PBP 79
use Carp;                            # PBP 283
use warnings;                        # PBP 431
use Socket;
our $VERSION = 1;
my $host = $ARGV[0], my $port = $ARGV[1];

# create the socket, connect to the port
socket SOCKET, PF_INET, SOCK_STREAM, ( getprotobyname 'tcp' )[2]
    or croak "Can't create a socket $OS_ERROR\n";
connect SOCKET, pack_sockaddr_in( $port, inet_aton($host) )
    or croak "Can't connect to port $port! \n";

# eclectic reporting
print "Connected to $host:$port\n" or croak "IO Error $OS_ERROR";

# close the socket
close SOCKET or croak "close: $OS_ERROR";
__END__
```

Use whichever scripting language you like with the `script` module.

can_reach as a Module

Next, we will implement `can_reach` as a proper Ansible Python module. You should invoke this module with these parameters:

```yaml
- name: Check if host can reach the database
  can_reach:
    host: example.com
    port: 5432
    timeout: 1
```

The module checks whether the host can make a TCP connection to *example.com* on port 5432. It will time out after one second if it does not make a connection.

We'll use this example throughout the rest of this chapter.

---

1 Note that this script complies to `perlcritic --brutal`.

Should You Develop a Module?

Before you start developing a module, it's worth asking a few basic questions: Is your module really something new? Does a similar module exist? Should you use or develop an action plug-in? Could you simply use a role? Should you create a collection instead of a single module? It is far easier to reuse existing code if you can, and it is easier to use Ansible than to program in Python. If you are a vendor with a Python API to your product, then it makes sense to develop a collection for it. Modules can be part of a collection, as discussed in Chapter 15.

Where to Put Your Custom Modules

Ansible will look in the *library* directory relative to the playbook. In our example, we put our playbooks in the *playbooks* directory, so we will put our custom module in *playbooks/library/can_reach*. `ansible-playbook` will look in the *library* directory automatically, but if you want to use it in Ansible ad hoc commands then add this line to *ansible.cfg*:

```
library = library
```

Modules can also be added in the *library* directory of an Ansible role or to collections. You can use the *.py* file extension, or the extension that is common for your scripting language.

How Ansible Invokes Modules

Before we implement the module, let's go over how Ansible invokes them:

1. Generate a standalone Python script with the arguments (Python modules only)
2. Copy the module to the host
3. Create an arguments file on the host (non-Python modules only)
4. Invoke the module on the host, passing the arguments file as an argument
5. Parse the standard output of the module

Let's look at each of these steps in more detail.

Generate a Standalone Python Script with the Arguments (Python Only)

If the module is written in Python and uses the helper code that Ansible provides (described later), then Ansible will generate a self-contained Python script that injects helper code, as well as the module arguments.

Copy the Module to the Host

Ansible will copy the generated Python script (for Python-based modules) or the local file *playbooks/library/can_reach* (for non-Python-based modules) to a temporary directory on the remote host. If you are accessing the remote host as the vagrant user, Ansible will copy the file to a path that looks like the following:

/home/vagrant/.ansible/tmp/ansible-tmp-1412459504.14-47728545618200/can_reach

Create an Arguments File on the Host (Non-Python Only)

If the module is not written in Python, Ansible will create a file on the remote host with a name like this:

/home/vagrant/.ansible/tmp/ansible-tmp-1412459504.14-47728545618200/arguments

If we invoke the module like this:

```
- name: Check if host can reach the database server
  can_reach:
    host: db.example.com
    port: 5432
    timeout: 1
```

then the arguments file will have the following content:

```
host=db.example.com port=5432 timeout=1
```

We can tell Ansible to generate the arguments file for the module as JSON, by adding the following line to *playbooks/library/can_reach*:

```
# WANT_JSON
```

If our module is configured for JSON input, the arguments file will look like this:

```
{"host": "www.example.com", "port": "80", "timeout": "1"}
```

Invoke the Module

Ansible will call the module and pass the arguments file as arguments. If it's a Python-based module, Ansible executes the equivalent of the following (with */path/to/* replaced by the actual path):

```
/path/to/can_reach
```

If not, Ansible will look at the first line of the module to determine the interpreter and execute the equivalent of this:

```
/path/to/interpreter /path/to/can_reach /path/to/arguments
```

Assuming the can_reach module is implemented as a Bash script and starts with #!/bin/bash, then Ansible should do something like this:

```
/bin/bash /path/to/can_reach /path/to/arguments
```

But this isn't strictly true. What Ansible *actually* does is a bit more complicated; it wraps the module in a secure shell command line to prepare the locale and to cleanup afterward:

```
/bin/sh -c 'LANG=en_US.UTF-8 LC_CTYPE=en_US.UTF-8 /bin/bash /path/to/can_reach \
/path/to/arguments; rm -rf /path/to/ >/dev/null 2>&1'
```

You can see the exact command that Ansible invokes by passing -vvv to `ansible-playbook`.

> Debian might need to be configured for these locale settings:
>
> ```
> localedef -i en_US -f UTF-8 en_US.UTF-8
> ```

Running Ansible Python modules remotely is a shell-centric implementation. Note that Ansible cannot use a restricted shell.

Expected Outputs

Ansible expects modules to output JSON. For example:

```
{"changed": false, "failed": true, "msg": "could not reach the host"}
```

As you'll see later, if you write your modules in Python, Ansible supplies helper methods that make it easy to generate JSON output.

Output Variables That Ansible Expects

Your module can return whatever variables you like, but Ansible has special treatment for certain returned variables.

changed

All Ansible modules should return a `changed` variable. The `changed` variable is a Boolean that tells whether the module execution caused the host to change state. When Ansible runs, it will show in the output whether a state change has happened. If a task has a `notify` clause to notify a handler, the notification will fire only if `changed` is `true`.

failed

If the module fails to complete, it should return `"failed": true`. Ansible will treat this task execution as a failure and will not run any further tasks against the host that failed unless the task has an `ignore_errors` or `failed_when` clause.

If the module succeeds, you can either return "failed": false or you can simply leave out the variable.

msg

Use the msg variable to add a descriptive message that describes the reason that a module failed.

If a task fails, and the module returns a msg variable, then Ansible will output that variable slightly differently than it does the other variables. For example, if a module returns the following:

```
{"failed": true, "msg": "could not reach www.example.com:81"}
```

then Ansible will output the following lines when executing this task:

```
failed: [fedora] ==> {"failed": true}
msg: could not reach www.example.com:81
```

After a host fails, Ansible tries to continue with the remaining hosts that did not fail.

Implementing Modules in Python

If you implement your custom module in Python, Ansible supplies the AnsibleMod ule Python class. That makes it easier to parse the inputs, return outputs in JSON format, and invoke external programs.

In fact, when writing a Python module, Ansible will inject the arguments directly into the generated Python file rather than require you to parse a separate arguments file. We'll discuss how shorthand input works later in this chapter.

We'll create our module in Python by creating a *can_reach* file. We'll start with the implementation and then break it down (see Example 19-3).

Example 19-3. can_reach

```
#!/usr/bin/env python3
""" can_reach ansible module """
from ansible.module_utils.basic import AnsibleModule                ❶


def can_reach(module, host, port, timeout):
    """ can_reach is a method that does a tcp connect with nc """
    nc_path = module.get_bin_path('nc', required=True)              ❷
    args = [nc_path, "-z", "-w", str(timeout), host, str(port)]
    # (return_code, stdout, stderr) = module.run_command(args)
    return module.run_command(args,check_rc=True)                   ❸


def main():
    """ ansible module that uses netcat to connect """
```

```
    module = AnsibleModule(                                    ❹
        argument_spec=dict(                                    ❺
            host=dict(required=True),
            port=dict(required=True, type='int'),             ❻
            timeout=dict(required=False, type='int', default=3) ❼
        ),
        supports_check_mode=True                              ❽
    )

    # In check mode, we take no action
    # Since this module never changes system state, we just
    # return changed=False
    if module.check_mode:                                      ❾
        module.exit_json(changed=False)                        ❿
    host = module.params['host']                               ⓫
    port = module.params['port']
    timeout = module.params['timeout']

    if can_reach(module, host, port, timeout)[0] == 0:
        msg = "Could reach %s:%s" % (host, port)
        module.exit_json(changed=False, msg=msg)              ⓬
    else:
        msg = "Could not reach %s:%s" % (host, port)
        module.fail_json(msg=msg)                             ⓭


if __name__ == "__main__":
    main()
```

❶ Imports the `AnsibleModule` helper class

❷ Gets the path of an external program

❸ Invokes an external program

❹ Instantiates the `AnsibleModule` helper class

❺ Specifies the permitted set of arguments

❻ A required argument

❼ An optional argument with a default value

❽ Specifies that this module supports check mode

❾ Tests whether the module is running in check mode

❿ Exits successfully, passing a return value

⓫ Extracts an argument

⓬ Exits successfully, passing a message

⓭ Exits with failure, passing an error message

Parsing Arguments

It's easier to understand the way `AnsibleModule` handles argument parsing by looking at an example. Recall that our module is invoked like this:

```
- name: Check if host can reach the database server
  can_reach:
    host: db.example.com
    port: 5432
    timeout: 1
```

Let's assume that the `host` and `port` parameters are required, and `timeout` is an optional parameter with a default value of 3 seconds.

You instantiate an `AnsibleModule` object by passing it an `argument_spec`, which is a dictionary in which the keys are parameter names and the values are dictionaries that contain information about the parameters:

```
module = AnsibleModule(
    argument_spec=dict(
        ...
```

In Example 19-2, we declare a required argument named `host`. Ansible will report an error if this argument isn't passed to the module when we use it in a task:

```
host=dict(required=True),
```

The variable named `timeout` is optional. Ansible assumes that arguments are strings unless specified otherwise. Our `timeout` variable is an integer, so we specify the type as `int` so that Ansible will automatically convert it into a Python number. If `timeout` is not specified, the module will assume it has a value of 3:

```
timeout=dict(required=False, type='int', default=3)
```

The `AnsibleModule` constructor takes arguments other than `argument_spec`. In the preceding example, we added this argument:

```
supports_check_mode = True
```

This indicates that our module supports check mode. We'll explain check mode a little later in this chapter.

Accessing Parameters

Once you've declared an `AnsibleModule` object, you can access the values of the arguments through the `params` dictionary, like this:

```
module = AnsibleModule(...)
host = module.params["host"]
port = module.params["port"]
timeout = module.params["timeout"]
```

Importing the AnsibleModule Helper Class

Ansible deploys a module to the host by sending a ZIP file containing the module
file along with the imported helper files. One consequence of this it that you can
explicitly import classes, such as the following:

```
from ansible.module_utils.basic import AnsibleModule
```

Argument Options

For each argument to an Ansible module, you can specify several options, as listed in
Table 19-1.

Table 19-1. Argument options

Option	Description
required	If True, argument is required
default	Default value if argument is not required
choices	A list of possible values for the argument
deprecated_aliases	A tuple or list of dictionaries with name, version, date, collection_name
aliases	Other names you can use as an alias for this argument
type	Argument type
elements	When type is list, elements can define the type of the list elements
fallback	A tuple of a lookup function and a list to pass to it
no_log	A Boolean that defines masking in logs
options	Implements the ability to create complex arguments in a dict of sub-options[a]
mutually_exclusive	A list of mutually exclusive sub-option names
required_together	A list of names of sub-options
required_one_of	A list of required mutually exclusive sub-options
required_if	A sequence of sequences
required_by	A dictionary mapping option names to sequences of option names

[a] Refer to the documentation for dependencies between module options (*https://oreil.ly/yJ74M*).

required

The required option is the only option that you should always specify. If it is True,
Ansible will return an error if the user fails to specify the argument.

In our can_reach module example, host and port are required, and timeout is not
required.

---

default

For arguments that have `required=False` set, you should generally specify a default value for that option. In our example:

```
timeout=dict(required=False, type='int', default=3)
```

If the user invokes the module like this:

```
can_reach: host=www.example.com port=443
```

then `module.params["timeout"]` will have the value 3.

choices

The `choices` option allows you to restrict the allowed arguments to a predefined list.

Consider the `distro` argument in the following example:

```
distro=dict(required=True, choices=['ubuntu', 'centos', 'fedora'])
```

If the user were to pass an argument that was not in the list—for example:

```
distro=debian
```

this would cause Ansible to throw an error.

aliases

The `aliases` option allows you to use different names to refer to the same argument. For example, consider the `package` argument in the `apt` module:

```
module = AnsibleModule(
    argument_spec=dict(
        ...
        package = dict(default=None, aliases=['pkg', 'name'], type='list'),
    )
)
```

Since `pkg` and `name` are aliases for the `package` argument, these invocations are all equivalent:

```
- apt:
    package: vim

- apt:
    name: vim

- apt:
    pkg: vim
```

type

The `type` option enables you to specify the type of an argument. By default, Ansible assumes all arguments are strings.

However, you can specify a type for the argument, and Ansible will convert the argument to the desired type. The types supported are as follows:

- `str`
- `list`
- `dict`
- `bool`
- `int`
- `float`
- `path`
- `raw`
- `jsonarg`
- `json`
- `bytes`
- `bits`

In our example, we specified the `port` argument as `int`:

```
port=dict(required=True, type='int'),
```

When we access it from the `params` dictionary, like this:

```
port = module.params['port']
```

the value of the `port` variable will be an integer. If we had not specified the type as `int` when declaring the `port` variable, the `module.params['port']` value would have been a string instead of an integer.

Lists are comma-delimited. For example, if you have a module named `foo` with a list parameter named `colors`:

```
colors=dict(required=True, type='list')
```

then you pass a `list` like this:

```
foo: colors=red,green,blue
```

For dictionaries, you can either use `key=value` pairs, delimited by commas, or you can use JSON inline.

For example, if you have a module named `bar`, with a `dict` parameter named `tags`:

```
tags=dict(required=False, type='dict', default={})
```

then you can pass the argument like this:

```
- bar: tags=env=staging,function=web
```

Or you can pass the argument like this:

```
- bar: tags={"env": "staging", "function": "web"}
```

The official Ansible documentation uses the term *complex args* to refer to lists and dictionaries that are passed to modules as arguments. See "Complex Arguments in Tasks: A Brief Digression" for how to pass these types of arguments in playbooks.

AnsibleModule Initializer Parameters

The `AnsibleModule` initializer method takes various arguments, listed in Table 19-2. The only required argument is `argument_spec`.

Table 19-2. AnsibleModule initializer arguments

Parameter	Default	Description
argument_spec	*(None)*	Dictionary that holds information about arguments
bypass_checks	False	If true, don't check any of the parameter constraints
no_log	False	If true, don't log the behavior of this module
check_invalid_arguments	True	If true, return error if user passed an unknown argument
mutually_exclusive	*(None)*	List of mutually exclusive arguments
required_together	*(None)*	List of arguments that must appear together
required_one_of	*(None)*	List of arguments where at least one must be present
add_file_common_args	False	Supports the arguments of the `file` module
supports_check_mode	False	If true, says module supports check mode

argument_spec

This is a dictionary that contains the descriptions of the allowed arguments for the module, as described in the previous section.

no_log

When Ansible executes a module on a host, the module will log output to the syslog, which on Ubuntu is at */var/log/syslog*.

The logging output looks like this:

```
Aug 29 18:55:05 ubuntu-focal python3[5688]: ansible-lineinfile Invoked with
dest=/etc/ssh/sshd_config.d/10-crypto.conf regexp=^HostKeyAlgorithms line=
state=present path=/etc/ssh/sshd_config.d/10-crypto.conf backrefs=False
create=False backup=False firstmatch=False unsafe_writes=False
search_string=None insertafter=None insertbefore=None validate=None
mode=None owner=None group=None seuser=None serole=None selevel=None
setype=None attributes=None
Aug 29 18:55:05 ubuntu-focal python3[5711]: ansible-stat Invoked with
path=/etc/ssh/ssh_host_ed25519_key follow=False get_md5=False
get_checksum=True get_mime=True get_attributes=True checksum_algorithm=sha1
```

```
Aug 29 18:55:06 ubuntu-focal python3[5736]: ansible-file Invoked with
path=/etc/ssh/ssh_host_ed25519_key mode=384 recurse=False force=False
follow=True modification_time_format=%Y%m%d%H%M.%S
access_time_format=%Y%m%d%H%M.%S unsafe_writes=False state=None
_original_basename=None _diff_peek=None src=None modification_time=None
access_time=None owner=None group=None seuser=None serole=None selevel=None
setype=None attributes=None
Aug 29 18:55:06 ubuntu-focal python3[5759]: ansible-lineinfile Invoked with
dest=/etc/ssh/sshd_config regexp=^HostKey /etc/ssh/ssh_host_ed25519_key
line=HostKey /etc/ssh/ssh_host_ed25519_key insertbefore=^# HostKey
/etc/ssh/ssh_host_rsa_key mode=384 state=present path=/etc/ssh/sshd_config
backrefs=False create=False backup=False firstmatch=False
unsafe_writes=False search_string=None insertafter=None validate=None
owner=None group=None seuser=None serole=None selevel=None setype=None
attributes=None
```

If a module accepts sensitive information as an argument, you might want to disable this logging. To configure a module so that it does not write to syslog, pass the no_tog=True parameter to the AnsibleModule initializer.

check_invalid_arguments

By default, Ansible will verify that all of the arguments that a user passed to a module are legal arguments. You can disable this check by passing the check_invalid_argu ments=False parameter to the AnsibleModule initializer.

mutually_exclusive

The mutually_exclusive parameter is a list of arguments that cannot be specified during the same module invocation. For example, the lineinfile module allows you to add a line to a file. You can use the insertbefore argument to specify which line it should appear before, or the insertafter argument to specify which line it should appear after, but you can't specify both.

Therefore, this module specifies that the two arguments are mutually exclusive, like this:

```
mutually_exclusive=[['insertbefore', 'insertafter']]
```

required_one_of

The required_one_of parameter expects a list of arguments with at least one that must be passed to the module. For example, the pip module, which is used for installing Python packages, can take either the name of a package or the name of a requirements file that contains a list of packages. The module specifies that one of these arguments is required like this:

```
required_one_of=[['name', 'requirements']]
```

add_file_common_args

Many modules create or modify a file. A user will often want to set some attributes on the resulting file, such as the owner, group, and file permissions.

You could invoke the `file` module to set these parameters, like this:

```
- name: Download a file
  get_url:
    url: http://www.example.com/myfile.dat
    dest: /tmp/myfile.dat

- name: Set the permissions
  file:
    path: /tmp/myfile.dat
    owner: vagrant
    mode: '0600'
```

As a shortcut, Ansible allows you to specify that a module will accept all of the same arguments as the `file` module, so you can simply set the file attributes by passing the relevant arguments to the module that created or modified the file. For example:

```
- name: Download a file
  get_url:
    url: http://www.example.com/myfile.dat
    dest: /tmp/myfile.dat
    owner: vagrant
    mode: '0600'
```

To specify that a module should support these arguments:

```
add_file_common_args=True
```

The `AnsibleModule` module provides helper methods for working with these arguments.

The `load_file_common_arguments` method takes the parameters dictionary as an argument and returns a parameters dictionary that contains all of the arguments that relate to setting file attributes.

The `set_fs_attributes_if_different` method takes a file parameters dictionary and a Boolean indicating whether a host state change has occurred yet. The method sets the file attributes as a side effect and returns `true` if there was a host state change (either the initial argument was true, or it made a change to the file as part of the side effect).

If you are using the common file arguments, do not specify the arguments explicitly. To get access to these attributes in your code, use the helper methods to extract the arguments and set the file attributes, like this:

```
module = AnsibleModule(
    argument_spec=dict(
        dest=dict(required=True),
```

```
        . . .
    ),
    add_file_common_args=True
)

# "changed" is True if module caused host to change state
changed = do_module_stuff(param)

file_args = module.load_file_common_arguments(module.params)

changed = module.set_fs_attributes_if_different(file_args, changed)
module.exit_json(changed=changed, ...)
```

 Ansible assumes your module has an argument named path or dest, which holds the path to the file. Unfortunately, this is not consistent, so check it with:

> $ **ansible-doc** module

bypass_checks

Before an Ansible module executes, it first checks that all of the argument constraints are satisfied and returns an error if they aren't. These include the following:

- No mutually exclusive arguments are present.
- Arguments marked with the required option are present.
- Arguments restricted by the choices option have the expected values.
- Arguments that specify a type have values that are consistent with the type.
- Arguments marked as required_together appear together.
- At least one argument in the list of required_one_of is present.

You can disable all of these checks by setting bypass_checks=True.

Returning Success or Failure

Use the exit_json method to return success. You should always return changed as an argument, and it's good practice to return msg with a meaningful message:

```
module = AnsibleModule(...)
...
module.exit_json(changed=False, msg="meaningful message goes here")
```

Use the fail_json method to express failure. You should always return a msg parameter to explain to the user the reason for the failure:

```
module = AnsibleModule(...)
...
module.fail_json(msg="Out of disk space")
```

Invoking External Commands

The `AnsibleModule` class provides the `run_command` convenience method for calling an external program, which wraps the native Python `subprocess` module. It accepts the arguments listed in Table 19-3.

Table 19-3. run_command arguments

Argument	Type	Default	Description
`args (default)`	String or list of strings	*(None)*	The command to be executed (see the following section)
`check_rc`	Boolean	False	If `true`, will call `fail_json` if command returns a nonzero value, with stderr included
`close_fds`	Boolean	True	Passes as `close_fds` argument to `subprocess.Popen`
`executable`	String (path to program)	*(None)*	Passes as `executable` argument to `subprocess.Popen`
`data`	String	*(None)*	Send to `stdin` if child process
`binary_data`	Boolean	False	If `false` and data is present, Ansible will send a newline to `stdin` after sending `data`
`path_prefix`	String (list of paths)	*(None)*	Colon-delimited list of paths to prepend to PATH environment variable
`cwd`	String (directory path)	*(None)*	If specified, Ansible will change to this directory before executing
`use_unsafe_shell`	Boolean	False	See the following section

If `args` is passed as a list, as shown in Example 19-4, then Ansible will invoke `subprocess.Popen` with `shell=False`.

Example 19-4. Passing args as a list

```
module = AnsibleModule(...)
...
module.run_command(['/usr/local/bin/myprog', '-i', 'myarg'])
```

If `args` is passed as a string, as shown in Example 19-5, then the behavior depends on the value of `use_unsafe_shell`. If `use_unsafe_shell` is `false`, Ansible will split `args` into a list and invoke `subprocess.Popen` with `shell=False`. If `use_unsafe_shell` is `true`, Ansible will pass `args` as a string to `subprocess.Popen` with `shell=True`.[2]

---

2 For more on the Python standard library `subprocess.Popen` class, see its documentation (*https://oreil.ly/trNKm*).

Example 19-5. Passing args as a string

```
module = AnsibleModule(...)
...
module.run_command('/usr/local/bin/myprog -i myarg')
```

Check Mode (Dry Run)

Ansible supports something called *check mode*, which is enabled when passing the -C or --check flag to ansible-playbook. It is similar to the *dry run* mode supported by many other tools.

When Ansible runs a playbook in check mode, it will not make any changes to the hosts when it runs. Instead, it will simply report whether each task would have changed the host, returned successfully without making a change, or returned an error.

 Modules must be explicitly configured to support check mode. If you're going to write your own module, I recommend you support check mode so that your module can be used in a dry run of playbooks.

To tell Ansible that your module supports check mode, set supports_check_mode to True in the AnsibleModule initializer method, as shown in Example 19-6.

Example 19-6. Telling Ansible the module supports check mode

```
module = AnsibleModule(
    argument_spec=dict(...),
    supports_check_mode=True)
```

Your module should confirm that check mode has been enabled by validating the value of the check_mode attribute of the AnsibleModule object, as shown in Example 19-7. Call the exit_json or fail_json methods as you would normally.

Example 19-7. Checking whether check mode is enabled

```
module = AnsibleModule(...)
...if module.check_mode:
    # check if this module would make any changes
    would_change = would_executing_this_module_change_something()
    module.exit_json(changed=would_change)
```

It is up to you, the module author, to ensure that your module does not modify the state of the host when running in check mode.

Documenting Your Module

You should document your modules according to the Ansible project standards so that HTML documentation for your module will be correctly generated and the `ansible-doc` program will display documentation for your module. Ansible uses a special YAML-based syntax for documenting modules.

Near the top of your module, define a string variable called `DOCUMENTATION` that contains the documentation, and a string variable called `EXAMPLES` that contains example usage. If your module returns information as JSON, document it in a variable called `RETURN`.

Example 19-8 shows an example for the documentation section for our `can_reach` module.

Example 19-8. Example of module documentation

```
DOCUMENTATION = r'''
---
module: can_reach
short_description: Checks server reachability
description: Checks if a remote server can be reached
version_added: "1.8"
options:
  host:
    description:
      - A DNS hostname or IP address
    required: true
  port:
    description:
      - The TCP port number
    required: true
  timeout:
    description:
      - The amount of time trying to connect before giving up, in seconds
    required: false
    default: 3
requirements: [nmap]
author: Lorin Hochstein, Bas Meijer
notes:
  - This is just an example to demonstrate how to write a module.
  - You probably want to use the native M(wait_for) module instead.
'''
EXAMPLES = r'''
# Check that ssh is running, with the default timeout
- can_reach: host=localhost port=22 timeout=1
# Check if postgres is running, with a timeout
- can_reach: host=example.com port=5432
'''
```

Ansible supports limited markup in the documentation. Table 19-4 shows the supported markup syntax, with recommendations about when you should use it.

Table 19-4. Documentation markup

Type	Syntax with example	When to use
URL	U(http://www.example.com)	URLs
Module	M(apt)	Module names
Italics	I(port)	Parameter names
Constant-width	C(/bin/bash)	File and option names

The existing Ansible modules are a great source of examples for documentation.

Debugging Your Module

The Ansible repository in GitHub has a couple of scripts that allow you to invoke your module directly on your local machine, without having to run it by using the `ansible` or `ansible-playbook` commands.

Clone the Ansible repository:

```
$ git clone https://github.com/ansible/ansible.git
```

Change directory to the repository root directory:

```
$ cd ansible
```

Create a virtual environment:

```
$ python3 -m venv venv
```

Activate the virtual environment:

```
$ source venv/bin/activate
```

Install development requirements:

```
$ python3 -m pip install --upgrade pip
$ pip install -r requirements.txt
```

Run the environment setup script for each new dev shell process:

```
$ source hacking/env-setup
```

Invoke your module:

```
$ ansible/hacking/test-module -m /path/to/can_reach -a "host=example.com port=81"
```

Since *example.com* doesn't have a service that listens on port 81, our module should fail with a meaningful error message. And it does:

```
* including generated source, if any, saving to:
/Users/bas/.ansible_module_generated
* ansiballz module detected; extracted module source to:
```

```
/Users/bas/debug_dir
***********************************
RAW OUTPUT

{"cmd": "/usr/bin/nc -z -v -w 3 example.com 81", "rc": 1, "stdout": "",
"stderr": "nc: connectx to example.com port 81 (tcp) failed: Operation timed
out\n", "failed": true, "msg": "nc: connectx to example.com port 81 (tcp)
failed: Operation timed out", "invocation": {"module_args": {"host":
"example.com", "port": 81, "timeout": 3}}}


***********************************
PARSED OUTPUT
{
        "cmd": "/usr/bin/nc -z -v -w 3 example.com 81",
        "failed": true,
        "invocation": {
                "module_args": {
                        "host": "example.com",
                        "port": 81,
                        "timeout": 3
                }
        },
        "msg": "nc: connectx to example.com port 81 (tcp) failed: Operation
timed out",
        "rc": 1,
        "stderr": "nc: connectx to example.com port 81 (tcp) failed: Operation
timed out\n",
        "stdout": ""
}
```

As the output suggests, when you run this test-module, Ansible will generate a Python script and copy it to ~/.ansible_module_generated. This is a standalone Python script that you can execute directly if you like.

Starting with Ansible 2.1.0, this Python script has a base64-encoded ZIP file with the actual source code from your module, as well as code to expand the ZIP file and execute the source code within it.

This file does not take any arguments; rather, Ansible inserts the arguments directly into the file in the ANSIBALLZ_PARAMS variable:

```
ANSIBALLZ_PARAMS = '{"ANSIBLE_MODULE_ARGS": {"_ansible_selinux_special_fs":
["fuse", "nfs", "vboxsf", "ramfs", "9p", "vfat"], "_ansible_tmpdir":
"/Users/bas/.ansible/tmp/ansible-local-12753r6nenhh",
"_ansible_keep_remote_files": false, "_ansible_version": "2.12.0.dev0",
"host": "example.com", "port": "81"}}'
```

Diving into debugging Ansible modules helps you understand Ansible, even if you don't write a module.

Implementing the Module in Bash

If you're going to write an Ansible module for Linux/Unix, we recommend writing it in Python because, as you saw earlier in this chapter, Ansible provides helper classes for writing modules in Python. PowerShell is used to create modules that manage Windows systems. However, you can write modules in other languages as well. Perhaps you need to write in another language because your module depends on a third-party library that's not implemented in Python. Or maybe the module is so simple that it's easiest to write it in Bash.

In this section, we'll work through an example of implementing the module as a Bash script. It's going to look quite like the implementation in Example 19-1. The main difference is parsing the input arguments and generating the outputs that Ansible expects.

We're going to use the JSON format for input and use a tool called jq (*http://stedo lan.github.io/jq/*) for parsing out JSON on the command line. This means that you'll need to provision jq on the hosts before invoking this module. Example 19-9 shows the complete Bash implementation of our module.

Example 19-9. can_reach module in Bash

```bash
#!/bin/bash -e
# WANT_JSON
# Read the variables from the file with jq
host=$(jq -r .host <"$1")
port=$(jq -r .port <"$1")
timeout=$(jq -r .timeout <"$1")
# Default timeout=3
if [[ $timeout = null ]]; then
    timeout=3
fi
# Check if we can reach the host
if nc -z -w "$timeout" "$host" "$port"; then
    echo '{"changed": false}'
else
    echo "{\"failed\": true, \"msg\": \"could not reach $host:$port\"}"
fi
```

We add `WANT_JSON` in a comment to tell Ansible that we want the input to be in JSON syntax. Michael DeHaan called this type of JSON "Baby JSON"; in 2013 he wrote: "Ansible also supports 'baby JSON' which is just a list of key=value pairs, so you don't technically have to output JSON."

Specifying an Alternative Location for Bash

Note that our module assumes that Bash is located at */bin/bash*. However, not all systems will have the Bash executable in that location. You can tell Ansible to look elsewhere for the Bash interpreter by setting the `ansible_bash_interpreter` variable on hosts that install it elsewhere.

For example, let's say you have a FreeBSD host named *fileserver.example.com* that has Bash installed in */usr/local/bin/bash*. You can create a host variable by creating the file *host_vars/fileserver.example.com* that contains the following:

```
ansible_bash_interpreter: /usr/local/bin/bash
```

Then, when Ansible invokes this module on the FreeBSD host, it will use */usr/local/bin/bash* instead of */bin/bash*.

Ansible determines which interpreter to use by looking for the *shebang* (#!) and then looking at the base name of the first element. In our example, it will see this line:

```
#!/bin/bash
```

Ansible will then look for the base name of */bin/bash*, which is *bash*. It will then use the `ansible_bash_interpreter` if the user specified one.

 If your shebang calls */usr/bin/env*, for example `#!/usr/bin/env bash`, Ansible will mistakenly identify the interpreter as `env` because it will call `basename` on */usr/bin/env* to identify the interpreter.

Here's the takeaway: don't invoke `env` in shebang. Instead, explicitly specify the location of the interpreter and override with `ansible_bash_interpreter` (or equivalent) when needed.

Conclusion

In this chapter, we covered how to write modules in Python, as well as in other languages, and how to avoid writing your own full-blown modules by using the `script` module. If you want to dive deeper into modules, a great place to start is to read the dev guide for developing modules (*https://oreil.ly/YCSdz*). The best way to learn how to write Ansible modules is to read the source code (*https://oreil.ly/G4CUl*) on GitHub for the modules that ship with Ansible.

## CHAPTER 20

Making Ansible Go Even Faster

Once you start using Ansible on a regular basis, you'll often find yourself wishing that your playbooks could run more quickly. This chapter presents strategies for reducing the time it takes Ansible to execute playbooks.

SSH Multiplexing and ControlPersist

If you've made it this far in the book, you know that Ansible uses SSH as its primary transport mechanism for communicating with servers. In particular, it uses the system SSH program by default.

Because the SSH protocol runs on top of the TCP protocol, when you make a connection to a remote machine with SSH, you need to make a new TCP connection. The client and server must negotiate this connection before you can actually start doing useful work. The negotiation takes a small amount of time, but it adds up if you have to do it many times, so it becomes a "penalty."

When Ansible runs a playbook it makes many SSH connections, to do things such as copy over files and run modules. Each time Ansible makes a new SSH connection to a host, it has to pay this negotiation penalty.

OpenSSH is the most common implementation of SSH; if you are on Linux or macOS, it is almost certainly the SSH client you have installed on your local machine. OpenSSH supports an optimization called *SSH multiplexing*, also referred to as *ControlPersist*, which allows multiple SSH sessions to the same host to share the same TCP connection. This means that the TCP connection negotiation happens only the first time, thus eliminating the negotiation penalty.

When you enable multiplexing, here is what happens:

- The first time you try to SSH to a host, OpenSSH starts one connection.
- OpenSSH creates a Unix domain socket (known as the *control socket*) that is associated with the remote host.
- The next time you try to SSH to a host, OpenSSH will use the control socket to communicate with the host instead of making a new TCP connection.

The main connection stays open for a user-configurable amount of time (Ansible uses a default of 60 seconds), and then the SSH client will close the connection.

Manually Enabling SSH Multiplexing

Ansible enables SSH multiplexing automatically, but to give you a sense of what's going on behind the scenes, let's work through the steps of manually enabling SSH multiplexing and using it to SSH to a remote machine.

Example 20-1 shows an entry to configure SSH to use multiplexing in the *~/.ssh/config* file.

Example 20-1. ~/.ssh/config for enabling SSH multiplexing

```
ControlMaster auto
ControlPath ~/.ssh/sockets/%r@%h:%p
ControlPersist 10m
```

`ControlMaster auto` enables SSH multiplexing and tells SSH to create the main connection and the control socket if they do not exist yet.

`ControlPersist 10m` tells SSH to close the master connection if there have been no SSH connections for 10 minutes.

`ControlPath ~/.ssh/sockets/%r@%h:%p` tells SSH where to put the control Unix domain socket files on the filesystem.

- `%l` is a placeholder for the local hostname, including the domain.
- `%h` is a placeholder for the target hostname.
- `%p` is a placeholder for the port.
- `%r` is a placeholder for the remote login username.
- `%C` is a placeholder for the hash of `%l%h%p%r`.

If we want to SSH with these options as the Vagrant user:

```
$ ssh -i ~/.vagrant.d/insecure_private_key vagrant@192.168.56.10.nip.io
```

SSH will create a control socket at *~/.ssh/sockets/vagrant@192.168.56.10.nip.io:22* the first time you SSH to the server. Arguments to ControlPath can use the tilde syntax to refer to a user's home directory. We recommend that any ControlPath you use for opportunistic connection sharing include at least %h, %p, and %r (or alternatively %C) and that you place it in a directory that is not writable by other users. This ensures that shared connections are uniquely identified.

You can check whether a master connection is open by using the -O check flag:

```
$ ssh -O check vagrant@192.168.56.10.nip.io
```

It will return output like this if the control master is running:

```
Master running (pid=5099)
```

Here's what the control master process looks like if you use ps 5099:

```
PID   TT  STAT     TIME COMMAND
5099  ??  Ss     0:00.00 ssh: /Users/bas/.ssh/sockets/vagrant@192.168.56.10.
nip.io:22 [mux]
```

You can also stop the master connection by using the -O exit flag, like this:

```
$ ssh -O exit vagrant@192.168.56.10.nip.io
```

You can see more details about these settings on the *ssh_config* manual page:

```
$ man 5 ssh_config
```

We tested the speed of making an SSH connection. The following times how long it takes to initiate an SSH connection to the server and run the */usr/bin/true* program, which simply exits with a return code 0:

```
$ time ssh -i ~/.vagrant.d/insecure_private_key \
    vagrant@192.168.56.10.nip.io \
    /usr/bin/true
```

The first time we ran it, the timing part of the output looked like this:[1]

```
real    0m0.319s
user    0m0.018s
sys     0m0.011s
```

The time we really care about is the total time: 0m0.319s total. This tells us it took 0.319 seconds to execute the whole command. (Total time is also sometimes called *wall-clock time*, since it's how much time elapses in the real world: that is, you could measure it by watching a clock on the wall.)

---

1 The output format may look different, depending on your shell and OS. We're running Bash on macOS.

The second time we ran it, the output looked like this:

```
real    0m0.010s
user    0m0.004s
sys     0m0.006s
```

The total time went down to 0.010s, for a savings of about 0.3s for each SSH connection after the first one. Recall that Ansible uses at least two SSH sessions to execute each task: one session to copy the module file to the host, and another session to execute the module file.[2] This means that SSH multiplexing should save you roughly one or two seconds for each task that runs in your playbook.

SSH Multiplexing Options in Ansible

Ansible uses the options for SSH multiplexing shown in Table 20-1.

Table 20-1. Ansible's SSH multiplexing options

Option	Value
ControlMaster	auto
ControlPath	~/.ssh/sockets/%r@%h:%p
ControlPersist	60s

We've never needed to change Ansible's default `ControlMaster` values. `ControlPersist=10m` reduces the overhead of creating sockets, but there is a trade-off when you sleep your laptop with active multiplexing: it takes that amount of time to pick up networking changes that break your connectivity.

We *did* need to change the value for the `ControlPath` option. That's because the operating system sets a maximum length on the path of a Unix domain socket, and if the `ControlPath` string is too long, then multiplexing won't work. Unfortunately, Ansible won't tell you if the `ControlPath` string is too long; it will simply run without using SSH multiplexing.

You can test it out on your control machine by manually trying to SSH using the same `ControlPath` that Ansible would use:

```
$ CP=~/.ansible/cp/ansible-ssh-%h-%p-%r
$ ssh -o ControlMaster=auto -o ControlPersist=60s \
    -o ControlPath=$CP \
    ubuntu@ec2-203-0-113-12.compute-1.amazonaws.com \
    /bin/true
```

---

2 One of these steps can be optimized away by using pipelining, described later in this chapter.

If the `ControlPath` is too long, you'll see an error that looks like Example 20-2.

Example 20-2. ControlPath too long

```
"/Users/lorin/.ansible/cp/ansible-ssh-ec2-203-0-113-12.compute-1.amazonaws.
com-22-ubuntu.KIwEKEsRzCKFABch"
too long for Unix domain socket
```

This is a common occurrence when connecting to Amazon EC2 instances, because EC2 uses long hostnames.

The workaround is to configure Ansible to use a shorter `ControlPath`. The official documentation (*https://oreil.ly/V6qpw*) recommends setting this option in your *ansible.cfg* file:

```
[ssh_connection]
control_path = %(directory)s/%%h-%%r
```

Ansible sets `%(directory)s` to `$HOME/.ansible/cp`. The double percent signs (%%) are needed to escape these characters because percent signs are special characters for files in the *.ini* format.

> If you have SSH multiplexing enabled and you change a configuration of your SSH connection—say, by modifying the `ssh_args` configuration option—the change won't take effect if the control socket is still open from a previous connection.

More SSH Tuning

When you are in charge of all your servers, or simply responsible enough to look at their security, you'll want to consider optimizing the configuration of the SSH client and servers. The SSH protocol uses several algorithms to negotiate and establish a connection, to authenticate the server and the client hosts, and to set the user and session parameters. Negotiating takes time, and algorithms differ in speed and security. If you manage servers with Ansible on a daily basis, then why not look a bit closer at their SSH settings?

Algorithm Recommendations

Major Linux distributions ship with a "compatible" configuration for the SSH server. The idea is that everyone will be able to connect and log in to the server using whatever client software they like, from whatever source IP address, as long as they know a valid user login method. Better take a closer look if that is what you want!

Bas researched the performance of the SSH connections of Ansible by changing the order and values of `ssh_args` and replaying *tests.yml* ad nauseam, but came to the conclusion that most of it has already been optimized. Bas did, however, find two `ssh_args` values that shave some microseconds, if combined with the multiplexing options discussed earlier:

```
ssh_args = -4 -o PreferredAuthentications=publickey
```

The `-4` selects the inet protocol family (ipv4) exclusively, and `PreferredAuthentications` reorders the user authentication to the socket of `ssh-agent`.

For `sshd_config`, Bas selects the fastest algorithm first and allows a few secure alternatives for compatibility, but in reverse order for speed.

For additional speed, Bas changed the key pair types to a modern standard. Elliptic curve 25519 is both faster and more secure than RSA (*https://oreil.ly/7KzzL*), so he uses it with `PublicKeyAuthentication` and for host keys.

When Bas generated his key pair on his machine, he used the `-a 100` option for brute-force protection:

```
$ ssh-keygen -t ed25519 -a 100 -C bas
```

This task ensures that Bas's key has exclusive access to the deploy user:

```
- name: Change ssh key to ed25519
  authorized_key:
    user: deploy
    key: "{{ lookup('file', '~/.ssh/id_ed25519.pub') }}"
    exclusive: true
```

These tasks ensure that the host key is generated and configured:

```
- name: Check the ed25519 host key
  stat:
    path: /etc/ssh/ssh_host_ed25519_key
  register: ed25519

- name: Generate ed25519 host key
  command: ssh-keygen -t ed25519 -f /etc/ssh/ssh_host_ed25519_key -N ""
  when:
    - not ed25519.stat.exists|bool
  notify: Restart sshd
  changed_when: true

- name: Set permissions
  file:
    path: /etc/ssh/ssh_host_ed25519_key
    mode: '0600'

- name: Configure ed25519 host key
  lineinfile:
    dest: /etc/ssh/sshd_config
    regexp: '^HostKey /etc/ssh/ssh_host_ed25519_key'
```

```
        line: 'HostKey /etc/ssh/ssh_host_ed25519_key'
        insertbefore: '^# HostKey /etc/ssh/ssh_host_rsa_key'
        mode: '0600'
        state: present
      notify: Restart sshd
```

Bas also ensures that his SSH server's configuration matches his SSH client configuration, so the first negotiated offer fits both ends. Adding optimization options in client configuration does not improve performance as much as adding them for server side, because these files are read for each SSH connection.

Pipelining

Recall how Ansible executes a task:

1. It generates a Python script based on the module being invoked.

2. It copies the Python script to the host.

3. It executes the Python script.

Ansible supports an optimization called *pipelining*. Pipelining, if supported by the connection plug-in, reduces the number of network operations required to execute a module on the remote server, by executing many Ansible modules without actual file transfer. Ansible executes the Python scripts by piping them to the SSH session instead of copying them. This saves time because it tells Ansible to use one SSH session instead of two.

Enabling Pipelining

Pipelining is off by default because it can require some configuration on your remote hosts, but we like to enable it because it is *a big speed-up* you can implement in Ansible. To enable it, change your *ansible.cfg* file as shown in Example 20-3.

Example 20-3. Enable pipelining in ansible.cfg

```
[connection]
pipelining = True
```

Configuring Hosts for Pipelining

For pipelining to work on Linux, you need to make sure that `requiretty` is not enabled in your */etc/sudoers* file on your hosts. Otherwise, you'll get errors that look like Example 20-4 when you run your playbook.

Example 20-4. Error when `requiretty` is enabled

```
failed: [centos] ==> {"failed": true, "parsed": false}
invalid output was: sudo: sorry, you must have a tty to run sudo
```

If `sudo` on your hosts is configured to read files from the */etc/sudoers.d*, then the simplest way to resolve this is to add a *sudoers* config file that disables the `requiretty` restriction for the user with which you use SSH.

If the */etc/sudoers.d* directory is present, your hosts should support adding *sudoers* config files in that directory. You can use the `ansible` command-line tool to check for the directory:

```
$ ansible vagrant -a "file /etc/sudoers.d"
```

If the directory is present, the output will look like this:

```
centos | CHANGED | rc=0 >>
/etc/sudoers.d: directory
ubuntu | CHANGED | rc=0 >>
/etc/sudoers.d: directory
fedora | CHANGED | rc=0 >>
/etc/sudoers.d: directory
debian | CHANGED | rc=0 >>
/etc/sudoers.d: directory
```

If the directory is not present, the output will look like this:

```
vagrant3 | FAILED | rc=1 >>
/etc/sudoers.d: ERROR: cannot open `/etc/sudoers.d' (No such file or
directory)
vagrant2 | FAILED | rc=1 >>
/etc/sudoers.d: ERROR: cannot open `/etc/sudoers.d' (No such file or
directory)
vagrant1 | FAILED | rc=1 >>
/etc/sudoers.d: ERROR: cannot open `/etc/sudoers.d" (No such file or
directory)
```

If the directory is present, create a template file that looks like Example 20-5.

Example 20-5. templates/disable-requiretty.j2

```
Defaults:{{ ansible_user }} !requiretty
```

Then run the playbook shown in Example 20-6, replacing `vagrant` with your hosts. Don't forget to disable pipelining before you do, or the it will fail with an error.

Example 20-6. disable-requiretty.yml

```
---
- name: Do not require tty for ssh-ing user
  hosts: vagrant
```

```
  become: true

tasks:
  - name: Set a sudoers file to disable tty
    template:
      src: disable-requiretty.j2
      dest: /etc/sudoers.d/disable-requiretty
      owner: root
      group: root
      mode: '0440'
      validate: 'bash -c "cat /etc/sudoers /etc/sudoers.d/* %s | visudo -cf-"'
...
```

Validating Files

The `copy` and `template` modules support a `validate` clause. This clause lets you specify a program to run against the file that Ansible will generate. Use %s as a placeholder for the filename. For example:

```
validate: 'bash -c "cat /etc/sudoers /etc/sudoers.d/* %s|visudo -cf-"'
```

When the `validate` clause is present, Ansible will copy the file to a temporary directory first and then run the specified validation program. If the validation program returns success (0), Ansible will copy the file from the temporary location to the proper destination. If the validation program returns a nonzero return code, Ansible will return an error that looks like this:

```
SSH | 367
failed: [myhost] ==> {"checksum": "ac32f572f0a670c3579ac2864cc3069ee8a19588",
"failed": true}
msg: failed to validate: rc:1 error:
FATAL: all hosts have already failed -- aborting
```

Since bad sudoers files on a host can prevent us from accessing the host as root, it's always a good idea to validate the combination of the sudoers file, and the files (aka sudo snippets) you create in */etc/sudoers.d* by using the `visudo` program. For a cautionary tale about invalid sudoers files, see Ansible contributor Jan-Piet Mens's blog post "Don't Try This at the Office: /etc/sudoers" (*https://oreil.ly/B9H0n*).

Mitogen for Ansible

Mitogen is a third-party Python library for writing distributed self-replicating programs. Mitogen for Ansible (*https://oreil.ly/t6TcY*) is a completely redesigned UNIX connection layer and module runtime for Ansible. Requiring minimal configuration changes, it updates Ansible's slow and wasteful shell-centric implementation with pure-Python equivalents, invoked via highly efficient remote procedure calls to persistent interpreters tunnelled over SSH.

Please note that at the time of writing Mitogen only supports Ansible 2.9; later versions are not supported yet. No changes are required to target hosts, but on the Ansible controller you will need to install Mitogen with:

```
$ pip3 install --user mitogen
```

To configure Mitogen as a strategy plug-in in *ansible.cfg*:

```
[defaults]
strategy_plugins = /path/to/strategy
strategy = mitogen_linear
```

Fact Caching

Facts about your servers contain all kinds of variables that can be useful in your playbook. These facts are gathered at the beginning of a playbook, but this gathering takes time, so it is a candidate for tuning. One option is to create a local cache with this data; another option is not to gather the facts.

If your play doesn't reference any Ansible facts, you can turn off fact gathering for that play. You can disable fact gathering with the `gather_facts` clause in a play; for example:

```
- name: An example play that doesn't need facts
  hosts: myhosts
  gather_facts: false
  tasks:
    # tasks go here:
```

You can disable fact gathering by default by adding the following to your *ansible.cfg* file:

```
[defaults]
gathering = explicit
```

If you write plays that do reference facts, you can use fact caching so that Ansible gathers facts for a host only once—even if you rerun the playbook or run a different playbook that connects to the same host.

If fact caching is enabled, Ansible will store facts in a cache the first time it connects to hosts. For later playbook runs, Ansible will look up the facts in the cache instead of fetching them from the remote host, until the cache expires.

Example 20-7 shows the lines you must add to your *ansible.cfg* file to enable fact caching. The `fact_caching_timeout` value is in seconds, and the example uses a 24-hour (86,400-second) timeout.

As with all caching-based solutions, there's always the danger of the cached data becoming stale. Some facts, such as the CPU architecture (stored in the `ansible_architecture` fact), are unlikely to change often. Others, such as the date and time reported by the machine (stored in the `ansible_date_time` fact), are guaranteed to change often.

If you decide to enable fact caching, make sure you know how quickly the facts used in your playbook are likely to change, and set an appropriate fact-caching timeout value. If you want to clear the fact cache before running a playbook, pass the `--flush-cache` flag to `ansible-playbook`.

Example 20-7. Enable fact caching in ansible.cfg

```
[defaults]
gathering = smart# 24-hour timeout, adjust if needed
fact_caching_timeout = 86400
# You must specify a fact caching implementation
fact_caching = ...
```

Setting the `gathering` configuration option to `smart` in *ansible.cfg* tells Ansible to use *smart gathering*. This means that Ansible will gather facts only if they are not present in the cache or if the cache has expired. The caching mechanism is plug-in based, and a list of available plug-ins can be retrieved with:

```
$ ansible-doc -t cache -l
```

If you want to use fact caching, make sure your playbooks do *not* explicitly specify `gather_facts: true` or `gather_facts: false`. With smart gathering enabled in the configuration file, Ansible will gather facts only if they are not present in the cache.

You must explicitly specify a `fact_caching` implementation in *ansible.cfg*, or Ansible will not cache facts between playbook runs. As of this writing, there are three types of `fact_caching` implementations:

- File-based: JSON, YAML, Pickle
- RAM backed, nonpersistant: memory
- NoSQL: Redis, Memcached, MongoDB

Redis is the most-used implementation of fact caching.

JSON File Fact-Caching Backend

With the JSON file fact-caching backend, Ansible will write the facts it gathers to files on your control machine. If the files are present on your system, it will use those files instead of connecting to the host and gathering facts.

To enable the JSON file fact-caching backend, add the settings in Example 20-8 to your *ansible.cfg* file.

Example 20-8. ansible.cfg with JSON fact caching

```
[defaults]
gathering = smart
# 24-hour timeout, adjust if needed
fact_caching_timeout = 86400
# JSON file implementation
fact_caching = jsonfile
fact_caching_connection = /tmp/ansible_fact_cache
```

Use the `fact_caching_connection` configuration option to specify a directory where Ansible should write the JSON files that contain the facts. If the directory does not exist, Ansible will create it.

Ansible uses the file modification time to determine whether the fact-caching timeout has occurred yet. Using a JSON file is the easiest option for fact caching, but it is limited in multi-user/multi-controller scenarios, because of file permissions and/or file locations.

Redis Fact-Caching Backend

Redis is a popular key-value data store that is often used as a cache. It is especially useful when you scale to multiple machines. To enable fact caching by using the Redis backend, you need to do the following:

1. Install Redis on your control machine.
2. Ensure that the Redis service is running on the control machine.
3. Install the Python Redis package.
4. Modify *ansible.cfg* to enable fact caching with Redis.

Example 20-9 shows how to configure *ansible.cfg* to use Redis as the cache backend.

Example 20-9. ansible.cfg with Redis fact caching

```
[defaults]
gathering = smart
# 24-hour timeout, adjust if needed
```

```
fact_caching_timeout = 86400

fact_caching = redis
```

Ansible needs the Python Redis package on the control machine, which you can install using pip:[3]

```
$ pip install redis
```

You must also install Redis and ensure that it is running on your control machine. If you are using macOS, you can install Redis by using Homebrew. If you are using Linux, install Redis by using your native package manager.

Memcached Fact-Caching Backend

Memcached is another popular key-value data store that is often used as a cache due to its simplicity and low resource usage. To enable fact caching by using the Memcached backend, you need to do the following:

1. Install Memcached on your control machine.
2. Ensure that the Memcached service is running on the control machine.
3. Install the Python Memcached package.
4. Modify *ansible.cfg* to enable fact caching with Memcached.

Example 20-10 shows how to configure *ansible.cfg* to use Memcached as the cache backend.

Example 20-10. ansible.cfg with Memcached fact caching

```
[defaults]
gathering = smart# 24-hour timeout, adjust if needed
fact_caching_timeout = 86400
fact_caching = memcached
```

Ansible needs the Python Memcached package on the control machine, which you can install using pip. You might need to sudo or activate a virtualenv, depending on how you installed Ansible on your control machine.

```
$ pip install python-memcached
```

You must also install Memcached and ensure that it is running on your control machine. If you are using macOS, you can install Memcached by using Homebrew. If you are using Linux, install Memcached by using your native package manager.

---

3 You may need to sudo or activate a virtualenv, depending on how you installed Ansible on your control machine.

For more information on fact caching, check out the official documentation.

Parallelism

For each task, Ansible will connect to the hosts in parallel to execute the tasks. But Ansible doesn't necessarily connect to *all* of the hosts in parallel. Instead, the level of parallelism is controlled by a parameter, which defaults to 5. You can change this default parameter in one of two ways.

You can set the ANSIBLE_FORKS environment variable, as shown in Example 20-11.

Example 20-11. Setting ANSIBLE_FORKS

```
$ export ANSIBLE_FORKS=8
$ ansible-playbook playbook.yml
```

You also can modify the Ansible configuration file (*ansible.cfg*) by setting a forks option in the defaults section, as shown in Example 20-12. Bas expects a relation between the number of cores on your Ansible controller and the optimal number of forks: if you set the number too high, the context switches cost you performance. I set the number to 8 on my machine. There is also a relation to the memory in the control node. The more forks you use, the more memory the controlling process needs to keep track of the current running tasks. In production environments a number of 25 or 50 is a rather common value, of course depending on the total number of hosts.

Example 20-12. Configuring number of forks in ansible.cfg

```
[defaults]
forks = 8
```

Concurrent Tasks with Async

Ansible introduced support for asynchronous actions with the async clause to work around the problem of connection timeouts. If the execution time for a task exceeds that timeout, Ansible will lose its connection to the host and report an error. Marking a long-running task with the async clause eliminates the risk of a connection timeout.

However, asynchronous actions can also be used for a different purpose: to start a second task before the first task has completed. This can be useful if you have two tasks that both take a long time to execute and are independent (that is, you don't need the first to complete to execute the second).

Example 20-13 shows a list of tasks that use the async clause to clone a large Git repository. Because the task is marked as async, Ansible will not wait until the Git clone is complete before it begins to install the operating system packages.

Example 20-13. Using async to overlap tasks

```
- name: Install git
  become: true
  apt:
    name: git
    update_cache: true

- name: Clone Linus's git repo
  git:
    repo: git://git.kernel.org/pub/scm/linux/kernel/git/torvalds/linux.git
    dest: /home/vagrant/linux
  async: 3600                                    ❶
  poll: 0                                        ❷
  register: linux_clone                          ❸

- name: Install several packages
  apt:
    name:
      - apt-transport-https
      - ca-certificates
      - linux-image-extra-virtual
      - software-properties-common
      - python-pip
    become: true

- name: Wait for linux clone to complete
  async_status:                                  ❹
    jid: "{{ linux_clone.ansible_job_id }}"      ❺
  register: result
  until: result.finished                         ❻
  retries: 3600
```

❶ We specify that this is an async task that should take less than 3,600 seconds. If the execution time exceeds this value, Ansible will automatically stop the process associated with the task.

❷ We specify a poll argument of 0 to tell Ansible that it should immediately move on to the next task after it spawns this task asynchronously. If we had specified a nonzero value instead, Ansible would not move on to the next task. Instead, it would periodically poll the status of the async task to check whether it was complete, sleeping between checks for the amount of time in seconds specified by the poll argument.

❸ When we run async, we must use the register clause to capture the async result. The result object has an ansible_job_id value that we will use later to poll for the job status.

❹ We use the async_status module to poll for the status of the async job we started earlier.

❺ We must specify a `jid` value that identifies the `async` job.

❻ The `async_status` module polls only a single time. We need to specify an `until` clause so that it will keep polling until the job completes, or until we exhaust the specified number of retries.

Conclusion

You should now know how to configure SSH, pipelining, fact caching, parallelism, and async in order to get your playbooks to run more quickly. Next, we'll discuss networking and security with Ansible.

## CHAPTER 21

Networking and Security

Network Management

Managing and configuring network devices always makes us feel nostalgic. Log in to a console by telnet, type some commands, save the configuration to startup config, and you're done. For a long time, we had two types of management strategies for network devices:

- Buy an expensive proprietary software that configures your devices.
- Develop minimal tooling around your configuration files: back up your configs locally, make some changes by editing them, and copy the result back onto the devices through the console.

We have seen some movement in this space. The first thing we noticed was that network device vendors started to create or open their APIs for everyone. The second thing is that the Ansible community did not stop going lower down the stack, to the core: hardware servers, load-balancer appliances, firewall appliances, network devices, and even routers and specialized appliances. Red Hat coordinated Ansible for Network Automation in release 2.5 of Ansible. Between the 2.5 and 2.9 versions of Ansible, the focus was on network modules. For maintainability reasons, this idea has since been abandoned in favor of *collections*, and networking is maybe the best evidence that it was a good decision to follow up (*https://oreil.ly/MW1Ie*) on JP Mens's blog post (*https://oreil.ly/DizNw*) by focusing on `ansible-core` with the Ansible team, as well as to delegate certified content creation to Red Hat partners and the rest to the community. Network vendors jumped on the bandwagon, perhaps because they can publish such content autonomously.

Supported Vendors

The first question you'll ask is, "Is my preferred vendor or network operating system supported?" The list of vendor collections is long and too dynamic to print, but you can find it here (*https://oreil.ly/CEHsD*). The Community namespace has a lot of content that was developed independently of vendors. In addition, `ansible.netcommon` offers abstractions that can be used with different vendors, which also means that coordination and design have been applied (nice to have). Collections include, but are not limited to, these brands:

- Arista (*https://oreil.ly/AsBf2*)
- Checkpoint (*https://oreil.ly/sLvpl*)
- Cisco ACI (*https://oreil.ly/TNOAT*)
- Cisco Meraki (*https://oreil.ly/gExAe*)
- Cyberark (*https://oreil.ly/vMQse*)
- F5 Networks (*https://oreil.ly/GcDFd*)
- Fortinet (*https://oreil.ly/R1sDM*)
- IBM (*https://oreil.ly/fiiWQ*)
- Infoblox (*https://oreil.ly/yCcpH*)
- Juniper (*https://oreil.ly/Js4de*)
- Vyos (*https://oreil.ly/MnTbI*)

Some of these vendors offer virtual appliances that you can download for use with Vagrant. The Vagrantfile for this chapter in the sample code includes junos, nxosv, and vyos.

 Use network automation modules explicitly from installed collections. You should also make sure to use the fully qualified collection namespace when using modules, not the short names of the modules bundled with Ansible. When inspecting task files or playbooks, look for the modules to have dots, as in `cisco.iosxr.iosxr_l2_interfaces`.

Ansible Connection for Network Automation

You can manage network devices using Ansible, but there are some differences compared to managing machines running Windows, macOS, or Linux. Linux systems are universally managed over an SSH connection, and Windows machines can be managed over a WinRM connection. Other connections that we have used so far are local, docker, and raw. Using REST with the uri module doesn't count as an ansible_connection because we cannot use other modules over that "connection."

Since network appliances don't run Python, network automation needed another paradigm. Network automation runs on the control node and talks to the APIs of the network devices. A playbook for network automation typically has this in the header:

```
hosts: localhost
```

The ansible_connection from the control node to the device depends on the platform and the purpose of the modules you use. The transport protocol can be SSH or HTTP/HTTPS. HTTPS connections are typically used for REST APIs, while SSH can be used for CLI use, like the command and shell modules in "normal" Ansible. XML over SSH is unique for network configuration (netconf). You'll need to install the Python library ncclient to use it.

Privileged Mode

Several network devices support a separation between normal user mode and a *privileged mode* for critical tasks with ansible_become: true. You should note that this does not use the sudo method that we know in Linux. Instead, the method is called enable. We like to use become at the beginning of a task, right under the name, for ease of auditing.

You can configure the Ansible connection for each type of device with a couple of parameters. The vars block in the inventory is a natural choice to register these parameters. Aside from the protocol for the connection, Ansible needs to know the operating system of the network device, as shown in the inventory INI file in Example 21-1.

Example 21-1. playbooks/inventory/hosts

```
[arista:vars]
# https://galaxy.ansible.com/arista/eos
ansible_connection=ansible.netcommon.httpapi
ansible_network_os=arista.eos.eos
ansible_become_method=enable

[cisco:vars]
# https://galaxy.ansible.com/cisco/ios
ansible_connection=ansible.netcommon.network_cli
ansible_network_os=cisco.ios.ios
ansible_become_method=enable

[junos:vars]
# https://galaxy.ansible.com/junipernetworks/junos
ansible_connection=ansible.netcommon.netconf
ansible_network_os=junipernetworks.junos.junos
ansible_become_method=enable
```

Network Inventory

While we favor the simplicity of the INI format for inventory files and dynamic inventories for cloud and Vagrant, the YAML format is better suited for inventories of large network topologies with a hierarchy (Example 21-2). A best practice in modeling is answering the basic questions: What is it? Where is it? Who owns it? And when will it go through development, test, pilot, staging, and production?

Example 21-2. YAML inventory

```
backbone:
  hosts:
    rt_dc1_noc_p:
      ansible_host: 10.31.1.1
  vars:
    ansible_connection: ansible.netcommon.network_cli
    ansible_network_os: cisco.ios.ios
    ansible_become_method: enable

perimeter:
  hosts:
    proxy_dc1_soc_p:
      ansible_host: 10.31.2.1
    vars:
      ansible_become_method: sudo

network:
  children:
    backbone:
    perimeter:
```

You can view the inventory as a graph, to assess it, with this command:

```
ansible-inventory -i inventory/hosts.yml --graph
```

Network Automation Use Cases

The theory that you could carefully create network drawings to design an infrastructure for corporate IT that lasts has been falsified in recent decades by general entropy: think of IT developments, disruptive competition, global crises, and market volatility, to name a few adversaries of stability. Organizations need to adapt to changing conditions, and that implies change—continuous change—and agility.

The idea that multifunctional teams can work autonomously to serve business goals, leveraged by cloud-native technology purchased in distributed ways, worries the network operations centers and security operations centers (to put it mildly).

Ansible can examine the state of all appliances and hosts at scale to gather the facts you need for configuration management and situational awareness. It can configure devices, automate updates, and test whether things run as expected. In general,

Ansible Network Automation is a great step forward over configuring devices by hand.

Security

Every organization has different security requirements. There are several security baselines such as CIS (*https://oreil.ly/4oGAp*), DISA-STIG (*https://oreil.ly/UQ3f0*), PCI (*https://oreil.ly/eM8aP*), HIPAA (*https://oreil.ly/CVYED*), NIST (*https://oreil.ly/mq03N*), and FedRAMP (*https://www.fedramp.gov*) for different industries in the United States, including payment cards, health care, the federal government, and defense contractors. In Europe, national institutes like BSI Germany (*https://oreil.ly/jyRtY*), BSI UK (*https://oreil.ly/RNXOj*), and NCSC (*https://oreil.ly/pBdtI*) publish recommendations to help secure computers and their connections. If your government does not require a security standard, you can look at the examples provided by software foundations like Mozilla (*https://oreil.ly/vzWsX*).

Even before Red Hat bought Ansible, Inc., there was an opportunity to assure compliance with particular security baselines. In 2015, Ansible, Inc., assigned coordination of the open source `ansible-lockdown` project (*https://oreil.ly/0lzC8*) to the security company MindPointGroup.[1] A lot has happened since. This content has partially moved from PDF documents and spreadsheets to playbooks. One area where Ansible is gaining ground is security automation.

For hardening systems like network devices, clusters, and hosts, using Ansible seems like an excellent idea. Separation of concerns is a principle of control theory, so in practice you would seek a scanning tool to assess the results of the hardening playbooks based on the security profile of your choice.

The Center for Internet Security maintains cybersecurity benchmarks for a wide variety of operating systems and middleware, which explain configurations in detail. Security scanners are available commercially. OpenSCAP (*https://oreil.ly/l4EiB*) publishes a security guide (*https://oreil.ly/3oMj6*) for free that allows you to select a profile suitable for your industry to scan RHEL systems for compliance in great detail. Did you know you can even generate an Ansible playbook backed by Red Hat to remediate divergence? (How cool is that!) There are other hardening projects by independent developers on GitHub, for instance the DevSec Project (*https://devsec.io/project*) from Germany.

---

1 Bas committed a bit for CIS (*https://oreil.ly/mAxJw*) and DISA-STIG (*https://oreil.ly/EgDNP*) compliance.

Comply with Compliance?

Yet even with these tools at your fingertips, Thompson's question remains:[2] Whom do you trust? Drill down and you find more questions within that one: Do you trust an Ansible hardening playbook more than a vendor's scanning results? Is compliance the same as security? Do national standards restrict cryptography (*https://oreil.ly/68zJp*) in your country? How are your security decisions affected by surveillance (*https://oreil.ly/kC4cN*), intrusion detection, malware detection (*https://oreil.ly/BXdzQ*), intellectual property, civil rights, employment law, unions, and politics? Are cybersecurity concerns getting in the way of your organization reaching its goals? How private are dialogs, anyway?

In modern IT architectures, several factors affect the use of the internet and cryptography. SSL inspection is common in web proxy servers to avoid malware infection in PCs. SSL inspection allows IT administrators to see, and intervene in, website traffic from web browsers in the company. To avoid legal implications, these proxy servers support using lists of trusted and distrusted site categories. Web proxy servers can limit the internet use of employees with good intentions, but there can be security issues with software as well. Either way, proxy inspection can help avoid viruses and ransomware, but it can also block development and innovation.

It is also a good practice to create a software library proxy to streamline the supply chain for programmers. Chapter 23 will create an example of such a proxy with Sonatype Nexus. The web traffic of both business users and IT staff should be subject to a policy that eradicates the use of covert channels.

Secured, but Not Secure

The sample code for this chapter creates a Vagrant box named *ansiblebook/Bastion* (*https://oreil.ly/ajtGQ*) that is hardened to comply on the Operating System Protection Profile (OSPP) for RHEL 8.

> This configuration profile is consistent with CNSSI-1253, which requires US National Security Systems to adhere to certain configuration parameters. Accordingly, this configuration profile is suitable for use in US National Security Systems.

For these purposes, it should be secured, right? Of course!

The `ansible_role_ssh` in the sample code can enforce a (custom) system-wide crypto-policy. The `ansible_role_ansible` installs Python, Python requirements, Ansible, collections, and roles onto this hardened operating system. It deals with the restrictions of volume mount options, SELinux, and `fapolicyd`.

---

2 Ken Thompson, "Reflections on Trusting Trust" (*https://oreil.ly/f52cw*), *Communications of the ACM* 27, no. 8 (August 1984).

We published these two roles separately on GitHub so you can use them in other playbooks:

- `ansible_role_ssh` (*https://oreil.ly/H3Ha6*)
- `ansible_role_ansible` (*https://oreil.ly/c9XmX*)

In the kickstart configuration (Example 21-3), the `org_fedora_oscap` add-on uses `ospp` as a profile. OSPP is based on the crypto policy FIPS. The FIPS:OSPP crypto policy restricts the set of algorithms even further than FIPS does. At the moment FIPS excludes some cryptographic algorithms and US government agencies mandate the use of a particular set of algorithms evaluated by NIST.

Example 21-3. packer-playbook.yml

```
---
- name: Provisioner
  hosts: all
  become: true
  gather_facts: true
  vars:
    crypto_policy: FIPS:OSPP
    intended_user: vagrant
    home_dir: "/home/{{ intended_user }}"
  pre_tasks:
    - name: Generate 4096 bits RSA key pair for SSH
      user:
        name: "{{ intended_user }}"
        generate_ssh_key: true
        ssh_key_bits: 4096

    - name: Fetch ssh keys
      fetch:
        flat: true
        src: "{{ home_dir }}/.ssh/{{ item }}"
        dest: files/
        mode: '0600'
      loop:
        - id_rsa
        - id_rsa.pub

    - name: Install authorized_keys from generated file
      authorized_key:
        user: "{{ intended_user }}"
        state: present
        key: "{{ lookup('file','files/id_rsa.pub') }}"
        exclusive: false

    - name: Fix auditd max_log_file_action
      lineinfile:
        path: /etc/audit/auditd.conf
        regexp: '^max_log_file_action'
```

```
        line: max_log_file_action = rotate
        state: present
  roles:
    - ansible_book_ssh
    - ansible_book_ansible
```

The *ansiblebook/Bastion* box was provisioned with Packer, creating a larger-than-default key pair for Vagrant. You can launch it with Vagrant after downloading this (*https://oreil.ly/HTiwq*) 4096-bit RSA key; name it like in the Vagrantfile:

```
config.ssh.private_key_path = "./playbooks/files/id_rsa"
```

The Ansible playbook in Example 21-4 will run a security audit and create a report in your Downloads folder.

Example 21-4. vagrant-playbook.yml

```
---
- name: Security Audit
  hosts: bastion
  become: true
  gather_facts: true
  tasks:
    - name: 'Run the audit and create a report.'
      command:
        oscap xccdf eval \
          --report /tmp/report.html
          --profile ospp
          /usr/share/xml/scap/ssg/content/ssg-rhel8-ds.xml
      no_log: true
      ignore_errors: true

    - name: 'Fetch the report.'
      fetch:
        flat: true
        src: /tmp/report.html
        dest: "~/Downloads/ospp.html"
...
```

You'll notice that the machine passes 198 of the 200 security tests, rather good! It is hardened.

However, if you run `ssh-audit` (*https://oreil.ly/gepyo*) on this "hardened" system you'll see lots of weaknesses:

```
# key exchange algorithms
(kex) ecdh-sha2-nistp256    -- [fail] using weak elliptic curves
(kex) ecdh-sha2-nistp384    -- [fail] using weak elliptic curves
(kex) ecdh-sha2-nistp521    -- [fail] using weak elliptic curves
# host-key algorithms
(key) ecdsa-sha2-nistp256   -- [fail] using weak elliptic curves
                            `- [warn] using weak random number generator could
                            reveal the key
```

```
# encryption algorithms (ciphers)
(enc) aes256-cbc            -- [fail] removed (in server) since OpenSSH 6.7,
unsafe algorithm
                            `- [warn] using weak cipher mode
(enc) aes128-cbc            -- [fail] removed (in server) since OpenSSH 6.7,
unsafe algorithm
                            `- [warn] using weak cipher mode
# message authentication code algorithms
(mac) hmac-sha2-256         -- [warn] using encrypt-and-MAC mode
(mac) hmac-sha2-512         -- [warn] using encrypt-and-MAC mode
# algorithm recommendations (for OpenSSH 8.0)
(rec) -aes128-cbc           -- enc algorithm to remove
(rec) -aes256-cbc           -- enc algorithm to remove
(rec) -ecdh-sha2-nistp256   -- kex algorithm to remove
(rec) -ecdh-sha2-nistp384   -- kex algorithm to remove
(rec) -ecdh-sha2-nistp521   -- kex algorithm to remove
(rec) -ecdsa-sha2-nistp256  -- key algorithm to remove
(rec) -hmac-sha2-256        -- mac algorithm to remove
(rec) -hmac-sha2-512        -- mac algorithm to remove
```

Similar weaknesses can be found in the default setup of OpenSSH 8, and in the recommendations by states favoring surveillance over system security. You can use the SSH role with the default `crypto_policy: STRICT` to use the ed25519 curves. This is faster as well as safe, as the research of the Technische Universiteit Eindhoven has proven (*https://oreil.ly/Tz9u0*). The use of ed25519 curves is proposed for an updated version of FIPS, but the FIPS 186-5 document still has a "draft" status. The STRICT crypto policy passes `ssh-audit`. Note that you can only have a system that is compliant to a security baseline with weak crypto.

The emergence of quantum computers can have major implications for organizations that process sensitive information. The consequences are serious: data encrypted with popular cryptographic algorithms may already have been intercepted, awaiting decryption with a future quantum computer. OpenSSH changed in release 9 (*https://oreil.ly/lZgN1*); it now uses the NTRU algorithm and X25519 ECDH key exchange by default to prevent that.

Shadow IT

Is your device *secured* or *secure*? Are your security controls effective? Do the restrictions enforce the policy, or can you go around them? How about all the other devices in your company? Has your IT department secured the network infrastructure, the servers, data access, and your desktops so stringently that you find yourself emailing files to your personal address just to get useful work done? Are you reaching for other alternatives? Corporate governance can grind innovation initiatives to a halt with its approval processes, definitions of "done," and risk and compliance audits, not to mention technical security controls like end-point protection, SSL inspection, and air-gapped environments.[3] Employees either waste paid time jumping through all these hoops, or they create *shadow IT*.

Shadow IT involves any computing resources that are not procured or delivered under corporate governance. It includes private laptops, old PCs hidden under the desks, personal cloud subscriptions, personal servers, and so on. To leapfrog the competition, some corporations even create a greenfield company to avoid dealing with all the red tape accumulated over decades. If the central IT organization delivers systems that don't meet developers' expectations, the developers will create their own systems.

Sunshine IT

Modern software is best created by autonomous teams, enabled by platforms that don't hinder productivity across departments, regions, and most of all, the corporate firewall. These software teams have, to coin a phrase, *intelligence autonomy*; that is, they have access to any information, API, AI, SaaS, IaaS, PaaS, source code, library, or tool they need to get the job done. They can organize their own work and communicate in strict privacy. If you think about it, strategically, this is a competitive advantage. It might disrupt your position if you work in central IT, but fear not!

Sunshine IT is all about collaboration and enabling teams to shine by creating a common platform for them, centered around internet-facing APIs, self-service infrastructure, and secure collaboration. Next to the business-specific applications, an enabling technology stack relieves teams' burdens with elements like:

- Software-defined infrastructure: application centric/cloud-based
- Platform services: CI/CD as a service, container platforms
- Integration platform: API managers/event streaming/messaging
- Technology monitoring

So instead of autonomous development teams, sunshine IT is about collaboration between teams in an organization where some core elements can reinforce the autonomous teams.

Zero Trust

The idea of *zero trust*, a trending term coined by security expert John Kindervag, holds that the traditional "fortress" model of security operates on an outdated assumption: that everything inside an organization's network should be implicitly trusted, with bastions and firewalls to secure the perimeter. This implicit trust means

---

3 Kelly Shortridge has written an eloquent blog post (*https://oreil.ly/NCrp9*) about such security obstructionism.

a lack of granular security controls, so that once on the network, users—including threat actors and malicious insiders—are free to move laterally and access or exfiltrate sensitive data. This model no longer works in an age of cloud and container technologies. Salespeople will offer you identity management, explicit verification, automation, least privilege, and other buzzwords to try to sell more. Just point them to this quote from Kindervag:[4]

> The hallmark of zero trust is simplicity. When every user, packet, network interface, and device is untrusted, protecting assets becomes simple. To reduce the complexity of cybersecurity environments, organizations can prioritize security technologies and tools that support simplicity by automating repetitive and manual tasks, integrating, and managing multiple security tools and systems, and auto remediating known vulnerabilities.

There is a new generation of network security software that can be managed with simple apps. They allow administrators to create groups of trusted users whose systems can connect over untrusted networks. These offer fine-grained user control and cross-platform encryption.

Conclusion

To learn more about network automation with Ansible, see Network Getting Started (*https://oreil.ly/JLMz6*) and Network Advanced Topics (*https://oreil.ly/1NvKm*). If you'd like to experiment, install the roles and collections from Example 15-1. See the Mozilla Foundation's advice site (*https://oreil.ly/ViJ3a*) to learn more.

Security automation is an Ansible use case that could fill another book, so it's fortunate that Ansible has published a guide: *Security Automation* (*https://oreil.ly/JF7g6*). Continuing on the theme of automation, the next chapter will look at CI/CD and Ansible.

---

4 John Kindervag, "The Hallmark of Zero Trust Is Simplicity" (*https://oreil.ly/41KGi*), *Wall Street Journal*, April 15, 2021.

## CHAPTER 22

CI/CD and Ansible

Roles are the basic components used to compose infrastructure as code (IaC) with Ansible. Treating systems administration as software engineering and applying software development practices to IaC is one of the foundations of Agile operations. You can decrease errors, increase productivity, and achieve more successful changes and less downtime by staging these changes in software environments and automating the verification of changes. By assessing code quality and automated tests in isolated environments, you can eliminate errors before their blast radius gets too large.

This chapter describes how to set up the core of a continuous integration and continuous delivery (CI/CD) environment for software teams, consisting of a central repository proxy for binaries and libraries, a source control system, a code quality tool, and a continuous integration server. The example code provisions four virtual machines with Sonatype Nexus3, Gitea, SonarQube, and Jenkins. Jenkins can use Ansible ad hoc commands and Ansible playbooks via the Ansible plug-in. The Ansible Tower plug-in for Jenkins can access Ansible Automation Platform (still affectionally known as Tower) to request various things like starting job templates.

Continuous Integration

In 2006, Martin Fowler published an influential article on Continuous Integration (*https://oreil.ly/AO3QV*), a successful practice in software development, describing it as follows:

> a software development practice where members of a team integrate their work frequently, usually each person integrates at least daily—leading to multiple integrations per day. Each integration is verified by an automated build (including test) to detect integration errors as quickly as possible. Many teams find that this approach leads to significantly reduced integration problems and allows a team to develop cohesive software more rapidly.

These practices are often called for when development teams want to deliver software in a reliably repeatable way. As Fowler put it: "Anyone should be able to bring in a virgin machine, check the sources out of the repository, issue a single command, and have a running system on their machine."

Nowadays there are even bigger challenges: most modern systems are more complex, they often need more than one machine to run, and their infrastructure, configuration management, system operations, security, and compliance are often *in code* as well.

Developers store all of that code in version control and run various tasks on integration machines, so we can test it and store it safely in a repository to deploy it when we're ready to go live. Put simply, we want to automate that.

Elements in a CI System

Storing everything your system requires in a version control system (VCS) is a precondition for CI. There are two kinds of VCS: those for text-based data, such as source code of any kind, and artifact repositories for binary data, such as software packages of any kind.

Artifact repository

JFrog Artifactory and Sonatype Nexus are the most popular artifact repositories. The sample code that accompanies this book deploys Nexus as a proxy for Python libraries. Nexus is a Java program, and the playbook to deploy it can be as simple as this:

```
#!/usr/bin/env ansible-playbook
---
- name: Artefact Repository
  hosts: nexus
  become: true
  roles:

    - role: java
      tags: java
    - role: nexus
      tags: nexus
```

We have an inventory with a group named nexus with a named server in it. You can create an inventory with four servers that you want to use for this project; it is reusable. The roles are installed from Ansible Galaxy using the file *roles/requirements.yml*:

```
---
roles:
  - src: ansible-thoteam.nexus3-oss
    name: nexus
  - src: geerlingguy.java
    name: java
```

Next we create *group_vars/nexus*. For this example we'll set simple configuration options, such as:

```
nexus_config_pypi: true
nexus_config_docker: true
nexus_admin_password: 'changeme'
nexus_anonymous_access: true
nexus_public_hostname: "{{ ansible_fqdn }}"
nexus_public_scheme: http
httpd_setup_enable: false
```

Nexus has many configuration options and is scriptable.

Gitea

For source-code versioning, Git is the most popular VCS choice nowadays, widely implemented by global vendors and SaaS services. Well-known brands include GitHub (*https://github.com*), Atlassian's BitBucket (*https://bitbucket.org*), and GitLab (*https://gitlab.com*) (which is open source). In corporate environments it is typical to find BitBucket in use with other Atlassian tools, like Confluence and Jira. GitHub and GitLab have enterprise offerings and compete on feature sets. If you want to "roll your own Git," a lightweight option to consider is Gitea, an open source, self-hosted solution with a Github-like UI and a very accessible API.

Let's create a group called `git` in our inventory and a playbook to deploy Gitea with the database manager MySQL on the same host:

```
---
- name: Git Server
  hosts: git
  become: true
  collections:
    - community.mysql
  roles:
    - role: mysql
      tags: mysql
    - role: gitea
      tags: gitea
```

The collection and roles are installed from Ansible Galaxy using these entries in *roles/requirements.yml*:

```
collections:
  - community.mysql
roles:
  - src: do1jlr.gitea
    name: gitea

  - src: do1jlr.mysql
    name: mysql
```

In *group_vars/git* there is configuration for the database and Gitea:

```
# https://github.com/roles-ansible/ansible_role_gitea
gitea_db_host: '127.0.0.1:3306'
gitea_db_name: 'gitea'
gitea_db_type: 'mysql'
gitea_db_password: "YourOwnPasswordIsBetter"
gitea_require_signin: false
gitea_fqdn: "{{ ansible_fqdn }}"
gitea_http_listen: '0.0.0.0'
gitea_http_port: '3000'
# https://github.com/roles-ansible/ansible_role_mysql
mysql_bind_address: '127.0.0.1'
mysql_root_password: ''  # insecure
mysql_user_home: /home/vagrant
mysql_user_name: vagrant
mysql_user_password: vagrant
mysql_databases:
  - name: 'gitea'
mysql_users:
  - name: "{{ gitea_db_name }}"
    password: "{{ gitea_db_password }}"
    priv: "{{ gitea_db_name }}.*:ALL"
    state: present
```

This configuration is just the beginning of a Gitea install; it could evolve, in a more mature setup.

Code quality

Developers need software quality control tools, and measuring technical debt and identifying security hotspots both call for tooling too. SonarSource SonarQube is open source software that can help. To install SonarQube, use this playbook:

```
- name: Code Quality
  hosts: sonar
  become: true
  collections:
    - community.postgres
  roles:
    - role: utils
    - role: java
    - role: postgres
      tags: postgres
    - role: sonarqube
```

The collection and roles are installed from Ansible Galaxy using these entries in *roles/requirements.yml*:

```
---
collections:
  - community.postgresql
roles:
  - src: dockpack.base_utils
    name: utils
  - src: geerlingguy.java
    name: java
```

```
  - src: lrk.sonarqube
    name: sonarqube
  - src: robertdebock.postgres
    name: postgres
```

In *group_vars/sonar* there is configuration for the database and SonarQube, also known as Sonar, as well as the required packages. Sonar can be extended with plug-ins. There is a plug-in to run `ansible-lint`, which could be useful in software projects that use Ansible along with source code in other languages. SonarQube is a Java program, yet it supports many programming languages. It works well with the Postgres database; however, to create users we had to install some extra packages to build the database library Python needed. Here is what you'll need, at minimum:

```
base_utils:
  - gcc
  - make
  - python36-devel
  - unzip
java_packages:
  - java-11-openjdk-devel
```

CI server

Depending on how your organization manages source code, you might want your own build server to run automated tasks. GitHub has Actions and GitLab has Runners to run automated tasks in containers. Both options are available in the cloud as well as on-premises, with different commercial plans. An alternative is to run your own CI server, using, for instance, TeamCity, Atlassian Bamboo, or Jenkins.

Jenkins

Jenkins is the de facto standard CI server. It is a Java program and is highly customizable through plug-ins. There are several plug-ins to work with Git systems, including Gitea, GitHub, and BitBucket. Ansible and Ansible Tower plug-ins are available as well.

However, for system administrators, setting up Jenkins has long been a manual, siloed process that involves installing dependencies, running and configuring the Jenkins server, defining pipelines, and configuring jobs. Needless to say, that should be automated as much as possible.

We have created a group `jenkins` in our inventory and a playbook to deploy Jenkins, using roles written by Jeff Geerling (author of *Ansible for DevOps* and @geerlingguy on Ansible Galaxy and GitHub):

```
- name: CI Server
  hosts: jenkins
  become: true
  roles:
    - role: epel
```

```
        tags: epel
    - role: utils
        tags: utils
    - role: java
    - role: docker
        tags: docker
    - role: jenkins
        tags: jenkins
    - role: configuration
        tags: qa
```

Most roles are installed from Ansible Galaxy using these entries in *roles/require-ments.yml*:

```
---
roles:
  - src: dockpack.base_utils
    name: utils
  - src: geerlingguy.repo-epel
    name: epel
  - src: geerlingguy.docker
    name: docker
  - src: geerlingguy.java
    name: java
  - src: geerlingguy.jenkins
    name: jenkins
...
```

In *group_vars/jenkins* there is basic setup configuration, such as for plug-ins and a few tools that you'll need:

```
jenkins_plugins:
  - ansible
  - ansible-tower
  - ansicolor
  - configuration-as-code
  - docker
  - docker-build-step
  - docker-workflow
  - git
  - gitea
  - job-dsl
  - pipeline-build-step
  - pipeline-rest-api
  - pipeline-stage-view
  - sonar
  - timestamps
  - ws-cleanup
base_utils:
  - unzip
  - git
docker_users:
  - jenkins
  - vagrant
```

This code installs Docker and allows Jenkins to use it.

Jenkins and Ansible

Installing the plug-ins for Ansible and Ansible Tower adds only the Java archives with the *.jpi* filename extension; you'll need to install Python and Ansible yourself. There are many installation options, but for this example, let's create a role for Jenkins and test some roles using it.

Jenkins configuration as code

If you are convinced by the ideas of configuration management, then you'll want to configure Jenkins automatically. It has an API that is used in the geerlingguy.jen kins role, with methods such as get_url and uri. Internally, Jenkins is configured mostly by XML files. There are a few Ansible modules, as listed in Table 22-1.

Table 22-1. Ansible modules for configuring Jenkins

Module	Purpose
jenkins_job	Manage Jenkins jobs
jenkins_job_facts	Get information about Jenkins jobs
jenkins_job_info	Get information about Jenkins jobs
jenkins_plugin	Add or remove the Jenkins plug-in
jenkins_script	Executes a Groovy script in the Jenkins instance

Groovy is a JVM scripting language that Jenkins uses internally.

You can also use Jenkins from the command line, provided that you download the Java jarfile from the API:

```
- name: Get Jenkins CLI for automation
  get_url:
    url: "http://127.0.0.1:8080/jnlpJars/jenkins-cli.jar"
    dest: /var/lib/jenkins/jenkins-cli.jar
    mode: '0755'
    timeout: 300
  retries: 3
  delay: 10
```

For a complex pluggable automation system like Jenkins, you should rather use a minimal amount of Ansible, to have it manage itself. The plug-in configuration-as-code (casc) uses a YAML file to configure different parts of the Jenkins setup. Jenkins can install some tools itself given this YAML config file, which we install with the template module as follows:

```
tool:
  ansibleInstallation:
    installations:
    - home: "/usr/local/bin"
      name: "ansible"
  git:
```

```
    installations:
    - home: "git"
      name: "Default"
jdk:
  installations:
  - properties:
    - installSource:
        installers:
        - jdkInstaller:
            acceptLicense: true
            id: "jdk-8u221-oth-JPR"
maven:
  installations:
  - name: "Maven3"
    properties:
    - installSource:
        installers:
        - maven:
            id: "3.8.4"
mavenGlobalConfig:
  globalSettingsProvider: "standard"
  settingsProvider: "standard"
sonarRunnerInstallation:
  installations:
  - name: "SonarScanner"
    properties:
    - installSource:
        installers:
        - sonarRunnerInstaller:
            id: "4.6.2.2472"
```

Not all tools are supported. We installed Git with the `utils` role.

The great advantage of this method is that Jenkins will install these tools on demand, on the build agents that need them. (*Build agents* are extra servers that you add when there is more load.) Here is how to configure Jenkins with YAML files. Note that Jenkins needs to be restarted with an extra Java property that tells it where to find these files:

```
- name: Ensure casc_configs directory exists
  file:
    path: "{{ casc_configs }}"
    state: directory
    owner: jenkins
    group: root
    mode: '0750'

- name: Create Jenkins jobs configuration
  template:
    src: jenkins.yaml.j2
    dest: "{{ casc_configs }}/jenkins.yaml"
    owner: jenkins
    group: root
    mode: '0440'
```

```
- name: Enable configuration as code
  lineinfile:
    dest: /etc/sysconfig/jenkins
    regexp: '^JENKINS_JAVA_OPTIONS='
    line:>-
      JENKINS_JAVA_OPTIONS="-Djava.awt.headless=true
      -Djenkins.install.runSetupWizard=false
      -Dcasc.jenkins.config={{ casc_configs }}"
    state: present
    mode: '0600'
  notify: Restart Jenkins

- name: Flush handlers
  meta: flush_handlers

- name: Wait for Jenkins
  wait_for:
    port: 8080
    state: started
    delay: 10
    timeout: 600
```

Install the YAML file in the directory */var/lib/jenkins/casc_configs* and configure the Java property -Dcasc.jenkins.config=/var/lib/jenkins/casc_configs. This tells Jenkins to look there for configurations to apply.

Jenkins job configurations as code

You can implement an extra level of automation with the job-dsl (*https://oreil.ly/ AXKGW*) plug-in. Here's how the Jenkins plug-in documentation (*https://oreil.ly/ QuJRE*) describes it:

> Jenkins is a wonderful system for managing builds, and people love using its UI to configure jobs. Unfortunately, as the number of jobs grows, maintaining them becomes tedious, and the paradigm of using a UI falls apart. Additionally, the common pattern in this situation is to copy jobs to create new ones. But these "children" have a habit of diverging from their original "template," making it difficult to maintain consistency between jobs.
>
> The Job DSL plug-in attempts to solve this problem by allowing jobs to be defined in a programmatic form in a human-readable file. You can write such a file without being a Jenkins expert, fortunately, since the configuration from the web UI translates intuitively into code.

In short, you generate Jenkins jobs based on a seed job. To configure Jenkins to do so, you'll add an extra block in the YAML casc template:

```
jobs:
  - file: /home/jenkins/jobs.groovy
```

Now you need a Groovy file to describe the jobs. As Ansible adepts, we grab for a Jinja2 template, jobs.groovy.j2:

```
{% for repo in git_repositories %}
pipelineJob('{{ repo }}') {
  triggers {
    scm ''
  }
  definition {
    cpsScm {
      scm {
        git {
          remote {
            url('https://{{ git_host }}/{{ git_path }}/{{ repo }}.git')
          }
        }
      }
      scriptPath('Jenkinsfile')
    }
  }
}
{% endfor %}
```

This template needs the following variables defined:

```
git_host: github.com
git_path: ansiblebook
git_repositories:
  - ansible_role_ssh
  - ansible_role_ansible
  - ansible_role_web
```

This *jobs.groovy* file is now installed. You can use the command module to activate the jobs with `jenkins-cli.jar`, a Java command-line tool for Jenkins:

```
- name: Create Job DSL plugin seed job
  template:
    src: jobs.groovy.j2
    dest: /home/jenkins/jobs.groovy
    owner: jenkins
    mode: '0750'

- name: Activate jobs configuration with Jenkins CLI
  command: |
    java -jar jenkins-cli.jar \
    -s http://127.0.0.1:8080/ \
    -auth admin:{{ jenkins_admin_password }} \
    reload-jcasc-configuration
  changed_when: true
  args:
    chdir: /var/lib/jenkins
```

Running CI for Ansible Roles

Molecule (discussed in Chapter 14) is a great framework to use for quality assurance of Ansible roles. To automate a Jenkins job, you'll add a Groovy script to the root directory for each source repository that we want to use Jenkins for. This script should be named `Jenkinsfile`. The Jenkinsfile in the example defines a Jenkins stage for each Molecule stage that we want to use, with an informational stage up front:

```
pipeline {
  agent any
  options {
    disableConcurrentBuilds()
    ansiColor('vga')
  }
  triggers {
    pollSCM 'H/15 * * * *'
    cron 'H H * * *'
  }
  stages {
    stage ("Build Environment") {
      steps {
        sh '''
          source /usr/local/bin/activate
          python -V
          ansible --version
          molecule --version
        '''
      }
    }
    stage ("Syntax") {
      steps {
        sh '(source /usr/local/bin/activate && molecule syntax)'
      }
    }
    stage ("Linting") {
      steps {
        sh '(source /usr/local/bin/activate && molecule lint)'
      }
    }
    stage ("Playbook") {
      steps {
        sh '(source /usr/local/bin/activate && molecule converge)'
      }
    }
    stage ("Verification") {
      steps {
        sh '(source /usr/local/bin/activate && molecule verify)'
      }
    }
    stage ("Idempotency") {
      steps {
        sh '(source /usr/local/bin/activate && molecule idempotence)'
      }
    }
  }
}
```

Defining these stages allows you to see your progress at a glance in Jenkins (Figure 22-1).

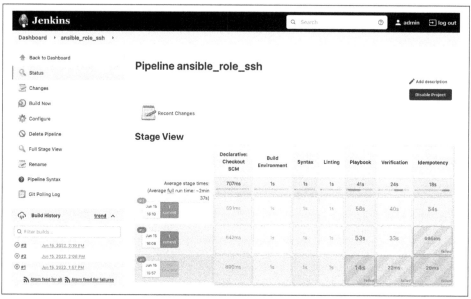

Figure 22-1. Jenkins pipeline for Ansible role

Jenkinsfiles have many possibilities. This is just a simple example of a pipeline job that maps well to Molecule's stages, but it leaves other tasks unimplemented. The Jenkins documentation has more information on pipelines (*https://oreil.ly/YOtO4*).

Staging

Most organizations that develop software have a blueprint for staging. Staging means running separate environments for different purposes in the life cycle of software. You develop software on a virtual desktop, and the software is built on the dev environment, tested on the test environment, and then deployed for "acceptance" and eventually production. There are many ways to do this, but in general you'd like to find problems as early as possible. It is a good practice to use network separation and security controls like firewalls, access management, and redundancy. Figure 22-2 depicts such staging environments.

A basic setup quickly becomes a rather complex beast to manage, but Jenkins and especially Jenkins agents that are confined to such environments can help automate the staging process in a reasonably secure way.

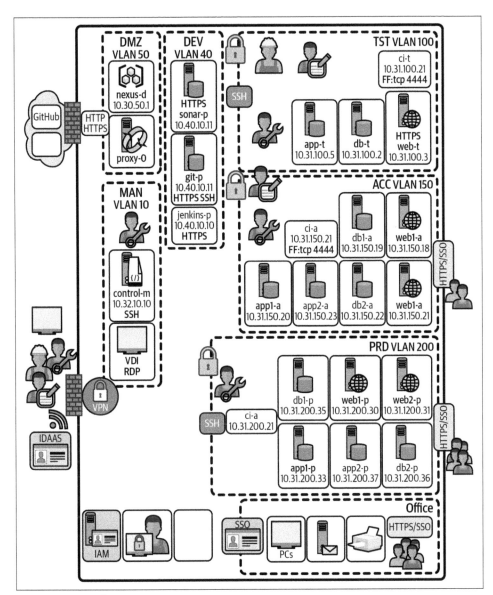

Figure 22-2. Different staging environments

Ansible Plug-in

The Ansible Jenkins plug-in creates the user interface for a build step in a Jenkins job. If you would like to use a pipeline job with a Jenkinsfile, then you can use a snippet like this to run a playbook as part of your pipeline:

```
ansiblePlaybook become: true, colorized: true, credentialsId: 'Machines',
disableHostKeyChecking: true, installation: 'ansible', inventory:
'inventory/hosts', limit: 'webservers', playbook: 'playbooks/playbook.yml',
tags: 'ssh', vaultCredentialsId: 'ANSIBLE_VAULT_PASSWORD'
```

Use the Snippet Generator to parameterize the build step (Figure 22-3).

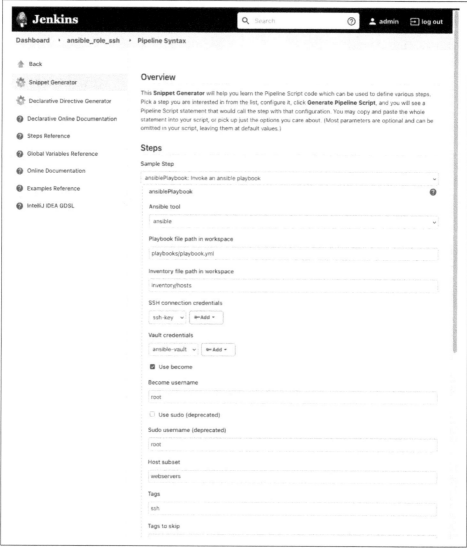

Figure 22-3. Jenkins Snippet Generator for Ansible playbook build step

The advantage of using Jenkins to run playbooks is central execution and logging. It is a natural fit for development teams that already know and use Jenkins. Ansible needs to be present on the Jenkins server or on the Jenkins agents that will execute the jobs.

Ansible Tower Plug-in

If you're automating your enterprise production environment with Ansible Automation Controller (see Chapter 23), you'll also want to make use of the Ansible Tower plug-in if you develop applications. Ansible Automation Controller allows for better scaling, both in the number of teams that can use it and in role-based access control. Ansible Automation Controller also has more security features than Jenkins.

To separate concerns for internal control, organizations often create staging environments and limit access to production environments. Developers might be given the rights to start a job or workflow with a well-defined combination of playbooks, machines, credentials, and other pre-filled options. Using Jenkins to start a job template can be a great step toward continuous delivery! With Jenkins Snippet Generator, it is possible to create fine-grained access to Ansible Automation Controller to start a playbook with specified parameters (a job template; Figure 22-4). You can store credentials safely in Ansible Automation Controller and delegate their use to the Jenkins job. This means that the developers won't need to log in to the inventory to deploy their app. They might not bother, or they might not be allowed to for compliance/risk reasons.

This plug-in could be used after software has been built and tested in a staging environment, to deploy the app into production. You can compose such a final build step in the Jenkinsfile with the Snippet Generator using the following code:

```
ansibleTower jobTags: 'appdeploy', jobTemplate: '1234', jobType: 'run', limit:
'web', throwExceptionWhenFail: false, towerCredentialsId:
'ANSIBLE_VAULT_PASSWORD', towerLogLevel: 'false', towerServer: 'tower'
```

Figure 22-4. Jenkins Snippet Generator for Ansible Tower job template build step

Conclusion

Ansible is a great tool in continuous delivery of complex software systems. It can not only manage the development environment, but also integrate deeply into software staging processes by automating all kinds of chores that kill productivity when done manually.

## CHAPTER 23

Ansible Automation Platform

Ansible Automation Platform is a commercial software product offered by Red Hat. Ansible Automation Platform 2 is the next-generation automation platform for the enterprise. It consists of a rearchitected *Automation Controller 4*, formerly known as Tower/AWX, and the *Automation Hub*, an on-premises repository for Ansible content that replaces the on-premises Ansible Galaxy. You can curate the Automation Hub to match your organization's governance policies or simply sync it with community content. Example 23-1 is a file that can be uploaded by the administrator of the Automation Hub (see Figure 23-1). It defines the collections that the Automation Hub will serve on the local network. The Automation Hub needs internet connectivity to download these.

Example 23-1. requirements.yml for community content on Automation Hub

```
---
collections:
  # Install collections from Ansible Galaxy.
  - name: ansible.windows
    source: https://galaxy.ansible.com
  - name: ansible.utils
    source: https://galaxy.ansible.com
  - name: awx.awx
    source: https://galaxy.ansible.com
  - name: community.crypto
    source: https://galaxy.ansible.com
  - name: community.docker
    source: https://galaxy.ansible.com
  - name: community.general
    source: https://galaxy.ansible.com
  - name: community.kubernetes
    source: https://galaxy.ansible.com
...
```

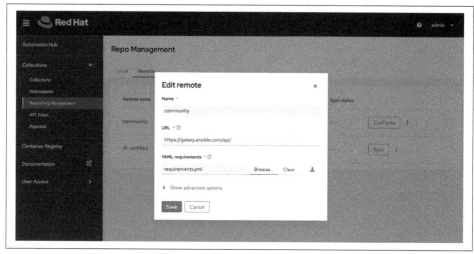

Figure 23-1. Uploading the requirements file

You can configure multiple servers for the `ansible-galaxy` command in *ansi-ble.cfg* if you use the Private Automation Hub in Ansible Automation Platform 2 (Example 23-2).

Example 23-2. ansible.cfg

```
[galaxy]
server_list = automation_hub, release_galaxy, my_org_hub, my_test_hub

[galaxy_server.automation_hub]
url=https://cloud.redhat.com/api/automation-hub/
auth_url=https://sso.redhat.com/auth/realms/redhat-external/protocol/openid-connect/token
token=my_ah_token

[galaxy_server.release_galaxy]
url=https://galaxy.ansible.com/
token=my_token

[galaxy_server.my_org_hub]
url=https://automation.my_org/
username=my_user
password=my_pass

[galaxy_server.my_test_hub]
url=https://automation-test.my_org/
username=test_user
password=test_pass
```

Staging environments like `my_test_hub` can be used for testing local collections, published eventually in `my_org_hub`.

The architecture of Ansible Automation Platform 2 benefits from developments in container technology. It is more scalable and secure than the previous generation. The biggest difference is that it decouples the control plane from the execution environments, as shown in Figure 23-2.

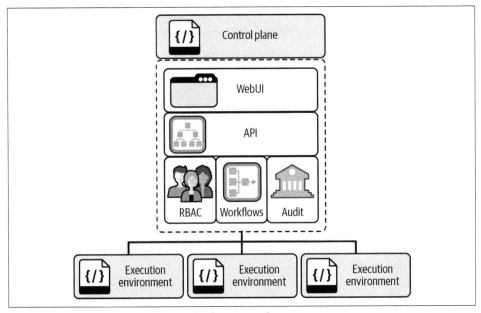

Figure 23-2. Ansible Automation Platform 2 Architecture

Ansible Tower used Python virtual environments to manage dependencies, but this method presented challenges for Tower operations teams. Ansible Automation Platform 2 introduces automation execution environments; in other words, it runs the automation in container images that include Ansible, Ansible content, and any other dependencies, as shown in Figure 23-3.

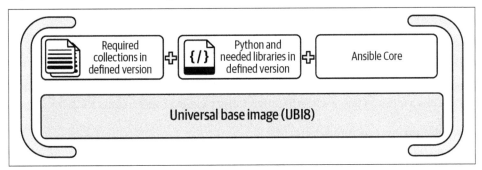

Figure 23-3. Ansible Execution Environment

Ansible Execution Environments are based on `ansible-builder` (*https://oreil.ly/ NlgNY*) (discussed later in this chapter).

Ansible Automation Platform can be installed in RedHat OpenShift or on Red Hat Enterprise Linux 8 hosts (rhel/8). The sample code for this chapter creates a development cluster on VirtualBox with Vagrant. A Packer configuration is included to create a rhel/8 VirtualBox box (Packer is discussed in Chapter 16).

The Automation Controller provides more granular user- and role-based access policy management combined with a web user interface, shown in Figure 23-4, a RESTful API.

Figure 23-4. Ansible Automation Controller dashboard

Subscription Models

Red Hat offers support (*https://oreil.ly/qsiFg*) as an annual subscription model with three subscription types, each with different service-level agreements (SLAs):

- Self-Support (no support and SLA)
- Standard (support and SLA: business hours)
- Premium (support and SLA: 24 hours a day, 7 days a week)

All subscription levels include regular updates and releases of Ansible Automation Platform.

As a developer, you can get free access to the many technology resources Red Hat has to offer. All you need to do is register (*https://oreil.ly/Q7UDb*) for a Red Hat Developer Subscription for Individuals.

Ansible Automation Platform Trial

Red Hat provides a free 60-day trial license (*https://oreil.ly/wSoD5*) with the feature set of the Self-Support subscription model for up to 100 managed hosts.

Once you register as a developer and apply for the trial, you'll be able to export the license manifest (*https://oreil.ly/7j8MF*) to activate your instance, as shown in Figure 23-5.

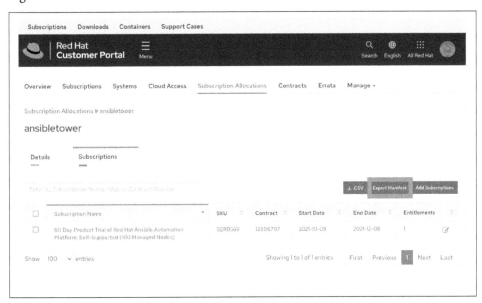

Figure 23-5. Managing subscriptions

 After acquiring Ansible, Inc., in 2015, Red Hat started working on an open source version of Ansible Tower called AWX. This installs in Kubernetes with the AWX Operator. See the documentation (*https://oreil.ly/NjaVt*) for instructions. The AWX source is available on GitHub (*https://oreil.ly/heqzB*).

For a quick evaluation setup using Vagrant, use the source "ansiblebook" on Github (*https://oreil.ly/FRY0I*):

```
$ git clone https://github.com/ansiblebook/ansiblebook.git
$ cd ansiblebook/ch23 && vagrant up
```

If the Vagrant machine is not reachable at *https://server03/*, you may need to run the following command inside the Vagrant machine to bring up the network interface associated with the IP address 192.168.56.13:

```
$ sudo systemctl restart network.service
```

What Ansible Automation Platform Solves

Ansible Automation Platform is not just a web user interface on top of Ansible: it extends Ansible's functionality with access control, projects, inventory management, and the ability to run jobs by job templates. Let's take a closer look at each of these in turn.

Access Control

In large corporations, Ansible Automation Platform helps manage automation by delegating control. You can create an organization for each department, and a local system administrator can set up teams with roles and add employees to them, giving each person as much control of the managed hosts and devices as they need to do their job.

Ansible Automation Platform was built with separation of duties in mind—a powerful idea, if applied well. Imagine that the developers of a playbook are not the same people as the owners of the infrastructure. Try creating a repository for your playbooks and another one for your inventory, so a team with their own machines can create another *inventory* to reuse your playbooks. Ansible Automation Platform has the concept of *organizations* with *teams*, each with distinct levels of permissions.

Ansible Automation Platform acts as a gatekeeper to hosts. No team or employee is required to have direct access to the managed hosts, which reduces complexity and increases security. Figure 23-6 shows Ansible Automation Platform's user management web interface. With a product like this it is also possible to use other authentication systems, such as Azure AD, GitHub, Google OAuth2, LDAP, RADIUS, SAML, or TACACS+. Connecting Ansible Automation Platform with existing authentication systems such as LDAP directories can reduce administrative cost per user.

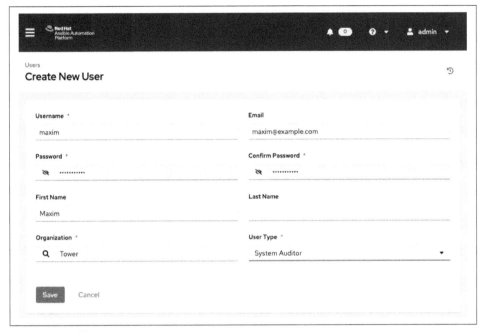

Figure 23-6. User management

Projects

A *project* in Ansible Automation Platform terminology is nothing more than a bucket holding logically related playbooks and roles.

In classic Ansible projects, static inventories are often kept alongside the playbooks and roles. Ansible Automation Platform handles inventories separately. Anything related to inventories and inventory variables that is kept in projects, such as group variables and host variables, will not be accessible later on.

 The target (for example, hosts: `<target>`) in these playbooks is essential. Choose wisely by using a common name across playbooks. This allows you to use the playbooks with different inventories. We will discuss this further later in the chapter.

As it is a best practice, we keep our projects with our playbooks in revision control on a source code management (SCM) system, and recommend that you do as well. The project management in Ansible Automation Platform can be configured to download these projects from your SCM servers and supports major open source SCM systems such as Git, Mercurial, and Subversion.

As a fallback if you do not want to use an SCM, you can set a static path under */var/lib/awx/projects*, where the project resides locally on the Ansible Automation Controller. You can also download a remote archive.

Since projects evolve over time, the projects on Ansible Automation Controller must be updated to stay in sync with the SCM. But no worries—Ansible Automation Platform has multiple solutions for updating projects.

First, ensure that Ansible Automation Platform has the latest state of your project by enabling "Update on Launch," as shown in Figure 23-7. Additionally, you can set a regularly scheduled update job on each project. Finally, you can manually update projects if you wish to maintain control of when updates happen.

Figure 23-7. Ansible Automation Controller project SCM update options

Inventory Management

Ansible Automation Platform allows you to manage inventories as dedicated resources, including managing access control. A common pattern is to put the production, staging, and testing hosts into separate inventories with their own credentials and variable values.

Within these inventories, you can add default variables and manually add groups and hosts. In addition, as shown in Figure 23-8, Ansible Automation Platform allows you to query hosts dynamically from a source (such as a Microsoft Azure Resource Manager) and put these hosts in a group.

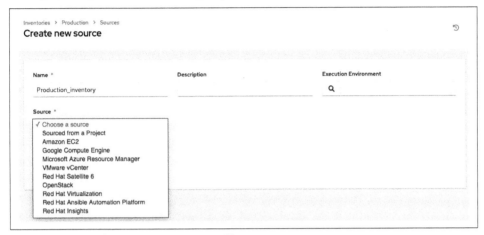

Figure 23-8. Ansible Automation Controller inventory source

Group and host variables can be added in form fields that will overwrite defaults.

You can even temporarily disable hosts by clicking a button (Figure 23-9), so they will be excluded from any job run.

Figure 23-9. Ansible Automation Platform inventory excluded hosts

Run Jobs by Job Templates

Job templates connect projects with inventories (Figure 23-10). They define how users are allowed to execute a playbook from a project to specific targets from a selected inventory.

Figure 23-10. Ansible Automation Platform job templates

Refinements can be applied on a playbook level, such as additional parameters and tags. Further, you can specify in what *mode* the playbook will run. For example, some users may be allowed to execute a playbook only in *check mode*, while others may be allowed to do so only on a subset of hosts but in *live mode*.

On the target level, you can select an inventory and, optionally, limit it to some hosts or a group.

An executed job template creates a new *job entry* (Figure 23-11).

Figure 23-11. Ansible Automation Platform job entries

In the detail view of each job entry (Figure 23-12), you'll find information not only about whether the job was successful but also the date and time it was executed, when it finished, who started it, and with which parameters. You can even filter by play to see all the tasks and their results. All of this information is stored and kept in the database, so you can audit it at any time.

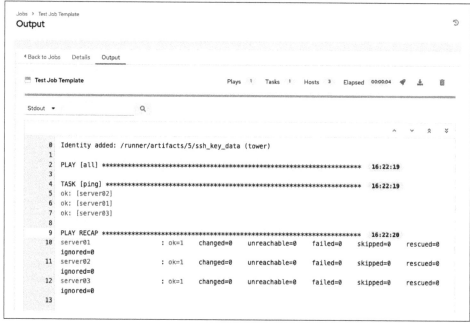

Figure 23-12. Ansible Automation Platform job detail view

RESTful API

The Ansible Automation Controller exposes a Representational State Transfer (REST) API that lets you integrate with existing build-and-deploy pipelines or continuous deployment systems.

Since the API is browsable, you can inspect the whole thing in your favorite browser by opening the URL *http://<tower_server>/api/v2/* to get all the available resources (Figure 23-13):

```
$ firefox https://server03/api/v2/
```

At the time of writing, the latest API version is v2.

Using the API can be a solution for integration, but to access the Ansible Automation Controller, there is an Ansible collection: `awx.awx`.

```
GET /api/v2/


HTTP 200 OK
Allow: GET, HEAD, OPTIONS
Content-Type: application/json
Vary: Accept
X-API-Node: server03
X-API-Product-Name: Red Hat Ansible Automation Platform
X-API-Product-Version: 4.0.0
X-API-Time: 0.009s

{
    "ping": "/api/v2/ping/",
    "instances": "/api/v2/instances/",
    "instance_groups": "/api/v2/instance_groups/",
    "config": "/api/v2/config/",
    "settings": "/api/v2/settings/",
    "me": "/api/v2/me/",
    "dashboard": "/api/v2/dashboard/",
    "organizations": "/api/v2/organizations/",
    "users": "/api/v2/users/",
    "execution_environments": "/api/v2/execution_environments/",
    "projects": "/api/v2/projects/",
    "project_updates": "/api/v2/project_updates/",
    "teams": "/api/v2/teams/",
    "credentials": "/api/v2/credentials/",
    "credential_types": "/api/v2/credential_types/",
    "credential_input_sources": "/api/v2/credential_input_sources/",
    "applications": "/api/v2/applications/",
    "tokens": "/api/v2/tokens/",
    "metrics": "/api/v2/metrics/",
    "inventory": "/api/v2/inventories/",
    "inventory_sources": "/api/v2/inventory_sources/",
    "inventory_updates": "/api/v2/inventory_updates/",
    "groups": "/api/v2/groups/",
    "hosts": "/api/v2/hosts/",
    "job_templates": "/api/v2/job_templates/",
    "jobs": "/api/v2/jobs/",
    "ad_hoc_commands": "/api/v2/ad_hoc_commands/",
    "system_job_templates": "/api/v2/system_job_templates/",
    "system_jobs": "/api/v2/system_jobs/",
    "schedules": "/api/v2/schedules/",
    "roles": "/api/v2/roles/",
    "notification_templates": "/api/v2/notification_templates/",
    "notifications": "/api/v2/notifications/",
    "labels": "/api/v2/labels/",
    "unified_job_templates": "/api/v2/unified_job_templates/",
    "unified_jobs": "/api/v2/unified_jobs/",
    "activity_stream": "/api/v2/activity_stream/",
    "workflow_job_templates": "/api/v2/workflow_job_templates/",
    "workflow_jobs": "/api/v2/workflow_jobs/",
    "workflow_approvals": "/api/v2/workflow_approvals/",
    "workflow_job_template_nodes": "/api/v2/workflow_job_template_nodes/",
    "workflow_job_nodes": "/api/v2/workflow_job_nodes/"
}
```

Figure 23-13. Ansible Automation Platform API version 2

AWX.AWX

So, how do you create a new user in Ansible Automation Controller or launch a job by using nothing but the API? Of course, you could use the all-time favorite command-line (CLI) HTTP tool, cURL, but Ansible has made an even more user-friendly way: playbooks!

 Unlike the Ansible Automation Platform application, Ansible Tower CLI is open source software, published on GitHub (*https://oreil.ly/ryjSo*) under the Apache 2.0 license.

Installation

To install `awx.awx`, use Ansible Galaxy:

```
$ ansible-galaxy collection install awx.awx
```

Since Ansible Automation Platform uses a preconfigured, self-signed SSL/TLS certificate, skip the verification in the template for the *tower_cli.cfg* file:

```
[general]
host = https://{{ awx_host }}
verify_ssl = false
oauth_token = {{ awx_token }}
```

Before you can access the API, you'll have to configure the credentials with the `admin_password` as an extra variable, like in Example 23-3.

Example 23-3. awx-config.yml

```
---
- name: Configure awx
  hosts: automationcontroller
  become: false
  gather_facts: false

  vars:
    awx_host: "{{ groups.automationcontroller[0] }}"
    awx_user: admin
    cfg: "-k --conf.host https://{{ awx_host }} --conf.user {{ awx_user }}"

  tasks:

    - name: Login to Tower
      delegate_to: localhost
      no_log: true
      changed_when: false
      command: "awx {{ cfg }} --conf.password {{ admin_password }} -k login"
      register: awx_login
```

```
- name: Set awx_token
  delegate_to: localhost
  set_fact:
    awx_token: "{{ awx_login.stdout | from_json | json_query('token') }}"

- name: Create ~/.tower_cli.cfg
  delegate_to: localhost
  template:
    src: tower_cli.cfg
    dest: "~/.tower_cli.cfg"
    mode: '0600'
...
```

This creates the file *~/.tower_cli.cfg* with the token. Now you can create a playbook to automate your Automation Controller—next-level automation!

Create an Organization

The data model listed in Figure 23-13 requires some objects to be present before others can be created, so the first thing you need to create is an organization:

```
---
- name: Configure Organization
  hosts: localhost
  gather_facts: false
  collections:
    - awx.awx

  tasks:

    - name: Create organization
      tower_organization:
        name: "Tower"
        description: "Tower organization"
        state: present

    - name: Create a team
      tower_team:
        name: "Tower Team"
        description: "Tower team"
        organization: "Tower"
        state: present
```

Everything links to either an organization or an inventory.

Create an Inventory

For the sake of the example code, we've created a simple inventory of the Ansible Automation Platform with the awx.awx collection. Normally you would use a tower_project pointing to a Git repository, and tie that as a tower_inventory_source to a tower_inventory:

```yaml
---
- name: Configure Tower Inventory
  hosts: localhost
  gather_facts: false
  collections:
    - awx.awx

  tasks:

    - name: Create inventory
      tower_inventory:
        name: "Tower Inventory"
        description: "Tower infra"
        organization: "Tower"
        state: present

    - name: Populate inventory
      tower_host:
        name: "{{ item }}"
        inventory: "Tower Inventory"
        state: present
      with_items:
        - 'server01'
        - 'server02'
        - 'server03'

    - name: Create groups
      tower_group:
        name: "{{ item.group }}"
        inventory: "Tower Inventory"
        state: present
        hosts:
          - "{{ item.host }}"
      with_items:
        - group: automationcontroller
          host: 'server03'
        - group: automationhub
          host: 'server02'
        - group: database
          host: 'server01'
```

If you create and destroy virtual machines using Ansible, then you manage the inventory that way.

Running a Playbook with a Job Template

If you are used to running playbooks using only Ansible Core on the command line, you are probably used to administrator privileges. Ansible Automation Platform has ways to model this into a secure setup that scales well.

Playbooks are stored in a source-control system like Git. A *project* corresponds to such a Git repository. You can import a project using the `tower_project` module:

```
- name: Create project
  tower_project:
    name: "test-playbooks"
    organization: "Tower"
    scm_type: git
    scm_url: https://github.com/ansible/test-playbooks.git
```

When you run an Ansible playbook on the command line, you probably set up SSH keys or another way to log in to the target systems in the inventory. Running the playbook that way is bound to your user account on the Ansible control host. If you use Ansible Automation Platform, then you store *machine credentials* in the (encrypted) platform database to access the machines in an inventory.

Although SSH keys are sensitive data, there is a way to add encrypted private keys to the Ansible Automation Controller and have it ask for the passphrase when a job template that uses it launches:

```
- name: Create machine credential
  tower_credential:
    name: 'Tower Credential'
    credential_type: Machine
    ssh_key_unlock: ASK
    organization: "Tower"
    inputs:
      ssh_key_data: "{{ lookup('file', 'files/tower_ed25519') }}"
```

Now that you have a project, an inventory, and access to the machines with the machine credential, you can create a *job template* to run a playbook from the project on the machines in the inventory:

```
- name: Create job template
  tower_job_template:
    name: "Test Job Template"
    project: "test-playbooks"
    inventory: "Tower Inventory"
    credential: 'Tower Credential'
    playbook: ping.yml
```

You'll probably want to automate running a job from a job template. The awx.awx collection makes this pretty straightforward. All you need to know is the name of the job template you want to launch:

```
- name: Launch the Job Template
  tower_job_launch:
    job_template: "Test Job Template"
```

Job templates are really useful for standard operational procedures. The examples given so far are easy to follow on a development system. When you work with multiple teams, ask for input when you launch a job template. This way you can delegate all kinds of standard tasks to teams on their infrastructure environments by asking for their inventory and their credentials.

Using Containers to Run Ansible

Containers simplify working with Ansible in two areas. One is in testing Ansible roles with Molecule (*https://oreil.ly/cQr6T*), which we discussed in Chapter 14.

The second argument for using containers appears when external dependencies create complexity, which might be different for each project or team. When you import Python libraries and external Ansible content like roles, modules, plug-ins, and collections, creating and using container images can help ensure they stay updated for long-term use. There are many moving parts: Linux packages, Python version, Ansible version, and Ansible roles and collections are updated constantly. It can be hard to get the same execution environment for Ansible on multiple machines or at different points in time. Execution environments (*https://oreil.ly/hpefh*) are a consistent, reproducible, portable, and sharable method to run Ansible Automation jobs on your laptop in the exact same way as they are executed on the AWX/Ansible Automation Platform.

Creating Execution Environments

Creating Ansible execution environments is an advanced topic that you might need when you work with Ansible Automation Platform 2. Execution environments evolved from the work on the Python library `ansible-runner` (*https://oreil.ly/bkOei*). They are built with Podman on RHEL 8 using a Python tool called `ansible-builder` (*https://oreil.ly/1vpq5*). (Podman is the container runtime for developers on RHEL 8).

Let's see how to create an execution environment. First, create a virtual environment to work with `ansible-builder` and `ansible-runner`:

```
$ python3 -m venv .venv
```

Activate the virtual environment and update your tools:

```
$ source .venv/bin/activate
$ python3 -m pip install --upgrade pip
$ pip3 install wheel
```

Then install `ansible-builder` and `ansible-runner`:

```
$ pip3 install ansible-builder
$ pip3 install ansible-runner
```

Ansible Builder needs a definition in a file named *execution-environment.yml*:

```
---
version: 1

ansible_config: 'ansible.cfg'

dependencies:
  galaxy: requirements.yml
  python: requirements.txt
```

```
    system: bindep.txt

additional_build_steps:
  prepend: |
    RUN pip3 install --upgrade pip setuptools
  append:
    - RUN yum clean all
```

Python libraries should be listed in *requirements.txt*, and Ansible requirements in *requirements.yml*. A new file type is used for binary dependencies, like the git and unzip packages. These are listed with their platform's package manager in *bindep.txt*:

```
git [platform:rpm]
unzip [platform:rpm]
```

Once you are happy with the definition of your execution environment, you can build it:

```
$ ansible-builder \
--build-arg ANSIBLE_RUNNER_IMAGE=quay.io/ansible/ansible-runner:stable-2.11-latest \
-t ansible-controller -c context --container-runtime podman
```

To use the execution environment, create a wrapper script around this command:

```
$ podman run --rm --network=host -ti \
    -v${HOME}/.ssh:/root/.ssh \
    -v ${PWD}/playbooks:/runner \
    -e RUNNER_PLAYBOOK=playbook.yml \
    ansible-controller
```

Conclusion

Ansible Automation Platform 2 is a product for enterprise-wide IT automation. The Automation Controller (formerly known as Ansible Tower) offers role-based access control, segregation of duties, and delegation. Ansible projects are retrieved from source control, credentials can be managed securely, inventory can be allocated, and every system change can be accounted for. This empowers organizations with hundreds of teams to manage tens of thousands of machines. No wonder the license cost is calculated over the number of hosts.

Automation Hub offers Ansible collections created by Red Hat's partners while enabling the administrators to curate community content and to restrict or replace access to Ansible Galaxy (*https://galaxy.ansible.com*).

In Ansible Automation Platform 2, the Ansible execution environments isolate software dependencies in containers, which offers greater flexibility than the virtual environments used in Ansible Tower. You can simply store Ansible's technical debt (particular versions needed, conflicting libraries, etc.) in several containers. Execution environments can be built by the teams, instead of by the administrator, which saves handovers.

## CHAPTER 24

Best Practices

In this chapter, we propose a set of best practices as a conversation starter, knowing that best practices don't transpose to other contexts very well. What works for Spotify or Netflix does not necessarily work for other companies. Our main goal is to get you thinking about these matters and discussing the ones that trigger your imagination or concern. The best practices are based on design principles and experience using Ansible in various settings. On the management level, we need to consider how practitioners perform and how to benchmark DevOps teams.

Simplicity, Modularity, and Composability

Michael DeHaan designed Ansible to automate the boring stuff in the simplest conceivable way because he wanted to spend his time doing more interesting things. Inexperienced users can now browse the Ansible Galaxy site (*https://galaxy.ansi ble.com*) for roles and collections to get something up and running within hours using Ansible.

Ever since DeHaan and Greg DeKoenigsberg started the Ansible community, they've been thinking and writing about best practices (*https://oreil.ly/ubBBZ*)—the documentation, however, changed its terminology from "best practices" (*https://oreil.ly/Yp36I*) in 2.9 to "tips and tricks" (*https://oreil.ly/0pOeP*) in 2.10. They point out that open source projects are more likely to gain and keep contributors when they have two particular properties: high modularity and high option value. *High modularity*, or *loose coupling*, allows freedom to add to Ansible. *High option value*, also known as *composability*, allows you to pick and choose: you might take from Galaxy what fits best in your situation, for instance, or choose Terraform for infrastructure provisioning and Ansible for systems management. Composability is also one of the foundations of the Tao of HashiCorp (*https://oreil.ly/Kohiw*).

Organize Content

- Use GitHub to share your Ansible content for collaboration and preservation.
- Use a repo per role, collection, project, and inventory.
- Track changes and approvals with a workflow like GitHub Flow (*https://oreil.ly/kgyjK*).
- Manage your dependencies: distributions, packages, libraries, tools.
- Magic happens when you put your files in the right places.
- Use the right tool for the job: try finding a module first.
- Don't solve complexity with Ansible; try writing a module with Python.

Decouple Inventories from Projects

- Make projects reusable to cater to multiple users.
- Let infrastructure owners define access to hosts in inventory.
- Use an inventory with group names based on function (or role).
- Combine projects and inventories, with separate Git repositories.
- Create staging environments to test properly before going live.
- Use the alternative directory layout (*https://oreil.ly/HH0VX*) to prepare for AWX/Ansible Automation Platform.

Decouple Roles and Collections

- Be aware that roles are ways of automatically loading vars, files, tasks, handlers, and templates based on a known file structure. Convention over configuration is a powerful pattern.
- Do one thing well with a role.
- Collections are a composite of roles, modules, plug-ins, etc. Test them as components.
- Group content by roles to allow for easy sharing with other users.
- Use the *roles/requirements.yml* manifest to express versioned dependencies.
- Separate project roles, shared roles, and Galaxy roles. Configure `roles_path` to search for these roles.
- Use top-level directories: files, templates for local implementation of role templates.

- The defaults are easy to override by the user with `group_vars`.
- The vars are not meant for the user to change.

Playbooks

- Make playbooks readable for nonspecialists (note to self).
- Think declarative, desired state, or simple state change.
- Safe defaults for newbies. Make IT simple for the whole team.
- When you can do something simply, do something simply.
- Playbooks are executable (with the #! shebang); vars files are not.

Code Style

- Format playbooks with native YAML style.
- Editors use file extensions for syntax coloring and linting.
- Always name your playbooks, plays, and tasks considering the logging.
- Comments start with a hashmark (#). Overuse comments and empty lines.
- To find problems in your content before you commit, use the rules of `ansible-lint` (*https://oreil.ly/HHMti*), `ansible-later` (*https://oreil.ly/zmXVV*), `yamllint` (*https://oreil.ly/4SW35*), SonarQube (*https://oreil.ly/07p8h*), Pylint (*https://oreil.ly/B6TRI*), ShellCheck (*https://oreil.ly/vX2mS*), Perl::Critic (*https://oreil.ly/hBnfg*), or any other linter required in your project.

Tag and Test All the Things

- Tags help organize execution of playbooks. You can run or skip parts of playbooks.
- Tags can help in testing. Add unit test tasks with the `unitTest` tag (*https://oreil.ly/kBZYZ*).
- Use Molecule (*https://oreil.ly/iTjBY*) for testing roles; verify the result.

Desired State

- Idempotency: the same operation should yield the same result, again and again.
- Ensure there are no changes unless things change.
- No uncertainty: describe the desired state and use variables to toggle state.

- Try to support check mode.
- Test states with a delegated driver: `molecule converge` and `molecule cleanup`.

Deliver Continuously

- Try to schedule provisioning and deployment as early and often as possible.
- Use the same playbooks in each environment with different credentials.
- Roll out changes to all environments in stages, in a visible way, by using Tower or Jenkins with ARA.
- Understand the `serial` keyword for rolling updates.

Security

- Make it easy to manage vault variables (*https://oreil.ly/15D7z*).
- Don't login as root. Don't use service accounts interactively.
- Design users and groups to minimize using privileges.
- Don't store logins and passwords in inventory.
- Encrypt logins, passwords, and tokens with `ansible-vault`.
- Use vault IDs for different access levels.
- Document `become` at the top of the task for easier auditing.
- Harden SSH (*https://oreil.ly/gTwbw*) and your system's attack surface.
- Run `ssh-audit` (*https://oreil.ly/BIJwU*) to validate SSH crypto (*https://oreil.ly/twN0f*).
- Consider using signed SSH keys (*https://oreil.ly/J1GUT*).

Deployment

- Create and store software packages in a repository, like Nexus (*https://oreil.ly/XOHiB*) or Artifactory (*https://oreil.ly/kI9AZ*).
- Releasing software is a one-bit decision, not a transfer of bytes.
- Manage applications' configuration with a central system or Git workflow.
- Create smoke tests to confirm proper startup, and validate the proper startup order.

Performance Indicators

If you are a team manager, scrum master, product owner, or another stakeholder in a software project, you'll need a yardstick. CALMS is a framework that assesses the ability to adopt DevOps processes, as well as a way of measuring success during a DevOps transformation. Jez Humble, coauthor of *The DevOps Handbook* (IT Revolution Press), coined the acronym, which stands for Culture, Automation, Lean, Measurement, and Sharing.

Key performance indicators for the adoption of best practices in software engineering include:

Collaboration
> Is the team sharing technical knowledge and proactively collaborating with other teams to integrate applications and environments?

Automation
> Is the team automating the deployment and promotion process for applications and environments?

Culture
> Is the team striving for improvement, best practices, and common principles when building and configuring applications and environments?

Measurement
> Is the team confirming functional and nonfunctional requirements (automatically) before promoting applications to production environments?

Sharing
> Is the team supplying and receiving the feedback they need to maintain control of the solutions they manage?

Benchmark Evidence

Proper application of Ansible best practices should be sufficient to provide evidence to all of the following challenges:

- Can we exactly reproduce any of our environments, including the version of the operating system, its patch level, the network configuration, the SW stack, the application deployed into it, and its configuration?

- Can we easily make an incremental change to any of these individual items and deploy the change to any, and all, of our environments?

- Can we easily see each change that occurred to a particular environment and trace it back to see exactly what the change was, who made it, and when?

- Can we satisfy all the compliance regulations to which we are subject?

- Is it easy for every member of the team to get the information they need, and to make changes? Or does our strategy get in the way of efficient delivery by increasing cycle time and decreasing feedback?

- When we onboard a new team member, do we give them an enthusiastic first impression?

Final Words

After writing all these pages for you, we can hardly claim that you can learn Ansible in two hours and deploy NGINX and Postgres in the third, but after reading *Ansible: Up and Running*, you may try teaching what you've learned to your coworkers, or even share a demo project in a Meetup. The Ansible community is global! If you are interested in joining the community, just go to Ansible's community page (*https:// oreil.ly/7KNaF*). Ansible discussion groups moved between RC, GitHub, Discord, and Reddit for online discussions and support.

If there's no Meetup close to you, then start one. If it's not active, then take the baton. That's how Bas started with the Ansible Benelux Meetup group in 2014. Meetups are a fantastic way to learn new things and to meet people who share the same interests. Bas has fond memories of the discussions, demonstrations, and workshops we held in various places around Amsterdam. Thanks, everybody!

Dear readers, we hope you got what you were after out of this book and the source code repositories, and that you have learned enough about Ansible for the tasks ahead of you. Good luck!

Bibliography

Barrett, Daniel, Richard Silverman and Robert Byrnes. *SSH The Secure Shell: The Definitive Guide*. Sebastopol, CA: O'Reilly Media, 2005.

Bauer, Kirk. *Automating UNIX and Linux Administration*. New York: Apress, 2003.

Clark, Mike. *Pragmatic Project Automation: How to Build, Deploy, and Monitor Java Applications*. Raleigh, NC: Pragmatic Bookshelf, 2004.

Conway, Damien. *Perl Best Practices*. Sebastopol, CA: O'Reilly Media, 2005.

Dobies, Jason, and Joshua Wood. *Kubernetes Operators*. Sebastopol, CA: O'Reilly Media, 2020.

Duvall, Paul, Steve Matyas, and Andrew Glover. *Continuous Integration: Improving Software Quality and Reducing Risk*. Upper Saddle River, NJ: Pearson Education, 2007.

Forsgren, Nicole, Jez Humble, and Gene Kim. *Accelerate: Building and Scaling High Performing Technology Organizations*. Portland, OR: IT Revolution, 2018.

Geewax, JJ. *Google Cloud Platform in Action*. Shelter Island, NY: Manning Publications, 2018.

Gift, Noah, and Jeremy Jones. *Python for Unix and Linux System Administration*. Sebastopol, CA: O'Reilly Media, 2008.

Hashimoto, Mitchell. *Vagrant: Up and Running*. Sebastopol, CA: O'Reilly Media, 2013.

Holzner, Steve. *Ant: The Definitive Guide*. Sebastopol, CA: O'Reilly Media, 2005.

Humble, Jeff, and David Farley. *Continuous Delivery: Reliable Software Releases through Build, Test, and Deployment Automation*. Upper Saddle River, NJ: Pearson Education, 2011.

Hunt, Andrew, and David Thomas. *The Pragmatic Programmer: From Journeyman to Master*. Boston, MA: Addison-Wesley, 2000.

Jaynes, Matt. *Taste Test: Puppet, Chef, Salt, Ansible*. Self-published, 2014.

Kernighan, Brian, and Rob Pike. *The UNIX Programming Environment*. Hoboken, NJ: Prentice Hall, 1984.

Kim, Gene, Jez Humble, Patrick DeBois, and John Willis. *The DevOps Handbook: How to Create World-Class Agility, Reliability, and Security in Technology Organizations*. Portland, OR: IT Revolution, 2016.

Kleppmann, Martin. *Designing Data-Intensive Applications*. Sebastopol, CA: O'Reilly Media, 2015.

Kurniawan, Yan. *Ansible for AWS*. Leanpub, 2016.

Limoncelli, Thomas A., Christina J. Hogan, and Strata R. Chalup. *The Practice of Cloud System Administration: Designing and Operating Large Distributed Systems*. Boston, MA: Addison-Wesley Professional, 2014.

Luksa, Marko. *Kubernetes in Action*. Shelter Island, NY: Manning Publications, 2018.

Mell, Peter, and Timothy Grance. *The NIST Definition of Cloud Computing*. NIST Special Publication 800-145, 2011.

Morris, Kief. *Infrastructure as Code: Dynamic Systems for the Cloud Age*. Sebastopol, CA: O'Reilly Media, 2021.

OpenSSH/Cookbook/Multiplexing, Wikibooks (*http://bit.ly/1bpeV0y*), October 28, 2014.

Oram, Andrew, and Steve Talbott. *Managing Projects with Make*. Sebastopol, CA: O'Reilly Media, 1986.

Reitz, Kenneth, and Tanya Schlusser. *The Hitchhiker's Guide to Python: Best Practices for Development*. Sebastopol, CA: O'Reilly Media, 2016.

Ryan, Mike, and Federico Lucifredi. *AWS System Administration*. Sebastopol, CA: O'Reilly Media, 2018.

Shafer, Andrew Clay. *Agile Infrastructure in Web Operations: Keeping the Data on Time*. Sebastopol, CA: O'Reilly Media, 2010.

Turnbull, James, and Jeffrey McCune. *Pro Puppet: Maximize and Customize Puppet's Capabilities for Your Environment*. New York: Apress, 2011.

Index

About the Authors

Bas Meijer is a freelance software engineer and devops coach. With a major from the University of Amsterdam, he has been pioneering web development since the early nineties. He worked in high-frequency trading, banking, cloud security, aviation, high-tech, and government. Bas has been an Ansible Ambassador since 2014 and a HashiCorp Ambassador from 2020–2021.

Lorin Hochstein is a senior software engineer on the Chaos Team at Netflix, where he works on ensuring that Netflix remains available. He is a coauthor of the *OpenStack Operations Guide* (O'Reilly), as well as numerous academic publications.

René Moser lives in Switzerland with his wife and three kids, likes simple things that work and scale, and has earned an Advanced Diploma of Higher Education in IT. He has been engaged in the open source community for the past 15 years, most recently working as an ASF CloudStack Committer and as the author of the Ansible CloudStack integration with over 30 CloudStack modules. He became an Ansible Community Core Member in April 2016 and is currently a senior system engineer at SwissTXT.

Colophon

The animal on the cover of *Ansible: Up and Running* is a Holstein Friesian (*Bos primigenius*), often shortened to Holstein in North America and Friesian in Europe. This breed of cattle originated in Europe in what is now the Netherlands, bred with the goal of obtaining animals that could exclusively eat grass—the area's most abundant resource—resulting in a high-producing, black-and-white dairy cow. Holstein Friesians were introduced to the United States from 1621 to 1664, but American breeders didn't become interested in the breed until the 1830s.

Holsteins are known for their large size, distinct black-and-white markings, and high production of milk. The black and white coloring is a result of artificial selection by the breeders. Healthy calves weigh 90–100 pounds at birth; mature Holsteins can weigh up to 1,280 pounds and stand at 58 inches tall. Heifers of this breed are typically bred by 13 to 15 months; their gestation period is 9½ months.

This breed of cattle averages about 2,022 gallons of milk per year; pedigree animals average 2,146 gallons per year and can produce up to 6,898 gallons in a lifetime.

In September 2000, the Holstein became the center of controversy when one of its own, Hanoverhill Starbuck, was cloned from frozen fibroblast cells recovered one month before his death, birthing Starbuck II. The cloned calf was born 21 years and 5 months after the original Starbuck.

Many of the animals on O'Reilly covers are endangered; all of them are important to the world.

Color illustration by Karen Montgomery, based on an antique line engraving from *Riverside Natural History*. The cover fonts are Gilroy Semibold and Guardian Sans. The text font is Adobe Minion Pro; the heading font is Adobe Myriad Condensed; and the code font is Dalton Maag's Ubuntu Mono.